CONCEPTS
OF
CRITICISM

by René Wellek

Edited and with an
Introduction by Stephen G. Nichols, Jr.

New Haven and London: Yale University Press

Library of Congress catalog card number: 63–7953
ISBN: 0–300–01033–8 (cloth),
        0–300–00255–6 (paper)

Set in Times Roman type,
and printed in the United States of America by
The Murray Printing Co., Westford, Mass.

20   19   18   17   16   15   14   13   12

Contents

Introduction

As a statement of purpose in one of his earliest theoretical articles, René Wellek said: "We have in mind . . . the clarification of . . . theoretical problems which can be solved only on a philosophical [i.e., conceptual] basis. Clearness on methodological issues should influence the direction of future research." Thus, in 1936, at a time when modern trends in criticism had hardly been recognized or named, Mr. Wellek was already concerned with the dangers imminent for the many methods of literary study which were then emerging in reaction to the critical attitudes of the nineteenth and early twentieth centuries. The dangers were many, but the common threat was that the inevitable confusion resulting from the almost simultaneous development of movements widely separated geographically and circumscribed by national, not to mention linguistic, boundaries would lead to a "veritable Tower of Babel." In this confusion there was a real possibility that a failure to define basic concepts would vitiate the work of the new literary scholarship. Accordingly, Mr. Wellek set out to formulate precise conceptual ideals for literary study. In view of the numerous ramifications of literature and literary scholarship, these ideals would have to be defined individually. Once formulated, however, they would continually interact in the practical pursuits of literary scholarship to point the way toward the optimum understanding of the meaning and values of literature.

The initial result of Mr. Wellek's efforts to formulate conceptual ideals for literary study on a large, systematic scale was the book he wrote with Austin Warren, *Theory of Literature*. Here, in a chapter by chapter development, the three central disciplines of literary scholarship—literary theory, criticism, and history—are defined and united in an effort to explain the many aspects of literary works and their study. Practical questions are studied in conjunction with theoretical problems whose antecedents go back at least as far as Aristotle's *Poetics*. Literature is examined in relation to its own world, in relation to other arts and sciences, and in relation to society in general. The component aspects of literary form, e.g. metrics, rhythm, image, symbol, rhetorical devices, are discussed along with the methods of literary study which use these formal aspects as a basis for critical analysis. The mode of existence of a literary work is closely considered. Such are the large questions posed in *Theory of Literature,* questions particularly relevant to the literary work itself.

In the present work Professor Wellek is specifically concerned with the *methods* of studying literary works. If justification be needed for the viewpoint of these essays, it is to be found in their purpose: to secure a firm base for the task of achieving a full understanding of imaginative literature. To this end each essay posits as its goal the development of a concept which will contribute to the better understanding of the literary work. In this sense we see that methods developed in writing *Theory of Literature* have played an important role in the creation of the present essays. That is, each article has a strong theoretical base postulating an ideal goal to be achieved by that aspect of literary study within the province of the particular essay. The justification of the ideal, its pertinence, is always measured in terms of its efficacy in explaining that aspect of literature under discussion. But Mr. Wellek does not appeal solely to the creative works themselves in order to demonstrate the appropriateness of the ideals formulated in the essays. To do so would be to ignore the results obtained by other critics and would merely add to the confusion of voices already plaguing literary study. True to the guiding principles outlined in the statement quoted initially, Mr. Wellek undertakes analytical reviews of the work done by other scholars as a basic part of his own method of approach to the questions discussed. In this way he succeeds not only in defining the ideal goals to be achieved by the new methods of criticism, but also in showing wherein these new methods have successfully attained their goals and wherein they have failed. As a result Mr. Wellek may be credited with bringing some order to the mass of new trends in criticism: in grouping them according to formative influences and according to similarities and effectiveness of method. In this latter effort we see the transition from the point of view of *Theory of Literature* to that utilized so effectively in *A History of Modern Criticism.*

Inasmuch as the essays were all written with the same unifying principle and goal in mind, they maintain a cohesive unity of purpose. Nevertheless, they were not all written at the same time or even in the order in which they appear here. They represent, rather, the results of intense concentration during the past eighteen years on the specific problems which the disciplines of literary theory, criticism, and history have had to face and must solve if they are to realize their potential. The most consistent problem discerned by Mr. Wellek has been the failure on the part of literary scholarship to attain a general and complete awareness of the basic concepts on which the three disciplines should be founded—concepts from which the basic questions to be asked of the literary works must be formulated. Accordingly, the first two essays, "Literary Theory, Criticism, and History" and "The Term and Concept of Literary Criticism" (consult the bibliography for place and date of original publication for those essays which have appeared previously), consider the terminology and functions of the disciplines which make up the field of literary scholarship. "Literary Theory, Criticism, and History" specifically combats recent attempts to conflate the basic distinctions among these areas, distinctions on which depends the meaningful structure of the whole field. "The Term and Concept of Literary Criticism" offers a historical consideration and working definition of criticism. Likewise "The Concept of Evolution in Literary History" is concerned with defining problems of methodology within another of the basic areas of literary study. The great problem of literary history today, as seen by Mr. Wellek, is the need for "a modern concept of time, modeled not on the metric chronology of the calendar and physical science, but on an interpenetration of the causal order in experience and memory." The pursuit of literary history divorced from the value judgments achieved by criticism is inconceivable as Wellek shows.

"Concepts of Form and Structure in Twentieth-Century Criticism" turns to the examination of two structural methods of analyzing literary works which have been widely used in this century. The terms "form" and "structure" have been so loosely used by such varied groups of critics that confusing and even conflicting usages of the terms have arisen. Mr. Wellek here untangles the various usages, marshaling them in an order roughly related to the various schools using the terms; then he analyzes the success of these usages in recent literary studies. Finally, he offers a positive means of choosing the best working concepts of "structure" for critical purposes. This article serves as a transition to the three essays which make up the central part of the book, essays dealing with specific problems of practical periodization. The essays—"The Concept of Baroque in Literary Scholarship," "The Concept of Romanticism in Literary History," "The Concept of Realism in Literary Scholarship" —are at once a review of previous attempts at characterizing works from these periods and, at the same time, an outline of the conceptual ideals which must be at the basis of future, hopefully more successful, attempts. Reinforcing the interaction of disciplines sketched in the first essay, Mr. Wellek shows in these articles that successful periodization is impossible as long as literary theory, criticism, and history are not utilized in concert to define the essence of the literature of a particular period. The impact of these three articles, and especially that of the baroque and romanticism studies which have been available for a longer time, has been such as to provoke a general re-examination of the problems raised in the studies. The whole question of periodization, released from the purely mechanistic principles characteristic of older attitudes opposed by Mr. Wellek, has now assumed a new vitality based upon its association with such immanent aspects of the individual work as style and ideology. In order to take cognizance of the work done since the baroque and romanticism articles were originally published, Mr. Wellek has written postscripts for them. The baroque postscript does not try to review the many hundreds of articles published since 1946 but does try to suggest wherein the original paper stands corrected and points out the new issues that have been raised. What is particularly striking for us, in retrospect, is the extent to which recent studies have attempted to utilize the concepts laid down in Mr. Wellek's original study. "Romanticism Re-examined" is a welcome reaffirmation of his views on the whole question of periodization in general and of the particular situation facing the romantic period.

"The Revolt Against Positivism in European Literary Scholarship" makes a transition back to broader questions —not of critical *definition* as in the first essays, but of critical *directions*— by tracing the origin of the modern critical methods from the revolt against positivism as practiced in the late nineteenth and early twentieth centuries. "The Crisis of Comparative Literature" and "American Literary

Scholarship" analyze specific failings in the direction of comparative literature as a discipline in the one case and of graduate schools in the other. The poor direction of comparative literature is of particular concern to literary scholarship because it is in comparative literature that freedom from the specific demands and boundaries faced by language departments should be found for pursuing the broader questions of literary theory. Similarly, the lack of freedom and vitality in graduate school curricula is of the gravest concern because it is through the graduate schools that our scholars receive their first professional training. The formative influence on these future scholars is particularly crucial in determining, as Mr. Wellek states, our success in attaining "better, more relevant, and more critical scholarship."

"Philosophy and Postwar American Criticism," one of the three previously unpublished pieces, represents a new approach by Mr. Wellek to the problem of imposing order on the chaos of critical voices. In this essay he examines the recent trends in American criticism from the point of view of their underlying philosophical orientation. He "takes the history of Western philosophy in its main representatives and currents—Plato, Aristotle, Thomism, British empiricism, Kant, Schelling, Hegel, etc.—in their chronological order and asks how far recent American critics profess allegiance to any of them." This article attempts to achieve what Mr. Wellek calls a "perspective by incongruity" and in so doing raises questions at the very core of American criticism.

"The Main Trends of Twentieth-Century Criticism" offers a final summation, along the lines of *A History of Modern Criticism,* of the main currents in contemporary literary criticism, showing the need within the field for a really concerted effort to attain a greater degree of awareness of the conceptual principles set forth in the preceding essays.

Such, then, is the purpose and structure of the book. In

closing it should be noted that the previously published articles are for the most part presented in the form in which they originally appeared. Some bibliographical revisions have been undertaken, and some reflections necessitated by work done since the articles first appeared have been amended. It is particularly fitting that these essays and the bibliography, striking testimonies of the enormous contribution René Wellek has made, not only in the United States, but, through translations, in other countries as well, should appear in time for his sixtieth birthday: August 22, 1963.

STEPHEN G. NICHOLS, JR.

New Haven, Connecticut
December 31, 1962

Literary Theory, Criticism, and History

In *Theory of Literature*[1] I tried to maintain the distinctions between certain main branches of literary study. "There is, first," I said, "the distinction between a view of literature as a simultaneous order and a view of literature which sees it primarily as a series of works arranged in a chronological order and as integral parts of the historical process. There is, then, the further distinction between the study of the principles and criteria of literature and the study of the concrete literary works of art, whether we study them in isolation or in chronological series."

"Literary theory" is the study of the principles of literature, its categories, criteria, and the like, while the studies of concrete works of art are either "literary criticism" (primarily static in approach) or "literary history." Of course, "literary criticism" is frequently used in such a way as to include literary theory.[2] I pleaded for the necessity of a collaboration among the three disciplines: "They implicate each other so thoroughly as to make inconceivable literary theory without criticism or history, or criticism without theory or history, or history without theory and criticism," and I concluded somewhat naively that "these distinctions are fairly obvious and rather widely accepted" (pp. 30–31).

1. René Wellek and Austin Warren, *Theory of Literature* (New York, 1949).

2. I have used the term thus widely in my *History of Modern Criticism* (New Haven, 1955).

Since these pages were written many attempts have been made either to obliterate these distinctions or to make more or less totalitarian claims for some one of these disciplines: either to say, e.g. that there is only history or only criticism or only theory or, at least, to reduce the triad to a duo, to say that there is only theory and history or only criticism and history. Much of this debate is purely verbal: a further example of the incredible confusion of tongues, the veritable Tower of Babel which seems to me one of the most ominous features of our civilization. It is not worth trying to disentangle these confusions if they do not point to actual issues. Terminological disagreements are inevitable, especially if we take into consideration the different associations and scope of such terms in the main European languages. For instance, the term *Literaturwissenschaft* has preserved in German its ancient meaning of systematic knowledge. But I would try to defend the English term "literary theory" as preferable to "science of literature," because "science" in English has become limited to natural science and suggests an emulation of the methods and claims of the natural sciences which seems, for literary studies, both unwise and misleading. "Literary scholarship" as a possible translation or alternative to "Literaturwissenschaft" seems also inadvisable, as it seems to exclude criticism, evaluation, speculation. A "scholar" has ceased to be so broad and wise a man as Emerson wanted the American scholar to be. Again, "literary theory" is preferable to "poetics," as, in English, the term "poetry" is still usually restricted to verse and has not assumed the wide meaning of German *Dichtung*. "Poetics" seems to exclude the theory of such forms as the novel or the essay and it has also the handicap of suggesting prescriptive poetics: a set of principles obligatory for practising poets.

I do not want to trace at length the history of the term "criticism" here, as it is properly the topic of the second essay. In English, the term criticism is often used to include literary theory and poetics. This usage is rare in German where the term *Literaturkritik* is usually understood in the very narrow sense of day-by-day reviewing. It might be interesting to show how this restriction has come about. In Germany, Lessing, certainly, and the Schlegels thought of themselves as literary critics, but apparently the overwhelming prestige of German philosophy, particularly the Hegelian system, combined with the establishment of a specialized literary historiography led to a sharp distinction between philosophical aesthetics and poetics on the one hand and scholarship on the other, while "criticism" taken over by politically oriented journalism during the thirties of the nineteenth century became degraded to something purely practical, serving temporal ends. The critic becomes a middleman, a secretary, even a servant, of the public. In Germany, the late Werner Milch, in an essay "Literaturkritik und Literaturgeschichte"[3] has tried to rescue the term by an argument in favor of "literary criticism" as a specific art-form, a literary genre. Its distinguishing characteristic is that in criticism everything must be related to *us,* while in literary history, literature is conceived as involved in a period, judged only relatively to the period. The only criterion of criticism is personal feeling, experience, the magic German word: *Erlebnis.* But Milch hardly touches on the distinction between literary criticism and theory. He rejects a general "science of literature," as all knowledge about literature has its place in history, and poetics cannot be divorced from historical relations.

I recognize that Milch's discussion raises interesting historical questions about the forms in which the insights of criticism have been conveyed, and that there is a real issue

3. *Germanisch-romanische Monatsschrift, 18* (1930), 1–15, reprinted in *Kleine Schriften zur Literatur- und Geistesgeschichte* (Heidelberg, 1957), pp. 9–24.

in the debate whether criticism is an art or a science (in the
old, wide sense). I shall be content to say here that criticism
has been conveyed in the most different art-forms, even in
poems, such as those of Horace, Vida, and Pope, or in brief
aphorisms, such as those by Friedrich Schlegel, or in abstractly, prosaically, even badly written treatises. The history
of the "literary review" (*Rezension*) as a genre raises historical and social questions, but it seems to me a mistake to
identify "criticism" with this one limited form. There still
remains the problem of the relation between criticism and
art. A feeling for art will enter into criticism: many critical
forms require artistic skills of composition and style; imagination has its share in all knowledge and science. Still, I do
not believe that the critic is an artist or that criticism is an
art (in the strict modern sense). Its aim is intellectual cog-
nition. It does not create a fictional imaginative world such
as the world of music or poetry. Criticism is conceptual
knowledge, or aims at such knowledge. It must ultimately
aim at systematic knowledge about literature, at literary
theory.

This point of view has recently been eloquently argued
by Northrop Frye in the "Polemical Introduction" to his
Anatomy of Criticism,[4] a work of literary theory which has
been praised as the greatest book of criticism since Matthew
Arnold. Frye, convincingly, rejects the view that literary
theory and criticism are a kind of parasite on literature, that
the critic is an artist *manqué* and postulates that "criticism
is a structure of thought and knowledge existing in its own
right" (p. 5). I agree with his general enterprise, his belief
in the necessity of a theory of literature. I want to argue
here only against his attempt to erect literary theory into
the uniquely worthwhile discipline and to expel criticism
(in our sense of criticism of concrete works) from literary
study. Frye makes a sharp distinction between, on the one

4. Princeton, 1957.

hand, both "literary theory" and "genuine criticism," which progresses toward making the whole of literature intelligible, and, on the other hand, a kind of criticism which belongs only to the history of taste. Obviously Frye has little use for the "public critic"—Sainte-Beuve, Hazlitt, Arnold, etc.—who represents the reading public and merely registers its prejudices. Frye laughs at "the literary chit-chat which makes the reputations of poets boom and crash in an imaginary stock exchange. That wealthy investor, Mr. Eliot, after dumping Milton on the market, is now buying him again; Donne has probably reached his peak and will begin to taper off; Tennyson may be in for a slight flutter but the Shelley stocks are still bearish" (p. 18). Frye is obviously right in ridiculing the "whirligig of taste"; but he must be wrong in drawing the conclusion that "as the history of taste has no organic connection with criticism, it can be easily separated."

In my own *History of Modern Criticism* I have discovered that it cannot be done.[5] Frye's view that "the study of literature can never be founded on value judgments," that the theory of literature is not directly concerned with value judgments, seems to me quite mistaken. He himself concedes that the "critic will find soon, and constantly, that Milton is a more rewarding and suggestive poet to work with than Blackmore" (p. 25). Whatever his impatience with arbitrary literary opinions may be or with the game of rankings, I cannot see how such a divorce as he seems to advocate is feasible in practice. Literary theories, principles, criteria cannot be arrived at *in vacuo:* every critic in history has developed his theory in contact (as has Frye himself) with concrete works of art which he has had to select, interpret, analyze and, after all, to judge. The literary opinions, rankings, and judgments of a critic are buttressed,

5. In his very generous review Mr. Frye apparently wished I had done so. Cf. *Virginia Quarterly, 32* (1956), 310–15.

confirmed, developed by his theories, and the theories are
drawn from, supported, illustrated, made concrete and
plausible by works of art. The relegation, in Frye's *Anatomy
of Criticism,* of concrete criticisms, judgments, evaluations
to an arbitrary, irrational, and meaningless "history of taste"
seems to me as indefensible as the recent attempts to doubt
the whole enterprise of literary theory and to absorb all literary study into history.

In the forties, during the heyday of the New Criticism,
historical scholarship was on the defensive. Much was done
to reassert the rights of criticism and literary theory and
to minimize the former overwhelming emphasis on biography and historical background. In the colleges a textbook,
Brooks and Warren's *Understanding Poetry*[6] (1938), was
the signal for the change. I believe my own *Theory of Literature* (1949) was widely understood as an attack on "ex-
trinsic" methods, as a repudiation of "literary history,"
though the book actually contains a final chapter on "Literary History" which emphatically argues against the neglect
of this discipline and provides a theory of a new, less external literary history. But in recent years the situation has
become reversed, and criticism, literary theory, the whole
task of interpreting and evaluating literature as a simultaneous order has been doubted and rejected. The New
Criticism, and actually any criticism, is today on the defensive. One type of discussion moves on an empirical level as
a wrangle about the interpretation of specific passages or
poems. The theoretical issue is there put often in very
sweeping and vague terms. A straw man is set up: the New
Critic, who supposedly denies that a work of art can be
illuminated by historical knowledge at all. It is then easy to
show that poems have been misunderstood because the
meaning of an obsolete word was missed or a historical or

6. Cleanth Brooks, Jr. and R. P. Warren, *Understanding Poetry;
an Anthology for College Students* (New York, 1938).

biographical allusion ignored or misread. But I do not believe that there ever was a single reputable "New" critic who has taken the position imputed to him. The New Critics, it seems to me rightly, have argued that a literary work of art is a verbal structure of a certain coherence and wholeness, and that literary study had often become completely irrelevant to this total meaning, that it had moved all too often into external information about biography, social conditions, historical backgrounds, etc. But this argument of the New Critics did not mean and could not be conceived to mean a denial of the relevance of historical information for the business of poetic interpretation. Words have their history; genres and devices descend from a tradition; poems often refer to contemporary realities. Cleanth Brooks—surely a New Critic who has focused on the close reading of poetry—has, in a whole series of essays (mainly on seventeenth century poems), shown very precisely some of the ways in which historical information may be necessary for the understanding of specific poems. In a discussion of Marvell's "Horatian Ode,"[7] Brooks constantly appeals to the historical situation for his interpretation, though he is rightly very careful to distinguish between the exact meaning of the poem and the presumed attitude of Marvell toward Cromwell and Charles I. He argues "that the critic needs the help of the historian—all the help he can get," but insists that "the poem has to be read as a poem—that what it 'says' is a question for the critic to answer, and that no amount of historical evidence as such can finally determine what the poem says" (p. 155). This seems a conciliatory, sensible attitude which holds firmly to the critical point of view and still admits the auxiliary value of historical information, and does not of course deny the separate enterprise of literary history.

Usually, however, the defenders of the historical point of

7. "Literary Criticism," in *English Institute Essays, 1946* (New York, 1947), pp. 127–58.

view are dissatisfied with such a concession. They remind us loudly that a literary work can be interpreted only in the light of history and that ignorance of history distorts a reading of the work. Thus Rosemond Tuve, in three very learned books,[8] has kept up a running battle against the modern readers of the metaphysical poets and of Milton. But the issues debated by her are far from clear-cut conflicts between historical scholarship and modern criticism. For instance, in her attack on Empson's reading of Herbert's "Sacrifice,"[9] she clearly has the upper hand not because she is a historian and Empson is a critic but because Empson is an arbitrary, willful, fantastic reader of poetry who is unwilling or unable to look at his text as a whole but runs after all sorts of speculations and associations. "All the Freudian stuff," says Empson disarmingly, "what fun!" He takes the line of Christ complaining, "Man stole the fruit, but I must climb the tree," to mean that Christ is "doing the stealing, that so far from sinless he is Prometheus and the criminal," that "Christ is climbing upwards, like Jack on the Beanstalk, and taking his people with him back to Heaven." Christ is "evidently smaller than Man or at any rate than Eve, who could pluck the fruit without climbing . . . the son stealing from his father's orchard is a symbol of incest," etc. (p. 294). Miss Tuve seems right in insisting that "I must climb the tree" means only "I must ascend the cross," and that "must" does not imply Christ's littleness or boyishness but refers to the command of God. Miss Tuve appeals, plausibly, to the concept of *figura,* of typology: Adam was considered as the type of Christ. Christ was the second Adam, the cross the other tree. Miss Tuve accumulates, in

8. *Elizabethan and Metaphysical Imagery* (Chicago, 1947); *A Reading of George Herbert* (Chicago, 1952); *Images and Themes in Five Poems by Milton* (Cambridge, Mass., 1957).

9. In William Empson, *Seven Types of Ambiguity* (London, 1930), pp. 286 ff.

A Reading of George Herbert, a mass of learning to show that there are liturgical phrases, Middle English and Latin poems, devotional treatises, etc., which anticipate the general situation of Herbert's poem, and that even many details of the complaint of Christ can be found long before Herbert in texts Herbert probably had never seen as well as in texts he might have known or knew for certain as an Anglican priest. All this is useful and even impressive as a study of sources and conventions, but it surely does not prove what she apparently hopes to prove: that Herbert's poem is somehow unoriginal, that Empson is mistaken in speaking of "Herbert's method" and its "uniqueness." Empson in his sly rejoinder[10] quite rightly argues that no amount of background study can solve the problem of poetic value. What is at issue is not a conflict between history and criticism but empirical questions about the correctness or incorrectness of certain interpretations. I think one must grant that Empson laid himself wide open to the charge of misreading but then one must say in his defense that nobody, literally nobody, had yet commented on that poem in any detail and that Empson's method, atomistic, associative, arbitrary as it is, is at least an ingenious attempt to come to grips with the problem of meaning. "Close reading" has led to pedantries and aberrations, as have all the other methods of scholarship; but it is surely here to stay, as any branch of knowledge can advance and has advanced only by a careful, minute inspection of its objects, by putting things under the microscope even though general readers or even students and teachers may be often bored by the procedure.

But these debates, like the debate between the Chicago critics and the New Critics or between the Chicago critics and the mythographs, concern rather specific problems of interpretation than our wider debate about the relationship of theory, criticism, and history. Far greater and more difficult

10. *Kenyon Review,* 12 (1950), 735–38.

issues are raised by those who have genuinely embraced the creed of "historicism," which after a long career in Germany and Italy, after its theoretical formulations by Dilthey, Windelband, Rickert, Max Weber, Troeltsch, Meinecke, and Croce, has finally reached the United States and has been embraced by literary scholars almost as a new religion. To give a characteristic recent example, Roy Harvey Pearce, in an article, "Historicism Once More,"[11]—strangely enough lauded and endorsed by J. C. Ransom—preaches a new historicism and concludes by quoting a poem by Robert Penn Warren with this climactic line, "The world is real. It is there" (*Promises 2*).

Warren, hardly an enemy of the New Criticism, is quoted as the key witness for "historicism," though his fine poem has nothing whatever to do with historicism and merely conveys, powerfully and movingly, a feeling for the reality of the past which might conceivably rather be called "existential." It asserts the kind of realization and wonder which Carlyle insisted upon in many of his later writings after he had repudiated his early adherence to German historicism. To quote Carlyle's examples: Dr. Johnson actually told a street-walker, "No, no, my girl, it won't do"; Charles I actually stayed the night in a hayloft with a peasant in 1651; King Lackland "was verily there," at St. Edmundsbury, and left *"tredecim sterlingii,* if nothing more, and did live and look in one way or the other, and a whole world was living and looking at him."[12] But such wonder, appropriate to the poet or Carlyle, is only the beginning of historicism as a method or a philosophy. Pearce's historicism is a confused mixture of existentialism and historicism, a string of bombastic assertions about humanity, the possibility of literature, and so on, with the constant polemical

11. Ibid., *20* (1958), 554–91.

12. Carlyle, *Works,* Centenary ed., (London, 1898–99), *Essays, 3,* 54–56; *Past and Present,* p. 46.

refrain that "criticism is a form of historical study" (p. 568). It is not worth trying to disentangle the hopeless muddles of Pearce's amazing stew of existence, eschatology, history, the "creative ground of all values," the whole weird mixture of Rudolph Bultmann, Américo Castro, Kenneth Burke, and Walter J. Ong, S.J., all quoted on one page. It is better to turn to a knowledgeable and sophisticated upholder of the historistic creed such as my late colleague and friend, Erich Auerbach.

In a review of my *History of Modern Criticism*[13] from which certain formulations passed, without explicit reference to my work, into the introduction of his posthumous book, *Literatursprache und Publikum in der lateinischen Spätantike und im Mittelalter,*[14] and into his English article "Vico's Contribution to Literary Criticism,"[15] Auerbach states most clearly the historistic creed:

> Our historistic way of feeling and judging is so deeply rooted in us that we have ceased to be aware of it. We enjoy the art, the poetry and the music of many different peoples and periods with equal preparedness for understanding. . . . The variety of periods and civilizations no longer frightens us. . . . It is true that perspectivistic understanding fails as soon as political interests are at stake; but otherwise, especially in aesthetic matters, our historistic capacity of adaptation to the most various forms of beauty is almost boundless. . . . But the tendency to forget or to ignore historical perspectivism is widespread, and it is, especially among literary critics, connected with the prevailing antipathy to philology of the 19th century type, this philology being

13. *Romanische Forschungen, 62* (1956), 387–97.
14. Bern, 1958.
15. *Studia philologica et letteraria in honorem L. Spitzer,* ed. A. G. Hatcher and K. L. Selig (Bern, 1958), pp. 31–37.

considered as the embodiment and the result of historicism. Thus, many believe that historicism leads to
antiquarian pedantry, to the overevaluation of biographical detail, to complete indifference to the values
of the work of art; therefore to a complete lack of
categories with which to judge, and finally to arbitrary
eclecticism. [But] it is wrong to believe that historical
relativism or perspectivism makes us incapable of evaluating and judging the work of art, that it leads to
arbitrary eclecticism, and that we need, for judgment,
fixed and absolute categories. Historicism is not eclecticism. . . . Each historian (we may also call him, with
Vico's terminology, "philologist") has to undertake
this task for himself, since historical relativism has a
twofold aspect: it concerns the understanding historian
as well as the phenomena to be understood. This is an
extreme relativism; but we should not fear it. . . . The
historian does not become incapable of judging; he
learns what judging means. Indeed, he will soon cease
to judge by abstract and unhistorical categories; he
even will cease to search for such categories of judgment. That general human quality, common to the
most perfect works of the particular periods, which
alone may provide for such categories, can be grasped
only in its particular forms, or else as a dialectical
process in history; its abstract essence cannot be expressed in exact significant terms. It is from the material itself that he will learn to extract the categories or
concepts which he needs for describing and distinguishing the different phenomena. These concepts are not
absolute; they are elastic and provisional, changeable
with changing history. But they will be sufficient to
enable us to discover what the different phenomena
mean within their own period, and what they mean
within the three thousand years of conscious literary

human life we know of; and finally, what they mean
to us, here and now. That is judgment enough; it may
lead also to some understanding of what is common to
all of these phenomena, but it would be difficult to
express it otherwise than as a dialectical process in
history. . . .

This is an excellent statement, moderately phrased, concrete in its proposals, supported by the authority of a scholar
who knew the relevant German tradition and had the experience of working within it. It contains, no doubt, a measure of truth which we all have to recognize, but still it rouses
ultimate, insuperable misgivings, a final dissatisfaction with
the "extreme relativism" accepted here so resignedly and
even complacently. Let me try to sort out some of the problems raised and marshal some answers to this influential
point of view. Let me begin at the most abstract level: the
assertion of the inevitable conditioning of the historian's
own point of view, the recognition of one's own limited
place in space and time, the relativism elaborated and emphasized by the "sociology of knowledge," particularly by
Karl Mannheim in *Ideologie und Utopie*.[10] This kind of
relativism was and is extremely valuable as a method of
investigating the hidden assumptions and biases of the investigator himself. But it surely can serve only as a general
warning, as a kind of *memento mori*. As Isaiah Berlin observes, in a similar context:

Such charges [of subjectiveness or relativity] resemble suggestions, sometimes casually advanced, that life
is a dream. We protest that "everything" cannot be a
dream, for then, with nothing to contrast with dreams,
the notion of a "dream" loses all specific reference. . . .
If everything is subjective or relative, nothing can be

16. Bonn, 1929, Eng. trans. London, 1936.

judged to be more so than anything else. If words like "subjective" and "relative," "prejudiced" and "biased," are terms not of comparison and contrast—do not imply the possibility of their own opposites, of "objective" (or at least "less subjective") or "unbiased" (or at least "less biased"), what meaning have they for us?[17]

The mere recognition of what A. O. Lovejoy has called, with a barbarous word formed on the analogy of the "egocentric predicament," the "presenticentric predicament"[18] does not get us anywhere: it merely raises the problem of all knowing; it leads only to universal skepticism, to theoretical paralysis. Actually the case of knowledge and even of historical knowledge is not that desperate. There are universal propositions in logic and mathematics such as two plus two equal four, there are universally valid ethical precepts, such, for instance, as that which condemns the massacre of innocent people, and there are many neutral true propositions concerning history and human affairs. There is a difference between the psychology of the investigator, his presumed bias, ideology, perspective and the logical structure of his propositions. The genesis of a theory does not necessarily invalidate its truth. Men can correct their biases, criticize their presuppositions, rise above their temporal and local limitations, aim at objectivity, arrive at some knowledge and truth. The world may be dark and mysterious, but it is surely not completely unintelligible.

But the problems of literary study need not actually be approached in terms of this very general debate about the relativity of all knowledge or even the special difficulties of all historical knowledge. Literary study differs from histor-

17. *Historical Inevitability* (Oxford, 1954), p. 61.
18. A. O. Lovejoy, "Present Standpoints and Past History," *Journal of Philosophy, 36* (1939), 477–89.

ical study in having to deal not with documents but with monuments. A historian has to reconstruct a long-past event on the basis of eye-witness accounts, the literary student, on the other hand, has direct access to his object: the work of art. It is open to inspection whether it was written yesterday or three thousand years ago, while the battle of Marathon and even the battle of the Bulge have passed irrevocably. Only peripherally, in questions which have to do with biography or, say, the reconstruction of the Elizabethan playhouse, does the literary student have to rely on documents. He can examine his object, the work itself; he must understand, interpret, and evaluate it; he must, in short, be a critic in order to be a historian. The political or economic or social historian, no doubt, also selects his facts for their interest or importance, but the literary student is confronted with a special problem of value; his object, the work of art, is not only value-impregnated, but is itself a structure of values. Many attempts have been made to escape the inevitable consequences of this insight, to avoid the necessity not only of selection but of judgment, but all have failed and must, I think, fail unless we want to reduce literary study to a mere listing of books, to annals or a chronicle. There is nothing which can obviate the necessity of critical judgment, the need of aesthetic standards, just as there is nothing which can obviate the need of ethical or logical standards.

One widely used escape door leads nowhere: the assertion that we need not judge, but that we simply need adopt the criteria of the past: that we must reconstruct and apply the values of the period we are studying. I shall not merely argue that these standards cannot be reconstructed with certainty, that we are confronted with insurmountable difficulties if we want to be sure what Shakespeare intended by his plays and how he conceived them or what the Elizabethan audience understood by them. There are different schools of scholarship which try to get at this past meaning by different routes: E. E. Stoll believes in reconstructing stage conventions; Miss Tuve appeals to rhetorical training, or liturgical and iconographic traditions; others swear by the authority of the NED; still others, like J. Dover Wilson, think that "the door to Shakespeare's workshop stands ajar" when they discover inconsistencies in punctuation or line arrangements from bibliographical evidence. Actually, in reconstructing the critical judgment of the past we appeal only to one criterion: that of contemporary success. But if we examine any literary history in the light of the actual opinions of the past we shall see that we do not admit and cannot admit the standards of the past. When we properly know the views of Englishmen about their contemporary literature, e.g., late in the eighteenth century, we may be in for some suprises: David Hume, for instance, thought Wilkie's *Epigoniad* comparable to Homer; Nathan Drake thought Cumberland's *Calvary* greater than Milton's *Paradise Lost*. Obviously, accepting contemporary evaluation requires our discriminating between a welter of opinions: who valued whom and why and when? Professor Geoffrey Barraclough, in a similar argument against historians who recommend that we should study "the things that were important *then* rather than the things that are important *now*," advises them to look, for instance, at thirteenth-century chronicles: "a dreary recital of miracles, tempests, comets, pestilences, calamities, and other wonderful things."[19] Clearly the standards of contemporaries cannot be binding on us, even if we could reconstruct them and find a common lowest denominator among their diversities. Nor can we simply divest ourselves of our individuality or the lessons we have learned from history. Asking us to interpret *Hamlet* only in terms of what the very hypothetical views of Shakespeare or his

19. *History in a Changing World* (Norman, Oklahoma, 1956), p. 22.

audience were is asking us to forget three hundred years of history. It prohibits us to use the insights of a Goethe or Coleridge, it impoverishes a work which has attracted and accumulated meanings in the course of history. But again this history itself, however instructive, cannot be binding on us: its authority is open to the same objections as the authority of the author's contemporaries. There is simply no way of avoiding judgment by us, by myself. Even the "verdict of the ages" is only the accumulated judgment of other readers, critics, viewers, and even professors. The only truthful and right thing to do is to make this judgment as objective as possible, to do what every scientist and scholar does: to isolate his object, in our case, the literary work of art, to contemplate it intently, to analyze, to interpret, and finally to evaluate it by criteria derived from, verified by, buttressed by, as wide a knowledge, as close an observation, as keen a sensibility, as honest a judgment as we can command.

The old absolutism is untenable: the assumption of one eternal, narrowly defined standard had to be abandoned under the impact of our experience of the wide variety of art, but on the other hand, complete relativism is equally untenable; it leads to paralyzing skepticism, to an anarchy of values, to the acceptance of the old vicious maxim: *de gustibus non est disputandum*. The kind of period relativism recommended as a solution by Auerbach is no way out: it would split up the concept of art and poetry into innumerable fragments. Relativism in the sense of a denial of all objectivity is refuted by many arguments: by the parallel to ethics and science, by recognition that there are aesthetic as well as ethical imperatives and scientific truths. Our whole society is based on the assumption that we know what is just, and our science on the assumption that we know what is true. Our teaching of literature is actually also based on aesthetic imperatives, even if we feel less definitely bound by them and seem much more hesitant to bring these assumptions out into the open. The disaster of the "humanities" as far as they are concerned with the arts and literature is due to their timidity in making the very same claims which are made in regard to law and truth. Actually we do make these claims when we teach *Hamlet* or *Paradise Lost* rather than Grace Metalious or, to name contemporaries of Shakespeare and Milton, Henry Glapthorne or Richard Blackmore. But we do so shamefacedly, apologetically, hesitatingly. There is, contrary to frequent assertions, a very wide agreement on the great classics: the main canon of literature. There is an insuperable gulf between really great art and very bad art: between say "Lycidas" and a poem on the leading page of the *New York Times,* between Tolstoy's *Master and Man* and a story in *True Confessions.* Relativists always shirk the issue of thoroughly bad poetry. They like to move in the region of near-great art, where disputes among critics are most frequent, as works are valued for very different reasons. The more complex a work of art, the more diverse the structure of values it embodies, and hence the more difficult its interpretation, the greater the danger of ignoring one or the other aspect. But this does not mean that all interpretations are equally right, that there is no possibility of differentiating between them. There are utterly fantastic interpretations, partial, distorted interpretations. We may argue about Bradley's or Dover Wilson's or even Ernest Jones' interpretation of Hamlet: but we know that Hamlet was no woman in disguise. The concept of adequacy of interpretation leads clearly to the concept of the correctness of judgment. Evaluation grows out of understanding; correct evaluation out of correct understanding. There is a hierarchy of viewpoints implied in the very concept of adequacy of interpretation. Just as there is correct interpretation, at least as an ideal, so there is correct judgment, good judgment. Auerbach's relativistic argument that nowadays we enjoy the art of all ages and peoples: neolithic cave-paintings, Chinese landscapes, Negro masks, Gregorian chants, etc., should and can be turned against the relativists. It shows that there is a common feature in all art which we recognize today more clearly than in earlier ages. There is a common humanity which makes every art remote in time and place, and originally serving functions quite different from aesthetic contemplation, accessible and enjoyable to us. We have risen above the limitations of traditional Western taste—the parochialism and relativism of such taste— into a realm if not of absolute then of universal art. There is such a realm, and the various historical manifestations are often far less historically limited in character than is assumed by historians interested mainly in making art serve a temporary social purpose and illuminate social history. Some Chinese or ancient Greek love lyrics on basic simple themes are hardly dateable in space or time except for their language. Even Auerbach, in spite of his radical relativism, has to admit "some understanding of what is common to all of these phenomena" and grants that we do not adopt relativism when our political (that is ethical, vital) interests are at stake. Logic, ethics and, I believe, aesthetics cry aloud against a complete historicism which, one should emphasize, in men such as Auerbach, is still shored up by an inherited ideal of humanism and buttressed methodologically by an unconsciously held conceptual framework of grammatical, stylistic and *geistesgeschichtlich* categories. In such radical versions as, e.g., George Boas' *A Primer for Critics*,[20] Bernard Heyl's *New Bearings in Esthetics and Art Criticism*,[21] or Wayne Shumaker's *Elements of Critical Theory*,[22] the theory leads to a dehumanization of the arts, to a paralysis of criticism, to a surrender of our primary con-

20. Baltimore, 1937 (renamed *Wingless Pegasus: A Handbook for Critics*, Baltimore, 1950).
21. New Haven, 1943.
22. Berkeley, 1952.

cern for truth. The only way out is a carefully defined and refined absolutism, a recognition that "the Absolute is in the relative, though not finally and fully in it." This was the formula of Ernst Troeltsch, who struggled more than any other historian with the problem of historicism and came to the conclusion that "historicism" must be superseded.[23]

We must return to the task of building a literary theory, a system of principles, a theory of values which will necessarily draw on the criticism of concrete works of art and will constantly invoke the assistance of literary history. But the three disciplines are and will remain distinct: history cannot absorb or replace theory, while theory should not even dream of absorbing history. André Malraux has spoken eloquently of the imaginary museum, the museum without walls, drawing on a world-wide acquaintance with the plastic arts. Surely in literature we are confronted with the same task as that of the art critic, or at least an analogous task: we can more directly and easily assemble our museum in a library but we are still faced with the walls and barriers of languages and historical forms of languages. Much of our work aims at breaking down these barriers, at demolishing these walls by translations, philological study, editing, comparative literature, or simply imaginative sympathy. Ultimately literature, like the plastic arts, like Malraux's voices of silence, is a chorus of voices—articulate throughout the ages —which asserts man's defiance of time and destiny, his victory over impermanence, relativity, and history.

23. Cf. "Historiography," in Hastings' *Encyclopaedia of Religion and Ethics*, 6 (Edinburgh, 1913), 722.

The Term and Concept of
Literary Criticism

The word "criticism" is so widely used in so many contexts
—from the most homely to the most abstract, from the criticism of a word or an action to political, social, historical,
musical, art, philosophical, Biblical, higher, and what-not
criticism—that we must confine ourselves to literary criticism
if we are to arrive at manageable distinctions. Even here
several difficult problems arise which can be clarified only
by a glance at the history of the term. Strangely enough
there seems to be practically no literature on the history of
the term "criticism" or even "critic," if we except Gudeman's
article on *kritikós* in antiquity.[1] Histories of criticism and
aesthetics as well as dictionaries such as the *NED* yield
something, though often surprisingly little. Histories of criticism discuss aesthetics, poetics, and literary theory but not
the theory of criticism or only very incidentally. I do not
know of any account which has examined or even recognized the three problems I want to raise here: (1) how and
why has the term "criticism" (*critica, la critique*) expanded
to embrace all study of literature and thus replaced "poetics"
or "rhetoric"; (2) how is it that in English we have a longer
form "criticism" in contrast to the Italian *critica* and the
French *la critique;* and (3) why, in Germany, did the term
Kritik shrink again in its meaning, become confined to daily

1. In Pauly-Wissowa-Kroll, *Real-Encyclopädie der classischen
Altertumswissenschaft, 11* (Stuttgart, 1921), 1912–15. A slightly
different account is in J. E. Sandys' *History of Classical Scholarship,
1* (3rd ed. Cambridge, 1926), 10–11.

reviewing and finally yield to new terms such as *Literatur-wissenschaft*? I cannot pretend to give an exact history of the terms which would establish precise historical priorities and date first occurences with accuracy, though I have consulted many dictionaries. But I am not primarily concerned with lexicography. I should rather like to treat the history of the term as a chapter in historical semantics as the late Leo Spitzer called his studies of such words as *Stimmung* and "milieu."[2] The history of the word will be treated as a point of reference for a history of ideas. The term is seen in its conceptual field, in relation to terms with which it competed or contrasted.

In Greek *krités* means "a judge," *krinein*, "to judge." The term *kritikós* as "a judge of literature" occurs as early as the end of the fourth century B.C. Philitas from the island Kos who came to Alexandria in 305 B.C. as the tutor of the future King Ptolemy II, was called "a poet and critic at the same time."[3] The Pergamon school of "critics" with Crates at their head stressed its distinction from the school of "grammarians" led by Aristarchus in Alexandria. We hear that Galen, in the second century A.D., wrote a lost treatise on the question of whether one could be a *kritikós* and at the same time be a *grammatikós*. But apparently the distinction disappeared and the use of the term *kritikós* declined. *Criticus* seems to be rare in classical Latin though it can be found in Cicero and was used of Longinus by Hieron in his *Epistolae*.[4] *Criticus* was a higher term than *grammaticus*, but obviously the *criticus* was also concerned with the interpre-

2. "Classical and Christian Ideas of World Harmony (Prolegomena to an Interpretation of the word *Stimmung*),"*Traditio, 2* (1944), 409–64 and *3* (1945), 307–64; *"Milieu* and *Ambiance,"* in *Essays in Historical Semantics* (New York, 1948), pp. 179–316.

3. Ποιητὴς ἅμα καὶ κριτικὸς, quoted in Rudolf Pfeiffer, *Philologia Perennis* (Munich, 1961), p. 5.

4. In the *Epistle ad Pisones* the word "critic" is not used though Horace speaks (445 ff.) of "vir bonus et prudens" who "versus

tation of texts and words. Rhetoricians such as Quintilian and of course philosophers such as Aristotle cultivated what in English would today be called literary criticism.

In the Middle Ages the word seems to occur only as a term in medicine: in the sense of "crisis" and "critical" illness. In the Renaissance the word was revived in its ancient meaning. Poliziano used the term in 1492, in a prolusion, *In priora Aristoteles analytica,* in which he exalts the grammarian or critic against the philosopher. He asserts proudly that "with the ancients this order (of grammarians) had so much authority that the censurers and judges of all writers were exclusively grammarians whom they therefore called also critics."[5] Grammarian, critic, philologist are almost interchangeable terms for the men engaged in the great enterprise of the revival of antiquity. With Erasmus "the art of criticism" (*ars critica*) is applied to the Bible as a tool in the service of an ideal of toleration. Among the later humanists the terms "critic" and "criticism" seem, however, limited specifically to the editing and correction of ancient texts. Kaspar Schoppe (1576–1649) describes the "only aim and task of critics" as "taking pains to improve the works of writers in either Greek or Latin,"[6] and the younger Scaliger, Joseph Justus (1540–1605) makes criticism even a subdi-

---

reprehendet inertes: Culpabit duros . . . mutanda notabit: Fiet Aristarchus." Both Batteux in his translation (*Les Quatres Poëtiques, 1* [Paris, 1771], 65) and E. H. Blakney ("Horace on the *Art of Poetry*" [1928], reprinted in Allan H. Gilbert, *Literary Criticism* [New York, 1940], p. 142) translate "un Critique éclairé et vrai" or "a kind and sensible critic."

5. *Angeli Politiani prelectio in Priora Aristotelis Analytica. Titulus Lamia* (Firenze, Antonio Miseomini, 1492): "At apud antiquos olim tantum auctoritatis hic ordo habuit / ut Censores essent / & Iudices / Scriptorum omnium soli Grammatici: Quos ob it etiam Criticos uocabant" (p. 27).

6. *De criticis et philologis veteribus et recentioribus* (1597): "Criticorum munus et officium unicum est operam dare ut, eorum

vision of grammar confined to distinguishing the spurious
lines of poets from the true, to restoring corrupt readings,
etc. Jan Wower of Leiden, in a *Tractatio de Polymathia*
(1602), divides *critica* into two parts: *iudicium,* which ascer-
tains the authenticity of an author's writings, and *emendatio,*
which improves misreadings.[7]

Surprisingly, the elder Julius Caesar Scaliger (1484–1558)
seems to be the main source of a new conception of criticism
at that time. In his posthumous *Poetics* (1561) the whole
sixth book, entitled "Criticus," is devoted to a survey and
comparison of the Greek and Roman poets with the emphasis on weighing and ranking and even censuring as in the
famous disparagement of Homer in favor of Virgil.

The penetration of the neo-Latin term into the vernaculars
was far slower and later than it is usually assumed. Certainly
the expansion of the term to include both the whole system
of literary theory and what we today would call practical
criticism and day-by-day reviewing happened only in the
seventeenth century. Modern books called "Literary criticism in the Renaissance" are entitled misleadingly since the
sixteenth century discussed these questions under the name
of poetics and rhetoric.

While I would not exclude the possibility of sporadic
occurrences of the term in books of rhetoric and poetics,
the first of the Italian books on poetics which uses the term
prominently seems to be only *Proginnasmi Poetici* of Udeno
Nisiely (a pseudonym for Benedetto Fioretti), published in
Florence in 1595,[8] but the decisive developments took place
in France, apparently at first under the influence of Scaliger

---

opera, melius sit omnibus utriusque linguae, Graecae dico et Latinae,
scriptoribus." See Antonio Bernardini and Gaetano Righi, *Il Concetto di Filologia e di cultura classica nel pensiero moderno* (Bari,
1947), p. 51.

7. Ibid., p. 100.
8. E.g., pp. 16, 17, 36, 44, 154.

and his Dutch disciples, Heinsius and Vossius. Chapelain called Scaliger "le grand critique" in 1623[9] and Guez de Balzac spoke of Heinsius in 1634 as a "poet, orator, philosopher, and critic."[10] In the *Discours* preceding his *Art Poëtique* (1639) La Mesnardière testifies to the spread of the term and the thing: "libraries are full of books by men of letters," he tells us, "devoted to poetic art, either in order to explain Aristotle, to justify their eulogies of some poems, or to support their censures when they have engaged in criticism."[11] The term—in various senses—seems to become generally accepted only in the sixties and seventies with Molière's *Critique de L'École des Femmes* (1663) and Richard Simon's *Histoire critique du Vieux Testament* (1678). Boileau's *L'Art poëtique* (1674) uses the term as a matter of course also in rhyme. La Bruyère in 1687 could complain of "critics and censurers" who appear in swarms and form factions retarding the progress of art.[12] A whole volume could be written to explain how criticism emancipated itself from its subordination to grammar and rhetoric, how the word "criticism" replaced "poetics" at least in part. It is a process obviously connected with the general critical spirit and its spread in the sense of increased skepticism, distrust of authority and rules, and later with the appeal to taste, sentiment, feeling, *je ne sais quoi,* etc. What had been a term strictly confined to the verbal criticism of classical writers became slowly identified with the whole problem of under-

9. Alfred C. Hunter, ed., *Opuscules critiques* (Paris, 1936), p. 108.

10. Quoted in Edith G. Kern, *The Influence of Heinsius and Vossius upon French Dramatic Theory* (Baltimore, 1949), p. 67.

11. Ibid., p. 7: "Les Bibliotheques sont pleines des productions des gens de lettres . . . qui ont travaillé sur cet Art soit pour expliquer Aristote, pour justifier leurs Eloges quand ils ont loué quelques Poëmes, ou pour appuyer leurs Censures, lorsqu'ils ont touché la Critique."

12. *Les Caractères* (1687), in the section "Des Ouvrages de l'esprit."

standing and judging and even with the theory of knowledge and knowing.

The development in England is parallel but has its special interesting features. The word "critic" hardly occurs in the Elizabethan age (though the *NED* cites "the prince of *Critici*" from Fulke's *Defense of the English Bible* in 1583 and quotes Florio's *Italian Dictionary* translating "critico" in 1598). The word certainly never occurs in the texts collected by Gregory Smith in *Elizabethan Critical Essays* or in the complete text of Puttenham's *Art of English Poesie*. Bacon's *Advancement of Learning* (1605) seems the earliest text which speaks of traditions of knowledge, "the one critical, the other pedantical."[13] The critical has five considerations: "(1) concerning the true correction and edition of authors, (2) concerning the exposition and explication of authors, (3) concerning the times, which in many cases give great light to true interpretations, (4) concerning some brief censure and judgment of the authors, and (5) concerning the syntax and disposition of studies." Soon afterwards (1607) Ben Jonson appeals to the "learned and charitable critick" and in his commonplace book, *Timber or Discoveries* (published 1640 but written possibly much earlier), translates Heinsius calling Aristotle "the first accurate Criticke" and speaking of the office of "a true Critick or Censor" as "judging sincerely of the Author and his matter."[14] The term and the thing are fully established when Rymer wrote his Preface (1674) to Rapin's *Reflections on Aristotle* saying that "in the last Century, Italy swarmed with Criticks," while "till of late years England was as free from Criticks, as it is from Wolves."[15]

13. *Of the Advancement of Learning*, ed. W. A. Wright (Oxford, 1891), p. 182.

14. J. E. Spingarn, ed., *Critical Essays of the Seventeenth Century, 1* (Oxford, 1908), 15, 55, 57. Cf. notes on pp. 228, 230.

15. Curt A. Zimansky, ed., *The Critical Works of Thomas Rymer* (New Haven, 1956), pp. 1–2.

This process parallels the French developments, but in English the noun "criticism" presents a peculiar problem. It seems at first glance obvious that it was formed to avoid the homonym "critic" meaning both an activity and a person. The evidence shows that the neologism was not entirely victorious for a long time. Richard Bentley in the *Phalaris Letters* (1697) uses the phrase "in way of critic" where we would say "criticism," and Steele in the *Tatler* (1710, No. 115) promises to "write a critick" upon a performance. Dr. Johnson still occasionally has "critick" with *ck* in the sense of "criticism." Obviously in order to distinguish this use from the name for the person, Addison wrote it with French spelling in 1721.[16] There is *A Critique on Milton's Paradise Regained* (London, 1732). Today the French double is again used widely, especially in the United States, sometimes with a rather arbitrary limitation of meaning. E.g. R. W. Stallman's well-known anthology *Critiques and Essays in Criticism* (New York, 1949) uses the word "critique" to refer to discussions of specific authors and "criticism" to mean theory. Mostly, I surmise, "critique" is used today to avoid an accumulation of "isms" (cf. *A Critique of Humanism*, 1930) or in order to give a somewhat superior air to a humble book review.

But "criticism" had anything but a humble career in English. The word was either formed with the Greek suffix *-ismos,* denoting nouns of action from verbs such as *baptizein;* or it may have been suggested simply by the analogy of the many abstract neo-Latin nouns for doctrines then coming into the English language such as Lutheranism, Protestantism, Platonism, Stoicism, skepticism, etc. The *NED* gives 1607 as the date of a quotation from Thomas Dekker: "I stand at the marke of criticisme to be shot at" where the use has nothing to do with literature. In Milton's *Apology*

16. Examples from *NED*. The Addison passage is from *The Dialogue on Medals* (1721).

for Smectymnuus (1642) Joseph Hall is attacked for his
satires: "For now the worm of Criticisme works in him, he
will tell us the derivation of German *rutters,* of meal and
of ink."[17] Here "criticism" is used in the sense in which it was
defined by Theophilus Gale in *Contra Gentiles* (1669), as
"the knowledge of languages anciently stiled Grammar, and
lately Criticisme."[18] Apparently the first author to use the
word in the new sense was Dryden who in 1677, in the
preface to *The State of Innocence,* says that by "criticism, as
it was first instituted by Aristotle, was meant a standard of
judging well." In 1679 Dryden wrote a preface to *Troilus
and Cressida* containing "The Grounds of Criticism in Tragedy" and thus the term was definitely launched.[19] In 1704
John Dennis published *The Grounds of Criticism in Poetry,*
and of course in 1711 Pope's *Essay on Criticism* established
the usage so firmly and widely that it is superfluous to follow
it further. The term was obviously even more widely and
broadly used than in France: e.g. Bouhours' *Manière de
Bien Penser* (1687) was translated as *The Art of Criticism*
(1705). Rapin's *Whole Critical Works* appeared in 1706
under that title though there is no such French collection,
and later in the century Lord Kames' *Elements of Criticism*
(1762) ambitiously formulated "the science of criticism" on
psychological grounds.

But is the form "criticism" exclusively English? No doubt
the term spread and expelled "critic" because it broke up the
homonym. But the long form "criticism" occurs also in the
Romance languages. I found it in Baltasar Gracián's *El
Heroe* (1637), "Aunque seguro el héroe del ostracismo de
Atena, peligra en el criticismo de España."[20] It seems to

17. Spingarn, ibid., p. 205.
18. *NED.*
19. W. P. Ker, ed., *Essays, 1* (Oxford, 1926), 179, 202 ff.
20. *Obras, 1* (Madrid, 1664), 534, or *Obras completas,* ed. E. Cor-
rea Calderón, (Madrid, 1944), p. 23. The English translation, *The
Heroe of Lorenzo, or the Way to Eminence and Perfection,* by Sir

occur early in the eighteenth century in Italian. Antonio
Maria Salvini (1653–1729) speaks of Pope as "un valent
Inglese nell' arte del criticismo,"[21] though the form is clearly
suggested by the title of Pope's *Essay*. "Criticismo" occurs
in Baretti's Italian-English *Dictionary* (1760), but Baretti
might be suspect as a friend of Johnson and a long-time resi-
dent of England. Even though "criticisme" or "criticismo"
may occur in French, Italian, and Spanish such usage seems
quite isolated before the nineteenth century. All French,
Spanish, and Italian dictionaries testify to its nineteenth-
century and present-day use as a term exclusively for Kant's
critical philosophy. Tommaseo quotes Rosmini; the Dictionary of the Spanish Academy has only examples from
Menéndez Pelayo late in the nineteenth century; Littré
quotes Renouvier and a passage dating from 1845. Kant
himself spoke of his "critical" philosophy and never called
it "criticism." I found only one passage in Kant where in
1790 he uses the term "Kriticism."[22] Schelling in 1796
applied the long form to Kant's thought contrasting it with
the dogmatism of traditional philosophy.[23] In a dictionary
of the critical philosophy (1799) the item "Critizismus"

John Skeffington (London, 1652) has: "Although our Heroe may
be secure from the Ostracism of Athens, yet he will be in the danger
of the Criticismes of Spain" (p. 145).

21. Quoted from *Prose toscane, 2* (1723), 243: in *Vocabolario
degli Accademici della Crusca* (Verona, 1806): "Ai quali con bello
estro rivolgendosi, felicemente cantò un valent Inglese nell' arte del
criticismo."

22. In "Ueber eine Entdeckung nach der alle neue Kritik der
reinen Vernunft durch eine ältere entbehrlich gemacht werden soll"
(1790), in *Gesammelte Schriften* (Akademie-ausgabe, Berlin, 1912),
1. Abteilung, *8*, 226–27: "Der Kriticism des Verfahrens mit allem,
was zur Metaphysik gehört, (der Zweifel des Aufschubs) ist dagegen
eine Maxime eines allgemeinen Misstrauens gegen alle synthetische
Sätze derselben."

23. "Philosophische Briefe über Dogmatismus und Kritizismus,"
in Niedhammer's *Philosophisches Journal* (1796).

sends us to "dogmatismus."[24] Jacobi wrote a treatise about Kantian "Kriticismus" (1801) and Hegel in the early Heidelberg *Encyclopädie* (1817) complains of Kant's "vernunftbescheidener Kriticismus."[25] But the long form seems to have been used very rarely in Germany during the heyday of Kant's influence. Only during the revival of Kant later in the nineteenth century did Alois Riehl use the term prominently as the title for *Der philosophische Kritizismus* (1876).

In Germany the term "Kritik," "kritisch" penetrated from France in the early eighteenth century. It is in the title of Gottsched's *Versuch einer kritischen Dichtkunst* (1730). Certainly Lessing, Herder, and the Schlegels considered themselves critics, and particularly August Wilhelm Schlegel and Adam Müller made elaborate attempts to define the position of criticism between theory and history and to assert its central importance for the study of literature.[26] But in Germany something happened to dislodge the term and concept and to narrow it more and more till it came to mean only day-by-day reviewing, arbitrary literary opinion. "Ästhetik," and the new term "Literaturwissenschaft" took over the old domain. In Wolfgang Kayser's *Das sprachliche Kunstwerk* (Bern, 1948) the term and the issues are not discussed at all though the word occurs in titles of the bibliography. In the new article on criticism in Merker-Stammler's standard *Reallexikon der deutschen Literaturgeschichte,* literary criticism is called "less a science than a form of *Publizistik.*" It means "the topical reviewing of literary novelties and the judging of literary and musical performances in the daily

24. In G. S. A. Mellin, *Wörterbuch der kritischen Philosophie* (Jena und Leipzig, 1799), under "Critizismus."

25. F. H. Jacobi, "Ueber das Unternehmen des Kriticismus, die Vernunft zum Verstande zu bringen," in Reinhold's *Beiträge,* 31. Heft (1801); and Hegel, *Sämtliche Werke,* ed. H. Glockner, 6 (Stuttgart, 1928), 7, also 313.

26. For a fuller account, see my *History of Modern Criticism,* 2 (New Haven, 1955), 55 ff., 292 ff.

press."[27] While in France Sainte-Beuve re-established the supremacy of the critic as a public figure and in England Matthew Arnold made criticism the key to modern culture and the salvation of England, in Germany criticism lost status drastically. Gervinus in the introduction to his *Geschichte der poetischen Nationalliteratur der Deutschen* (1835) expressly repudiates the task of criticism: "I have nothing to do with the aesthetic judgment of things: I am no poet and no belletristic critic."[28] Hermann Hettner writes in 1853 that "criticism is nothing but aesthetics of art and the characteristics of individual great works and epochs, the history of art and literature,"[29] and F. T. Vischer in his five volume *Aesthetik* discusses criticism only briefly in volume III (1854) under "the relation of the artist to the spectator."[30] A divorce between aesthetics, a philosophical discipline to which poetics was subordinated, and literary scholarship, which was mainly literary history, became a feature of the German intellectual scene of the nineteenth century. The critic became a mere middleman, a journalist of ephemeral significance. The reasons for this narrowing of the term in Germany seem fairly obvious: the overwhelming prestige of

27. *2* (Bern, 1959), 63 (by Werner Kohlschmidt): "Weniger Wissenschaft als vielmehr eine Form der Publizistik. . . . es meint jetzt vornehmlich die aktuelle Rezension literarischer Neuerscheinungen and die Berurteilung literarischer oder musikalischer Aufführungen in der Tagespresse."

28. *1*, 11: "Ich habe mit der aesthetischen Beurteilung der Sachen nichts zu tun, ich bin kein Poet und kein belletristischer Kritiker."

29. A review, "Ludwig Tieck als Kritiker," reprinted in *Schriften zur Literatur* (Berlin, 1959), p. 358: "Die Kritik . . . ist jetzt nichts anderes als die Ästhetik der Kunst als solcher und die Charakteristik der einzelnen grossen Kunstwerke und Kunstepochen, die Kunst- und Literaturgeschichte."

30. *3* (Stuttgart, 1854), 68, part of par. 507: "Das Verhältnis des Künstlers zum Zuschauer. Die Kunst der bürgerlichen Bildung; Kritik."

Hegelianism made aesthetics the concern of the academic philosopher while literary history, specialized along national lines, took over the discussion of the past. Criticism fell a victim to the general contempt with which the Enlightenment and its revival, *Das junge Deutschland,* was soon treated not only by the conservatives but also by the idealistic liberals.

One might expect that the influx of critical, positivistic, and scientific ideals later in the century would have changed the situation. No doubt, critics who called themselves critics played a significant role in the German naturalist movement of the nineties. But a new constellation had arisen which prevented the term criticism from recovering the ground it had lost. In Germany the term "Literaturwissenschaft" took the place of "criticism" as used in the West. It succeeded while similar combinations such as "science de la littérature" or "science of literature" failed in the West. Not that the idea of a science of literature was peculiar to Germany. In France there is a long tradition of such attempts and claims: thus J.-J. Ampère in his *Discours sur l'histoire de la poésie* (1830) expressly speaks of philosophy of literature and literary history as constituting the two parts of a "science littéraire."[31] I need only to allude to Taine, Brunetière, or Hennequin's *Critique scientifique* (1888) to make us recognize how important a trend this transfer of scientific methods to literary study was in France. In England E. S. Dallas and J. A. Symonds made similar attempts to found criticism scientifically on psychological or biological principles. But the term took root only in Germany. The term is used quite casually by Karl Rosenkranz in a review of several books in 1842 surveying the state of German "Literaturwissenschaft."[32] I found it again in a periodical in

31. Reprinted in *Mélanges d'histoire littéraire et de littérature, 1* (Paris, 1867), 2.

32. *Reden und Abhandlungen* (3. Folge, Leipzig, 1848), Studien, Fünfter Theil. There: "Die deutsche Literaturwissenschaft. 1836–

1865.[33] In 1887 Ernst Grosse lectured on *Die Literaturwissenschaft, ihr Ziel und ihr Weg*. Ernst Elster produced a systematic two-volume treatise *Prinzipien der Literaturwissenschaft* (*1*, Halle, 1897, *2*, 1911) which applied the principles and terms of Wundt's psychology.

Outside of Germany, however, the term "science of literature" made no headway. Lectures on *The Science of Literature* by a Netherlander, Henrik Clemens Muller, given at Edinburgh in 1898,[34] is an isolated exception to the rule and so is the four-volume work of a Rumanian, Michel Dragomirescou, *La Science de la littérature* (1928–29). The expression has cropped up again in Guy Michaud's *Introduction à une science de la littérature,* published in Istanbul in 1950. In English and French "science" became so much identified with natural science that the term could not survive, while in Germany "Wissenschaft" kept its old broader meaning and thus "Literaturwissenschaft," shorn of its naturalistic association, was picked up as the slogan for the new poetics and criticism directed against the prevailing literary history. In 1908 Rudolf Unger, a student of Dilthey, pleaded for a study of philosophical problems in modern "Literaturwissenschaft,"[35] but apparently only after the first world war did the term become the rallying cry of the new scholars. In

---

42. Eine Uebersicht," pp. 189–202. Theodor Mundt, *Geschichte der Literatur der Gegenwart* (Berlin, 1842), p. 2, refers to "Literaturgeschichte als eine besondere Wissenschaft," and "der Begriff der Literatur als einer zusammenhängenden nationalen Wissenschaft." I cannot find the compound "Literaturwissenschaft" though Kohlschmidt (see n. 27) refers to this book for the first occurrence of the term.

33. Richard Gosche, "Übersicht der literarhistorischen Arbeiten in den Jahren 1863 und 1864," in *Jahrbuch für Literaturgeschichte, 1* (Berlin, 1865), 221.

34. Published in Haarlem, 1904.

35. *Philosophische Probleme in der neueren Literaturwissenschaft* (Munich, 1908).

1920 a Pole, Sigmund von Lempicki, wrote *Geschichte der deutschen Literaturwissenschaft,* a book which excludes practical criticism but includes poetics and literary history, and in 1923 the *Vierteljahrschrift für Literaturwissenschaft und Geistesgeschichte* was founded and Paul Merker published his booklet, *Literaturgeschichte und Literaturwissenschaft,* which is based on this contrast.

In the English-speaking countries in the meantime, the hold of the word "criticism" was reconfirmed by such books as I. A. Richards' *Principles of Literary Criticism* (1924), by the vogue of the term "The New Criticism" since J. C. Ransom's book in 1941, and by Northrop Frye's *Anatomy of Criticism* (1957). In other American critics such as R. P. Blackmur and Kenneth Burke or in the English critic G. Wilson Knight the function and claims of criticism are similarly expanded to make criticism something like a total world view or even a system of philosophy.

In France, in spite of the prestige of Sainte-Beuve and Taine, the meaning of the word "critique" has narrowed somewhat, though later than in Germany, for different reasons, and with less drastic effects. With Ferdinand Brunetière "la critique universitaire" reached its peak of influence and with the reaction against the man and his doctrine a neutral factual "literary history" became victorious in the French universities (for which Gustave Lanson is somewhat unjustly held responsible). Criticism went its own ways outside of the Academy or mostly so. It seems characteristic of contemporary France that critics in the wide Anglo-American sense taught or teach largely in the Swiss universities: Albert Thibaudet, Albert Béguin, Marcel Raymond, Georges Poulet, to name a few. But in France the term "critique littéraire" is still inclusive and a term to conjure with. Gide, Valéry, Malraux, Mauriac are critics, and some philosophers care for the theory of literature. The hostility to criticism is rather a peculiarity of the French academic situation and the positivistic factualism so conspicuous in its doctrine of comparative literature than a widely shared contraction of the term "critique."

Meanwhile in Germany the contraction has stopped its course and the term is again acquiring its older and wider meaning. There is certainly a revival of interest in the history of German criticism. E. R. Curtius in a well-known passage of his *Europäische Literatur und lateinisches Mittelalter* (1948) eloquently pleaded for a recognition of German criticism during the classic age.[36] Emanating from East Germany is a full anthology of German criticism by Hans Mayer[37] who interprets the term in its old sense as including poetics and literary theory. The influence of English and American usage since the war and possibly the Russian example are felt in this trend.

I wonder whether the established English, French, and Italian usage of "criticism" does not in its very breadth obscure some meaningful distinctions. I still believe in the distinction between "literary theory"—a term which seems to me preferable to "poetics" because it definitely includes the prose forms and renounces prescription implied in the old term—and "literary criticism" in the more narrow sense as the study of concrete works of literature with emphasis on their evaluation. Croce as early as 1894 complained that the term "literary criticism" had come to mean merely an assemblage of the most diverse operations of the mind, held together merely by a common subject matter, the work of literature.[38] The German narrowing to daily book reviewing seems to me dangerous because it leaves evaluation to the journalist and isolates "Literaturwissenschaft" as a discipline

36. Bern, 1948, p. 304.

37. Hans Mayer, ed., *Meisterwerke deutscher Literaturkritik* (2 vols. Berlin, 1954–56).

38. In *La Critica letteraria* (Rome, 1894), reprinted in *Primi Saggi* (2nd ed. Bari, 1927), pp. 77 ff.

removed from contemporary literature and released from the task of discrimination and evaluation. An in-between solution seems to commend itself. We cannot legislate away the wide English, French, Italian, etc., usage of "criticism": I have myself used it in the title of my *History of Modern Criticism*. But let us try to keep the meaningful distinction between "theory," concerned with principles, categories, devices, etc., and "criticism" as a discussion of concrete works of literature, whenever there seems any reason to draw attention to this distinction. Nothing more can be done by us than to make recommendations. The meaning of a word is the meaning it assumes in its context and which has been imposed on it by its users. The attempts of different schools of modern philosophy—the "analytical" philosophy centered at Oxford, or the existential analysis of Heidegger—to discover one essential meaning of a term are doomed to failure. Words have their history, are given meaning by individuals and cannot be fixed and stabilized. A terminology, particularly in such an elusive subject as literary criticism, cannot be frozen even by the greatest authority or the most influential association of scholars. We can help to disentangle meanings, describe contexts, clarify issues and may recommend distinctions but we cannot legislate for the future.

The Concept of Evolution in
Literary History

Fifty and sixty years ago the concept of evolution dominated
literary history; today, at least in the West, it seems to have
disappeared almost completely. Histories of literature and
of literary genres are being written without any allusion to
the problem and apparently with no awareness of it.[1] The
attempts of F. W. Bateson to trace the history of English
poetry as a mirror either of linguistic or of social change,[2]
and the statistical investigations of Josephine Miles into the
changes in key-words and sentence patterns which determine
"eras in English poetry,"[3] are the only exceptions I know.
The reasons for this general rejection of the concept of literary evolution today can emerge only from a sketch of its
history.

The earliest instance is in Aristotle's *Poetics*. We are told

1. See e.g. Sir Herbert Grierson and J. C. Smith, *A Critical History of English Poetry* (New York, 1946), *A Literary History of
England*, ed. A. C. Baugh (New York, 1948), *Literary History of
the United States*, ed. R. Spiller et al. (New York, 1949), David
Daiches, *A Critical History of English Literature* (2 vols. New York,
1960). I reviewed these books in *Western Review, 12* (1947), 52–
54; *Modern Philology, 47* (1949), 39–45; *Kenyon Review, 11* (1949),
500–06; and *Yale Review, 50* (1961), 416–20, respectively.

2. See *English Poetry and the English Language* (Oxford, 1934)
and *English Poetry: A Critical Introduction* (London, 1950).

3. *The Vocabulary of Poetry* (Berkeley, 1946), *The Continuity
of Poetic Language* (Berkeley, 1951), and "Eras in English Poetry,"
PMLA, 70 (1955), 853–75.

that the origin of tragedy is in the dithyramb, and of comedy
in phallic songs, and then Aristotle adds the fateful sentence:
"From its early form tragedy was developed little by little as
the authors added what presented itself to them. After going
through many alterations, tragedy ceased to change, having
come to its full natural stature."[4] The analogy between the
history of tragedy and the life-cycle of a living organism is
here asserted for the first time. Tragedy reached maturity,
"natural stature," beyond which it could not grow, as man
cannot grow after he has reached the age of twenty-one. Evolution is conceived (as everywhere in Aristotle) as a "tel-
eological process in time directed toward one and only one
absolutely predetermined goal."[5]

Antiquity applied Aristotle's insight extensively: thus Dio-
nysius of Halicarnassus traced the evolution of Greek oratory
towards the supreme model of Demosthenes, and Quintilian
did the same for Roman eloquence culminating in Cicero.[6]
Velleius Paterculus, in a passage quoted throughout the history of criticism, even as late as by Sainte-Beuve, asserted the
alternation of periods of flowering and exhaustion, the impossibility of lasting perfection, the fatal necessity of decay.[7]

These ancient ideas were taken up by Renaissance and
neoclassical criticism: echoes can be found everywhere, but
I know of no systematic application to the history of literature before the middle of the eighteenth century, when the
growth of biological and sociological speculation (in Vico,
Buffon, and Rousseau) stimulated analogous thinking about
literature. John Brown's attempt at a general history of

4. Allan Gilbert's translation, quoted from *Literary Criticism:
Plato to Dryden* (New York, 1940), p. 74.

5. Quoted from Northrop's paper described in n. 31.

6. See J. W. H. Atkins, *Literary Criticism in Antiquity 2* (Cambridge, 1934), 123, 281.

7. See J. Kamerbeek Jr., "Legatum Velleianum," in *Levende
Talen,* No. 177 (December, 1954), pp. 476–90. Sainte-Beuve quotes
the passage in *Nouveaux Lundis, 9* (January, 1865), 290.

poetry (1763)[8] expounds an elaborate evolutionary scheme: a union of song, dance, and poetry is assumed among primitive nations, and all subsequent history is described as a separation of the arts, a dissolution of each art into genres, a process of fission and specialization, of degeneration linked to a general corruption of pristine manners. Brown's scheme, marred as it is by his illogical recommendation of a return to the original union of the arts, still foreshadows the later concept of an internal development of poetry. Brown writes a "history without names," in blocks and masses, seen in a perspective which embraces the oral poetry of all known nations.

Brown's sketch was published the year before Winckelmann's *Geschichte der Kunst im Alterthum* (1764), the first history of an art which traced an evolutionary scheme with a wealth of concrete knowledge. Within an over-all analogy of growth and decline, Winckelmann describes four stages of Greek sculpture: the grand youthful style of the earliest time, the mature perfection of the Periclean climax, the decline with its imitators, the sad end with late Hellenistic mannerism. Both Herder and Friedrich Schlegel proclaimed an ambition to become the Winckelmann of literature. In Herder's many sketches of literary history and in Friedrich Schlegel's fragmentary histories of Greek poetry,[9] the "organological" concept of evolution is employed with skill and consistency. Both Herder and Schlegel assume throughout a principle of continuity, the adage *natura non facit saltum*, which in Germany had been immeasurably strengthened by

8. *A Dissertation on the Rise, Union, and Power, the Progressions, Separations, and Corruptions of Poetry and Music* (London, 1763). A fuller account of Brown and other contemporaries is in my *Rise of English Literary History* (Chapel Hill, 1941).

9. In *Griechen and Römer* (1797), which contains a long paper, "Über das Studium der griechischen Poesie," written in 1794–95, and *Geschichte der Poesie der Griechen und Römer* (1798) which, however, breaks off before treating Greek tragedy.

the philosophy of Leibniz. But in detail, Herder, Schlegel, and their many followers vary in their attitudes toward the future and the implicit consequences of the determinism implied in their scheme. Thus Herder teaches that poetry must decline from the glories of primitive song, but at the time he believes that poetry, at least in Germany, can be saved from the blight of classical civilization and be returned to the racial wellspring of its power. Friedrich Schlegel conceives of Greek poetry as a complete array of all the different genres in a natural order of evolution. The evolution is described in terms of growth, proliferation, blossoming, maturing, hardening, and final dissolution, and it is thought of as necessary and fated. But this closed cycle is completed only in Greece —modern poetry is rather "universal progressive poetry," an open system, perfectible almost limitlessly. In the Grimms, the process is one of irreversible decay: there has been in the dim past the glory of natural poetry, and modern art poetry is but its sorry detritus.[10] What is common to all of these conceptions is the assumption of slow, steady change on the analogy of animal growth, of an evolutionary substratum in the main types of literature, of a determinism which minimizes the role of the individual, and of purely literary evolution in the general process of history.

Hegel introduced a strikingly different concept of evolution. Dialetics replaces the principle of continuity. Sudden revolutionary changes, reversals into opposites, annulments and, simultaneously, preservations constitute the dynamics of history. The "objective spirit" (of which poetry is only a phase) differs profoundly from nature. The biological analogy is dropped. Poetry is conceived as self-developing, in constant give-and-take with society and history, but distinct and even profoundly different, as a product of the spirit must

10. A much fuller discussion in my *History of Modern Criticism,* (New Haven, 1955), *1*, 189 f; *2*, 7 ff., 22, 284 f.

be, from the processes of nature. But in his *Lectures on Aesthetics* Hegel does not apply his method consistently: he makes many concessions to the older, "organological" point of view which he has met in the Schlegels. Though he traces an involved scheme of triads, from epic through lyric to a synthesis in tragedy, and from symbolic through classical to romantic art, the *Lectures* remain largely a poetics and aesthetics and do not incorporate history successfully, as they should according to his theory. Hegel's followers tried to apply his scheme to literary history, but most of them succeeded only in discrediting his method by forcing the complexities of reality into Hegelian formulas.[11]

With the advent of Darwin and Spencer evolutionism revived. Spencer himself suggested how the development of literature could be conceived in terms of a law of progression from the simple to the complex.[12] In many countries the ideas of the new evolutionism were eagerly applied to literary history. But it seems difficult to decide exact priorities and to distinguish the new, Darwinian and Spencerian *motifs* from returns to ideas of "organological" or of Hegelian evolution. The exact share of these three conceptions would need detailed investigation in case of each writer on the subject. In Germany, for instance, where the romantic tradition was very strong, it would be almost impossible to disentangle the different strands in the writings on *Völkerpsychologie* of H. Steinthal and M. Lazarus, or in those on the history of German literature and on poetics of Wilhelm Dilthey and Wil-

11. Cf. e.g. Karl Rosenkranz, *Handbuch einer allgemeinen Geschichte der Poesie* (3 vols. Halle, 1832), and the much later writings of the St. Louis Hegelians (Denton Snider, W. T. Harris) on Dante, Shakespeare, and Goethe.

12. "Progress: its Law and Cause" (1857), in *Illustrations of Universal Progress* (New York, 1880), pp. 24–30, and *First Principles* (1862) (New York, 1891), pp. 354–58.

helm Scherer.[13] Evolutionism should be called Darwinian
only when it implies the mechanistic explanation of the process (which was Darwin's special contribution) and when it
uses such ideas as "survival of the fittest," "natural selection,"
"transformation of species."

In England, John Addington Symonds applies the biological analogy to the history of Elizabethan drama (1884)
with ruthless consistency. He argues that Elizabethan drama
runs a well-defined course of germination, expansion, efflo-
rescence, and decay. This development is described as
"e-volution," as an unfolding of embryonic elements to
which nothing can be added and which run their course with
iron necessity to their predestined exhaustion. The initiative
of the individual is completely denied. Genius is incapable
of altering the sequence of the stages. Even the individuality
of different cycles of evolution disappears: Italian painting
passes through exactly the same stages as Elizabethan drama.
Literary history becomes a collection of cases which serve as
documents to illustrate a general scientific law. In practice,
Symonds escaped some of the rigidities of his scheme by his
innate aestheticism and by such a device as the concept of
the "hybrid," which allows for the blurring of types which
would otherwise be made to appear too sharply distinct.[14]

After Symonds, Richard Green Moulton applied evolutionism to *Shakespeare as a Dramatic Artist* (1885) and
reiterated his faith in the principle as late as 1915 in *The
Modern Study of Literature*. There is hardly any English or
American book in these decades which deals with oral literature and is not based on Darwinian conceptions. The New

13. See Erich Rothacker, *Einleitung in die Geisteswissenschaften,*
(2nd ed. Tübingen, 1930), pp. 80n. and 215, for good comments on
Steinthal, Lazarus, Wilhelm Scherer, and Dilthey.

14. In the preface to *Shakspere's Predecessors in the English
Drama* (London, 1884) Symonds says that he wrote the book substantially in 1862–65. "On the Application of Evolutionary Principles
to Art and Literature," in *Essays Speculative and Suggestive 1* (London, 1890), 42–83, contains a theoretical defense of his method.

Zealander H. M. Posnett treated *Comparative Literature* (1886) as a Spencerian progress from communal to individual life. F. Gummere's *Beginnings of Poetry* (1901) and A. S. Mackenzie's *The Evolution of Literature* (1911) may serve as later examples by American authors.

In France the two leading critics of the period, Taine and Brunetière, were preoccupied with the problem of evolution. Taine, however, is wrongly described as a naturalistic positivist: in spite of many terminological borrowings from physiology and biology, his concept of evolution remained purely Hegelian. He definitely disapproved of Comte and Spencer.[15] Hegel, whom he read as a student, taught him "to conceive of historical periods as *moments,* to look for internal causes, spontaneous development, the incessant becoming of things."[16] But Taine never thinks of evolution as a separate literary evolution. Literature is part of the general historical process conceived as an organized unity. Literature is dependent on society, represents society. It is also dependent on the *moment,* but *moment* for Taine usually means the "spirit of the age." Only once in all his writings does Taine think of *moment* as the position of a writer in a merely literary evolution. He contrasts French tragedy under Corneille and under Voltaire, the Greek theater under Aeschylus and under Euripides, and Latin poetry under Lucretius and under Claudian, in order to illustrate the difference between precursors and successors.[17]

Ferdinand Brunetière finds his starting point in this very

15. On Taine and Comte see, besides his article in *Journal des débats* (July 6, 1864), reproduced in V. Giraud, *Essai sur Taine* (6th ed. Paris, 1912), p. 232, D. D. Rosca, *L'Influence de Hegel sur Taine* (Paris, 1928), p. 262n. On Spencer see *Derniers Essais de critique et de l'histoire* (3rd ed. 1903), pp. 198–202. There is a more detailed treatment in my article, "Hippolyte Taine's Literary Theory and Criticism," in *Criticism 1* (1959), 1–18, 123–38.

16. *Derniers Essais,* ibid. p. 198.

17. Introduction to *Histoire de la littérature anglaise, 1* (2nd ed. 1866), xxx.

passage. *Moment* with him takes precedence over *milieu* and *race*. He resolutely envisages the ideal of an internal history of literature which "has in itself the sufficient principle of development."[18] What is to be established is the inner causality. "In considering all the influences which operate in the history of literature, the influence of works on works is the main one."[19] It is a double influence, positive and negative: we imitate or reject. Literature moves by action and reaction, convention and revolt. Novelty, originality, is the criterion which changes the direction of development. Literary history is the method which defines the points of change. So far Brunetière could be a Tainian or even a Hegelian. But he has also tried to transfer specifically biological concepts from Darwinism. He believes in the reality of genres as if they were biological species. He constantly parallels the history of genres with the history of human beings. French tragedy was born with Jodelle, matured with Corneille, aged with Voltaire, and died before Hugo. He cannot see that the analogy breaks down on every point; that French tragedies were not born with Jodelle but just were not written before him, and that they died only in the sense that *important* tragedies, according to Brunetière's definition, were not written after Lemercier. Racine's *Phèdre,* in Brunetière's scheme, stands at the beginning of the decline of tragedy, but it will strike us as young and fresh compared to the frigid Renaissance tragedies which, according to the scheme, represent the "youth" of French tragedy. Brunetière in his genre histories even uses the analogy of the struggle for existence to describe the rivalry of genres and argues that some genres are transmuted into other genres. French pulpit oratory of the seventeenth and eighteenth centuries was thus changed into the

18. *Études critiques sur l'histoire de la littérature française, 3* (Paris, 1890), 4.

19. Preface to *Manuel de l'histoire de la littérature française* (Paris, 1898), p. iii.

lyrical poetry of the Romantic movement. But the analogy will not withstand close inspection: at most, one could say that pulpit oratory expresses similar feelings (e.g., about the transience of things human) or fulfills similar social functions (the articulation of the sense of the metaphysical behind our lives). But surely no genre has literally changed into another. Nor can one be satisfied with Brunetière's attempt to compare the role of genius in literature, its innovative effect, to that of the Darwinian "sport," the mechanistic variation of character traits.[20]

Brunetière's followers pushed his schematism often to absurd extremes: thus Louis Maigron, in his *Le Roman historique* (1898), simply declares one book, Mérimée's *Chronique de Charles IX* (1829), to be the culmination point of the French historical novel, to which those preceding it (such as Vigny's *Cinq-mars,* 1826) provide the stepping stones, while all those which follow (such as Hugo's *Notre Dame de Paris,* 1831) demonstrate only slow decadence. Chronology is king: a neat gradation and recession must be construed at any price.

Later attempts to modernize and modify the concept of literary evolution failed. Thus John Matthews Manly was deeply impressed by the mutation theory of De Vries and proposed its application to literary history and especially to the history of medieval drama.[21] But "mutation" turns out to be simply the introduction of new principles which suddenly crystallize new types. Evolution, in the sense of slow continuous development, is given up in favor of an anomalous principle of special creation.

Evolutionism, especially in the form in which it was formulated by Brunetière, was not convincing. It was widely criticized and rejected, in part, of course, simply in the name

20. See E. R. Curtius, *Ferdinand Brunetière* (Strassburg, 1914).
21. "Literary Forms and the New Theory of the Origin of Species," *Modern Philology, 4* (1907), 577–95.

of genius and impressionistic appreciation. But the reaction
in the early twentieth century has deeper roots and raises
new issues. It was powerfully supported by the new philosophies of Bergson and Croce. Bergson's concept of creative
evolution, his intuitive act of true duration, rejected the
whole idea of a chronological order. It is no accident that his
central book, *Evolution créatrice* (1907), ends with an
attack on Spencer. Croce's onslaught on the very concept of
genre was almost universally convincing. His arguments for
the uniqueness of every work of art and his rejection of
artistic devices, procedures, and styles, even as topics of history, destroyed, in the eyes of many, the very basis of all
evolutionism. Croce's prediction and hope that literary history would come to consist entirely of essays and monographs (or handbooks and compendia of information) is
being fulfilled.[22]

All over the West, the antihistorical point of view in criticism reasserted itself at about the same time. It was in part a
reaction against critical relativism, against the whole anarchy
of values to which nineteenth century historicism had led,
and in part a new belief in a hierarchy of absolute values, a
revival of classicism. T. S. Eliot has most memorably formulated his sense of the simultaneity of all literature, the feeling
of a poet "that the whole of the literature of Europe from
Homer and within it the whole of the literature of his own
country has a simultaneous existence and composes a simultaneous order."[23] This sense of the timelessness of literature
(which Eliot oddly enough calls the "historical sense") is

22. "La Riforma della storia artistica e letteraria," in *Nuovi Saggi
di estetica* (2nd ed. Bari, 1927), pp. 157–80; and "Categorismo e
psicologismo nella storia della poesia," in *Ultimi Saggi* (Bari, 1935),
pp. 373–79. See my "Benedetto Croce, Literary Critic and Historian," in *Comparative Literature,* 5 (1953), 75–82.

23. "Tradition and the Individual Talent" (1917), in *Selected
Essays* (London, 1932), p. 14.

only another name for classicism and tradition. Eliot's view has been followed by almost all recent English and American critics. On occasion they may recognize the illumination which criticism derives from literary history and history in general,[24] but they have on the whole ignored the problem of literary historiography and evolution.

The story has been very different in Russia. There Spencerian evolutionism was stated most impressively in the grandiose attempts of Aleksandr Veselovsky to write a historical poetics on a worldwide scale. Veselovsky had been a pupil of Steinthal in 1862 in Berlin; he drew evolutionism also from many other sources, including the English ethnographers. More concretely, and with a much wider command of literatures and languages than anybody in the West, he traces the history of poetic devices, themes, and genres throughout oral and medieval literature. Yet Veselovsky's theoretical assumptions are extremely rigid. Content and form are sharply divorced. Poetic language is assumed as something given since immemorial times: it changes only under the impact of social and ideological changes. Veselovsky traces the break-up of the syncretism of original oral poetry and always looks for survivals of animism, myth, ritual, or customs in conventional poetic language. All poetic creativity is seen as occurring in the prehistoric times when man created language. Since then the role of the individual has been limited to modifying the inherited poetic language in order to give expression to the changed content of his own time. On the one hand Veselovsky conducts a genetic inquiry into the dim origins of poetry, on the other he studies "comparative literature," migrations and radiations of devices and motifs. His shortcomings are those of his period: he worships fact and science so excessively that he has no use for aesthetic

24. E.g. William K. Wimsatt, Jr., "History and Criticism: A Problematic Relationship," in *The Verbal Icon* (Louisville, Ky., 1954), pp. 253–66.

value; he views the work of art far too atomistically, dividing it into form and content, motifs and plots, metaphors and meters.[25]

Deservedly Veselovsky enjoyed enormous academic prestige and thus imposed the problem of literary evolution on the Russian Formalists. They shared his emphasis on the work of literature, his preoccupation with formal devices, his interest in the "morphology" of literary types. But they could not accept his view of evolution. They had grown up in a revolutionary atmosphere which radically rejected the past, even in the arts. Their allies were the Futurist poets. In contemporary Marxist criticism art had lost all autonomy and was reduced to a passive reflection of social and even economic change. This the formalists could not accept. But they could accept the Hegelian view of evolution: its basic principle of an immanent, dialectical alteration of old into new and back again. They interpreted this for literature largely as a wearing out or "automatization" of poetic conventions and then the "actualization" of such conventions by a new school using radically new and opposite procedures. Novelty became the one criterion of value.[26]

The formalist view was imported to Czechoslovakia, mainly through Roman Jakobson. It was applied most consciously to the problem of literary evolution by Jan Mukařovský, who restated its theory with a great awareness of the aesthetic and critical issues. His aim was to evaluate an individual work of art in relation to the dynamics of evolution. "A work of art will appear as a positive value when it regroups the structure of the preceding period, it will appear

25. On Veselovsky see Victor Erlich, *Russian Formalism: History–Doctrine* (The Hague, 1955); in Russian see B. M. Engel'gardt, *A. N. Veselovsky* (Petrograd, 1924), and V. Zhirmunsky's long introduction to Veselovsky, *Istoricheskaya Poetika* (Leningrad, 1940).

26. On the Russian formalists Erlich's book is the most informative, not only in English.

as a negative value if it takes over the structure without changing it."[27] Mukařovský argues in favor of a divorce between literary history and criticism: purely aesthetic evaluation belongs to criticism rather than to literary history. Criticism, he thinks, looks necessarily at a work as a fixed and realized structure, a stable and clearly articulated configuration, while history must see a poetic structure in constant movement, as a continuous reshuffling of elements and transformation of their relations. In history there is only one criterion of interest: the degree of novelty.

But Mukařovský (like the other Formalists) is unable to answer a basic question about the direction of change: if change is only alternation, action and reaction, it will be an ever-recurring oscillation around the same axis. But does evolution in fact proceed always in the opposite direction? And what is the opposite? Is the lyric the opposite of the epic, as Hegel assumed? Is accentual meter the opposite of syllabic? Is metonymy the opposite of metaphor? With Mukařovský's single criterion nothing can be said about the starting point of a series except that it is altogether new. We are asked to value initiators more highly than the great masters, to prefer Marlowe to Shakespeare, Wyatt to Spenser, Klopstock to Goethe. We are expected to forget that novelty need not be valuable or essential, that there may be after all, original rubbish. We are to avoid reflecting that the very material of literary history must be chosen in relation to values, that structures involve values, and that when structures are developing, values are developing also. History cannot be divorced from criticism as Mukařovský attempted to do. It is not entirely surprising that Mukařovský in recent years abandoned his Formalist scheme and embraced Marxism—of course, at the expense of his original insight into the nature and autonomy of art.

27. *Polákova Vznešenost přírody* (Prague, 1934), p. 9. Reprinted in *Kapitoly z české poetiky, 2* (Prague, 1948), 100–01.

Strangely enough neither Mukařovský nor any other Formalist writer has paid proper attention to the last collaborative effort of Yuryj Tynyanov and Roman Jakobson, an article "Questions of the Study of Literature and Language" (1927), in which the authors restate the problem of immanent evolution, but revise it significantly. The crucial passages are these:

> The idea of a purely synchronic system turned out to be an illusion. Every synchronic system has its past and its future as inseparable parts of the system. (Archaism is a fact of style: the literary and linguistic background may be felt as a worn-out, old-fashioned style; or on the other hand, innovating tendencies in language and literature may be conceived as renewals of the system.)
>
> The concept of a literary synchronic system does not coincide with the concept of a chronological period as it is ordinarily thought of, since it is composed not merely of literary works, chronologically proximate, but also of works, which are brought in from foreign literatures and older periods. Thus an undiscriminating catalogue of co-existing works is insufficient. The hierarchy of works in a given age is decisive.[28]

Though this is formulated somewhat too succinctly and is perhaps obscure, the passage does contain a radical criticism of literary evolutionism and suggests the right remedies: that is, the critic's (as well as the poet's) freedom to select from the past and the necessity for the critic (who may be also the poet) of multiple value judgment.

An analogy between literature and the human mind is inevitable: I am living not merely in the present reacting against the immediate past (as the evolutionists assume),

28. "Voprosy izučenija literatury i jazyka," in *Novyj Lef* (1927, No. 12), pp. 26–37.

but simultaneously in three times: in the past through memory, in the present, and, through anticipation, plans, and hopes, in the future. I may reach, at any moment, into my own remote past or into the remotest past of humanity. There is a constantly potential simultaneity in a man's mental development: it constitutes a structure which is virtual at any single moment. It is simply not true that an artist necessarily develops toward a single future goal: he can reach back to something he may have conceived twenty, thirty, or fifty years ago. He can start on a completely different track. His reaching out into the past for models or stimuli, abroad and at home, in art or in life, in another art or in thought, is a free decision, a choice of values which constitutes his own personal hierarchy of values, and will be reflected in the hierarchy of values implied in his works of art. It will eventually affect the hierarchy of values of a given period and should be discerned and interpreted by the critic.

Darwinian or Spencerian evolutionism is false when applied to literature because there are no fixed genres comparable to biological species which can serve as substrata of evolution. There is no inevitable growth and decay, no transformation of one genre into another, no actual struggle for life among genres. Hegelian evolutionism is right in denying the principle of gradation, in recognizing the role of conflict and revolution in art, in seeing the relationship of art to society as a dialectical give-and-take, but it is wrong in its rigid determinism and its schematism of triads. The Formalist version of it is wrong in the attempt to arrive at value in a value-proof way. What is needed (and this is implied in the passage quoted from Tynyanov and Jakobson) is a modern concept of time, modeled not on the metric chronology of the calendar and physical science, but on an interpenetration of the causal order in experience and memory. A work of art is not simply a member of a series, a link in a chain. It may stand in relation to anything in the past. It is not only a structure to be analyzed descriptively, as the Russian and Czech Formalists assume. It is a totality of values which do not adhere to the structure but constitute its very nature. All attempts to drain value from literature have failed and will fail because its very essence is value.

Finally, a science of literature which divorces literary study from criticism (i.e. value judgment) is impossible. Taine, who at first tried to expel value from criticism, came himself to the conclusion that he was mistaken and recanted in his *Philosophie de l'art*,[29] construing a double scheme of social and aesthetic value. R. G. Moulton failed when he advocated an "inductive criticism," and so did Emile Hennequin when he thought he could base a purely scientific criticism on a study of the psychology of the author and a sociology of the audience.[30] I. A. Richards failed when he tried to reduce poetry to a kind of tonic for our nerves, as he could not concretely describe the "patterning of our impulses," supposedly achieved by poetry, and could not relate this mysterious state of mind to any concrete work. And the Russian Formalists failed when they wanted to reduce all value to one: that of novelty.

Yet the denial of a "science" of criticism is by no means a recommendation of pure subjectivity, of "appreciation" and arbitrary opinion. Literary scholarship must become a systematic body of knowledge, an inquiry into structures, norms, and functions which contain and *are* values. Criticism cannot be expelled from literary history. The problem of an internal literary history, the central question of evolution, will have to be newly approached with a realization that

29. See section "De l'idéal dans l'art," first published separately in 1867. Good comment in Sholom J. Kahn, *Science and Aesthetic Judgment. A Study of Taine's Critical Method* (New York, 1953).

30. On Moulton, see "Science in Criticism," in J. M. Robertson, *Essays towards a Critical Method* (London, 1889), pp. 1–148. Emile Hennequin's *La Critique scientifique* (1888) was reviewed by Brunetière in *Questions de critique* (Paris, 1889), pp. 297–324.

time is not a mere uniform sequence of events and that value cannot be only novelty. The question is immensely complex, for at any moment the whole past is implicated and all values are implied. We must discard easy solutions and face reality in all its concrete density and diversity.[31]

31. I know of no history of evolutionism in literature. The treatment of evolutionary concepts in historiography and philosophy in Ernst Troeltsch, *Der Historismus und seine Probleme* (Tübingen, 1922), is most illuminating. I have profited from F. S. C. Northrop's "Evolution in its Relation to the Philosophy of Nature and the Philosophy of Culture," in *Evolutionary Thought in America,* ed. Stow Persons (New Haven, 1950), pp. 44–84, and from Hans Meyerhoff, *Time in Literature* (Berkeley, 1955).

Concepts of Form and Structure in
Twentieth-Century Criticism

It would be easy to collect hundreds of definitions of "form" and "structure" from contemporary critics and aestheticians and to show that they contradict each other so radically and basically that it may be best to abandon the terms. The temptation is great to throw up one's hands in despair, to pronounce the case another instance of the Babylonian confusion of tongues which seems to be a characteristic of our civilization. The only alternative to despair is, one could argue, the "analytical philosophy" proposed by a group of British philosophers inspired by the Austrian Ludwig Wittgenstein. They declare philosophy and thus also aesthetics to be "the examination of the ways in which language is used"[1] and would, by patient analysis, arrive at something like a series of dictionary definitions. Actually some years ago the Polish phenomenologist, Roman Ingarden, wrote an elaborate paper[2] in which he disentangled nine different meanings of the contrast between form and content. Here I shall have a more modest, quite different aim in view: I should like to sketch some fairly obvious distinctions between the concepts of form and structure as these are employed by some of the prominent critics of our time, and thus suggest some main trends of twentieth-century criticism.

It is no overstatement to say that there is wide agreement

1. W. Elton, *Aesthetics and Language* (Oxford, 1954), p. 12.
2. "Das Form-Inhalt-Problem im literarischen Kunstwerk," *Helicon, 1* (1938), 51–67.

today that the old distinction between form and content is untenable. I quote a recent formulation by Harold Osborne:

> The form of a poem, the prosodic structure, the rhythmic interplay, the characteristic idiom, are nothing any more when abstracted from the content of meaning; for language is not language but noise except in so far as it expresses meaning. So, too, the content without the form is an unreal abstraction without concrete existence, for when it is expressed in different language it is something different that is being expressed. The poem must be perceived as a whole to be perceived at all. There can be no conflict between form and content . . . for neither has existence without the other and abstraction is murder to both.[3]

This recognition of the inseparability and reciprocity of form and content is of course as old as Aristotle. It was reasserted by German romantic criticism and by devious ways, via Coleridge or the French Symbolists or De Sanctis, descends to twentieth-century criticism, to Croce, to the Russian Formalists, to the American New Criticism, to German "Formgeschichte." In general, the older rhetorical Renaissance and neoclassicist use which refers "form" to elements of a verbal composition—rhythm, meter, structure, diction, imagery, and "content" to message and doctrine, has been abandoned as we recognize that " 'Form' in fact embraces and penetrates 'message' in a way that constitutes a deeper and more substantial meaning than either abstract message or separable ornament."[4] The old views survive, for instance, in Marxist criticism which is a version of nineteenth-century didacticism interested in propaganda, message, and ideology.

3. *Aesthetics and Criticism* (London, 1955), p. 289.
4. W. K. Wimsatt and Cleanth Brooks, *Literary Criticism* (New York, 1957), p. 748.

Still, there are even some Marxist critics who, in theory,
admit the importance of form: especially the Hungarian
Georg Lukács has been able to assimilate some of the insights
of Hegelian aesthetics to his materialistic ideology and to recognize the importance of "aesthetic form as serving the purpose of expressing all essential moments of universality."[5]

In general, then, the reciprocity between form and content
seems well established in modern criticism. I shall try to
show, nevertheless, that in practice very different consequences have been drawn from this insight.

In Croce's *Estetica* (1902), the unity of a work of art, the
identity of form and content is asserted with great vigor.
Croce rejects the idea that there is any abstractable content
and says that "the aesthetic fact is form, and nothing but
form."[6] But one misunderstands Croce if one thinks of him
as "formalist." The terms are used in almost the opposite
sense to the traditional, as he himself recognizes: "Some call
'content' the internal fact or expression (for us, on the contrary, form), and 'form' the marble, the colours, the rhythm,
the sounds (for us the antithesis of 'form')."[7] "Form" in
Croce is "expression-intuition," another term for the work
of art, but the work of art is in Croce, we must realize, a
purely internal event. "What is external is no longer a work
of art,"[8] says Croce, speaking quite consistently within his
epistemological system, a total monistic idealism. Croce even
admits that what he calls form could also be called content. "It is merely a question of terminological convenience,
whether we should present art as content or as form, provided
it is always recognized that the content is formed, and the
form filled, that feeling is figured feeling and the figure a

5. "Einführung in die Aesthetik Tschernyschewskijs" (1952), in
Beiträge zur Geschichte der Aesthetik (Berlin, 1954), p. 159.

6. Eng. trans., *Aesthetic* (2nd ed. London, 1922), p. 16.

7. Ibid., p. 98.

8. Ibid., p. 51.

figure that is felt."[9] Hence if we examine Croce's practical criticism we are constantly made aware that he does not discuss formal problems (in the old sense) at all, but always tries to define the leading sentiment, the master faculty of an author. The concern of his criticism is not with the objective, verbal structure and not of course with the raw material outside of art such as the theme or the intellectual doctrine, but with the feelings, attitudes, and preoccupations embodied in the work of art. Croce arrives, e.g. at the formula that Corneille was dominated by one passion, that of free will, and that Ariosto was inspired by a desire for cosmic harmony. His criticism is really ethical, even psychological if we recognize that Croce makes the distinction between an empirical and a poetic personality, and studies only the latter. The emphasis on the unity and uniqueness of the work of art results, in Croce's practical criticism, often in abstract and, to my mind, rather empty generalizations. The term "form" in Croce has reversed its meaning: it is the same as what Hegel calls *Gehalt,* or substance.

Valéry in France is at the opposite pole from Croce: no wonder that Croce detested him. Valéry, like all modern critics, recognizes the collaboration of sound and sense in poetry which he thinks of as a kind of compromise between the two. "The value of a poem resides in the indissolubility of sound and sense."[10] But Valéry emphasizes "form" in the sense of pattern, words in a pattern, words formalized so that "content" disappears, at least in theory. He quotes Mistral with approval, "There is nothing but form,"[11] and approves of Mallarmé for whom "the material is no longer the cause of the 'Form'; it is one of the effects."[12] Valéry can say para-

9. "Breviario di Estetica," in *Nuovi Saggi di estetica* (3rd ed. Bari, 1948), p. 34.
10. *Variété, 5* (30th ed. Paris, 1948), 153.
11. *Vues* (Paris, 1948), p. 173.
12. Ibid., p. 188.

doxically that "content is nothing but an impure form—that
is to say a mixed form."[13] He praises Hugo because with
Hugo "the form is always master. . . . Thought becomes a
means and not the end of expression,"[14] and he says of himself: "I subordinate 'content' to 'form' when I am nearer my
best state—I am always inclined to sacrifice the former to
the latter."[15] This formalism extends to the origin of a poem
in the poet's mind. "Sometimes something wants to express
itself, at other times, some means of expression wants something it can serve."[16] The technical, the formal suggestions
come first: "A charming, touching, 'profoundly human' (as
fools say) idea comes sometimes from the need of linking
two stanzas, two developments."[17] "The principal persons
of a poem are always the smoothness and the vigor of the
verses."[18] Valéry rapturously praises the value of conventions and conventional forms such as the sonnet, since he
aims to achieve the ideal work of art, unified, nonrelative,
nontemporal, imperishable, something beyond the decay of
nature and man, something absolute, "a closed system of all
parts in which nothing can be modified."[19] Valéry has no use
for the diffuse novel and is puzzled by the violence of drama.
He offers an austere ideal of pure poetry with Mallarmé and
himself as its only successful practitioners.

At first sight, Valéry and T. S. Eliot seem to resemble each
other closely. But this is deceptive, at least with regard to
form: Eliot in his critical writings hardly ever refers to form.
He is concerned with the creative process, with emotions and

13. *Variété, 3* (45th ed. Paris, 1949), 26.
14. *Vues,* p. 180.
15. "Propos me concernant," in Berne-Jouffroy, *Présence de Valéry* (Paris, 1944), p. 20.
16. *Variété, 5,* 161.
17. *Tel Quel, 2* (36th ed. Paris, 1948), 76.
18. *Variété, 1* (91st ed. Paris, 1948), 78.
19. Quoted in Charles Du Bos, *Journal 1921–23* (Paris, 1946),
p. 222 (January 30, 1923).

feelings, with the problem of "belief," with tradition, or at most with the difference between the diction of poetry and that of drama. In his usual noncommittal manner he does echo the great issue: "In the perfect poet form and content fit and are the same thing; it is always true to say that form and content are the same thing, and always true to say that they are different things."[20] He is interested in the pattern of imagery, the "figure in the carpet": an image he draws from a well-known story by Henry James. Still he makes almost nothing of the term or concept "form."

Similarly the other most influential English critic of the century, I. A. Richards, hardly bothers about "form." He can say that the "close cooperation of the form with the meaning is the chief secret of Style in poetry,[21] but only in order to deny that there can be any sound values, any metrical effects, apart from meaning. Form is totally dispensed with, dissolved into impulses and attitudes. Moreover, Richards' main disciple, William Empson, is not concerned with "form." He studies the ambiguities of poetic language in single passages and words and in a 1952 study, *The Structure of Complex Words,* engages rather in a special kind of lexicography than in literary criticism. Another prominent English critic, F. R. Leavis, who has combined motifs from Eliot and Richards, is also indifferent to form. "Technique can be studied and judged only in terms of the sensibility it expresses, otherwise it is an unprofitable abstraction."[22] Leavis deceptively emphasizes linguistic, verbal values, but he leaves the verbal surface very quickly in order to discuss the particular emotion or ethos an author conveys. In practice, Leavis' method is strangely similar to Croce's.

The only prominent English literary critic who is preoc-

20. Introduction to Ezra Pound, *Selected Poems* (London, 1928), p. x.
21. *Practical Criticism* (New York, 1949), p. 233.
22. *Education and the University* (London, 1943), p. 113.

cupied with "form" is Herbert Read. He has a close interest in the fine arts and knows Clive Bell and Roger Fry and their theories of "significant form." But he is nearer the romantics (especially Coleridge)[23] and T. E. Hulme, who drew from Worringer the distinction between Abstraction and Empathy, abstract and organic form. Read defends organic form and sees beyond word-music, image and metaphor, structure and conception "structure which is the embodiment of words in a pattern or form."[24] But, in practice, Read is another "emotionalist" like Eliot, only with a more romantic taste, who looks for the "nexus of emotion,"[25] for "sensibility," and finally for the psychic personality which he studies with the tools of Freud and Jung.

The situation in American criticism is entirely different though it is not unfair to say that the New Critics derive from Eliot and Richards. The blanket term "New Criticism" largely obscures the extreme diversity of recent American criticism, the deep contradictions and divergences between the main critics. The problem of form is an excellent test case. For our purposes we can ignore the many fine critics whose chief concern is social, political, or psychological, such as Edmund Wilson or Lionel Trilling. We can divide modern American critics into three groups: Kenneth Burke and Blackmur go together; Ransom, Winters, and Allen Tate form a group, and Cleanth Brooks and W. K. Wimsatt agree in principle. Kenneth Burke combines the methods of Marxism, psychoanalysis, and anthropology with semantics in order to devise a system of human behavior and motivation which uses literature only as a starting point or illustration. In his early books there is still concern for "form," but

23. Cf. *The True Voice of Feeling, Studies in English Romantic Poetry* (London, 1953).

24. *Collected Essays in Literary Criticism* (London, 1948), p. 60.

25. Ibid, p. 71.

"form" is defined as "an arousing and fulfillment of desires. A work has form in so far as one part of it leads a reader to anticipate another part to be gratified by the sequence."[26] The whole burden is thus shifted, as in Richards, to the emotional responses of the reader. In *The Philosophy of Literary Form* form is completely subordinated to an interpretation of poetry as a series of "strategies for the encompassing of situations."[27] Poetry in practice is an act of the poet's self-purification. Blackmur, who is strongly influenced by Burke, has a similar psychologistic concept of form: "its final purpose is to bring into being an instance of the feeling of what life is about,"[28] but Blackmur is much more intimately concerned than Burke with literature, with words, diction, meter, and on occasion, with the "principle of composition" —what he oddly enough calls "executive form."[29]

J. C. Ransom, usually considered the founder of the New Criticism, and Yvor Winters may be classed together—in spite of their disagreements—as critics who have relapsed into ancient dualisms. Ransom distinguishes between "texture" and "structure" in poetry. "Texture" is the seemingly irrelevant detail, the concrete local life of a poem which by its very logical irrelevancies reconstitutes the *Dinglichkeit,* the "body," the qualitative richness of the world, while "structure" is the indispensable logical statement which poetry must make about reality.[30] The dualism of form and content, message and decoration seems here reintroduced. It is quite bluntly reaffirmed by the highly moralistic Yvor

26. *Counter-Statement,* (2nd ed. Los Altos, Calif., 1953), p. 124.
27. *The Philosophy of Literary Form* (Baton Rouge, 1941), p. 1.
28. *The Lion and the Honeycomb* (New York, 1955), p. 268.
29. Ibid., p. 273.
30. See *The World's Body* (New York, 1938), especially the chapter, "Poetry: A Note in Ontology"; and *The New Criticism* (Norfolk, Conn., 1941), the chapter, "Wanted: An Ontological Critic."

Winters: poetry makes a defensible rational statement about a given human experience.[31] Form is something moral: an imposition of order on matter.[32] Form is even a decisive part of the "moral content," which allows some final reconciliation of feelings and technique. A similar dualism is concealed in Allen Tate's concept of "tension" which punningly combines "extension" and "intension," with "intension" meaning something very similar to Ransom's "texture."

The real "formalist" among the American critics is Cleanth Brooks, who definitely has rejected these dichotomies and has grasped more clearly than any American critic the organic point of view. Brooks, however, comes also from the direction of Richards and Empson and writes, at least in his earlier essays, with a deceptively psychological vocabulary. He analyzes poems as structures of tensions, of paradoxes and ironies. Irony and paradox are terms used very broadly in Brooks: irony is "a general term for the kind of qualification which the various elements in a context receive from the context."[33] Thus the contextual unity, the wholeness, the formal coherence and integrity of a poem are analyzed, and the "heresy of paraphrase," i.e. any attempt to reduce a poem to its prose content, is rejected. Brooks does not succumb to the false biological analogies of the organistic concept of form but holds firmly to a totality which in spite of highly varied metaphorical terms such as "resolutions," "balances," and "harmonization" is seen as a genuinely linguistic and formal structure. Brooks is primarily a critic and analyst of individual poems. Statements on purely philosophic abstract levels of an organistic theory have, however, become common in American aesthetics: in William K. Wimsatt, who has recently collaborated with Brooks on a short history of *Literary Criticism;* in Susanne Langer who,

31. *In Defence of Reason* (Denver, 1947), p. 11.
32. Ibid., 64n.
33. *The Well Wrought Urn* (New York, 1947), p. 191.

drawing on Cassirer and Bell, defines art "as the creation of forms symbolic of human feeling"[34]; in Morris Weitz's *Philosophy of the Arts* (1950); and in Eliseo Vivas.

The concept of "organic form," of "unity in variety," of "the reconciliation of opposites" derives from Coleridge and through him from the German romantics. In Germany, however, its tradition had died out, at least in practice. During the nineteenth century the formalism of Herbart, which conceived of form as the sensuous surface or the combination of sounds, was an important movement in aesthetics, especially for the fine arts and music (E. Hanslick), but influenced literary criticism only slightly. German literary scholarship became either philological or, in the twentieth century, increasingly *geistesgeschichtlich* and psychological, influenced by the towering figure of Dilthey and his concept of *Erlebnis*. Even the George-school, which did recover a feeling for form can, in its criticism, hardly be described as "formalistic." Gundolf, in his book on Goethe seeks to construct his subject's "Gestalt," a term which suggests an obscure synthesis of biography and criticism. In this heroically stylized figure no distinction, Gundolf argues, can be made between "Erlebnis" and work, with the result that Gundolf again confuses life and art.

In more strictly academic scholarship Oskar Walzel has turned attention again to formal problems: though the terms have been used before, he has, I believe, contributed to a replacement in Germany of the old "Form-Stoff" dichotomy by rechristening it: *Gehalt und Gestalt*. But his work is either concerned with individual technical devices or with *Die wechselseitige Erhellung der Künste*, the transfer of the categories devised by Wölfflin for art history to literary history. It is a theory of the evolution of styles. Certain broadly conceived types are interpreted mainly in terms of intellectual history or of obscure changes in the manner of "seeing." This

---

34. *Feeling and Form* (New York, 1953), p. 40.

seems to me true also of Paul Böckmann's *Formgeschichte der deutschen Dichtung* (1949). "Formgeschichte" is here defined: "Geschichte der Auffassungsformen des Menschlichen"[35]: i.e. form is changed into some attitude toward the world, into man's self-knowledge and self-interpretation or it remains a "Formwille" or even, paradoxically, "Formgedanke." Böckmann and many other German scholars operate with the term "inner form," which comes from the neo-Platonic tradition through Shaftesbury to Winckelmann, Goethe, and Wilhelm von Humboldt but remains as vague as ever, since one cannot draw a line between it and "outer form." "Inner form" seems only a metaphor for psychological and philosophical attitudes grouped around some assumed center. Böckmann's book seems to me slightly disguised *Geistesgeschichte.* Neither formal nor critical but historical and relativistic, it is concerned with showing the change from medieval symbolism to *Ausdruckskunst,* to romantic self-expression.

The term "organic form" has also been revived in Germany with strong emphasis on its biological analogies by Günther Müller and Horst Oppel. The analogy between the work of art and a living being is so strongly exploited by these two authors that they are in constant danger of obliterating the distinction between art and life, between a work of art made by man and an animal or tree. Müller speaks, e.g. of the time scheme of a novel as if it were the skeleton of an animal.[36] Literary scholarship is to become a branch of biology.

In some countries, especially in France, existentialism has meant a turn to the study of literature as philosophy. In Germany, surprisingly, existentialism has focused on the text of the literary work, on its projected structure—since German

35. Hamburg, 1949, p. 13.
36. See *Die Gestaltfrage in der Literaturwissenschaft und Goethes Morphologie* (Halle, 1941), and "Morphologische Poetik" in *Heli-*

existentialism distrusts *Geistesgeschichte,* sociology, and psychology. In Max Kommerell and in Emil Staiger especially there is a new awareness of the problem of form, though these writers are hardly concerned with overall form but rather with the interpretation of single passages, or the theory of genres related to time and tense. In Friedrich Bollnow's distinguished book on Rilke the dangers of the existentialist attitude from a literary point of view, are demonstrated most clearly: the poems are treated almost as sequences of philosophical statements which are to be accepted as binding truths or rejected as untrue.

It seems to me that in spite of the basic truth of the insight of organicism, the unity of content and form, we have arrived today at something like a deadend. A final glance at Russian "Formalism," discussed more fully in "The Revolt against Positivism," may support this conclusion and suggest, at least, one way out. The movement is hardly known in the West, since it was suppressed in Russia, and its texts are exceedingly difficult of access. But there is now a good description in English by Victor Erlich, *Russian Formalism,*[37] which allows us to know the basic theories very accurately. "Form," for the Russians, became a slogan so all-inclusive that it meant simply everything that makes a work of art. The Russian Formalists argued in a context of revolt against the ideological criticism around them, against the idea of "form" as a mere container into which ready-made "content" is poured. They argued, like many critics before and after, for the inextricable unity of form and content, the impossibility of drawing a line between the "linguistic elements" and the "ideas" expressed in them. Content implies some element of form. The events told in a novel, for instance, are parts

---

con, 5 (1943); and Oppel, *Morphologie der Literaturwissenschaft* (Mainz, 1947).

37. The Hague, 1955.

of the content while the way they are arranged into a plot is presumably part of the form. Dissociated from this way of arrangement, they have, however, no artistic effect whatsoever. Even in the language of the aesthetic surface, considered usually as part of the form, the words themselves, usually aesthetically indifferent, must be differentiated from the manner in which individual words make up units of meaning, which alone have aesthetic effect. The Russian Formalists have, often quite inconsistently, chosen two solutions: one is simply the extension of the term "form." "Form is what makes a linguistic utterance a work of art." Thus Victor Shklovsky can say that the "Formalist method does not deny the ideology or the content of art, but considers the so-called content as one of the aspects of form."[38] Victor Zhirmunsky admits that "if by 'formal' we mean 'aesthetic,' all facts of content become in art formal phenomena." This allows him to say "Love, sorrow, tragic inner strife, a philosophical idea, etc., do not exist in poetry as such but only in their concrete form."[39] Roman Jakobson draws from this insight the consequence of the irresponsibility of the artist. "It is as absurd to attribute ideas and feelings to a poet as it was for a medieval audience to beat an actor for playing Judas. Why should the poet have greater responsibility for the conflict of ideas than for a duel by swords or pistols?"[40] Ideas are like colors on a canvas; means toward an end, functioning in an artistic totality which we call "form."

But usually the Russian formalists saw that it is not sufficient simply to make "form" absorb "content." They replace the traditional dichotomy by a new one: by a contrast between the extra-artistic, nonaesthetic materials and the sum of artistic devices. "Device" (*priyom*) became for them the

38. Loc. cit., p. 160.
39. Loc. cit., p. 159.
40. *Novyeshaya russkaya poeziya* (Prague, 1921), pp. 16–17.

only legitimate subject matter of literary study with the result that "form" was replaced by a mechanistic concept of the sum of techniques or procedures which could be studied separately or in diverse interlocking combinations. The Russian Formalists, especially in their early work, analyzed poetic language as a special language, characterized by a purposeful "deformation" of ordinary speech, by what they called strikingly the "organized violence" committed against it. They studied the sound stratum, vowel harmonies, consonant clusters, rhyme, prose rhythm, and meter, leaning heavily on the results of modern linguistics, its concept of the phoneme and its functional method. They were positivists with a scientific, almost technological ideal of literary scholarship. Their concept of form seems to make it a sum of relations between elements. Though their tools were immeasurably finer, they returned to the old rhetorical "formalism."

But when Russian formalism was exported to Poland and Czechoslovakia in the period between the two wars it came into contact with the German tradition of *Ganzheit, Gestalt,* wholeness, totality, and with the philosophical insights into the nature of the object of contemplation which can be found in Husserl's phenomenology or in a different way in the philosophy of symbolic forms of Cassirer. The Czech group around the Prague Linguistic Circle (now defunct) called the doctrine "structuralism" rather than "formalism" because they felt that the term "structure" (which must not be misinterpreted as referring to anything purely architectural) does more justice to the totality of the work of art and is less weighed down by suggestions of externality than "form." They saw that "form" cannot be studied merely as a sum of devices and that it is not purely sensuous, or even purely linguistic inasmuch as it projects a "world" of motifs, themes, characters, and plots. The Polish phenomenologist Roman Ingarden has, in his *Das literarische Kunstwerk* (1931), given the most coherent account of a theory which sees that the work of art is a totality but a totality composed of different heterogeneous strata.[41] Such a concept of the literary work of art avoids two pitfalls: the extreme of organicism which leads to a lumpish totality in which discrimination becomes impossible, and the opposite danger of atomistic fragmentation. A book like Wolfgang Kayser's *Das sprachliche Kunstwerk* (1948) seems to point in the right direction even though it may be difficult to accept some of his distinctions. A concept of stratification, developed also in my (and Austin Warren's) *Theory of Literature* (1949), allows us to return to concrete analytical work without having to surrender the basic insights into the wholeness, totality, and unity of content and form.

But again, it seems to me that even a complete analysis of the structure of a work of art does not exhaust the task of literary scholarship. As I have said before, a work of art is a totality of values which do not adhere merely to the structure but constitute its very essence. All attempts to drain value from literature have failed and will fail because its very essence is value. Literary study cannot and must not be divorced from criticism, which is value judgment. It would be the task of another paper to plead that we cannot divorce form and structure from concepts such as value, norm, and function and that it is impossible to have a science of form and structure or style which is not part of an aesthetics and a canon of criticism.

41. Halle, 1931, p. 24. "Die wesensmässige Struktur des literarischen Werkes liegt m. E. darin, dass es ein aus mehreren heterogenen Schichten aufgebautes Gebilde ist."

The Concept of Baroque in
Literary Scholarship

1

All students of English will realize that the use of the term "baroque" in literature is a recent importation from the continent of Europe. A full-scale history of the term, which has never been attempted,[1] would be of considerable interest, even though I do not believe that the history of any term needs to be decisive for its present-day use, and though I realize that a term cannot be returned to any of its original meanings; least, of course, by the dictum of one man.

"Baroque" as Karl Borinski and Benedetto Croce have shown by convincing quotations,[2] is derived from *baroco,* the name for the fourth mode of the second figure in the scholastic nomenclature of syllogisms. It is a syllogism of the type: "Every P is M; some S are not M, hence some S are not P"; or to give Croce's example: "Every fool is stubborn; some people are not stubborn, hence some people are not fools." This type of argument was felt to be sophistical and far-fetched as early as 1519 when Luis Vives ridiculed the Parisian professors as "sophists in *baroco* and *baralip-*

1. J. Isaacs, "Baroque and Rococo: A History of Two Concepts," *Bulletin of the International Committee of the Historical Sciences,* 9 (1937), 347–48, is only a very brief abstract of an unpublished lecture.

2. Karl Borinski, *Die Antike in Poetik und Kunsttheorie 1* (Leipzig, 1914), 199, 303; Benedetto Croce, *Storia della Età barocca in Italia* (Bari, 1929), pp. 20 ff.

ton."[3] Croce gives several examples of the use of such phrases as "ragioni barrochi" from 1570 on. The etymology found in the *NED* and elsewhere which would derive the term from the Spanish *barrueco,* an oddly-shaped pearl, must apparently be abandoned. In the eighteenth century the term emerges with the meaning of "extravagant," "bizarre." In 1739 it is used thus by the Président de Brosses, and in the sense of "decorative, playfully free" by J. J. Winckelmann in 1755.[4] In Quatremère de Quincy's *Dictionnaire historique de l'architecture* (1795–1825), it is called "une nuance du bizarre" and Guarino Guarini is considered the master of the baroque.[5] Jakob Burckhardt seems to have stabilized its meaning in art history as referring to what he considered the decadence of the High Renaissance in the florid architecture of the Counter Reformation in Italy, Germany, and Spain. In 1843 he had used the term *rococo* in exactly the same sense as he later used baroque and suggested that every style has its rococo: a late, florid, decadent stage.[6] This suggestion of Burckhardt's of an extension of the term was taken up by Wilamowitz-Moellendorff, the famous classical philologist, who in 1881 wrote about "ancient baroque," i.e. Hellenistic art. L. von Sybel, in his *Weltgeschichte der Kunst* (1888)[7] has a chapter on ancient Roman baroque. The same

3. Quoted in Gustav Schnürer, *Katholische Kirche und Kultur in der Barockzeit* (Paderborn, 1937), p. 68, from *In pseudodialeticos.*
4. Charles de Brosses, *Le Président de Brosses en Italie,* ed. R. Colomb, *2* (Paris, 1885), 15; J. J. Winckelmann, *Sendschreiben* (1744), p. 113, quoted by Borinski, *Die Antike,* p. 303, and *Gedanken über die Nachahmung der griechischen Werke* (Dresden, 1756), p. 87.
5. Quoted by Heinrich Wölfflin, *Renaissance und Barock* (Munich, 1888), p. 10.
6. Wölfflin, ibid., refers to Burckhardt's "Über die vorgotischen Kirchen am Niederrhein," in Lersch's *Niederrheinisches Jahrbuch* (1843).
7. See n. 5.

year is the date of Heinrich Wölfflin's *Renaissance und Barock,* a detailed monograph chiefly concerned with the development of architecture in Rome. Wölfflin's work is highly important not only because it gave a first reliable technical analysis of the development of the style in Rome in appreciative terms, but because it also contains a few pages on the possibility of applying baroque to literature and music. With Wölfflin began the revaluation of baroque art, soon taken up by other German art historians such as Gurlitt, Riegl, and Dehio, and soon to be followed in Italy by Giulio Magni and Corrado Ricci, and in England by Martin S. Briggs and Geoffrey Scott. The latter wrote a fervent defence, oddly enough called *The Architecture of Humanism* (1914).[8] After the first World War, admiration and sympathy for even the most grotesque and tortured forms of baroque art reached its peak in Germany; there were a good many individual enthusiasts in other countries, such as Eugenio d'Ors in Spain, Jean Cassou in France, and Sacheverell Sitwell in England.[9] In art history, today, baroque is recognized as the next stage of European art after the Renaissance. The term is used not only in architecture, but also in sculpture and painting, and covers not only Tintoretto and El Greco but also Rubens and Rembrandt.

8. Cornelius Gurlitt, *Geschichte des Barockstils in Italien* (Stuttgart, 1887); *Geschichte des Barockstils und des Rococo in Deutschland* (Stuttgart, 1889); Alois Riegl, *Barockkunst in Rom* (Vienna, 1908); Guilio Magni, *Il Barocco a Roma* (3 vols. Turin, 1911–13); Corrado Ricci, *Baroque Architecture and Sculpture in Italy* (London, 1912); Martin Shaw Briggs, *Baroque Architecture* (London, 1913). Geoffrey Scott, *The Architecture of Humanism* (London, 1914 [2nd ed. New York, 1924]).

9. Eugenio d'Ors, *Du Baroque* (Paris, 1935); Sacheverell Sitwell, *Southern Baroque Art* (London, 1931), *Spanish Baroque Art* (London, 1931), *German Baroque Sculpture* (London, 1938); Jean Cassou, "Apologie de l'art baroque," in *L'Amour de l'art* (September, October, 1927).

Baroque is also fully established as a term in the history of music. It was apparently well-known in the eighteenth century, as Rousseau's *Dictionnaire de Musique* (1764) lists it as a term for music with "confused harmony" and other vices.[10] But the Czech music historian August W. Ambros seems to have been the first to use it as a period term, in 1878.[11] Today it is the current label for seventeenth-century music and seems to be applied widely to Schütz, Buxtehude, Lully, Rameau, and even Bach and Handel.[12] There are now also baroque philosophers: Spinoza has been called baroque and I have seen the term applied to Leibniz, Comenius, and even Berkeley.[13] Spengler spoke of baroque painting, music, philosophy, and even psychology, mathematics, and physics. Baroque is now used in general cultural history for practically all manifestations of seventeenth century civilization.[14]

10. *1* (Amsterdam, 1769), 62 (1st ed. 1764).

11. W. August Ambros, *Geschichte der Musik, 4* (Breslau, 1878), 85–86.

12. E.g. in Oscar Thompson's *Dictionary of Music and Musicians* (New York, 1943). Leichtentritt, Paul Lang, McKinney and Anderson, and apparently most other current histories of music have sections on the baroque. Cf. also Robert Haas, *Die Musik des Barocks* (Potsdam-Wildpark, 1929).

13. Carl Gebhardt, "Rembrandt und Spinoza, Stilgeschichtliche Betrachtungen zum Barockproblem," *Kant-studien, 32* (1927), 161–81, argues that Rembrandt and Spinoza are both baroque and closely similar. Karl Joël's *Wandlungen der Weltanschauung, 1* (Tübingen, 1938) has a chapter on baroque philosophy. See Hermann Schmalenbach, *Leibniz* (Munich, 1921), especially pp. 11–18; Dietrich Mahnke, "Der Barock-Universalismus des Comenius," *Zeitschrift für Geschichte der Erziehung, 21* (1931), 97–128, and *22* (1932), 61–90; "Der Zeitgeist des Barock und seine Verewigung in Leibnizens Gedankenwelt," *Zeitschrift für deutsche Kulturphilosophie, 2* (1936), 95–126.

14. Oswald Spengler, *Der Untergang des Abendlandes, 1* (Munich, 1923), 400 (1st ed. 1918); Egon Friedell, *Kulturgeschichte*

So far as I know, Wölfflin was the first to transfer the term baroque to literature. In a remarkable page of *Renaissance und Barock* (1888)[15] he suggests that the contrast between Ariosto's *Orlando Furioso* (1516) and Tasso's *Gerusalemme liberata* (1584) could be compared to the distinction between Renaissance and baroque. In Tasso, he observes a heightening, an emphasis, a striving for great conceptions absent in Ariosto, and he finds the same tendency in Berni's reworking of Boiardo's *Orlando innamorato*. The images are more unified, more sublime; there is less visual imagination (*Anschauung*), but more mood (*Stimmung*). Wölfflin's suggestions do not seem to have been taken up for a long time. A search through a large number of writings on marinism, gongorism, euphuism, *préciosité,* and German *Schwulst* has failed to produce more than one or two passages where a literary work or movement is actually called baroque before 1914, though baroque art was discussed as a parallel phenomenon under that name.[16] This seems to be true of the writings of Benedetto Croce before the first World War. In *Saggi sulla letteratura italiana del seicento* (1910), the literature is never called baroque, though Croce discusses the parallel with baroque in the arts and even warns against the "exaggeration" in the appreciation of seventeenth-century literature "to which the present fashion which in the plastic arts has returned to the baroque could easily seduce us."[17]

In 1914, however, a Danish scholar, Valdemar Vedel,

---

der *Neuzeit,* 2 (Munich, 1929); Willi Flemming, *Deutsche Kultur im Zeitalter des Barocks* (Potsdam, 1937); Schnürer, *Katholische Kirche.*

15. Pp. 83–85.

16. Corrado Ricci, *Baroque Architecture and Sculpture in Italy* (New York, 1912), calls Marino "the Baroque poet *par excellence*" (p. 1). This would be the first use of the term applied to literature known in English.

17. Bari, 1910, cf. xix, xx, 404, etc.

published a paper "Den digteriske Barokstil omkring aar
1600."[18] He draws there a close parallel between Rubens
and French and English poetic style between 1550 and 1650.
Literature is, like the art of Rubens, decorative, colorful,
emphatic. Vedel lists favorite themes and words in literature
which he considers applicable to the art of Rubens: grand,
high, flourish, red, flame, horses, hunt, war, gold, the love
of show, swelling bombast, mythological masquerade. But
Vedel's article, possibly because it was in Danish, was completely ignored. The radiating point for the spread of the
term was Germany and especially Munich where Wölfflin,
a Swiss by birth, was a professor. His colleague in German
literature, Karl Borinski, wrote a long book, *Die Antike in
Poetik und Kunsttheorie* (1914), with the subtitle for Volume I, *Mittelalter, Renaissance und Barock,* where he discusses especially the conceptist theories of Gracián and
sketches the history of the term in a learned and substantially
accurate note.[19]

In 1915 Wölfflin published a new book, *Kunstgeschichtliche Grundbegriffe,*[20] where Renaissance and baroque are
contrasted as the two main types of style, and criteria for
their distinction are worked out very concretely. This book
made a tremendous impression on several German literary
historians struggling with the problem of style. It seemed to
invite imitation and possibly transfer to literary history. In
1916, without mentioning Wölfflin, Fritz Strich gave a stylistic analysis of German seventeenth-century lyrical poetry
which he called "baroque."[21] Oskar Walzel, in the same year,

18. In *Edda, 2* (Kristiana, 1914), 17–40.
19. See n. 2.
20. Munich, 1915. Eng. trans. M. D. Hottinger, *Principles of Art
History* (New York, 1932).
21. "Der lyrische Stil des 17. Jahrhunderts," in *Abhandlungen
zur deutschen Literaturgeschichte, Festschrift für Franz Muncker*
(Munich, 1916), pp. 21–53.

followed with a paper which claimed Shakespeare as belonging to the baroque.[22] In 1917 Max Wolff rejected Walzel's claim but admitted baroque in Shakespeare's *Venus and Adonis,* in the *Rape of Lucrece,* and in Lyly.[23] In 1918 Josef Nadler published the three-volume edition of his *Literaturgeschichte der deutschen Stämme und Landschaften,*[24] an original attempt to write the history of German literature "from below," from the local literature of the German cities and provinces. Nadler, whose orientation was then strongly Austrian and Roman Catholic, used the term baroque very prominently to describe the Jesuit Counter Reformation literature of southern Germany.

But all these items I have described up till now are comparatively isolated. The enormous vogue of baroque as a literary term arose in Germany only about 1921–22. In 1921 Rudolf von Delius published an anthology of German baroque poetry and in the next year no fewer than four such anthologies were issued.[25] Josef Gregor wrote a book on the Vienna baroque theater[26] and Arthur Hübscher started the long line of philosophers on the baroque with a piece, "Barock als Gestaltung antithetischen Lebensgefühls."[27] Herbert Cysarz, one of the most prolific and pretentious of

22. "Shakespeares dramatische Baukunst," *Jahrbuch der Shakespearegesellschaft, 52* (1916), 3–35, reprinted in *Das Wortkunstwerk, Mittel seiner Erforschung* (Leipzig, 1926), pp. 302–25.

23. "Shakespeare als Künstler des Barocks," *Internationale Monatsschrift, 11* (1917), 995–1021.

24. Regensburg, 1918.

25. *Die deutsche Barocklyrik* (Stuttgart, 1921); Max Pirker, *Das deutsche Liebeslied in Barock und Rokoko* (Zurich, 1922); Fritz Strich, "Die deutsche Barocklyrik," in *Genius, 3* (Munich, 1922); W. Unus, *Die deutsche Lyrik des Barock* (Berlin, 1922); R. Wiener, *Pallas und Cupido. Deutsche Lyrik der Barockzeit* (Vienna, 1922).

26. *Das Wiener Barocktheater* (Vienna, 1922).

27. "Grundlegung einer Phaseologie der Geistesgeschichte," *Euphorion, 24* (1922), 15; Ergänzungsheft, 517–62, 759–805.

the German writers on literary baroque, published his first large, boldly-conceived book, *Deutsche Barockdichtung*, in 1924.[28] Since then interest in the German seventeenth century has risen by leaps and bounds and produced a large literature permeated by the term baroque. I would be hesitant to dogmatize about the exact reasons for this revival of German baroque poetry; part of it may be due to Spengler, who had used the term vaguely in the *Decline of the West*,[29] and part is due, I think, to a misunderstanding. Baroque poetry was felt to be similar to the most recent German expressionism, to its turbulent, tense, torn diction and tragic view of the world induced by the aftermath of the war; part was a genuine change of taste, a sudden comprehension for an art despised before because of its conventions, its supposedly tasteless metaphors, its violent contrasts and antitheses.

German scholars soon applied their newly found criterion to other European literatures. Theophil Spoerri was, in 1922, I believe, the first to carry out Wölfflin's suggestions as to the difference between Ariosto and Tasso.[30] Ariosto is shown by Wölfflin's criteria to be Renaissance; Tasso, baroque. Marino and the Marinists appeared baroque. Spain was also easily assimilable, since Gongorism and conceptism presented clearly parallel phenomena which had but to be christened baroque. But all other Spanish literature, from Guevara in the early sixteenth century to Calderón in the late seventeenth century, was soon claimed as baroque. Wilhelm Michels in a paper on "Barockstil in Shakespeare und Cal-

28. Leipzig, 1924; see his earlier article, "Vom Geist des deutschen Literaturbarocks," *Deutsche Vierteljahrschrift für Literaturwissenschaft und Geistesgeschichte, 1* (1923), 243–68.

29. *Der Untergang des Abendlandes* (Munich, 1923), pp. 236, 308, 399–400, etc.

30. *Renaissance und Barock bei Ariost und Tasso. Versuch einer Anwendung Wölfflin'scher Kunstbetrachtung* (Bern, 1922).

derón" (1929)[31] used the acknowledged baroque characteristics of Calderón to argue that Shakespeare also shows the
same stylistic tendencies. There seems to be only some disa-
greement among the German writers as to the status of
Cervantes: Helmut Hatzfeld as early as 1927 had spoken
of Cervantes as "Jesuitenbarock"[32] and had argued that his
world view is that of the Counter Reformation. In a later
paper, "El predominio del espíritu español en las literaturas
del siglo XVII,"[33] Hatzfeld tried to show that Spain is eter-
nally, basically baroque and that it was historically the
radiating center of the baroque spirit in Europe. The perma-
nently Spanish features which are also those of baroque
were only temporarily overlaid by the Renaissance. Ludwig
Pfandl, however, who wrote the fullest history of Spanish
literature during the Golden Age,[34] limits baroque to the
seventeenth century and expressly exempts Cervantes. Both
Vossler and Spitzer, however, consider even Lope de Vega
baroque (in spite of Lope's objections to Góngora).[35]

French literature was also described by German scholars
in terms of the baroque. Neubert and Schürr[36] talked, at
first somewhat hesitatingly, of baroque undercurrents and
features in seventeenth-century France. Schürr claimed Rabelais as early baroque and described the *précieux*, the writers

31. *Revue Hispanique, 85* (1929), 370–458.

32. *Don Quixote als Sprachkunstwerk* (Leipzig, 1927), p. 287.

33. In *Revista de Filología Hispánica, 3* (1941), 9–23.

34. *Geschichte der spanischen Nationalliteratur in ihrer Blütezeit,*
(Freiburg im Breisgau, 1929), p. 289.

35. Karl Vossler, *Lope de Vega und sein Zeitalter* (Munich, 1932),
pp. 89–105 especially; Leo Spitzer, *Die Literarisierung des Lebens in
Lopes Dorotea* (Bonn, 1932).

36. V. Klemperer, H. Hatzfeld, F. Neubert, *Die romanischen Lit-
eraturen von der Renaissance bis zur französischen Revolution* (Wildpark-Potsdam, 1928); Friedrich Schürr, *Barock, Klassizismus und
Rokoko in der französischen Literatur. Eine prinzipielle Stilbetrach-
tung* (Leipzig, 1928).

of the sprawling courtly novels and of burlesques, as baroque, a style which was defeated by the new classicism of Boileau, Molière, La Fontaine, and Racine. Others advocated the view that these French classics themselves are baroque. Apparently Erich Auerbach, in 1929, was the first to voice this view.[37] Leo Spitzer endorses it with some qualifications. In a brilliant analysis of the style of Racine,[38] he has shown how Racine always tones down baroque features, how Racine's baroque is tame, subdued, classical. Though Hatzfeld does not completely deny the obviously striking distinctions of French classicism, he is the one scholar who most insistently claims all French classicism as baroque. In an early paper[39] he discusses the French religious poetry of the seventeenth century, showing its similarity to Spanish mysticism and its stylistic similarities to general baroque. In a long piece in a Dutch review[40] he has accumulated many observations to show that French classicism is only a variant of baroque. French classicism has the same typically baroque tension of sensuality and religion, the same morbidity, the same pathos as Spanish baroque. Its form is similarly paradoxical and antithetical, "open" in Wölfflin's sense. The discipline of French classicism is simply a universal characteristic of the "rule over the passions," recommended by the Counter Reformation everywhere.

English literature, even outside of the attempts to claim Shakespeare as baroque, was also soon brought in line. As

37. Reported by Leo Spitzer, "Klassische Dämpfung in Racines Stil," in *Romanische Stil- und Literaturstudien, 1* (Marburg, 1931), 255n. In talking with me Auerbach repeatedly denied Spitzer's report.

38. Cf. n. 37. The paper appeared first in *Archivum Romanicum, 12* (1928), 361–472.

39. "Der Barockstil der religiösen klassischen Lyrik in Frankreich," *Literaturwissenschaftliches Jahrbuch der Görresgesellschaft, 4* (1929), 30–60.

40. "Die französische Klassik in neuer Sicht. Klassik als Barock," *Tijdschrift voor Taal en Letteren, 23* (1935), 213–81.

far as I know, Friedrich Brie's *Englische Rokokoepik* (1927) is the first attempt of this sort.[41] There Pope's *Rape of the Lock* is analyzed as rococo, but in passing a contrast to the baroque Garth and Boileau is drawn. Fritz Pützer in "Prediger des englischen Barocks stilistisch untersucht" (1929) then claimed almost all English pulpit oratory from Latimer to Jeremy Taylor as baroque.[42] F. W. Schirmer in several articles and in his *Geschichte der englischen Literatur*[43] uses the term for the metaphysicals, Browne, Dryden, Otway, and Lee, excluding Milton from the baroque expressly. This was also the conclusion of Friedrich Wild[44] who called even Ben Jonson, Massinger, Ford, and Phineas Fletcher baroque. The idea of an antithesis of sensualism and spiritualism in English seventeenth-century poetry was in the mean time carried out in a rather mechanical fashion by Werner P. Friederich,[45] a work which was accepted as a Harvard Ph.D. thesis under J. L. Lowes. There are a good many other German theses on English literary baroque: Wolfgang Jünemann[46] compared Dryden's *Fables* with their sources to show how Dryden translated, e.g. Chaucer into a baroque style; Wolfgang Mann[47] examined Dryden's

41. Munich, 1927.
42. Diss. Bonn, 1929.
43. "Die geistesgeschichtlichen Grundlagen der englischen Barockliteratur," *Germanisch-romanische Monatsschrift, 19* (1931), 273–84; "Das Problem des religiösen Epos im siebzehnten Jahrhundert in England," *Deutsche Vierteljahrschrift für Literaturwissenschaft und Geistesgeschichte, 14* (1936), 60–74; *Geschichte der englischen Literatur* (Halle, 1937).
44. "Zum Problem des Barocks in der englischen Dichtung," *Anglia, 59* (1935), 414–22.
45. *Spiritualismus und Sensualismus in der englischen Barocklyrik. Wiener Beiträge, 57* (Vienna, 1932).
46. *Drydens Fabeln und ihre Quellen, Britannica,* No. 5 (Hamburg, 1932).
47. *Drydens heroische Tragödien als Ausdruck höfischer Barockkultur* (1932). Diss. Tübingen.

heroic tragedies as an expression of courtly baroque culture. A Zurich thesis by Elisabeth Haller[48] analyses the baroque style of Thomas Burnet's *Theory of the Earth* in comparison with its Latin and German translations. The view that all English seventeenth-century civilization is baroque has been pushed farthest by Paul Meissner,[49] who includes also Milton and who has devised a whole scheme of contraries covering all activities and stages of the English seventeenth century. In a piece which stresses the Spanish influence in England, Hatzfeld goes so far as to call Milton "the most hispanized poet of the age, who to the foreigner appears the most baroque."[50] Bernhard Fehr finally has extended the frontiers of English baroque by finding it in Thomson and Mallet and even tracing it in the verse form of Wordsworth.[51] Thus all literatures of Europe in the seventeenth century (and in part of the sixteenth century) are conceived of by German scholars as a unified movement. E.g. in Schnürer's bulky volume, *Katholische Kirche und Kultur der Barockzeit* (1937),[52] Spain, Portugal with Camões, Italy, France, Germany, Austria, but also Poland, Hungary, and Yugoslavia are treated as baroque. It is a coherent view which needs discussion, acceptance, refutation, or modification.

I have reviewed the Germans first because they were the originators and instigators of the movement (if one ignores the isolated Dane, Vedel). But the idea was taken up soon

48. *Die barocken Stilmerkmale in der englischen, lateinischen und deutschen Fassung von Dr. Thomas Burnets Theory of the Earth, Swiss Studies in English,* 9 (Bern, 1940). See my review in *Philological Quarterly, 21* (1942), 199–200.

49. *Die geisteswissenschaftlichen Grundlagen des englischen Literaturbarocks* (Munich, 1934).

50. *Revista de Filología Hispánica, 3* (1941), 22.

51. "The Antagonism of Forms in the Eighteenth Century," *English Studies, 18* (1936), 115–21, 193–205, and *19* (1937), 1–13, 49–57.

52. See n. 3.

by scholars of other nationalities. In 1919 the term made its first conquest outside Germany. F. Schmidt-Degener published a piece on "Rembrandt en Vondel" in *De Gids*[53] where Rembrandt is made out an opponent of baroque taste, while the poet Vondel, Flemish by descent and a convert to Catholicism, is drawn as the typical representative of the European baroque. The author looks with distinct disfavor on the baroque, its sensual mysticism, its externality, its verbalism in contrast to the truly Dutch and at the same time universal art of Rembrandt. To judge from a little book by Heinz Haerten, *Vondel und der deutsche Barock* (1934),[54] the revaluation of baroque has also triumphed in Holland. There Vondel is claimed as the very summit of Northern, Teutonic baroque. In general, seventeenth-century Dutch literature seems by the Dutch themselves to be now described as baroque.

The next country to succumb to the invasion was Italy. Giulio Bertoni had reviewed Spoerri without showing much interest[55]; Leonello Venturi early expounded Wölfflin.[56] But late in 1924 Mario Praz finished a book, *Secentismo e Marinismo in Inghilterra*,[57] which, in its title, avoids the term baroque, but in its text, actually two monographs on Donne and Crashaw, freely refers to baroque in literature and to the literary baroque in England. Praz studied especially the contacts of Donne and Crashaw with Italian and neo-Latin literature, and he knew the work of Wölfflin. In July 1925

53. *83* (1919), 222–75. A German translation by Alfred Pauli was published as *Rembrandt und der holländische Barock,* / *Studien der Bibliothek Warburg,* No. 9, (Leipzig, 1928).

54. *Disquisitiones Carolinae. Fontes et Acta Philologica et Historica,* ed. Th. Baader, *6* (Nijmegen, 1934).

55. In *Giornale storico della letteratura Italiana,* 81 (1923), 178–80.

56. "Gli schemi del Wölfflin," in *L'Esame,* 1 (1922), 3–10.

57. Florence, 1925. The preface is dated November, 1924. Cf. pp. 94, 110n., 113.

Benedetto Croce read a paper in Zurich on the concept of
the baroque which was then published in German translation.[58] There he discusses the term without, it seems, much
consciousness of its newness in literature, though he vigorously protests against many of the current German theories
and pleads for a revival of the original meaning of baroque
as a kind of artistic ugliness. Though Croce tried again and
again to defend his negative attitude to the baroque, he himself adopted the term as a label for the Italy of the seventeenth century. His largest book on the period, *Storia della
Età barocca in Italia,*[59] has the term on the title page. After
1925 he discussed even his beloved Basile in terms of baroque.[60] Baroque thus seems victorious in Italy.

The history of the penetration of the term into Spain is
not so clear to me. Eugenio d'Ors in an extravagant book,
Du Baroque (1935), known to me only in the French translation,[61] includes reflexions and aphorisms which are carefully dated but of which I have no means to find out whether
they were actually printed at that time in Spanish. One piece,
dated 1921, calls Milton's *Paradise Lost* baroque, and in the
later sections d'Ors finds baroque all throughout history in
Góngora and Wagner, in Pope and Vico, in Rousseau and
El Greco, in the Portugal of the fifteenth century and today.
A less fanciful application of the term has appeared in
Spain since 1927, the tercentenary of Góngora's death.
There was an anthology in honor of Góngora which spoke of

58. *Der Begriff des Barock. Die Gegenreformation. Zwei Essays*
(trans. Berthold Fenigstein), Zurich, 1925. Practically identical with
Chapters 2 and 1 of *Storia della Età barocca in Italia* (Bari, 1929).

59. *Storia* (above).

60. Introduction to Basile's *Lo Cunto de li Cunti* (2 vols. Bari,
1925). The paper on Basile in *Saggi sulla Letteratura Italiana del
Seicento* (Bari, 1910) does not use the term. The English translation
by N. M. Penzer, introducing the *Pentamerone of Giambatista Basile*
(2 vols. London, 1932), contaminates the two pieces.

61. Paris, 1935.

him as a baroque poet.[62] Then Dámaso Alonso published an edition of the *Soledades*[63] which has a page on Góngora's *barroquismo* with an express recognition of the novelty of the term. In the same year, Ortega y Gasset, in reviewing Alonso, called "Góngorism, Marinism, and Euphuism merely forms of baroque." "What is usually called classical in poetry is actually baroque, e.g. Pindar who is just as difficult to understand as Góngora."[64] Another famous Spanish scholar, Américo Castro, has also begun using baroque, first I believe for Tirso da Molina, but also for Góngora and Quevedo. In an unpublished paper on the "Baroque as Literary Style" Castro rejects the view that Rabelais or Cervantes are baroque, but accepts Pascal and Racine as well as Góngora and Quevedo.[65]

France is, I think, the one major country which has almost completely refused to adopt the term. There are a few exceptions. André Koszul calls Beaumont and Fletcher baroque in 1933, and refers in his bibliography to some of the German work.[66] A French student of German literature, André Moret, wrote a good thesis on the German baroque lyric adopting the term as a matter of course.[67] The one French book I know which makes much of the term is de

62. Gerardo Diego, *Antología poética en honor de Góngora* (Madrid, 1927). Reviewed by Dámaso Alonso in *Revista de Occidente, 18* (1927), 396–401.

63. Madrid, 1927, especially pages 31–32.

64. "Góngora, 1627–1927," in *Espíritu de la Letra* (Madrid, 1927), quoted from Ortega y Gasset, *Obras, 2* (Madrid, 1943), 1108–09.

65. "El Don Juan de Tirso y el Molière como personajes barrocos," in *Hommage à Ernest Martinenche* (Paris, 1937), pp. 93–111.

66. "Beaumont et Fletcher et le Baroque," *Cahiers du Sud, 10* (1933), 210–16.

67. *Le Lyrisme baroque en Allemagne* (Lille, 1936). Cf. also "Vers une Solution du Problème du baroque," *Revue Germanique, 38* (1937), 373–77.

Reynold's *Le XVIIe Siècle: Le Classique et le Baroque.*[68]
M. Reynold recognizes a conflict between the baroque and
the classic in seventeenth-century France: the temperament
of the time, its passion and its will seem to him baroque;
Corneille, Tasso, and Milton are called so, but the actual
French classicists appear as victors over something which
endangered their balance and poise. One should note that
Gonzague de Reynold is a professor at Fribourg, where the
late Schnürer was his colleague, and that he taught for years
at the University of Bern, to which Strich had gone from
Munich. Most French literary historians, such as Baldensperger, Lebègue, and Henri Peyre,[69] have raised their voices
vigorously against the application of the term to French literature; I have not found any evidence that even the new
French defenders of *préciosité* and its historical importance,
such as Fidao-Justiniani, Mongredien, and Daniel Mornet,[70]
have any inclination to use the term even for their protégés.
Recently, Marcel Raymond in a volume in honor of Wölfflin
has tried to distinguish Renaissance and baroque elements
in Ronsard with subtle, though extremely elusive results.
Madame Dominique Aury edited an anthology of French
baroque poets which elicited a fine essay by Maurice Blanchot.[71]

68. Montreal, 1944.
69. Fernand Baldensperger, "Pour une Révaluation littéraire du
XVIIe siècle classique," *Revue d'histoire littéraire de la France, 44*
(1937), 1–15, especially 13–14; Raymond Lebègue, *Bulletin of the
International Committee of Historical Sciences, 9* (1937), 378; Henri
Peyre, *Le Classicisme français* (New York, 1942), cf. pp. 181–83.
70. F. Fidao-Justiniani, *L'Esprit classique et la préciosité* (Paris,
1914); Georges Mongredien, *Les Précieux et les précieuses* (Paris,
1939); Daniel Mornet, "La Signification et l'évolution de l'idée de
préciosité en France au XVIIe siècle," *Journal of the History of
Ideas, 1* (1940), 225–31, and *Histoire de la littérature française
classique,* 1600–1700 (Paris, 1940).
71. "Classique et baroque dans la poésie de Ronsard," in *Concin-
nitas: Festschrift für Heinrich Wölfflin* (Bâle, 1944); Dominique

Baroque as a literary term has also spread to the Slavic countries with a Catholic past. It is used in Poland widely for the Jesuit literature of the seventeenth century, and in Czechoslovakia there has been a sudden interest in the half-buried Czech literature of the Counter Reformation which is always called baroque. The editions of baroque poets and sermons and discussions became especially frequent in the early thirties. There is also a small book by Václav Černý (1937) which discusses the baroque in European poetry, including in it even Milton and Bunyan.[72] The term seems to be used in Hungarian literary history for the age of Cardinal Pasmány, and by Yugoslavs to denote Gundulić and his great epic *Osman*. I have found no evidence that the Scandinavians speak of any period of their literature as baroque, though Valdemar Vedel, the Danish scholar who wrote the first article on poetic baroque back in 1914, has since written a book on Corneille which analyzes his style as baroque, and though there is recent Danish work on German baroque drama.[73]

To England and America the term, as applied to literature, came late, much later than the revival of interest in Donne and the metaphysicals. Grierson and T. S. Eliot do not use it, though Eliot apparently spoke of a baroque pe-

---

Aury, *Les Poètes précieux et baroques du xviie siècle* (Paris, 1942). Maurice Blanchot, "Les poètes baroques du XVIIe siècle," in *Faux Pas* (Paris, 1943), pp. 151–56.

72. Julius Kleiner, *Die polnische Literatur* (Wildpark-Potsdam, 1929), uses the term, e.g. of Casimir (Sarbiewski), the neo-Latin poet, p. 15; studies and editions by J. Vašica (e.g. *České literárni baroko*, Prague, 1938), V. Bitnar, Zdeněk Kalista, F. X. Šalda, Arne Novák, etc.; Václav Černý, *O básnickém baroku* (Prague, 1937).

73. *Deux Classiques français: Corneille et son temps—Molière.* French trans. by Mme. E. Cornet (Paris, 1935); cf. pp. 6, 7, 189, 190, 235; cf. also Erik Lunding's *Tysk Barok og Barokforskning* (Copenhagen, 1938), and *Das schlesische Kunstdrama* (Copenhagen, 1940).

riod in his unpublished Clark lectures on the metaphysical poets.[74] In an epilogue to a new edition of Geoffrey Scott's *Architecture of Humanism* (1924)[75] the parallel between Donne and Thomas Browne on the one hand and baroque architecture on the other is drawn expressly, though the literature itself is not called baroque. A rather flimsy essay by Peter Burra, published in *Farrago* in 1930, is called "Baroque and Gothic Sentimentalism"[76] but uses the term quite vaguely for periods of luxuriance as an alternative for Gothic. The more concrete literary use seems to come from Germany: J. E. Crawford Fitch published a book on Angelus Silesius in 1932 which uses the term occasionally,[77] and in 1933, the philosopher E. I. Watkin, a close student of German Catholic literature, discussed Crashaw as baroque.[78] Watkin, of course, must have known the book by Mario Praz. Crashaw is again, in 1934, the center of a study of the baroque by T. O. Beachcroft.[79] In 1934 F. W. Bateson published his little book *English Poetry and the English Language,*[80] where he applied the term baroque to Thomson, Gray, and Collins. He uses Geoffrey Scott's *Architecture of Humanism* quite independently, without being aware of the Continental uses, and without realizing that Scott is dependent on Wölfflin. Since then the term baroque occurs in English scholarship more frequently, but not, it seems to me, prominently. Recently F. P. Wilson[81] used it to characterize

74. See Mario Praz, "Donne's Relation to the Poetry of his Time," in *A Garland for John Donne, ed.* T. Spencer (Cambridge, Mass., 1932), 58–59.

75. New York, 1924, p. 268.

76. Reprinted privately, London, 1931.

77. *Angelus Silesius* (London, 1932).

78. In *The English Way: Studies in English Sanctity from St. Bede to Newman,* ed. Maisie Ward (London, 1933), pp. 268–96.

79. "Crashaw and the Baroque Style," *Criterion, 13* (1934), 407–25.

80. Oxford, 1934, pp. 76–77.

81. *Elizabethan and Jacobean* (Oxford, 1945), p. 26.

Jacobean in contrast to Elizabethan literature, and E. M. W. Tillyard[82] applied it in passing to Milton's epistolary prose.

In the United States, as early as 1929, Morris W. Croll christened a very fine analytical paper on seventeenth-century prose style "baroque."[83] Before, in several papers on the history of prose style, he had called the same traits of the anti-Ciceronian movement "Attic," a rather obscure and misleading term. Croll knew Wölfflin's work and used his criteria, though very cautiously. In the next year George Williamson, in his *Donne Tradition,* singled out Crashaw as "the most baroque of the English metaphysicals" and calls him a "true representative of the European baroque poet, contrasting with Donne therein."[84] Williamson, of course, had read Mario Praz. Since then Helen C. White in her *Metaphysical Poets*[85] used the term for Crashaw, and Austin Warren's book on Crashaw has the subtitle: *A Study in Baroque Sensibility* (1939).[86] Quite recently the term seems to be used even more widely and broadly. Harry Levin has applied the word to Ben Jonson, Wylie Sypher included the metaphysicals and Milton, and Roy Daniells, a Canadian, has argued that the later Shakespeare is baroque as well as Milton, Bunyan, and Dryden.[87]

82. John Milton, *Private Correspondences and Academic Exercises* (Cambridge, 1932), xi.

83. "The Baroque Style in Prose," in *Studies in English Philology: A Miscellany in Honor of Frederick Klaeber,* ed. K. Malone and M. B. Ruud (Minneapolis, 1929), pp. 427–56. Cf. "Juste Lipse et le mouvement anticicéronien à la fin du XVIe et au debut du XVIIe siècle," *Revue du seizième siècle, 2* (1914), 200–42; "Attic Prose in the Seventeenth Century," *Studies in Philology, 18* (1921), 79–128; "Attic Prose, Lipsius, Montaigne, and Bacon," in *Schelling Anniversary Papers* (New York, 1923), pp. 117–50; "Muret and the History of Attic Prose," P.MLA, *39* (1924), 254-309.

84. Cambridge, Mass., 1930, pp. 116, 123.

85. New York, 1936, pp. 84, 198–99, 247, 254, 306, 370, 380.

86. Baton Rouge, 1939.

87. Roswell Gray Ham, *Otway and Lee: Biography from a Baroque Age* (New Haven, 1931), p. 70; Harry Levin, introduction

The term is also used for the echoes of English seven-teenth-century literature in America. Zdeněk Vančura, a Czech scholar who visited Mr. Croll's seminar in Princeton, applied his description of baroque style to seventeenth-century American prose,[88] to Nathaniel Ward and Cotton Mather. Austin Warren finally has brilliantly analyzed the newly discovered early eighteenth-century American poet, Edward Taylor, as Colonial baroque.[89] Thus baroque is widely used today in the discussion of literature and is likely to spread even more widely.

2

This brief sketch of the spread of the term may have sug-gested the various status of baroque in the different countries —its complete establishment in Germany, its recent success in Italy and Spain, its slow penetration into English and American scholarship, and its almost complete failure in France. It is possible to account for these differences easily enough. In Germany the term succeeded because it found a vacuum: terms such as the first and second Silesian school, which were used before, were obviously inadequate and purely external. Baroque has become a laudatory term in the fine arts and could easily be used for the literature whose beauties were discovered during the change of taste caused by expressionism. Furthermore, the general revolt against

---

to *Ben Jonson: Selected Works* (New York, 1938), pp. 30, 32; Wylie Sypher, "The Metaphysicals and the Baroque," *Partisan Review, 11* (1944), 3–17; Roy Daniells, "Baroque Form in English Literature," *University of Toronto Quarterly, 14* (1945), 392–408.

88. "Baroque Prose in America," *Studies in English by Members of the English Seminar of Charles University, 4* (Prague, 1933), 39–58.

89. "Edward Taylor's Poetry: Colonial Baroque," *Kenyon Review, 3* (1941), 355–71, reprinted in *Rage for Order* (Chicago, 1948), pp. 1–18.

positivistic methods in literary scholarship enhanced interest in period terms. Discussions as to the essence of the Renaissance, romanticism, and baroque occupied German literary scholars tired of the minutiae of research and eager for sweeping generalizations. In Italy there had been long recognized the phenomenon of Marinism and *secentismo,* but baroque seemed a preferable substitute, as not being associated with a single poet and as not a mere century label. In Spain baroque has also superseded *gongorismo, culteranismo, conceptismo,* as it is a more general term, free from associations with a single style or with some peculiar critical doctrine or technical device. In France baroque has been rejected, partly because the old meaning of "bizarre" is still felt very vividly, and partly because French classicism is a distinct literary movement inimical to the ideals of contemporary baroque movements in Spain and Italy. Even Hatzfeld, who is no doubt right in stressing some affinities with the general European Counter Reformation and some concrete influences of Spain on French classicism, has to speak of the French "Sonderbarock,"[90] a prefix which seems to weaken his thesis considerably. The *précieux,* whatever their affinities with Spain and Italy may have been, are also clearly distinct in their lightness and secularity from the heavier, predominantly religious art which one associates with southern baroque. In England the reluctance to adopt the term has somewhat similar reasons: the memory of Ruskin's denunciations of baroque seems to be lingering in English minds, and this distaste cannot be corrected by the sight of any considerable baroque architecture in England. The term "metaphysical" is too well established (though admittedly misleading), and today too honorific to be felt in any serious need of replacement. As for Milton, he seems too individual

---

90. "Die französische Klassik in neuer Sicht. Klassik als Barock," *Tijdschrift voor Taal en Letteren, 23* (1935), 222.

and Protestant to be easily assimilated to baroque, still associated in most minds with Jesuits and the Counter Reformation. Besides, the English seventeenth century does not impress the historian as a unity: its earlier part up to the closing of the theaters in 1642 is constantly assimilated to the Elizabethan Age; its later part from 1660 on has been annexed by the eighteenth century. Even those who would sympathize with the view that there is a continuity of artistic tradition from Donne and Chapman to the last writings of Dryden cannot overlook the very real social changes of the civil wars, which brought with them a considerable change of taste and general "intellectual climate." Here in America, where we are unimpeded or uninspired by the sight of baroque buildings and even pseudo-baroque imitations and can think of baroque only as an episode in Colonial literature, nothing hinders the spread of the term. On the contrary, there is the danger, to judge from a few recent loosely worded review articles, that it will be bandied about too freely and will soon lose any definite meaning. Thus an analysis of its possibilities may be welcome.

3

In discussing such a term as baroque we have to realize that it has the meanings which its users have decided to give it. We can, however, distinguish between those meanings and recommend those which seem to us most useful, that is, which best clarify the complexity of the historical process. It seems to me, it would be an extreme and false nominalism to deny that such concepts as the baroque are *organs* of real historical knowledge, that in reality there are pervasive styles, or turning points in history which we are able to discern and which such terms help us in distinguishing. In such an analysis we have to take up at least three different aspects of meaning: the extension of the term, the valuation it implies on the part of the speaker, and its actual referent.

There is, first of all, the important distinction between those who use baroque as a term for a recurrent phenomenon in all history and those who use it as a term for a specific phenomenon in the historical process, fixed in time and place. The first use really belongs to a typology of literature, the second to its history. Croce, Eugenio d'Ors, Spengler and many other Germans consider it a typological term. Croce argues that the term should be returned to its original meaning, "a form of artistic ugliness," and that the phenomenon can be observed among the Silver Latin poets as well as in Marino or in D'Annunzio. Rather curiously, however, Croce abandoned this use for practical purposes and prefers to call baroque only "that artistic perversion, dominated by a desire for the stupefying, which can be observed in Europe from the last decades of the sixteenth to the end of the seventeenth century."[91] In Germany, Spengler and Worringer and, following them, Walzel in literature, used baroque as an alternative term for Gothic and romanticism, assuming an underlying identity of all these periods opposed to the other sequence of classical antiquity, Renaissance, and neoclassicism.[92] Georg Weise has argued that the baroque is rather the specifically Nordic tendency towards arbitrary inorganic decoration which occurs in the history of the arts and of literature always at the end of a period. Baroque becomes in him a synonym for the florid, precious, decorative style recurrent in all ages and countries. Old Irish poetry, Wolfram von Eschenbach, the French *rhétoriqueurs,* and Góngora are some of the examples cited.[93] Eugenio d'Ors has called such pervasive stylistic types "eons" and sees baroque as a

---

91. *Storia della Età barocca in Italia,* pp. 32–33.

92. Oskar Walzel, *Gehalt und Gestalt im Kunstwerk des Dichters* (Wildpark-Potsdam, 1925), pp. 265 ff., 282 ff.

93. "Das 'gotische' oder 'barocke' Stilprinzip der deutschen und nordischen Kunst," *Deutsche Vierteljahrschrift für Literaturwissenschaft und Geistesgeschichte, 10* (1932), 206–43.

historical category, an *idée-événement,* a "constant" which
recurs almost everywhere. He even indulges in drawing up a
table of the different variants or subspecies of *homo baroc-
chus,*[94] where we find an archaic baroque, a Macedonian, an
Alexandrian, a Roman, a Buddhist, a Gothic, a Franciscan,
a Manuelian (in Portugal), a Nordic, a Palladian (in Italy
and England), a Jesuit, a rococo, a romantic, a *fin-de-siècle,*
and some other varieties of baroque. It pervades all art history from the ruins of Baalbek to the most recent modernism, all literature from Euripides to Rimbaud, and all other
cultural activities including philosophy as well as the discoveries of Harvey and Linné. The method is pushed to absurd
extremes: half of the world's history and creations are baroque, all which are not purely classical, not flooded by the
dry light of the intellect. The term thus used may have the
merit of drawing attention to this recurrence of an emotional
art of stylistic overelaboration and decoration, but it has
become so broad and vague when cut off from its period
moorings that it loses all usefulness for concrete literary
study. To divide the world of literature into Renaissance and
baroque or classicism and baroque is no better than dividing
it into classicism and romanticism, realism and idealism. At
the most, we achieve a separation into sheep and goats. The
historian of literature will be interested far more in baroque
as a term for a definite period.

In discussing baroque as a period term we should, however, realize that, also as a period concept, baroque cannot
be defined as a class concept in logic can be defined. If it
were, all individual works of a period could be subsumed
under it. But this is impossible, as a work of art is not an
instance of a class, but is itself a part of the concept of a
period which it makes up together with other works. It thus
modifies the concept of the whole. We shall never define
romanticism or baroque or any other of these terms exhaus-

94. *Du Baroque,* pp. 161 ff.

tively, because a period is a time section dominated by some system of literary norms. Period is thus only a regulative concept, not a metaphysical essence which must be intuited nor, of course, a purely arbitrary linguistic label. We must be careful in such an analysis not to fall into the errors of medieval realism or of modern extreme nominalism. Periods and movements "exist" in the sense that they can be discerned in reality, can be described and analyzed. It would, however, be foolish to expect a single noun or adjective such as baroque to carry unimpeded and still clearly realized a dozen different connotations.[95]

Even as a period term the chronological extension of its use is most bafflingly various. In England it may include Lyly, Milton, and even Gray and Collins. In Germany it may include Fischart, Opitz, and even Klopstock. In Italy, Tasso as well as Marino and Basile; in Spain, Guevara, Cervantes, Góngora, and Quevedo as well as Calderón; in France, Rabelais, Ronsard, Du Bartas, the *précieux*, but also Racine and even Fénelon. Two or even almost three centuries may be spanned; or at the other extreme, the term may be limited to a single author in English, Richard Crashaw, or to a single style such as marinism or gongorism. The widest use, which includes the most heterogeneous authors of several centuries, should obviously be discouraged as there is always the danger of sliding back into a general typology. But the limitation to a single literary style seems not broad enough. There the existing terms like conceptism, marinism, gongorism, metaphysical poetry, might serve as well and serve with less confusion. The term baroque is most acceptable, it seems to me, if we have in mind a general European movement whose conventions and literary style

95. For a more detailed discussion of the theoretical problems involved see my "Periods and Movements in Literary History," in *English Institute Annual, 1940* (New York, 1941), pp. 73–93, and *Theory of Literature* (New York, 1949).

can be described fairly concretely and whose chronological limits can be fixed fairly narrowly, from the last decades of the sixteenth century to the middle of the eighteenth century in a few countries. Baroque points out that Sir Thomas Browne and Donne, Góngora and Quevedo, Gryphius and Grimmelshausen have something in common, in one national literature and all over Europe.

4

Baroque can be used pejoratively, or as a neutral descriptive term, or as a term of praise. Croce advocates a return to the pejorative use and goes so far as to say that "art is never baroque and baroque is never art."[96] He recognizes that Du Bartas and Góngora and some German poets of the seventeenth century were real poets, but considers that by this very fact they raised themselves into the realm of the one and indivisible realm of poetry where there cannot be different styles and diverse standards. Croce is quite alone, however, in this use, which must be mostly influenced by the low opinion he has of seventeenth-century Italian poetry. Baroque as a descriptive neutral term prevails. There is no need to follow Croce in suspecting all baroque enthusiasts of setting up a "heretical" standard of poetry expressly got up to include the great works of the baroque style. As in all styles, there may be great baroque artists, imitators, and mere bunglers. There are good and bad baroque churches as there are good and bad baroque poems. There is Góngora, Théophile, Donne, Herbert, Marvell, Gryphius, but also the mass of quibbling conceited verse which fills Saintsbury's *Minor Poets of the Caroline Period,* Croce's *Lirici marinisti,* and Cysarz's three-volume *Barocklyrik.*[97]

Among the Germans baroque has assumed an honorific

96. *Storia della Età barocca in Italia,* p. 37.
97. Saintsbury (3 vols. Oxford, 1905–21); Croce (Bari, 1910); the introduction for this volume was published only in *Saggi sulla letteratura italiana del seicento* (Bari, 1910) as "Sensualismo e Ingeg-

meaning, if only because it appears on the side of the angels in the series of Gothic-baroque-romanticism against classical antiquity, Renaissance, and neoclassicism. Enthusiasm for German baroque literature seems to have gone very far in Germany: especially Herbert Cysarz and Günther Müller are the sinners who have written in oracular adoration of works which seem derivative and frigid as well as formless and sprawling. Günther Müller especially accepts the German baroque in toto as a great *geistesgeschichtlich* achievement.[98] As its art appears to him communal, an expression of courtly culture, he feels relieved of the duties of a critic. A scholarly movement which had begun in praise of the baroque because of its supposed affinities with subjective expressionism has ended in the reduction of baroque art to a mere sociological category, "the courtly." There are other absurdities. Nadler prefers Bidermann's *Cenodoxus* to the *Divine Comedy* and Müller considers the *Aramena* of Duke Anton Ulrich von Braunschweig a greater work of art than Grimmelshausen's *Simplizissimus*. These excesses which could be paralleled by some of the extravaganzas which have been written in recent years on Vondel, Góngora, and Donne seem to confirm the view that baroque itself is neither good nor bad, but a historical style which had its great and small practitioners.

5

The most important question remains: What is the precise content of the word baroque? Two fairly distinct trends of description can be observed: one which describes it in terms

nosità nella lirica del seicento," pp. 353–408; Cysarz (3 vols. Leipzig, 1937); the introduction to Vol. I is substantially identical with *Deutsches Barock in der Lyrik* (Leipzig, 1936).

98. *Deutsche Dichtung von der Renaissance bis zum Ausgang des Barocks* (Wildpark-Potsdam, 1928), and "Höfische Kultur der Barockzeit," in Hans Naumann and Günther Müller, *Höfische Kultur* (Halle, 1929).

of style and one which prefers ideological categories or emotional attitudes. The two may be combined to show how certain stylistic devices express a definite view of the world.

The use of the term baroque in literature began with a transfer of Wölfflin's categories to literature; Walzel took one of the pair of contraries in Wölfflin, closed and open form, and applied it to Shakespeare.[99] Studying the composition of Shakespeare's plays, he came to the conclusion that Shakespeare belongs to the baroque. The number of minor characters, the unsymmetrical grouping, the varying emphasis on different acts of a play, are all traits supposed to show that Shakespeare's technique is the same as that of baroque, i.e. is "asymmetrical, atectonic," while Corneille and Racine (later to be pronounced baroque by other Germans) belong rather to the Renaissance because they composed their tragedies around a central figure and distributed the emphasis among the acts according to the Aristotelian pattern. Walzel's slogan of the baroque Shakespeare has caught on amazingly in Germany: there is even a book by Max Deutschbein, *Shakespeares Macbeth als Drama des Barock*,[1] which presents us with a graphic picture of the composition of Macbeth. An ellipse is drawn with the words "Grace" and "Realm of Darkness" written around it and "Lady Macbeth" and the "Weird sisters" placed at the focal points. We are then told that this represents the "inner form" of *Macbeth* and that the play is baroque since the baroque style "has a predilection for the oval groundplan, as shown frequently in the groundplans of baroque churches and castles." To dismiss the whole preposterous undertaking of construing a parallel on the basis of a completely arbitrary pattern of "inner form," it is not even necessary to doubt whether the ellipse is as frequent in baroque churches as Deutschbein's theory demands. Similarly Bernhard Fehr[2] has

99. See n. 22, above.
1. Leipzig, (1936?), pp. 26–28.
2. See n. 51, above.

argued that Thomson and Mallet and even Wordsworth wrote baroque blank verse since Fehr represents its run-on lines and subclauses by graphic patterns which remind him of the serpentine lines and even of the corkscrew pillars of baroque churches. He does not face the conclusion that any run-on line verse and any prose or verse with subclauses from Cicero to Fehr would have to be pronounced baroque by his criteria. But even the more sober transfer of Wölfflin's categories seems to have achieved very little for a definition of the baroque. Among these categories, four—"painterly," "open form," "unity," "relative clarity"—can be applied to baroque literature fairly easily, but they achieve little more than ranging baroque literature against harmonious, clearly outlined, well-proportioned classical literature. The dangers of this transfer become obvious in F. W. Bateson's argument that Thomson, Young, Gray, and Collins are all baroque since they fulfill the Wölfflinian categories of picturesqueness and inexactness and in their diction show the equivalent of "baroque ornament."[3] If their personifications, invocations, and stock phrases are baroque, then any poetic diction from the Silver Latin poets through the Scottish Chaucerians and the Italian sonneteers has to be classified as baroque. Baroque becomes simply a term for anything decorative, tawdry, and conventionalized. The transfer of the Wölfflinian categories to literature must lead to the giving up of a clear period concept and sliding back into a typology which can achieve only a most superficial and rough classification of all literature into two main types.

Even the many attempts to define baroque in terms of its most obvious stylistic devices run into the same difficulty. If we say that baroque literature uses conceits or is written in an ornate prose style, we cannot draw any kind of line which shall rule out the predecessors of the baroque and even styles which historically arose without any connection with the baroque. Thus conceits can be found in Lucan, in the church

3. See n. 80, above.

fathers, and in the mystics of the thirteenth century. Ornate, labored, and figured prose flourished throughout the Middle Ages, especially in the tradition of the Latin *cursus*. If we consider conceit the "elaboration of a figure of speech to the farthest stage ingenuity can carry," then we cannot distinguish between many forms of Petrarchism of the fifteenth and sixteenth centuries and the cult of Marinism. Petrarch himself must then be called baroque. If an ornate mannered prose is baroque, then many church fathers were baroque. This is a very real issue for all the many scholars who have tried to trace the sources and antecedents of Gongorism and Marinism. D'Ancona and D'Ovidio decide that Marinism was caused by Spanish influences, Belloni and Vento consider it a development of Petrarchism, Scopa traces it back to the church fathers, and Gobliani has found baroque in Seneca and Lucan:[4] in short, no clear line can be drawn on such grounds between the baroque and a good half of the world's preceding literature.

Far more useful and hopeful seem the attempts to narrow down the repertory of stylistic devices characteristic of the baroque to a few specific figures or specific types of schemes. It can be said that antithesis, asyndeton, antimetabole, oxymoron, and possibly even paradox and hyperbole are favorite figures of baroque literature. But are they peculiar to the baroque? Viëtor and Curtius[5] have traced the supposedly

4. Alessandro d'Ancona, "Del' secentismo della poesia cortegiana del secolo XV," in *Studi sulla letteratura italiana dei primi secoli* (Ancona, 1884), pp. 151–237; F. d'Ovidio, "Un Punto di Storia Letteraria; Secentismo Spagnolismo?" in *Nuova Antologia, 65* (1882), 661–68; Antonio Belloni, *Il Seicento,* (Milano [1899?]), pp. 456–66; Sebastiano Vento, "L'Essenza del Secentismo," *Rivista d' Italia, 28* (1925), 313–35; B. Scopa, *Saggio di nuove ricerche sulla origine del secentismo* (Napoli, 1907); H. Gobliani, *Il Barrochismo in Seneca e in Lucano* (Messina, 1938).

5. K. Viëtor, "Vom Stil und Geist der deutschen Barockdichtung," *Germanisch-romanische Monatsschrift, 14* (1926), 145–84, and

baroque asyndeton back through the Middle Ages to Quintilian, Cicero, and even Horace. The same could be done easily for the other figures. This objection is also fatal to the paper of Wilhelm Michels[6] who claims Shakespeare and Calderón as baroque on the basis of a stylistic analysis which lists parallels, bombast, mythology, hyperbole as expression of the quantitative urge and word play, dissection, allegory, antithesis, abstraction, the use of *sententiae* as expression of the qualitative urge (*Trieb*).

Individual stylistic devices can, however, be defined fairly clearly at least for some baroque authors or schools. The metaphysicals and their use of "conceit" seem to lend themselves very well to such sharp discrimination from the Elizabethans or the neoclassicists. If one, however, examines the definitions proposed, scarcely any one seems to set off the metaphysicals clearly from the preceding or following styles. John Crowe Ransom, Allen Tate, and Cleanth Brooks favor the view that a metaphysical poem is coextensive with its imagery, that it contains a "single extended image to bear the whole weight of the conceptual structure" or, at least, has a conceptual development in imaginistic terms.[7] But this type of definition fits only a very few poems such as Henry King's "Exequy" and is true only of the last stanzas of Donne's "A Valediction: Forbidding Mourning" where the famous metaphor of the compasses is first introduced. It does not fit, at all, an undoubted metaphysical poem such as Donne's "Twicknam Garden" which does not contain a

---

Probleme der deutschen Barockliteratur (Leipzig, 1928); E. R. Curtius, "Mittelalterlicher und barocker Dichtungsstil," *Modern Philology, 48* (1941), 325–33.

6. See n. 31, above.

7. J. C. Ransom, "Honey and Gall," *Southern Review,* 6 (1940), 10; Allen Tate, *Reason in Madness* (New York, 1941), p. 68; Cleanth Brooks, *Modern Poetry and the Tradition* (Chapel Hill, 1939), pp. 15, 39, 43, etc.

single extended image. Rosemond Tuve[8] has argued that metaphysical imagery was caused by the vogue of Ramist logic, but she, herself, cannot draw a clear distinction between the imagery of Sidney and Donne with her criteria. The most convincing analysis is a variation and elaboration of Dr. Johnson's suggestion that *"discordia concors*: a combination of dissimilar images, or discovery of occult resemblances in things apparently unlike"[9] is characteristic of metaphysical wit. Henry W. Wells spoke of the "radical image" by which he means a metaphor where vehicle and tenor meet only at one point[10]; Douds and others speak of conceit when its terms are "imaginatively removed to the farthest possible degree;"[11] Mrs. Brandenburg prefers the term "dynamic image" stressing the neutrality of the minor terms and the imaginative distance between the major and minor terms.[12] Leonard Unger[13] has analyzed many poems by Donne to show that they do not fit the definitions hitherto propounded and that a "complexity of attitudes" is rather the pervading characteristic of most of Donne's poems. But such a well-known piece as "Go and catch a falling star" shows no such complexity. His analysis is probably true only of a certain type of Donne's dramatic monologues in the *Songs and Sonnets.* Among other traditionally baroque authors, Góngora has attracted most interest for his very defi-

8. "Imagery and Logic: Ramus and Metaphysical Poetics," *Journal of the History of Ideas, 3* (1942), 365–400; elaborated in *Elizabethan and Metaphysical Imagery* (Chicago, 1947).

9. "Life of Abraham Cowley," in *Lives of the English Poets.*

10. *Poetic Imagery* (New York, 1924).

11. John Beal Douds, "Donne's Technique of Dissonance," PMLA, *52* (1937), 1051–61.

12. Alice Stayert Brandenburg, "The Dynamic Image in Metaphysical Poetry," PMLA, *57* (1942), 1039–45.

13. *Donne's Poetry and Modern Criticism* (Chicago, 1950). Reprinted in Unger's *The Man in the Name* (Minneapolis, 1956), 30–104.

nite style. Dámaso Alonso, Leo Spitzer, and Walther Pabst[14] have written careful analyses especially of the imagery and the syntax of Góngora. Alonso speaks of Góngora's metaphors as achieving "the erection of an unreal wall between meaning and object," while Pabst draws elaborate charts of the enormously intricate relationships among the metaphorical clusters of Góngora. But these analyses apply only to one very individual artist and among his works only to two poems, the *Polifemo* and the *Soledades*.

Also in the study of baroque prose style much concrete work has been accomplished. Croll has demonstrated that the style of *Euphues* is derived from medieval Latin prose and is based on *schemata verborum,* on sound figures.[15] It thus has nothing whatever to do with the new anti-Ciceronian movement in prose style which modeled itself on the style of Tacitus and Seneca and which Croll at first called "Attic" and later rechristened baroque.[16] The epigrammatic "terse" Senecan style and the asymmetrical, non-Ciceronian, sprawling period, which Croll calls "loose" style, came to dominate the seventeenth century and can be illustrated from Montaigne, Pascal, Bacon, St. Evremond, Halifax, and Sir William Temple as well as from Sir Thomas Browne, Fuller, and Jeremy Taylor. This style was ousted at the end of the seventeenth century by the simple style recommended by the

14. See n. 62, above. Also Dámaso Alonso, "Alusion y elusion en la poesía de Góngora," *Revista de Occidente, 19* (1928), 177–202 and *La Lengua poética de Góngora* (Madrid, 1935); Walther Pabst, "Góngoras Schöpfung in seinen Gedichten *Polifemo* und *Soledades,*" *Revue Hispanique, 80* (1930), 1–229; Leo Spitzer, "Zu Góngora's *Soledades,*" in *Volkstum und Kultur der Romanen, 2* (1929), 244 ff., reprinted in *Romanische Stil- und Literaturstudien, 2* (Marburg, 1931), 126–40, and "La Soledad Primera de Góngora," *Revista de Filología Hispánica, 2* (1940), 151–76.

15. Introduction to *John Lyly, Euphues: His Anatomy of Wit, Euphues and his England,* ed. Harry Clemon (London, 1916).

16. See n. 83, above.

Royal Society and inspired by scientific ideals of clarity and objectivity. But if we accept the results of these careful analyses in the history of imagery and prose style, are we prepared to accept their consequences for the term "baroque"? Some of these run completely counter to accepted usage. For instance, if we exclude all Petrarchan imagery from baroque, we arrive at the paradoxical conclusion that Marino himself was not baroque but merely an overingenious Petrarchist. The most baroque, in the conventional view, of all German poets, Lohenstein and Hoffmannswaldau, who were very close to Marino, would not fit the definition. Only Góngora, the best metaphysicals, and a few poems in Théophile, Tristan l'Hermite, and in Gryphius and possibly a few other Germans would live up to these specifications, which approximate baroque imagery to symbolist techniques. In prose style, it is true, we would succeed in excluding *Euphues* and the *Arcadia* from the baroque but we would have to exclude also most baroque preachers and orators in Italy, Austria, and elsewhere, such as the well-known Abraham à Santa Clara who, like Lyly, were primarily using schemes of sound.[17] Are we prepared to call the style of Montaigne, Bacon, and Pascal baroque? We are definitely on the horns of dilemma: either we take baroque in a wide sense and open the door to the inclusion of Petrarchism, Euphuism, and thus of Shakespeare and Sidney, or we narrow it down and then we exclude some of the traditionally most baroque authors such as Marino and the second Silesian school.

6

It is probably necessary to abandon attempts to define baroque in purely stylistic terms. One must acknowledge that all stylistic devices may occur at almost all times. Their

17. See the well-known imitation of his style in Friedrich Schiller's *Wallensteins Lager (Die Kapuzinerpredigt)*.

presence is only important if it can be considered as symptomatic of a specific state of mind, if it expresses a "baroque soul." But what is the baroque mind or soul? A majority of the discussions of baroque have been frankly ideological or socio-psychological. Baroque, first, has been associated with specific races, social classes, professions of faith, or a political and religious movement, the Counter Reformation. Obviously, post-Tridentine Catholicism is, at first sight, closely related to the rise of baroque; and there are many scholars who simply identify baroque and Jesuitism.[18] Actually, this point of view cannot be upheld without ignoring most obvious literary affinities and relationships. The cases of Germany, Bohemia, and America need only be considered. In all three countries there is an unmistakable Protestant baroque which cannot be dismissed by a specious label such as "pseudo-Renaissance"[19] and cannot be reduced to Catholic influences, as Martin Sommerfeld has tried to argue.[20] Though there are German scholars such as Nadler and Günther Müller who magnify the Catholic share in the baroque and there are others like Schulte who refuse to recognize the existence of Protestant baroque, the counterarguments seem to me completely convincing, even though I would not go to the extreme of considering, as Cysarz does, baroque primarily a Protestant creation. Certainly Gryphius and the Silesians were Protestants and a convert such as Angelus Silesius did his most characteristic writing when he

18. E.g. Werner Weisbach, *Der Barock als Kunst der Gegenreformation* (Berlin, 1921), and "Barock als Stilphänomen," *Deutsche Vierteljahrschrift für Literaturwissenschaft und Geistesgeschichte, 2* (1924), 225–56.

19. W. Schulte, "Renaissance und Barock in der deutschen Dichtung," *Literaturwissenschaftliches Jahrbuch der Görresgesellschaft, 2* (1926), 47–61.

20. "The Baroque Period in German Literature." *Essays Contributed in Honor of William Allan Neilson, Smith College Studies in Modern Languages, 21* (1939), 192–208.

was still a Lutheran. In Bohemia there is a similar division. The last Bishop of the Bohemian Brethren, Jan Amos Komenský (known as Comenius), was a radical Protestant who died in exile in Holland, but was still a very baroque writer. Of course, there were also Jesuits in Bohemia who wrote in the baroque style. In America there was at least one metaphysical poet, Edward Taylor, who was a Congregationalist. There were Dutch baroque poets who were Protestant and Calvinist even after excluding Vondel, who became a convert to Catholicism. Among the English poets, most were Anglicans and thus can be argued to be in the Catholic tradition; but it seems impossible to dissociate Andrew Marvell, the successor of Milton as Cromwell's Latin Secretary, from the metaphysicals. It can hardly be denied that there are, at least, baroque elements even in Milton. The French are also divided between the two professions of faith, especially if we consider Du Bartas and D'Aubigné, two staunch Huguenots, to be baroque. Certainly neither Théophile, who was condemned to death for atheism, nor Tristan L'Hermite, the two possibly most gifted French poets who could be called baroque, strike one as inspired by the Counter Reformation. We must conclude that baroque was a general European phenomenon which was not confined to a single profession of faith. Nor can it, to my mind, be limited to one national spirit or one social class. Günther Müller calls baroque the expression of "courtly culture," and it has been frequently thought of as aristocratic and upper class. But there is a definitely bourgeois baroque, especially in Northern Germany and in Holland, and baroque has widely filtered down to the peasant masses in Germany and in Eastern Europe. E.g. much of the popular poetry of the Czechs comes from this age and shows baroque traits in style, in verse form, and in religious feeling. It seems to me also impossible to claim one nation as the radiating center of the baroque or to consider baroque a specific national style. Since Strich's first article, which tried to discover a similarity between the German baroque lyric and Old Teutonic poetry, some Germans have claimed baroque as *urdeutsch* or at least peculiarly Nordic or Teutonic. Others have, it seems to me, rightly protested against this identification of German and baroque and have pointed out its obvious foreign origins and analogues.[21] Another German scholar, Helmut Hatzfeld, has, on the other hand, argued that all baroque is the effect of the Spanish spirit,[22] which, since Lucan and Seneca, has been essentially baroque. According to Hatzfeld, even French classicism and most Elizabethan and English seventeenth-century literature illustrate the dominance of the Spanish spirit in seventeenth-century Europe. *Lo hispanico* and the baroque have become almost identical.[23] One need not deny the importance of Spanish influences in order to come to the conclusion that this type of argument is a gross exaggeration: baroque obviously arose in the most diverse countries, almost simultaneously, in reaction against preceding art forms. The metaphysicals are not reducible to Spanish influence, even though Donne may have traveled in Spain besides taking part in the burning of Cadiz. There was simply no Spanish poetry at that time which could have served as model for Donne.

Much better chances of success attend the attempts at defining baroque in more general terms of a philosophy or a world view or even a merely emotional attitude toward the world. Gonzague de Reynold speaks of baroque voluntarism and pessimism.[24] Eugenio d'Ors characterizes it in terms of pantheism, a belief in the naturalness of the supernatural, the

---

21. Carl Neumann, "Ist wirklich Barock und Deutsch das nämliche?" *Historische Zeitschrift, 138* (1928), 544–46.
22. See n. 33, above.
23. See n. 39, above.
24. See n. 68, above.

identification of nature and spirit.[25] Spitzer makes much of the baroque feeling that life is a dream, an illusion or a mere spectacle.[26] None of these formulas and labels can, however, be seriously considered as peculiar to baroque. Arthur Hübscher was, I believe, the inventor of the slogan about the *antithetisches Lebensgefühl des Barock*,[27] which has found much favor and has given rise to a number of German books which all describe baroque in terms of one opposition or a number of oppositions. Thus Emil Ermatinger[28] describes the baroque as a conflict between asceticism and worldliness, the spirit and the flesh. W. P. Friederich[29] has applied the same dichotomy of spiritualism and sensualism to English seventeenth-century poetry. Cysarz[30] operates largely with the tension between the classical form and the Christian *ethos* and sentiment of baroque literature. Paul Hankamer,[31] in a less obvious way, describes the tension as that between life and spirit, out of which the baroque knew only two ways of escape—ascetic denial of life or irony. Ludwig Pfandl has written a large book on the Spanish literature of the Golden Age[32] which speaks of the supposedly innate Spanish dualism of realism and idealism which during the baroque age was "expanded and exaggerated" into an antithesis of naturalism and illusionism. Possibly the *reductio ad absurdum* of this method is reached in Paul Meissner's book on the English

25. See first n. 9, above.

26. E.g. in "Zur Auffassung Rabelais'," in *Romanische Stil- und Literaturstudien, 1* (Marburg, 1931), 133–34, and in *Die Literarisierung des Lebens in Lopes Dorotea* (Bonn, 1932), p. 58.

27. See n. 27, above.

28. *Barock und Rokoko in der deutschen Dichtung* (Leipzig, 1926).

29. See n. 45, above.

30. See first n. 28, above.

31. *Deutsche Gegenreformation und deutsches Barock in der Dichtung* (Stuttgart, 1935), pp. 101, 217, 253.

32. See n. 34, above.

literary baroque.[33] Meissner defines baroque as a conflict of antithetic tendencies and pursues this formula for the "time spirit" relentlessly through all human activities from technological inventions to philosophical speculation, from traveling to religion. Meissner never stops to ask the question whether we could not impose a completely different scheme of contraries on the seventeenth century and even on exactly the same quotations culled from his wide reading, or whether the same contraries would not apply to almost any other age. While one need not deny a general impression of the violent disharmonies of the baroque age and even of the intensified conflict between the traditional Christian view of the world and the newly rising secularism, it is by no means clear that these tensions and conflicts on which these scholars have based the schematism of their books are peculiar to baroque. For instance, the supposedly baroque feeling for the physical horrors of death and putrefaction can be easily matched and even surpassed in the late fifteenth century, as Huizinga or Mâle show with ample documentary evidence.[34] Theodore Spencer has devoted a whole chapter of his book *Shakespeare and the Nature of Man* to the "Renaissance conflict,"[35] describing the tensions and contradictions of the Renaissance very much in the fashion in which the Germans describe the baroque age. What appears baroque to many observers may be also medieval or simply universally Christian, such as the paradoxes of the Christian faith, or even generally human, like the fear of death or lust for the other sex. Attempts to reduce the nature of the baroque to one con-

33. See n. 49, above. A fuller discussion of this and the preceding book is in my "The Parallelism between Literature and the Arts," in *English Institute Annual, 1941* (New York, 1942), pp. 37–39.

34. Johan Huizinga, *The Waning of the Middle Ages* (London, 1937), pp. 129–35; Emile Mâle, *L'Art religieux de la fin du moyen âge en France* (Paris, 1908), pp. 375 ff.

35. New York, 1942, pp. 21–50.

trary dichotomy like that of sensualism and spiritualism, fail
to take account of the fact that there are definitely baroque
poets who do not show this particular conflict or show it
only peripherally. Marino seems unproblematic, an unspirit-
ual sensualist, and many religious poets such as Traherne
scarcely know the temptations of the flesh even in the disguise of mystical love.

7

The most promising way of arriving at a more closely
fitting description of the baroque is to aim at analyses which
would correlate stylistic and ideological criteria. Already
Strich had tried to interpret them in such a unity. The ideological conflicts, the "tensions of the lyrical motion," find
expression in stylistic antitheses, in paradoxes, in syntactic
contortions, in a heaving up of the heavy burden of language.[36] Américo Castro derives the style of the period from
the division of the man of this age which he perceives in himself. The precious and rare style of the baroque artists is an
expression of aggression, a sublime form of independence, of
the conflict between the individual and the insecure world.[37]
But all these and similar formulations, while true as far as
they go, lack the requirement of specific application exclusively to the baroque. Conflicts between the ego and the
world, conflicts within the individual combined with a tortu-
ous or precious style can be found all over the history of
literature from Iceland to Arabia and India. Some more
concrete analytical studies seem to me more convincing. In
a paper on the baroque style of the religious classical lyric
in France,[38] Helmut Hatzfeld has made an attempt to interpret stylistic characteristics such as gemination, "chaotic"

36. See first n. 21, above.
37. See n. 65, above.
38. See n. 39, above.

asyndeton, and a phenomenon which he calls "veiled antithesis" in relation to such attitudes as the melting together of heaven and earth, the glorification and exaltation of God, the morbid eroticism of the time. One can be critical of Hatzfeld's conclusions as to the baroque nature of French classicism, as his material is confined to a very specialized genre, the religious lyric and within it to modernizations of medieval hymns, the psalms, and the *Song of Songs,* but it is scarcely possible to doubt the skill with which style and mind, device and spirit are brought together. It seems to me that the later articles which expand Hatzfeld's analysis to the whole of French classicism and finally to the whole European movement of the baroque conceived by him as dominated by the Spanish spirit, never achieve again the same admirable concreteness and close integration of formal and ideological analysis. Austin Warren in his book on Crashaw also succeeds in closely correlating aesthetic method and religious belief. Crashaw's imagery "runs in streams; the streams run together, image turning into image. His metaphors are sometimes so rapidly juxtaposed as to mix. The effect is often that of phantasmagoria. For Crashaw, the world of the senses is evidently enticing; yet it was a world of appearances only—shifting, restless appearances. By temperament and conviction he was a believer in the miraculous: and his aesthetic method may be interpreted as a genuine equivalent of his belief, as its translation into a rhetoric of metamorphosis."[39] For many other writers it will be possible to see an indubitable connection between the emblematic image and their belief in the pervasive parallelism between macrocosmos and microcosmos, in some vast system of correspondences which can be expressed only by sensuous symbolism. The prevalence of synaesthesia which in the Renaissance apparently occurs only under such traditional figures as the music of the spheres, but during the baroque boldly hears

39. See n. 86 (p. 192), above.

colors and sees sounds,[40] is another indication of this belief in a multiple web of interrelations, correspondences in the universe. Most baroque poets live with a world picture suggested by traditional Christian gradualism, and have found an aesthetic method where the imagery and the figures "link seemingly alien, discontinuous spheres."[41]

Such analyses will be most successful with poets like Crashaw where the integration of belief and expression is complete. But it seems to me impossible to deny that this connection is frequently very loose in the baroque age, possibly more so than in other ages. In Hatzfeld's long piece on French classicism a peculiarity of baroque literature and all baroque art is seen in the "paradoxical relation of content and form." "French classicism with its noble and simple language which disguises the passions burning behind it"[42] is proved baroque on the basis of this tension between content and form. Leo Spitzer characterizes Racine in similar terms and stresses elsewhere, in connection with an analysis of Lope de Vega's *Dorotea,* the baroque artists' sceptical attitude toward language. He comes to the conclusion that baroque artists were conscious of the "distance between word and thing, that they perceive the linkage between meaning and form at the same time as they see its falling-apart." To quote Spitzer's paradoxical formulas: the baroque artist "says something with full consciousness that one cannot actually say it. He knows all the difficulty of translation from intention to expression, the whole insufficiency of linguistic

40. Albert Wellek, "Renaissance- und Barock-synästhesie," *Deutsche Vierteljahrschrift für Literaturwissenschaft und Geistesgeschichte, 9* (1931), 534–84.

41. Austin Warren, "Edward Taylor's Poetry," *Kenyon Review, 3* (1941), 356.

42. See first n. 40 (p. 263), above. Hatzfeld quotes Fritz Neubert, "Zur Wort- und Begriffskunst der französischen Klassik," in *Festschrift für Eduard Wechssler* (1929), p. 155.

expression."[43] That is why his style is precious, cultist, recherché. A case in point seems to me also German baroque poetry which by many Germans since its rediscovery has been interpreted as expressing a turbulent, torn, convulsed soul struggling with its language, piling up asyndetons and epithets. Strich considers even antithesis, word play, and onomatopoeia as evidences of an intense lyrical impulse.[44] But surely the attempt to see an anticipation of Romantic subjectivism in the baroque is doomed to failure. The figures and metaphors, hyperboles and catachreses frequently do not reveal any inner tension or turbulence and may not be the expression of any vital experience (*Erlebnis*) at all, but may be the decorative overelaborations of a highly conscious, sceptical craftsman, the pilings-up of calculated surprises and effects.

We may solve this final difficulty by distinguishing two main forms of baroque: that of the mystics and tortured souls such as Donne and Angelus Silesius, and another baroque which must be conceived as a continuation of rhetorical humanism and Petrarchism, a courtly "public" art which finds its expression in the opera, the Jesuit drama, and the heroic plays of Dryden. Possibly this dualism is not so sharp as it has been stated just now. It can be argued that the autobiographical content of even such an extremely unusual artist as Donne has been very much exaggerated by critics like Gosse[45] and that even the most ardently mystical poets like Crashaw or Angelus Silesius share in a communal, traditional and ritualistic religion. Even their description of per-

---

43. *Die Literarisierung des Lebens in Lopes Dorotea* (Bonn, 1932), pp. 11–12. Spitzer refers to Franz Heinz Mautner's "Das Wortspiel und seine Bedeutung," *Deutsche Vierteljahrschrift für Literaturwissenschaft und Geistesgeschichte,* 9 (1931), 679.

44. See first n. 21, above.

45. Cf. e.g. Allen R. Benham, "The Myth of John Donne the Rake," *Philological Quarterly,* 20 (1941), 465-73.

sonal experiences and conflicts are symbolic of man and
would be misinterpreted if seen as anticipations of the romantic ego. Thus Faguet seems to me mistaken when he
interprets French poetry around 1630 by comparisons with
Lamartine.[46] Similarly Viëtor[47] sees the seventeenth century
too much through the spectacles of Goethe's subjective
poetry, when he discovers a trend towards modern subjectivism and irrationalism in German baroque poetry which, after
all, culminated in the very impersonal art of the second Silesian school. A poet such as Fleming has been shown to have
developed toward a more personal, subjective expression, but
stylistically he broke away from the baroque antithetical,
hyperbolical style and tended towards the simple, the concrete, and the popular.[48] Subjectivism and baroque rarely
go hand in hand. Góngora, though an extremely individual
writer, did not therefore in any way become subjective:
rather his most characteristic poetry became almost symbolistic, "absolute" poetry which could be welcomed and
praised by Mallarmé. The question of the correlation between style and philosophy cannot be solved, it seems to me,
by the fundamental assumption of German stylistics that a
"mental excitement which deviates from the normal habitus
of our mental life, must have coordinated a linguistic devia-
tion from normal linguistic usage."[49] One must, at least,
admit that stylistic devices can be imitated very success-

46. Emile Faguet, *Histoire de la poésie française de la Renaissance
au Romantisme* (Paris, n.d.), *2*, 145, 171 ff; *3*, 185, and *Petite Histoire de la littérature française* (Paris n.d.), pp. 100–01.

47. See second n. 5, above.

48. Hans Pyritz, *Paul Flemings deutsche Liebeslyrik* (Leipzig,
1932), in *Palaestra, 180,* especially pp. 209 ff.

49. Leo Spitzer, "Zur sprachlichen Interpretation von Wortkunst-
werken," *Neue Jahrbücher für Wissenschaft und Jugendbildung, 6*
(1930), 649; Reprinted in *Romanische Stil- und Literaturstudien, 1*
(Marburg, 1931), 4.

fully and that their possible original expressive function can disappear. They can become, as they did frequently in the baroque, mere empty husks, decorative tricks, craftman's clichés. The whole relationship between soul and word is looser and more oblique than it is frequently assumed.

If I seem to end on a negative note, unconvinced that we can define baroque either in terms of stylistic devices or a peculiar world view or even a peculiar relationship of style and belief, I would not like to be understood as offering a parallel to Lovejoy's paper on the "Discrimination of Romanticisms." I hope that baroque is not quite in the position of "romantic" and that we do not have to conclude that it has "come to mean so many things, that by itself, it means nothing."[50] In spite of the many ambiguities and uncertainties as to the extension, valuation, and precise content of the term, baroque has fulfilled and is still fulfilling an important function. It has put the problem of periodisation and of a pervasive style very squarely; it has pointed to the analogies between the literatures of the different countries and between the several arts. It is still the one convenient term which refers to the style which came after the Renaissance but preceded actual neoclassicism. For a history of English literature the concept seems especially important since there the very existence of such a style has been obscured by the extension given to the term Elizabethan and by the narrow limits of the one competing traditional term: "metaphysical." As Roy Daniells has said, the century is "no longer drawn apart like a pack of tapered cards."[51] The indubitable affinities with contemporary Continental movements would stand out more clearly if we had a systematic study of the enormous mass of translating and paraphrasing from Italian, French, and Spanish which was going on throughout the seventeenth

50. PMLA, *39* (1924), 229–53, especially 232.
51. See n. 87 (pp. 407–08), above.

century even from the most baroque Continental poets.[52]
Baroque has provided an aesthetic term which has helped us
to understand the literature of the time and which will help
us to break the dependence of most literary history from peri-
odisations derived from political and social history. Whatever
the defects of the term baroque—and I have not been sparing
in analyzing them—it is a term which prepares for synthesis,
draws our minds away from the mere accumulation of observations and facts, and paves the way for a future history of
literature as a fine art.[53]

52. The edition of Drummond of Hawthornden by R. Kastner
(Manchester, 1913), his scattered papers on his sources; R. C. Wal-
lerstein's "The Style of Drummond in its Relation to his Translations," PMLA, *48* (1933), 1090–1177; the work of Mario Praz and
Austin Warren on Crashaw (see Notes 57, 86), of Pierre Legouis
on Marvell *(André Marvell, Poète, Puritain, Patriote* [Paris, 1928]);
Mario Praz's "Stanley, Sherburne, and Ayres as Translators and Imitators," *Modern Language Review, 20* (1925), 280–94, 419–31;
H. Thomas, "Three Translators of Góngora and other Spanish Poets
during the Seventeenth Century," *Revue Hispanique, 48* (1920),
180–256, are some of the studies which would be useful for such a
monograph.

53. For surveys of scholarship, mostly German, see Leonello Vin-
centi, "Interpretazione del Barocco Tedesco," *Studí Germanici 1*
(1935), 39–75; James Mark, "The Uses of the Term *baroque,"
Modern Language Review, 33* (1938), 547–63; Erich Trunz, "Die
Erforschung der deutschen Barockdichtung," *Deutsche Vierteljahrschrift für Literaturwissenschaft und Geistesgeschichte, 18* (1940),
Referatenheft, 1–100. See also two unfavorable discussions: Hans
Epstein, *Die Metaphysizierung in der literaturwissenschaftlichen
Begriffsbildung und ihre Folgen, Germanische Studien, 73* (Berlin,
1929), and Hans K. Kettler, *Baroque Tradition in the Literature of
the German Enlightenment, 1700–1750. Studies in the Determina-
tion of a Literary Period* (Cambridge [1943?]).

This essay was written in 1945 and read, in a shortened version, at a symposium of the Modern Language Association meeting in Chicago at Christmas that year. Since then the discussion of baroque in literature has grown by leaps and bounds. It would be necessary to write a report several times the length of this one if the new developments were to be treated on the same scale. The bibliography originally appended to this paper would have to be supplemented by many hundred items. Here I can only suggest on what points this paper has been corrected and what main new issues have been raised in the great debate.

My history of the term "baroque" and its transfer to literature needs correction. The controversy on the origin of the term is by no means concluded, but apparently the outline of the early fortunes of the term is inaccurate. I accepted the derivation of the term "baroque" from the scholastic syllogism supported by Benedetto Croce. This etymology has been buttressed for Italy, at least, by many new quotations, particularly through the researches of Carlo Calcaterra.[1] But, on the other hand, it seems now proven that the older derivation from the Portuguese (rather than Spanish) word *barroco* as a jewelers' term for the irregular, odd-shaped pearl is correct, not for the Italian noun, but for the French adjective. To judge from the evidence presented in the papers by Giovanni Getto, Otto Kurz, Giuliano Briganti, and Bruno

1. "Il problema del Barocco," in *Problemi ed orientamenti critici di lingua e di letteratura italiana,* ed. Attilio Momigliano, *3* (Milan, 1949), 405–501.

Migliorini,[2] we must speak of a confluence of these two words of different etymologies. In the late eighteenth and the early nineteenth centuries the adjective "baroque" was widely used as an equivalent of "bizarre," and the noun "baroque" became established as a term for "bad taste" in architecture, at first hardly distinguished from "Gothic" or "rococo." My description of the spread and transfer of the term from the fine arts to literature is substantially correct, though I missed an important passage in Nietzsche's *Menschliches, Allzumenschliches* (1878). Nietzsche recognizes a baroque stage in art after the Renaissance, which he, however, conceives also as a recurrent phenomenon in history, occurring always at the decadence of great art as a decline into rhetoric and theatricality. In other contexts Nietzsche spoke of the baroque style of the Greek dithyramb and the baroque phase of Greek eloquence.[3] Heinrich Wölfflin remains the focal figure for the transfer of the term to literature by his book *Renaissance und Barock* (1888). I underrated, however, the number of isolated instances of a literary use of the term before 1914. As Andreas Angyal has shown,[4] many come from the Austrian-Hungarian Empire, where the taste for baroque architecture and the spiritual attitudes of the Counter Reformation were still alive. In 1893 a Polish scholar, Edward Porębowicz from Cracow, put the word baroque on the title page of his monograph on a seventeenth-

2. Getto, "La polemica sul Barocco," in *Letteratura e critica nel tempo* (Milan, 1954), pp. 131–218; Kurz, "Barocco: storia di una parola," *Lettere Italiane, 12* (1960), 414–44; Briganti, "Barocco; Storia della parola e fortuna critica del concetto," in *Enciclopedia universale dell' Arte, 2* (1958), 346–59; Migliorini, "Etimologia e storia del termine 'barocco,'" in *Manierismo, Barocco, Rococò, Convegno internazionale,* Rome, 21–24 April 1960 (Rome, Accademia Nazionale dei Lincei, 1962), pp. 39–49.

3. *Werke* (19 vols. Leipzig, 1903–19), *3,* 76–8; *11,* 105; *3,* 72.

4. "Der Werdegang der internationalen Barockforschung," in *Forschungen und Fortschritte, 28* (1954), 377–84.

century Polish poet, Andrzej Morsztyn.[5] In J. W. Nagl and Jakob Zeigler's *Deutsch-österreichische Literaturgeschichte* (1899) a long chapter is devoted to "österreichische Barocke und deutsche Renaissance-literatur." There the style is described as "decorative and symbolic," and seen as an expression of the Counter Reformation surviving in Austrian literature as late as in the dramas of Franz Grillparzer and Ferdinand Raimund.[6] There are other instances from Hungarian and Croatian before 1914. In Spain, an isolated instance of "barroquismo literario" in Menéndez Pelayo's *Historia de las ideas estéticas* (1886) even antedates Wölfflin.[7] In Italy, I missed a casual use by Carducci in 1860 and an essay by Enrico Nencioni, entitled "Barrochismo" (1894), which, impressionistically, relates the arts and poetry of the age. In the introduction to a reissue, the paper was, oddly enough, referred to by D'Annunzio as "Del Barocco."[8] Still, the basic argument of my history that the transfer of the term to literature occurred on a full scale in Germany early in the nineteen twenties and that it radiated thence to the other countries is valid. In a paper by Václav Černý the different reasons for the acceptance of the term in the individual

5. *Andrzej Morsztyn, przedstawiciel baroku v poezji polskiej,* Rozprawy Akademii umiejętności, ser. 2, *6* (Krakow, 1894), 225–317

6. *1* (Vienna, 1899), 652–817, esp. 656. Note that "die Barocke" is a feminine noun while today "der Barock" has become standard.

7. *3* (Santander, 1947), 488. Menéndez Pelayo discusses a Portuguese critic of the eighteenth century, Luis Antonio de Verney, and recognizes a certain merit "en su lucha contra el barroquismo literario del siglo anterior, contra lo que él llamaba el *sexcentismo*." See Luis Monguió, "Contribución a la cronología de barroco y barroquismo en España," *PMLA, 64* (1949), 1230n.

8. Carducci, in a "Prolusione" delivered at Bologna, 22 November 1860, refers to "Barocco dei secentisti" (Giosuè Carducci, *Opere, Edizione Nazionale, 5* [Bologna, 1941], 520). Nencioni's essay appeared first in *La Vita italiana nel seicento* (Milan, 1894), reprinted in *Saggi critici di letteratura italiana. Preceduta da uno scritto di Gabriele d'Annunzio* (Florence, 1898).

countries are brought out somewhat more sharply than in my sketch.[9]

One statement, though true in 1945, is now out of date. France is not any more "the one country which has almost completely refused to adopt the term." In France and in French there has been a veritable spate of writings on the baroque and on baroque literature. The discussion of the extent and the value of the term is as lively as ever and has been surveyed knowledgeably by the indefatigable propagandist of the term, Helmut A. Hatzfeld, and by R. A. Sayce, Václav Černý, Franco Simone, Marcel Raymond, and others.[10] The discovery by Alan Boase, an Englishman, of Jean de Sponde, a late sixteenth-century poet, the reprinting of the almost forgotten La Ceppède, the many anthologies of

9. "Les origines européennes des études baroquistes," *Revue de littérature comparée, 24* (1950), 25–45.

10. *Der gegenwärtige Stand der romanistischen Barockforschung,* Bayerische Akademie der Wissenschaften, Philosophische-historische Klasse: Sitzungsberichte (Munich, 1961), Heft 4, is Mr. Hatzfeld's newest survey. Cf. his "A Critical Survey of the Recent Baroque Theories," *Boletín del Instituto Caro y Cuervo, 4* (1948), 1–33; "A Clarification of the Baroque Problem in the Romance Literatures," *Comparative Literature, 1* (1949), 113–39; *Literature through Art* (New York, 1952); "The Baroque from the Viewpoint of the Literary Historian," *Journal of Aesthetics and Art Criticism, 14* (1955), 156–64; "Italia, Spagna e Francia nello sviluppo della letteratura barocca," in *Lettere Italiane* (1957), pp. 1–29; Professor Hatzfeld compiled also the annotated list on "The Baroque" in David C. Cabeen and Jules Brody's *A Critical Bibliography of French Literature, 3 (The Seventeenth Century,* ed. N. Edelman), (Syracuse, 1961), 78–84. R. A. Sayce, "The Use of the Term Baroque in French Literary History," *Comparative Literature, 10* (1958), 246–53; Václav Černý, "Le baroque et la littérature francaise," *Critique, 12* (1956), 517–33, 617–35; Franco Simone, "I contributi europei all' identificazione del barocco francese," *Comparative Literature, 6* (1954), 1–25, and "Per la definizione di un barocco francese," *Rivista di letterature moderne, 5* (1954), 165–92; Marcel Raymond, "Le Baroque littéraire français," in *Manierismo, Barocco, Rococò* (Rome, 1962), pp. 107–26.

French poetry unearthing little-known poems between Ronsard and Malherbe have definitely established a consciousness that there existed in France a fine poetic tradition which was neither Renaissance nor classical, and can best be described as baroque.[11] But the attempts, mainly by writers outside of France, to extend the term baroque to French classicism have not found acceptance in France, though they have, I think, established at least the survival of the baroque in classicism, or the struggle between baroque and classical elements even late in the century and even in such a classic as Racine.[12] At any rate, seventeen years ago such a widespread acceptance of the term in France seemed inconceivable.

In Italy the discussion and interest in baroque has increased considerably, and the negative attitude of Croce has become rare. Especially the work of Calcaterra, who showed the survival of the baroque in Arcadia and appreciated the sensual and sensuous art of Marino, fortified the change of taste. A peculiar feature of the Italian interest in the baroque is the convening of no less than three congresses devoted to a discussion of the term and age.[13]

In Spain and Germany baroque is so completely estab-

11. Cf. François Ruchon and Alan Boase, *La Vie et l'œuvre de Jean de Sponde* (Paris, 1949); Jean de Sponde, *Poésies* (Geneva, 1949); François Ruchon, *Essai sur la vie et l'œuvre de Jean de la Ceppède* (Geneva, 1953), Travaux d'humanisme et Renaissance No. 8. See Alan Boase, "Poètes anglais et français de l'époque baroque," *Revue des sciences humaines*, Sect. 55–56 (1949), 155–84.

12. Hatzfeld and Spitzer. But see also Buffum below and Philip Butler, *Classicisme et baroque dans l'œuvre de Racine* (Paris, 1959).

13. Carlo Calcaterra (see also Note 1), *Il Parnasso in Rivolta* (Milan, 1940, ed. Ezio Raimondi, Bologna, 1961); *Il Barocco in Arcadia e altri scritti sul settecento* (Bologna, 1950); *Retorica e Barocco. Atti del III congresso internazionale di studi umanistici* (Venice, 1954, Rome, 1955); *La Critica stilistica e il barocco letterario. Atti del secondo congresso internazionale di studi italiani*, ed. Ettore Caccia (Florence, 1957); *Manierismo, Barocco, Rococò* (Rome, 1962).

lished as a general term for their seventeenth century that
little change can be reported. I have, however, the impression that in Germany the initial enthusiasm for the time and
taste, fostered as it was by expressionism, has somewhat
abated, though research and learned comment has revived
since the war and flourishes as vigorously as ever.[14]

In my remarks on the Slavic countries I was not sufficiently
informed about the isolated Russian uses and the attempt of
Dmitri Čyževskyj to describe different forms of the baroque
in the Slavic literatures.[15] Since 1945 one must speak rather
of a regression and contraction of the use of the term in the
Slavic countries in spite of good historical research and a
well-informed survey, in German, by a Hungarian scholar.[16]
Today, the problem is almost completely ignored in Russia,
while in Poland and Czechoslovakia baroque is inevitably
identified with the Counter Reformation and thus looked
upon with disfavor by an official literary policy promoting
realism and enlightenment.[17]

14. On Spain see Oreste Macrì, *La historiografía del barocco literario español* (Bogotà, 1961); Also "La storiografia sul Barocco
letterario spagnolo," in *Manierismo, Barocco, Rococò*, pp. 149–98.
On German research see Erik Lunding, "Stand und Aufgaben der
deutschen Barockforschung," in *Orbis Litterarum, 8* (1950), 27–91;
Curt von Faber du Faur, *German Baroque Literature* (New Haven,
1958), is much more than a catalogue of the collection in the Yale
University Library; Leonello Vincenti, "Il Barocco nei paesi di lingua
tedesca e in Olanda," in *Manierismo, Barocco, Rococò*, pp. 201–15.

15. See Dmitri Čyževskyj, *Outline of Comparative Slavic Literature* (Boston, 1952), and "Die Slavistische Barockforschung," in *Die
Welt der Slawen, 1* (1956), 293–307, 431–45. Cf. A. Angyal, "Das
Problem des slawischen Barocks," in *Wissenschaftliche Zeitschrift
der Ernst Moritz Arndt Universität Greifswald, 6* (1956–57), 67–77.

16. Andreas Angyal, *Die slawische Barockwelt* (Leipzig, 1961);
cf. also his *Barock in Ungarn* (Budapest, 1947).

17. See the comment in Angyal's article quoted in Note 15, and
the thin and embarrassed treatment of Czech baroque in *Dějiny české
literatury*, ed. Jan Mukařovský, *1* (Prague, 1959), a monumental
history of Czech literature published by the Czech Academy.

Also, the hope of the usefulness of the term in English literary studies I expressed has not been fulfilled. Not that the word is not used much more frequently than two decades ago, but precisely its importance for drawing English seventeenth-century literature together in a unity, by stressing the continuity from Donne to Dryden, its affinity with similar Continental trends, and its analogy with developments in the fine arts, has not been recognized very widely. Baroque, in English literary studies, is used in all kinds of contexts, but usually with an arbitrary limitation to a few authors. Thus Tucker Brooke uses "Baroque glory" as a label for Donne's prose, Thomas Browne, Jeremy Taylor, and James Howell.[18] Douglas Bush calls Giles Fletcher's *Christ's Victory and Triumph* "the chief monument of baroque devotional poetry," but elsewhere insists that Crashaw is "the one conspicuous English incarnation of the 'baroque sensibility.'" The simplest definition of baroque is to him "poetry like Crashaw's."[19] David Daiches, in his *Critical History of English Literature* (1960), similarly refers only to Giles Fletcher, to Sylvester's translation of Du Bartas, and to Crashaw as baroque.[20] In the books of M. M. Mahood and of Wylie Sypher, baroque is used predominantly for Milton,[21] but, generally speaking, the term "metaphysical" has held out extremely

18. In Albert C. Baugh, ed., *Literary History of England* (New York, 1948), pp. 613–23, 627, 644.

19. *English Literature in the Earlier Seventeenth Century* (Oxford, 1945), pp. 86, 140–41, 362.

20. New York, 1960, pp. 354, 356, 372–73.

21. M. M. Mahood, *Poetry and Humanism* (New Haven, 1950), see esp. the chapter "Milton: The Baroque Artist," and pp. 132 ff.; Sypher, *Four Stages of Renaissance Style* (Garden City, N.Y., 1955). Two moderately sceptical discussions of baroque in England are: Rudolf Stamm, "Englischer Literaturbarock?" in *Die Kunstformen des Barockzeitalters* (Bern, 1956), pp. 383–412, and Mario Praz, "Il Barocco in Inghilterra," in *Manierismo, Barocco, Rococò*, pp. 129–46.

well. Its application has been even extended to Continental poetry by Odette de Mourgues and Frank J. Warnke.[22] Thus the situation of the term baroque in the different countries is about the same as it is described in Section 2, though resistance against it has considerably weakened in France.

On most other points the paper requires no correction. The attempts to make baroque a recurrent type throughout history are open to the same objections. The pejorative use of the term to which Croce clung seems to be disappearing, as has the indiscriminate enthusiasm of some German scholars and critics. The attempts to define baroque have proliferated but cannot convince as long as they restate descriptions in terms of single stylistic devices or limit baroque to the spirit of the Counter Reformation or to the influence of Spain. Helmut A. Hatzfeld has restated this view[23] in combination with many stylistic and ideological considerations, but is, to my mind, refuted by the existence of a definitely Protestant baroque arising independently of Spanish influence. Ingenious proposals, such as Willi Flemming's to make the fugue *the* compositional principle of baroque, or that of G. J. Geers to reduce baroque to "an expression of the unconscious irrational fear of freedom,"[24] remain idiosyncratic *aperçus*.

22. Odette de Mourgues, *Metaphysical, Baroque & Précieux Poetry* (Oxford, 1953); Frank J. Warnke, *European Metaphysical Poetry* (New Haven, 1961).

23. See n. 10. Fritz Strich, "Der europäische Barock," in *Der Dichter und die Zeit* (Bern, 1947), pp. 71–131, expounds this view without referring to Hatzfeld. In another article, "Die Übertragung des Barockbegriffs von der bildenden Kunst auf die Dichtung," in *Die Kunstformen des Barockzeitalters,* ed. R. Stamm (Bern, 1956), pp. 243–65 (reprinted as "Der literarische Barock," in *Kunst und Leben* [Bern, 1960], pp. 42–58), Strich abandons the emphasis on Spain and defends his early transfer of Wölfflin's principles of art history to literature.

24. Willi Flemming, "Die Fuge als epochales Kompositionsprinzip des deutschen Barock," *Deutsche Vierteljahrschrift für Liter-*

Much more promising are the attempts to approach the problem of the baroque through a study of the history of poetic theories. Joseph A. Mazzeo[25] has described the baroque poetic of correspondences mainly from Italian sources. He has criticized the linking of the baroque conceit with the emblem, and thus with intellectual play, made particularly by Mario Praz, exaggerating to my mind the incompatibility of the two theories. Austin Warren in his book on Crashaw sees that there is no contradiction between the emblem influence (limited though it may be) and the more general concept of a poetic of correspondences. I quoted the central passage from Warren, who surely puts his finger on something that is obviously common to Baroque all over Europe. Starting from different texts and premises, Guido Morpurgo Tagliabue tried to see baroque in the tradition of the seventeenth-century interpretation of Aristotelian rhetoric.[26] Baroque is a combination of dialectic and rhetoric and leads to an eminently social culture. Baroque does not express the anguish of the age but rather its repose and pacification. The Italian perspective and the reliance on theory rather than on actual works of art obscures the contradictions and divisions of the time and does not allow an actual analysis of style.

In general, most recent attempts to define the baroque combine stylistic and ideological criteria. Great efforts are being made to avoid the pitfalls of a mechanical transfer of the Wölfflinian categories to literature and to discuss style

---

aturwissenschaft und Geistesgeschichte, 32 (1958), 483–515; G. J. Geers, "Towards the Solution of the Baroque Problem," *Neophilologus, 44* (1960), 299–307.

25. "A Critique of some Modern Theories of Metaphysical Poetry," *Modern Philology, 50* (1952–53), 88–96, and "Metaphysical Poetry and the Poetic of Correspondencies," *Journal of the History of Ideas, 14* (1953), 221–34.

26. "Aristotelismo e barocco," in *Retorica e barocco* (Rome, 1955), pp. 119–95.

concretely in reference to specific texts. Only a few examples
might be cited. Imbrie Buffum, in two books on French literature,[27] studies texts very closely using simple empirical criteria such as the use of the color red or the description of the
divinity in terms of radiant light in D'Aubigné in order to
arrive at familiar conclusions about metamorphosis, incarnation, illusion, etc. Buffum's baroque is optimistic, Christian,
didactic, and includes even Montaigne. Marcel Raymond and
his pupil Jean Rousset use Wölfflin as their starting point.
Rousset has devised a new dichotomy: Circe and the Pea-
cock, the principle of metamorphosis and the principle of
ostentation, and has illustrated it by many little known texts
from French plays and poems.[28]

A different line is taken by Lowry Nelson in his *Baroque
Lyric Poetry* (1961). He wants to escape the traditional preoccupation with imagery and the conceit and shows, very
concretely, by an analysis of specific texts such as Milton's
"Nativity Ode" and "Lycidas" and Góngora's *Polifemo,* how
these poets manipulate the time and tense paradoxically and
how they achieve what he calls "dramaticality": i.e. how they
exploit a rhetorical situation, the role of a speaker, addressing
an audience in a specific situation.[29] Though Nelson's study
is limited to a few great authors and poems it moves in the
right direction: without cloudy and turgid speculation it
bridges the gulf between stylistic study and an insight into
changed mental attitudes, into the intellectual climate of the
time.

Possibly the most widespread feature of baroque discus-

27. *Agrippa D'Aubigné's Les Tragiques. A Study of the Baroque
Style in Poetry* (New Haven, 1951); *Studies in the Baroque from
Montaigne to Rotrou* (New Haven, 1957).

28. Marcel Raymond, *Baroque & renaissance poétique* (Paris,
1955); Jean Rousset, *La Littérature de l'âge baroque en France*
(Paris, 1953).

29. New Haven, 1961, esp. pp. 153 ff.

sion in recent years has been the attempt to replace the term completely or to break it up into several components which either follow each other chronologically or are conceived as existing simultaneously. E. R. Curtius suggested that Baroque should be replaced by the term "Mannerism."[30] His pupil Gustav René Hocke has written two volumes on Mannerism which collect a fascinating mass of materials and observations from all the arts and literatures to document the persistence of the bizarre and grotesque from antiquity to surrealism and dada.[31] Though the emphasis is on the seventeenth century and almost every conceivable topic is raised, Mr. Hocke succeeds only in creating the impression of literature and art as a labyrinth, as anything irregular, abstruse, absurd, fantastic, and weird goes into his wonderful ragbag. But the problem of definition is not furthered. More fruitfully, Wylie Sypher conceived of mannerism as the second of his *Four Stages of Renaissance Style* (1955). In close parallel to the development of Italian painting, Sypher interprets the history of English poetry as a sequence of Renaissance, which includes Spenser; Mannerism (Shakespeare and Donne); Baroque, mainly represented by *Paradise Lost;* and Late Baroque, for which Dryden and Racine serve as examples. Sypher characterizes brilliantly and sensitively, but his analogizing is frequently hazardous and willful, and the assumed stages of style are imposed with disconcerting schematic literal-mindedness; "Lycidas," he knows, is

30. *Europäische Literatur und lateinisches Mittelalter* (Bern, 1948), pp. 273 ff.

31. *Die Welt als Labyrinth. Manier und Manie in der europäischen Kunst* (Hamburg, 1957); *Manierismus in der Literatur, Sprachalchemie und esoterische Kombinationskunst* (Hamburg, 1959). On mannerism see Georg Weise, "Manierismo e letteratura," in *Rivista di letterature moderne*, N. S. 2, *11* (1960), 5–52, and "Storia del termine 'manierismo,' " in *Manierismo, Barroco, Rococò*, pp. 27–38. Cf. Ezio Raimondi, "Per la nozione di manierismo letterario," ibid., pp. 57–79.

mannerist, *Paradise Lost* baroque, *Paradise Regained* late baroque. There is a "mannerist temperament," even a "mannerist God," a "mannerist conscience," a "mannerist sense of reprobation," etc.: in short, the book falls into all the traps of German *Geistesgeschichte*. His difficulties are compounded by the remoteness between Italian painting of the sixteenth and seventeenth centuries and the concrete issues of English poetry in the seventeenth.[32]

A different attempt to bring order into the welter of terminology is that of Odette de Mourgues, in her *Metaphysical, Baroque and Précieux Poetry*. While Sypher is fanciful and metaphorical, Madame de Mourgues is engaged in acute logical discriminations. Metaphysical is to her the poetry of Scève early in the sixteenth century, of La Ceppède, of Jean de Sponde, etc., a poetry of paradoxical ratiocination, while baroque poetry is rather "a distortion of the universe through sensibility" concerned with the mystical, the morbid, macabre, cosmic, apocalyptic, and absurd. Précieux poetry is social witty poetry addressed to a specific coterie. Madame de Mourgues primarily studies French poetry, but she constantly relates it to English poetry with the result that baroque appears there as a term of disapproval limited in practice to Crashaw.[33] Baroque has shrunk to a minor and disparaged trend of the time. In Frank J. Warnke's *European Metaphysical Poetry,* an anthology of well-translated poems with a long introduction, "metaphysical" is similarly extended to include much Continental poetry, but, in difference from Madame de Mourgues, Warnke considers baroque the generic style of which "metaphysical" is a variation or a subspecies.[34]

Louis L. Martz, in a well-documented study on *The*

32. *Four Stages of Renaissance Style,* e.g. pp. 17, 105, 131, 132, 134, 138, 162, etc.
33. *Metaphysical Baroque & Précieux Poetry,* cf. pp. 66–75, 77.
34. Esp. pp. 4 ff.

Poetry of Meditation, has suggested an alternative term: "the meditative tradition," which cuts across the usual style terms, emphasizing the technique of meditation derived from St. Ignatius as a structural model for the poetry usually called "metaphysical" in England.[35] Like the term "metaphysical" or "précieux," it is also extended into the present age: meditative poems were composed by Hopkins and Yeats. No doubt new terminologies can be devised: they will justify themselves if they serve their purpose as instruments of insight, as "regulative ideas" of our conception of the historical process.

There seems to me no contradiction between a recognition of the inevitable arbitrariness and multiple connotations of a term and a defense and even recommendation of its use. One commentator found the conclusion of my article "astonishing," and even "comical,"[36] but it seems to me still good sense to recommend the term, while recognizing all its difficulties and the increasing welter of its meanings. It raises the problem of periodisation, of the analogies between the arts; it is the one term for the style between the Renaissance and classicism which is sufficiently general to override the local terms of schools; and it suggests the unity of a Western literary and artistic period. The discussion of baroque has contributed enormously to our understanding of a time and art which was for a long time ignored, disparaged, or misinterpreted. This alone is sufficient justification for its continued use.

35. New Haven, 1954.
36. Bernard C. Heyl, "Meanings of Baroque," *Journal of Aesthetics and Art Criticism, 19* (1961), 276.

The Concept of Romanticism in
Literary History

1

The Term "Romantic" and Its Derivatives

The terms "romanticism" and "romantic" have been under attack for a long time. In a well-known paper, "On the Discrimination of Romanticisms," Arthur O. Lovejoy has argued impressively that "the word 'romantic' has come to mean so many things that, by itself, it means nothing. It has ceased to perform the function of a verbal sign." Lovejoy proposed to remedy this "scandal of literary history and criticism" by showing that "the 'Romanticism' of one country may have little in common with that of another, that there is, in fact, a plurality of Romanticisms, of possibly quite distinct thought-complexes." He grants that "there may be some common denominator to them all; but if so, it has never been clearly exhibited."[1] Moreover, according to Lovejoy, "the romantic ideas were in large part heterogeneous, logically independent, and sometimes essentially antithetic to one another in their implications."[2]

As far as I know, this challenge has never been taken up by those who still consider the terms useful and will continue to speak of a unified European romantic movement. While

1. *PMLA, 29* (1924), 229–53; reprinted in *Essays in the History of Ideas* (Baltimore, 1948), pp. 228–53, see esp. pp. 232, 234, 235, 236.
2. "The Meaning of Romanticism for the Historian of Ideas," *Journal of the History of Ideas, 2* (1941), 261.

Lovejoy makes reservations and some concessions to the older view, the impression seems widespread today, especially among American scholars, that his thesis has been established securely. I propose to show that there is no basis for this extreme nominalism, that the major romantic movements form a unity of theories, philosophies, and style, and that these, in turn, form a coherent group of ideas each of which implicates the other.

I have tried elsewhere to make a theoretical defense of the use and function of period terms.[3] I concluded that one must conceive of them, not as arbitrary linguistic labels nor as metaphysical entities, but as names for systems of norms which dominate literature at a specific time of the historical process. The term "norms" is a convenient term for conventions, themes, philosophies, styles, and the like, while the word "domination" means the prevalence of one set of norms compared with the prevalence of another set in the past. The term "domination" must not be conceived of statistically: it is entirely possible to envisage a situation in which older norms still prevailed numerically while the new conventions were created or used by writers of greatest artistic importance. It thus seems to me impossible to avoid the critical problem of evaluation in literary history. The literary theories, terms, and slogans of a time need not have prescriptive force for the modern literary historian. We are justified in speaking of "Renaissance" and "baroque," though both of these terms were introduced centuries after the events to which they refer. Still, the history of literary criticism, its terms and slogans affords important clues to the modern historian, since it shows the degree of self-consciousness of the artists themselves and may have profoundly influenced the practice of writing. But this is a question which has to be

3. Cf. "Periods and Movements in Literary History," *English Institute Annual 1940* (New York, 1941), pp. 73–93, and *Theory of Literature*, with Austin Warren (New York, 1949), esp. pp. 274 ff.

decided case by case, since there have been ages of low self-consciousness and ages in which theoretical awareness lagged far behind practice or even conflicted with it.

In the case of romanticism the question of the terminology, its spread and establishment, is especially complicated because it is contemporary or nearly contemporary with the phenomena described. The adoption of the terms points to an awareness of certain changes. But this awareness may have existed without these terms, or these terms may have been introduced before the actual changes took place, merely as a program, as the expression of a wish, an incitement to change. The situation differs in different countries; but this is, of course, in itself no argument that the phenomena to which the terms refer showed substantial differences.

The semantic history of the term "romantic" has been very fully studied in its early stages in France, England, and Germany, and for the later stages in Germany.[4] But, unfortunately, little attention has been paid to it in other countries and, even where materials are abundant, it is still difficult to ascertain when, for the first time, a work of literature and which works of literature were designated as "romantic," when the contrast of "classical-romantic" was introduced, when a contemporary writer referred to himself first as a

4. Fernand Baldensperger, " 'Romantique'—ses analogues et équivalents," *Harvard Studies and Notes in Philology and Literature, 14* (1937), 13–105, is the fullest list. Unfortunately there is no interpretation and it goes only to 1810. Richard Ullmann and Helene Gotthard, *Geschichte des Begriffs "Romantisch" in Deutschland* (Berlin, 1927), *Germanische Studien, 50,* is most valuable and tells the story to the 1830s, but the arrangement is confusing and confused. Logan P. Smith, *Four Words, Romantic, Originality, Creative, Genius,* Society for Pure English, tract no. 17 (London, 1924), reprinted in *Words and Idioms* (Boston, 1925), is still the only piece on English developments and is for this purpose valuable; the comments on the further story in Germany are injudicious. The book by Carla Apollonio, *Romantico: Storia e Fortuna di una parola* (Florence, 1958), is confined to Italy.

"romanticist," when the term "romanticism" was first adopted in a country, etc. Some attempt, however imperfect in detail, can be made to straighten out this history on an international scale and to answer some of these questions.

We are not concerned here with the early history of "romantic" which shows an expansion of its use from "romance-like," "extravagant," "absurd," etc., to "picturesque." If we limit ourselves to the history of the term as used in criticism and literary history, there is little difficulty about its main outlines. The term "romantic poetry" was used first of Ariosto and Tasso and the medieval romances from which their themes and "machinery" were derived. It occurs in this sense in France in 1669, in England in 1674,[5] and certainly Thomas Warton understood it to mean this when he wrote his introductory dissertation to his *History of English Poetry* (1774), "The Origin of Romantic Fiction in Europe." In Warton's writings and those of several of his contemporaries a contrast is implied between this "romantic" literature, both medieval and Renaissance, and the whole tradition of literary art as it came down from classical antiquity. The composition and "machinery" of Ariosto, Tasso, and Spenser are defended against the charges of neoclassical criticism with arguments which derive from the Renaissance defenders of Ariosto and Tasso and the medieval romances from which such good neoclassicists as Jean Chapelain.[6] An attempt is

5. Jean Chapelain speaks of "l'epique romanesque, genre de poésie sans art" in 1667. In 1669 he contrasts "poésie romanesque" and "poésie héroïque." René Rapin refers to "poésie romanesque du Pulci, du Boiardo, et de l'Arioste" in 1673. Thomas Rymer translates this as "Romantick Poetry of Pulci, Bojardo, and Ariosto" a year later. Baldensperger, ibid., pp. 22, 24, 26.

6. For the antecedents of Warton's and Hurd's arguments, see Odell Shepard's review of Clarissa Rinaker's *Thomas Warton* in *JEGP*, 16 (1917), 153, and Victor M. Hamm, "A Seventeenth Century Source for Hurd's *Letters on Chivalry and Romance*," *PMLA*, 52 (1937), 820.

made to justify a special taste for such "romantic" fiction and its noncompliance with classical standards and rules, even though these are not challenged for other genres. The dichotomy implied has obvious analogues in other contrasts common in the eighteenth century: between the ancients and moderns, between artificial and popular poetry, the "natural" poetry of Shakespeare unconfined by rules and French classical tragedy. A definite juxtaposition of "Gothic" and "classical" occurs in Hurd and Warton. Hurd speaks of Tasso as "trimming between the Gothic and the Classic," and of the *Faerie Queene* as a "Gothic, not a classical poem." Warton calls Dante's *Divine Comedy* a "wonderful compound of classical and romantic fancy."[7] Here the two famous words meet, possibly for the first time, but Warton probably meant little more than that Dante used both classical mythology and chivalric motifs.

This use of the term "romantic" penetrated into Germany. In 1766 Gerstenberg reviewed Warton's *Observations on the Fairy Queen,* considering them far too neoclassical, and Herder used the learning, information, and terminology of Warton and his English contemporaries. He distinguished sometimes between the "romantic" (chivalric) and the "Gothic" (Nordic) taste, but mostly the words "Gothic" and "romantic" were used by him interchangeably. He notes as early as 1766 that from the mixture of the Christian religion and chivalry arises "italienischer, geistlich, frommer, romantischer Geschmack."[8] This usage then penetrated into the first handbooks of general history of literature: into Eichhorn's *Literärgeschichte* (1799) and into the first volumes, devoted to Italian and Spanish literature, of Friedrich Bouterwek's monumental *Geschichte der Poesie und Bered-*

7. Examples from L. P. Smith, ibid.; Warton's *History of English Poetry, 3* (London, 1781), 241, on Dante.

8. Herder's *Werke,* ed. Bernhard Suphan (Berlin, 1899) *32,* 30. Other examples in Ullmann-Gotthard.

samkeit seit dem Ende des dreizehnten Jahrhunderts (1801–05). There the term "romantisch" is used in all combinations: style, manners, characters, poetry are called "romantisch." Sometimes Bouterwek uses the term "altromantisch" to refer to the Middle Ages, and "neuromantisch" to refer to what we would call the Renaissance. This usage is substantially identical with Warton's except that its realm has been expanded more and more: not only medieval literature and Ariosto and Tasso but also Shakespeare, Cervantes, and Calderón are called "romantic." It simply means all poetry written in a tradition differing from that descended from classical antiquity. This broad historical conception was later combined with a new meaning: the typological, which is based on an elaboration of the contrast between "classical" and "romantic" and is due to the Schlegels. Goethe, in a conversation with Eckermann in 1830, said that Schiller invented the distinction "naive and sentimental" and that the Schlegels merely renamed it "classical and romantic."[9] At that time Goethe had become very antagonistic to recent literary developments in France and Germany and had even formulated the contrast: "Klassich ist das Gesunde, romantisch das Kranke."[10] He disliked the Schlegels for personal and ideological reasons. But his pronouncement is certainly not accurate history. Clearly Schiller's *Über naive und sentimentalische Dichtung* was a statement of a typology of styles which did influence Friedrich Schlegel's turn towards modernism from his earlier Hellenism.[11] But Schiller's contrast is not identical with that of the Schlegels, as is obvious from the mere fact that Shakespeare is "naiv" in Schiller and "romantisch" in Schlegel.

9. Goethe to Eckermann, March 21, 1830.
10. Goethe, *Werke,* Jubiläumsausgabe, *38,* 283.
11. The best analysis is in A. O. Lovejoy, "Schiller and the Genesis of German Romanticism," *MLN, 35* (1920), 1–10, 136–46; reprinted in *Essays in the History of Ideas* (Baltimore, 1948), pp. 207–27.

Much attention has, comprehensibly, been paid to the exact usage of these terms by the Schlegels.[12] But, if we look at the history of the word "romantic" from a wide European perspective, many of these uses must be considered purely idiosyncratic, since they had no influence on the further history of the term and did not even determine the most influential statement formulated by August Wilhelm Schlegel himself in the *Lectures on Dramatic Art and Literature* (1809–11), which has rightly been called the "Message of German Romanticism to Europe."[13] The terms "Romantik" and "Romantiker" as nouns were apparently inventions of Novalis, in 1798–99. But, with Novalis, "Romantiker" is a writer of romances and fairy tales of his own peculiar type, "Romantik" is a synonym of "Romankunst" in this sense.[14] Also the famous fragment, No. 116, of the *Athenaeum* (1798) by Friedrich Schlegel, which defines "romantic poetry" as "progressive Universalpoesie" connects it with the idea of such a romantic novel. In the later "Gespräch über die Poesie" (1800), however, the term assumed again its concrete historical meaning: Shakespeare is characterized as laying the foundation of romantic drama and the romantic is found also in Cervantes, in Italian poetry, "in the age of chivalry, love, and fairy tales, whence the thing and the word are derived." Friedrich Schlegel, at this time, does not consider his own age romantic, since he singles out the novels of

12. See A. O. Lovejoy, "The Meaning of 'Romanticism' in Early German Romanticism," *MLN, 31* (1916), 385–96, and *32* (1917), 65–77; reprinted, *Essays,* pp. 183–206.

13. Josef Körner, *Die Botschaft der deutschen Romantik an Europa* (Augsburg, 1929), a sketch of the reception of A. W. Schlegel's lectures outside Germany.

14. Cf. "Der Romantiker studiert das Leben wie der Maler, Musiker und Mechaniker Farben, Ton und Kraft," *Schriften,* ed. Samuel-Kluckhohn, *3,* 263; "Romantik," *3,* 74–75, 88. These passages date from 1798–99, but only the first saw the light in the 1802 edition of Novalis' *Schriften,* ed. F. Schlegel and L. Tieck, *2,* 311.

Jean Paul as the "only romantic product of an unromantic age." He uses the term also quite vaguely and extravagantly as an element of all poetry and claims that all poetry must be romantic.[15]

But the descriptions and pronouncements which were influential, both in Germany and abroad, were those of the older brother, August Wilhelm Schlegel. In the lectures on aesthetics, given at Jena in 1798, the contrast of classical and romantic is not yet drawn explicitly. But it is implied in the lengthy discussion of modern genres, which include the romantic novel culminating in the "perfect masterwork of higher romantic art," *Don Quixote,* the romantic drama of Shakespeare, Calderón, and Goethe, and the romantic folk poetry of the Spanish romances and Scottish ballads.[16]

In the Berlin lectures, given from 1801 to 1804, though not published until 1884,[17] Schlegel formulated the contrast, classical and romantic, as that between the poetry of antiquity and modern poetry, associating romantic with the progressive and Christian. He sketched a history of romantic literature which starts with a discussion of the mythology of the Middle Ages and closes with a review of the Italian poetry of what we would today call the Renaissance. Dante, Petrarch, and Boccaccio are described as the founders of modern romantic literature, though Schlegel, of course, knew that they admired antiquity. But he argued that their form and expression were totally unclassical. They did not dream of preserving the forms of antiquity in structure and composition. "Romantic" includes the German heroic poems such as the *Nibelungen,* the cycle of Arthur, the Charlemagne

15. Reprinted in Friedrich Schlegel's *Jugendschriften,* ed. J. Minor, 2, 220–21, 365, 372.

16. *Vorlesungen über philosophische Kunstlehre,* ed. W. A. Wünsche, (Leipzig, 1911) pp. 214, 217, 221.

17. *Vorlesungen über schöne Literatur und Kunst,* ed. J. Minor (3 vols. Heilbronn, 1884); see especially *1,* 22.

romances, and Spanish literature from *Cid* to *Don Quixote*. The lectures were well attended and from them these conceptions penetrated into print in the writings of other men than the Schlegels. Schlegel printed parts in his *Spanisches Theater* (1803). In the unpublished lectures of Schelling on *Philosophie der Kunst* (1802–03),[18] in Jean Paul's *Vorschule der Aesthetik* (1804), and in Friedrich Ast's *System der Kunstlehre* (1805)[19] we find the contrast elaborated. But the most important formulation was in the *Lectures* of A. W. Schlegel delivered at Vienna in 1808–09 and published in 1809–11. There romantic-classical is associated with the antithesis of organic-mechanical and plastic-picturesque. There clearly the literature of antiquity and that of neoclassicism (mainly French) is contrasted with the romantic drama of Shakespeare and Calderón, the poetry of perfection with the poetry of infinite desire.

It is easy to see how this typological and historical usage could pass into the designation of the contemporary movement, since the Schlegels were obviously strongly anticlassicist at that time and were appealing to the ancestry and models of the literature they had designated as romantic. But the process was surprisingly slow and hesitant. Jean Paul speaks of himself as "Biograph von Romantikern" in 1803, but seems only to refer to figures in his novels. In 1804 he refers to "Tieck und andere Romantiker," meaning writers of fairy tales. But the designation of contemporary literature as romantic was apparently due only to the enemies of the Heidelberg group which today we are accustomed to call the Second Romantic School. J. H. Voss attacked them for their reactionary Catholic views in 1808 and published a parodistic *Klingklingelalmanach* with the subtitle: *Ein Taschen-*

18. Printed only in *Sämmtliche Werke*, 1st. sect., *5* (Stuttgart, 1859). Schelling had read the MS of Schlegel's Berlin lectures.

19. Ast had attended A. W. Schlegel's lectures at Jena in 1798. His very imperfect transcript was published in 1911. See n. 16.

buch für vollendete Romantiker und angehende Mystiker. The *Zeitschrift für Einsiedler,* the organ of Arnim and Brentano, adopted the term with alacrity. In the *Zeitschrift für Wissenschaft und Kunst* (1808), the merit of "unsere Romantiker" seems to be praised for the first time. The first historical account of "die neue literarische Partei der sogenannten Romantiker" can be found only in the eleventh volume (1819) of Bouterwek's monumental *Geschichte,* where the Jena group and Brentano are discussed together.[20] Heine's much later *Romantische Schule* (1833) included Fouqué, Uhland, Werner, and E. T. A. Hoffmann. Rudolf Haym's standard work, *Die romantische Schule* (1870) is limited to the first Jena group: the Schlegels, Novalis, and Tieck. Thus, in German literary history, the original broad historical meaning of the term has been abandoned and "Romantik" is used for a group of writers who did not call themselves "Romantiker."

The broad meaning of the term as used by August Wilhelm Schlegel, however, spread abroad from Germany in all directions. The northern countries seem to have been the first to adopt the terms: Jens Baggesen, as early as 1804, wrote (or began to write) a parody of *Faust* in German, of which the subtitle runs *Die romantische Welt oder Romanien im Tollhaus.*[21] Baggesen was, at least formally, the editor of the *Klingklingelalmanach.* Adam Öhlenschläger brought conceptions of German romanticism to Denmark in the first decade of the nineteenth century. In Sweden the group around the periodical *Phosphoros* seems to have discussed the terms first. In 1810, a translation of part of Ast's *Aesthetik* was published and was extensively reviewed in *Phosphoros* with references to Schlegel, Novalis, and Wack-

20. See Ullmann-Gotthard, pp. 70 ff.
21. Apparently published only in Jens Baggesen's *Poetische Werke in deutscher Sprache, 3* (Leipzig, 1836). A statement on date of composition is given there.

enroder.[22] In Holland we find the contrast between classical poetry and romantic poetry elaborated by N. G. Van Kampen in 1823.[23]

In the Latin world, and in England as well as in America, the intermediary role of Madame de Staël was decisive. For France it can be shown, however, that she was anticipated by others, though far less effectively. Warton's usage of the term was apparently rare in France, though it occurs in Chateaubriand's *Essai sur les révolutions* (1797), a book written in England, where the word is coupled with "Gothique" and "tudesque," and spelled in the English way.[24] But with the exception of such small traces, the word is not used in a literary context until the German influence was felt directly. It occurs in a letter by Charles Villers, a French emigrant in Germany and first expounder of Kant, published in the *Magasin encyclopédique* in 1810. Dante and Shakespeare are spoken of as "sustaining *La Romantique*" and the new spiritual sect in Germany is praised because it favors *"La Romantique."*[25] Villers' article was hardly noticed: a translation of Bouterwek's *Geschichte der spanischen Literatur* by Phillipe-Albert Stapfer, in 1812, also elicited no interest, though it was reviewed by the young Guizot. The decisive year was 1813: then Simonde de Sismondi's *De la littérature du midi de l'Europe* was published in May and June. In October Madame de Staël's *De l'Allemagne* was finally published in London, though it had been ready for print in 1810.

22. *Phosphoros* (Upsala, 1810), pp. 116, 172–73.

23. "Verhandeling over de vraag: welk is het onderscheidend verschil tussen de klassische poezy der Ouden en de dus genoemde Romantische poezy der nieuweren?" *Werken der Hollandsche Maatschappij van Fraaije Kunsten en Wetenschappen, 6* (Leyden, 1823), 181–382.

24. See Baldensperger, p. 90.

25. Reprinted in Edmond Eggli-Pierre Martino, *Le Débat romantique en France, 1* (Paris, 1933), 26–30. A continuation of this excellent collection, which goes only to 1816, is much to be desired.

In December 1813 A. W. Schlegel's *Cours de littérature dramatique* appeared in a translation by Madame Necker de Saussure, a cousin of Madame de Staël. Most importantly, *De l'Allemagne* was reprinted in Paris in May 1814. All these works, it need hardly be shown, radiate from one center, Coppet, and Sismondi, Bouterwek, and Madame de Staël are, as far as the concept of "romantic" is concerned, definitely dependent on Schlegel.

There is no need to rehearse the story of A. W. Schlegel's associations with Madame de Staël. The exposition of classical-romantic in Chapter 11 of *De l'Allemagne,* including its parallel of classical and sculpturesque, romantic and picturesque, the contrast between Greek drama of event and modern drama of character, the poetry of Fate versus the poetry of Providence, the poetry of perfection versus the poetry of progress, clearly derive from Schlegel. Sismondi disliked Schlegel personally and was shocked by many of his "reactionary" views. In details, he may have drawn much more from Bouterwek than from Schlegel, but his view that the Romance literatures are essentially romantic in spirit, and that French literature forms an exception among them, is definitely derived from Schlegel, as are his descriptions of the contrast between Spanish and Italian drama.[26]

These three books, Sismondi's, Madame de Staël's, and Schlegel's, were reviewed and discussed very heatedly in France. M. Edmond Eggli has collected a whole volume of almost five hundred pages of these polemics, covering only the years 1813–16.[27] The reaction was fairly mild to the scholarly Sismondi, violent to the foreign Schlegel, and

26. Best accounts of these relationships are Carlo Pellegrini, *Il Sismondi e la storia delle letterature dell' Europa meridionale* (Geneva, 1926), Comtesse Jean de Pange, *Auguste-Guillaume Schlegel et Madame de Staël* (Paris, 1938), and Jean-R. de Salis, *Sismondi, 1773–1842* (Paris, 1932).
27. See n. 25.

mixed and frequently baffled to Madame de Staël. In all of these polemics, the enemies are called *Les romantiques,* but it is not clear what recent literature is referred to except these three books. When Benjamin Constant published his novel *Adolphe* (1816), he was attacked as strengthening *"le genre romantique."* The melodrama also was called contemptuously by this name and German drama identified with it.[28]

But up to 1816 there was no Frenchman who called himself a romantic nor was the term "romantisme" known in France. Its history is still somewhat obscure: curiously enough, "Romantismus" is used as a synonym of bad rhyming and empty lyricism in a letter written by Clemens Brentano to Achim von Arnim in 1803,[29] but so far as I know this form had no future in Germany. In 1804 Sénancour refers to "romantisme des sites alpestres,"[30] using it thus as a noun corresponding to the use of "romantic" as "picturesque." But, in literary contexts, it does not seem to occur before 1816 and then it is used vaguely and jocularly. There is a letter in the *Constitutionnel,* supposedly written by a

28. The definition of "romantique" by E. Jouy in 1816, quoted by Eggli, p. 492, sums up the contemporary view of the history very neatly: *"Romantique*: terme de jargon sentimental, dont quelques écrivains se sont servis pour caractériser une nouvelle école de littérature sous la direction du professeur Schlegel. La première condition qu' on y exige des élèves, c'est de reconnaître que nos Molière, nos Racine, nos Voltaire, sont de petits génies empêtrés dans les règles, qui n'ont pu s'élever à la hauteur du beau idéal, dont la recherche est l'object du *genre romantique.* Ce mot envahisseur n'a d'abord été admis qu'à la suite et dans le sens du mot *pittoresque,* dont on aurait peut-être dû se contenter; mais il a passé tout à coup du domaine descriptif, qui lui était assigné, dans les espaces de l'imagination."

29. "Es ist aber auch jetzt ein solch Gesinge und ein solcher Romantismus eingerissen, dass man sich schämt auch mit beizutragen." Reinhold Steig, *Achim von Arnim und die ihm nahe standen, 1* (Stuttgart, 1894), 102. Letter, dated Frankfurt, Oct. 12, 1803. This item is not mentioned in the very full collections of Ullmann-Gotthard or by any other student of the history of the term.

30. *Obermann,* letter 87, quoted by Eggli, p. 11.

man residing near the Swiss frontier, within sight of Madame de Staël's castle, who complains of his wife's enthusiasm for the "romantic" and tells of a poet who cultivates "le genre tudesque" and has read to them "des morceaux pleins de *romantisme,* les purs mystères du baiser, la sympathie primitive et l'ondoyante mélancolie des cloches."[31] Shortly afterwards, Stendhal, then at Milan, who had read Schlegel's lectures immediately after the publication of the French translation, called Schlegel in letters a "petit pédant sec" and "ridicule" but complained that, in France, they attack Schlegel and think that they have defeated "le Romantisme."[32] Stendhal seems to have been the first Frenchman who called himself a romantic: "Je suis un romantique furieux c'est-à-dire, je suis pour Shakespeare contre Racine et pour Lord Byron, contre Boileau."[33]

But that was in 1818 and Stendhal was then voicing adherence to the Italian romantic movement. Thus Italy enters importantly into our story, since it was the first Latin country to have a romantic movement which was aware of its being romantic. There, of course, the controversy had penetrated also in the wake of Madame de Staël's *De l'Allemagne,* which was translated as early as 1814. H. Jay's violently antiromantic *Discours sur le genre romantique en littérature,* published in 1814, appeared immediately in an Italian translation.[34] The role of Madame de Staël's article on translations from German and English is well known. It elicited Lodovico di Breme's defense, who refers, however, to the whole dispute

31. July 19, 1816, reprinted in Eggli, pp. 472–73.

32. Letters to Louis Crozet, Sept. 28, Oct. 1, and Oct. 20, 1816, in *Correspondance,* ed. Divan (Paris, 1934), *4,* 371, 389, and *5,* 14–15. Marginalia to Schlegel in *Mélanges intimes et marginalia,* ed. Divan (Paris, 1936), *1,* 311–26. Most are malicious and even angry.

33. Letter to Baron de Mareste, Apr. 14, 1818, *Correspondance,* *5,* 137.

34. Originally in *Le Spectateur,* no. 24 (1814), *3,* 145; reprinted in Eggli, pp. 243–56. In Italian in *Lo Spettatore,* no. 24, *3,* 145, apparently a parallel publication.

as a French affair, and obviously thinks of "romantic" in terms which would have been comprehensible to Herder or even Warton. He quotes Gravina's arguments in favor of the composition of Ariosto's *Orlando Furioso* and sees that the same criteria apply to "Romantici settentrionali, Shakespeare e Schiller," in tragedy.[35] Giovanni Berchet's *Lettera semiseria di Grisostomo*, with its translations from Bürger's ballads, is usually considered the manifesto of the Italian romantic movement; but Berchet does not use the noun nor does he speak of an Italian romantic movement. Tasso is one of the poets called "romantici," and the famous contrast between classical poetry and romantic poetry as that between the poetry of the dead and the living is suggested.[36] The peculiarly "contemporaneous," political character of the Italian romantic movement is here anticipated. In 1817 Schlegel's *Lectures* were translated by Giovanni Gherardini, but the great outburst of pamphlets—the whole battle—came only in 1818, when the term "romanticismo" is used first by antiromantic pamphleteers, Francesco Pezzi, Camillo Piciarelli, and Conte Falletti di Barolo, who wrote *Della Romanticomachia,* and there draws the distinction between "genere romantico" and "il romanticismo."[37] Berchet, in his ironical comments, professes not to understand the distinction.[38] Ermes Visconti, in his formal articles on the term, uses shortly afterwards only "romantismo."[39] But "romanticismo"

35. "Intorno all'ingiustizia di alcuni giudizi letterari italiani" (1816), in *Polemiche,* ed. Carlo Calcaterra (Turin, 1923), pp. 36–38.

36. In Giovanni Berchet, *Opere,* ed. E. Bellorini, *2* (Bari, 1912), 19, 20, 21.

37. See *Discussioni e polemiche sul romanticismo* (1816–26), ed. Egidio Bellorini, *1* (Bari, 1943), 252, 358–59, 363. Bellorini was unable to procure the pamphlet by Piciarelli. The first occurrence of the word is in an article by Pezzi on Byron's *Giaour* in *Gazzetta di Milano* (Jan. 1818).

38. *Il Conciliatore,* no. 17 (Oct. 29, 1818), pp. 65–66.

39. "Idee elementari sulla poesia romantica," in *Il Conciliatore,* no. 27 (Dec. 3, 1818), p. 105.

seems to have been well established by 1819, when D. M. Dalla used it in the title of his translation of the thirtieth chapter of Sismondi's *Literature of the South,* as *Vera Definizione del Romanticismo,* though the French original shows no trace of the term. Stendhal, who had used the term "romantisme," and continued to use it, was now temporarily converted to "romanticisme," obviously suggested by the Italian term. Stendhal wrote two small papers "Qu' est-ce que le romanticisme?" and "Du Romanticisme dans les beaux arts" which, however, remained in manuscript.[40] The first paper of *Racine et Shakespeare,* published in the *Paris Monthly Review* (1822), uses "romanticisme" for the first time in French in print.

But, in the meantime, "romantisme" seems to have become general in France. François Mignet used it in 1822, Villemain and Lacretelle in the following year.[41] The spread and acceptance of the term was assured when Louis S. Auger, director of the French Academy, launched a *Discours sur le Romantisme,* condemning the new heresy in a solemn session of the Academy on April 24, 1824. In the second edition of *Racine et Shakespeare* (1825), Stendhal himself gave up his earlier form "romanticisme" in favor of the new "romantisme." We shall not try to recount the familiar story of the romantic *cénacles,* the romantic periodicals of the twenties, all leading up to the preface to *Cromwell* and the great battle of *Hernani.*[42] Clearly, just as in Italy, a broadly

40. These papers were published only in 1854 and 1922, respectively. See *Racine et Shakespeare,* ed. Divan (Paris, 1928), pp. 175, 267.

41. *Courier français* (Oct. 19, 1822), quoted by P. Martino, *L'Époque romantique en France* (Paris, 1944), p. 27. Mignet says that Scott "a résolu selon moi la grande question du romantisme." Lacretelle, in *Annales de la littérature et des arts, 13* (1823), 415, calls Schlegel "le Quintilien du romantisme"; quoted in C. M. Des Granges, *Le Romantisme et la Critique* (Paris, 1907), p. 207.

42. The most useful account is René Bray, *Chronologie du romantisme* (Paris, 1932).

typological and historical term, introduced by Madame de Staël, had become the battle cry of a group of writers who found it a convenient label to express their opposition to the ideals of neoclassicism.

In Spain the terms "classical" and "romantic" occurred in newspapers as early as 1818, once with a specific reference to Schlegel. But apparently an Italian exile, Luigi Monteggia, who came to Spain in 1821, was the first to write elaborately on "romanticismo" in *Europeo* (1823), where shortly afterward López Soler analyzed the debate between "románticos y clasicistas." The group of Spanish writers who called themselves "románticos" was, however, victorious only around 1838 and it soon disintegrated as a coherent "school."[43]

Among Portuguese poets, Almeida Garrett seems to have been the first to refer to "nos romanticos" in his poem, *Camões,* written in 1823 in Le Havre during his French exile.[44]

The Slavic countries received the term at about the same time as the Romance. In Bohemia the adjective "romantický" in connection with a poem occurs as early as 1805, the noun "romantismus" in 1819, the noun "romantika," a formation from the German, in 1820, the noun "romantik" (meaning romanticist) only in 1835.[45] But there never was a formal romantic school.

43. E. Allison Peers, "The Term Romanticism in Spain," *Revue Hispanique, 81* (1933), 411–18. Monteggia's article is reprinted in *Bulletin of Spanish Studies, 8* (1931), 144–49. For the later history, see E. Allison Peers, *A History of the Romantic Movement in Spain* (2 vols. Cambridge, 1940), and Guillermo Díaz-Plaja, *Introducción al estudio del romanticismo español* (Madrid, 1942).

44. Theophilo Braga, *Historia do Romantismo em Portugal* (Lisbon, 1880), p. 175.

45. These dates come from the very complete collections of the Dictionary of the Czech Academy. I owe this information to the kindness of the late Professor Antonín Grund of Masaryk University at Brno, Czechoslovakia.

In Poland, Casimir Brodzinski wrote a dissertation concerning classicism and romanticism in 1818. Mickiewicz wrote a long preface to his *Ballady i Romanse* (1822) in which he expounded the contrast of classical and romantic, referring to Schlegel, Bouterwek, and Eberhard, the author of one of the many German aesthetics of the time. The collection contains a poem, "Romantyczność," a ballad on the theme of *Lenore*.[46]

In Russia, Pushkin spoke of his *Prisoner from the Caucasus* as a "romantic poem" in 1821, and Prince Vyazemsky, reviewing the poem during the next year, was apparently the first to discuss the contrast between the new romantic poetry and the poetry still adhering to the rules.[47]

We have left the English story, the most unusual development, for the conclusion. After Warton there had begun in England an extensive study of medieval romances and of "romantic fiction." But there is no instance of a juxtaposition of "classical" and "romantic," nor any awareness that the new literature inaugurated by the *Lyrical Ballads* could be called romantic. Scott, in his edition of *Sir Tristram,* calls his text "the first classical English romance."[48] An essay by John Forster, "On the Application of the Epithet Romantic,"[49] is merely a commonplace discussion of the relation between imagination and judgment with no hint of a literary application except to chivalrous romances.

The distinction of classical-romantic occurs for the first time in Coleridge's lectures, given in 1811, and is there clearly derived from Schlegel, since the distinction is associ-

46. *Poezje,* ed. J. Kallenbach (Kraków, 1930), pp. 45, 51.

47. N. V. Bogoslovsky, ed., *Pushkin o literature* (Moscow-Leningrad, 1934), pp. 15, 35, 41, etc. Vyazemsky's review in *Syn otechestva* (1822) was reprinted in *Polnoe Sobranie Sochinenii, 1* (Petersburg, 1878), 73–78.

48. Edinburgh, 1804, p. xlvii.

49. *Essays in a Series of Letters* (London, 1805).

ated with that of organic and mechanical, painterly and
sculpturesque, in close verbal adherence to Schlegel's phrasing.[50] But these lectures were not published at that time, and
thus the distinction was popularized in England only through
Madame de Staël, who made Schlegel and Sismondi known
in England. *De l'Allemagne,* first published in London, appeared almost simultaneously in an English translation. Two
reviews, by Sir James Mackintosh and William Taylor of
Norwich, reproduce the distinction between classical and
romantic, and Taylor mentions Schlegel and knows of
Madame de Staël's indebtedness to him.[51] Schlegel was in the
company of Madame de Staël in England in 1814. The
French translation of the *Lectures* was very favorably reviewed in the *Quarterly Review,*[52] and in 1815 John Black,
an Edinburgh journalist, published his English translation.
This was also very well received. Some reviews reproduce
Schlegel's distinction quite extensively: for instance, Hazlitt's
in the *Edinburgh Review.*[53] Schlegel's distinctions and views
on many aspects of Shakespeare were used and quoted by
Hazlitt, by Nathan Drake in his *Shakespeare* (1817), by

50. Coleridge's *Shakespearean Criticism,* ed. Thomas M. Raysor
(Cambridge, Mass., 1930), *1,* 196–98, *2,* 265, and *Miscellaneous
Criticism,* ed. T. M. Raysor (Cambridge, Mass., 1936), pp. 7, 148.
Coleridge himself says that he received a copy of Schlegel's *Lectures*
on Dec. 12, 1811; see Coleridge's *Unpublished Letters,* ed. Earl L.
Griggs (London, 1932), *2,* 61–67. A MS by Henry Crabb Robinson,
written about 1803, "Kant's Analysis of Beauty," now in the Williams
Library, London, contains the distinction of classical-romantic; see
my *Immanuel Kant in England* (Princeton, 1931), p. 158.

51. *Edinburgh Review, 22* (Oct. 1813), 198–238; *Monthly Review, 72* (1813), 421–26, *73* (1814), 63–68, 352–65, especially 364.

52. *Quarterly Review, 20* (Jan. 1814), 355–409. I do not know
the author: he is not given in the list of contributors in the *Gentle-
man's Magazine,* 1844, or in W. Graham's *Tory Criticism in the
Quarterly Review* (New York, 1921).

53. Feb. 1816, reprinted in *Complete Works,* ed. Howe, *16,* 57–
99.

Scott in his *Essay on Drama* (1819), and in *Ollier's Literary Magazine* (1820), which contains a translation of Schlegel's old essay on *Romeo and Juliet*. The use to which Coleridge put Schlegel in his lectures given after the publication of the English translation needs no repetition.

The usual impression that the classical-romantic distinction was little known in England seems not quite correct.[54] It is discussed in Thomas Campbell's *Essay on Poetry* (1819), though Campbell finds Schlegel's defense of Shakespeare's irregularities on "romantic principles" "too romantic for his conception." In Sir Edgerton Brydges' *Gnomica* and *Sylvan Wanderer* there is striking praise of romantic medieval poetry and its derivations in Tasso and Ariosto in contrast to the classical abstract poetry of the eighteenth century.[55] We find only a few practical uses of these terms at that time: Samuel Singer, in his introduction to Marlowe's *Hero and Leander,* says that "Musaeus is more classical, Hunt more romantic." He defends Marlowe's extravagances which might excite the ridicule of French critics: "but here in England their reign is over and thanks to the Germans, with the Schlegels at their head, a truer philosophical method of judging is beginning to obtain among us."[56] De Quincey in 1835 attempted a more original elaboration of the dichotomy by stressing the role of Christianity and the difference in the attitudes toward death; but even these ideas are all derived from the Germans.[57]

But none of the English poets, we must stress, recognized himself as a romanticist or recognized the relevance of the

54. Further examples in Herbert Weisinger, "English Treatment of the Classical-Romantic Problem," in *Modern Language Quarterly, 7* (1946), 477–88.

55. Issues dated Apr. 20, 1819, and Oct. 23, 1818.

56. London, 1821, p. lvii.

57. Cf. a full discussion in my "De Quincey's Status in the History of Ideas," *Philological Quarterly, 23* (1944), 248–72.

debate to his own time and country. Neither Coleridge nor Hazlitt, who used Schlegel's *Lectures,* made such an application. Byron definitely rejects it. Though he knew (and disliked) Schlegel personally, had read *De l'Allemagne,* and even tried to read Friedrich Schlegel's *Lectures,* he considered the distinction "romantic-classical" as merely a Continental debate. In a planned dedication of *Marino Falieri* to Goethe he refers to "the great struggle, in Germany, as well as in Italy, about what they call 'classical' and 'romantic' —terms which were not subjects of classification in England, at least when I left it four or five years ago." Byron contemptuously says of the enemies of Pope in the Bowles-Byron controversy, "nobody thought them worth making a sect of." "Perhaps there may be something of the kind sprung up latterly, but I have not heard of much about it, and it would be such bad taste that I shall be very sorry to believe it." Still, during the next year, Byron used the concepts in what seems to be a plea for the relativity of poetic taste. He argues that there are no invariable principles of poetry, that reputations are bound to fluctuate. "This does not depend upon the merits [of the poets] but upon the ordinary vicissitudes of human opinion. Schlegel and Mmé de Staël have endeavoured also to reduce poetry to two systems, classical and romantic. The effect is only beginning." But there is no consciousness in Byron that he belongs to the romantics. An Austrian police spy in Italy knew better. He reported that Byron belongs to the *Romantici* and "has written and continues to write poetry of this new school."[58]

58. There is a copy of *De l'Allemagne,* with a long note by Byron, in the Harvard Library. Madame de Staël sent Byron Schlegel's *Lectures;* see Byron's *Letters and Journals,* ed. Lord Prothero, *2,* 343. On Friedrich Schlegel's *Lectures,* cf. *Letters, 5,* 191–93. The dedication of *Marino Falieri,* dated Oct. 17, 1820, ibid., *5,* 100–04. The letter to Murray on Bowles, Feb. 7, 1821, ibid., *5,* 553–54n. The police spy, Sept. 10, 1819, quoted ibid., *4,* 462.

The actual application of the term "romantic" to English literature of the early nineteenth century is much later. Also the terms, "a romantic," "a romanticist," "romanticism," are very late in English and occur first in reports or notes on Continental phenomena. An article in English by Stendhal in 1823 reviews his own book, *Racine et Shakespeare,* singling out the section on "Romanticism" for special praise.[59] Carlyle entered in his notebook in 1827 that "Grossi is a Romantic and Manzoni a romanticist." In his "State of German Literature" (1827) he speaks of the German "Romanticists." "Romanticism" occurs in his article on Schiller (1831), where he says complacently that "we are troubled with no controversies on Romanticism and Classicism, the Bowles controversy on Pope having long since evaporated without result."[60] There are, it seems, no instances of the application of these terms by Carlyle to the history of English literature. As late a book as Mrs. Oliphant's *Literary History of England between the End of the Eighteenth and the Beginning of the Nineteenth Centuries* (1882) shows no trace of the terms and their derivatives. She speaks merely of the Lake School, the Satanic School, and the Cockney Group. W. Bagehot used "romantic" with "classical" in a way which shows that they were not associated in his mind with a definite, established period of English literature: he speaks of Shelley's "classical imagination" (1856) and in 1864 contrasts the "classical" Wordsworth with the "romantic" Tennyson and the "grotesque" Browning.[61]

59. In the *New Monthly Magazine, 3* (1823), 522–28, signed Y. I. See Doris Gunnell, *Stendhal et l'Angleterre* (Paris, 1909), pp. 162–63.

60. *Two Notebooks,* ed. C. E. Norton (New York, 1898), p. 111. *Miscellanies* (London, 1890), *1,* 45, and *3,* 71. Cf. also *2,* 276. The *NED* gives much later examples of first occurrences: for "a romantic," 1882; for "romanticist," 1830; for "romanticism," 1844.

61. *Literary Studies,* ed. R. H. Hutton (London, 1905), *1,* 231 and *2,* 341.

But this does not seem to be the entire story. Among the handbooks of English literature, Thomas Shaw's *Outlines of English Literature* (1849) is the earliest exception. He speaks of Scott as the "first stage in literature towards romanticism" and calls Byron the "greatest of romanticists," but separates Wordsworth for his "metaphysical quietism."[62] It may be significant that Shaw compiled his handbook originally for his classes at the Lyceum in St. Petersburg, where by that time, as everywhere on the Continent, the terms were established and expected.

In David Macbeth Moir's *Sketches of the Poetical Literature of the Past Half Century* (1852), Matthew Gregory Lewis is set down as the leader of the "purely romantic school" of which Scott, Coleridge, Southey, and Hogg are listed as disciples, while Wordsworth is treated independently. Scott is treated under the heading "The Revival of the Romantic School," though the term is not used in the text of the chapter.[63] W. Rushton's *Afternoon Lectures on English Literature* (1863) discusses the "Classical and Romantic School of English Literature as represented by Spenser, Dryden, Pope, Scott and Wordsworth."[64] The further spread and establishment of the term for English Literature of the early nineteenth century is probably due to Alois Brandl's *Coleridge und die romantische Schule in England,* translated by Lady Eastlake (1887), and to the vogue of Pater's discussion of "Romanticism" in *Appreciations* (1889); it is finally established in books such as those of W. L. Phelps and Henry A. Beers.

If we survey the evidence assembled we can hardly escape several conclusions which seem important for our argument.

62. *A Complete Manual* (New York, 1867), pp. 290 ff., 316, 341, 348, 415.

63. 2nd ed., Edinburgh, 1852; six lectures delivered in 1850–51; cf. pp. 17, 117, 213.

64. London, 1863. The lectures were given in Dublin.

The self-designation of writers and poets as "romantic" varies in the different countries considerably; many examples are late and short lived. If we take self-designation as the basic criterion for modern use, there would be no romantic movement in Germany before 1808, none in France before 1818 or (since the 1818 example was an isolated instance, Stendhal) before 1824, and none at all in England. If we take the use of the word "romantic" for any kind of literature (at first medieval romances, Tasso, and Ariosto) as our criterion, we are thrown back to 1669 in France, 1673 in England, 1698 in Germany. If we insist on taking the contrast between the terms "classical and romantic" as decisive, we arrive at the dates 1801 for Germany, 1810 for France, 1811 for England, 1816 for Italy, etc. If we think that a realization of the quality of romanticism is particularly important, we would find the term "Romantik" in Germany in 1802, "romantisme" in France in 1816, "romanticismo" in Italy in 1818, and "romanticism" in England in 1823. Surely, all these facts (even though the dates may be corrected) point to the conclusion that the history of the term and its introduction cannot regulate the usage of the modern historian, since he would be forced to recognize milestones in his history which are not justified by the actual state of the literatures in question. The great changes happened, independently of the introduction of these terms, either before or after them and only rarely approximately at the same time.

On the other hand, the usual conclusion drawn from examinations of the history of the words, that they are used in contradictory senses, seems to me greatly exaggerated. One must grant that many German æstheticians juggle the terms in extravagant and personal ways, nor can one deny that the emphasis on different aspects of their meaning shifts from writer to writer and sometimes from nation to nation, but on the whole there was really no misunderstanding about the meaning of "romanticism" as a new designation for poetry,

opposed to the poetry of neoclassicism, and drawing its inspiration and models from the Middle Ages and the Renaissance. The term is understood in this sense all over Europe,
and everywhere we find references to August Wilhelm
Schlegel or Madame de Staël and their particular formulas
opposing "classical" and "romantic."

The fact that the convenient terms were introduced sometimes much later than the time when actual repudiation of
the neoclassical tradition was accomplished does not, of
course, prove that the changes were not noticed at that time.

The mere use of the terms "romantic" and "romanticism"
must not be overrated. English writers early had a clear
consciousness that there was a movement which rejected
the critical concepts and poetic practice of the eighteenth
century, that it formed a unity, and had its parallels on the
continent, especially in Germany. Without the term "romantic" we can trace, within a short period, the shift from the
earlier conception of the history of English poetry as one of
a uniform progress from Waller and Denham to Dryden
and Pope, still accepted in Johnson's *Lives of the Poets,* to
Southey's opposite view in 1807, that the "time which
elapsed from the days of Dryden to those of Pope is the dark
age of English poetry." The reformation began with Thomson and the Wartons. The real turning point was Percy's
Reliques, "the great literary epocha of the present reign."[65]
Shortly afterwards, in Leigh Hunt's *Feast of the Poets* (1814)
we have the view established that Wordsworth is "capable
of being at the head of a new and great age of poetry; and
in point of fact, I do not deny that he is so already, as the
greatest poet of the present."[66] In Wordsworth's own postscript to the 1815 edition of the *Poems,* the role of Percy's
Reliques is again emphasized: "The poetry of the age has

65. Introduction to *Specimens of the Later English Poets* (London, 1807), pp. xxix and xxxii.
66. P. 83.

been absolutely redeemed by it."[67] In 1816 Lord Jeffrey acknowledged that the "wits of Queen Anne's time have been gradually brought down from the supremacy which they had enjoyed, without competition, for the best part of a century." He recognized that the "present revolution in literature" was due to the "French revolution—the genius of Burke—the impression of the new literature of Germany, evidently the original of our Lake School of poetry."[68] In Nathan Drake's book on *Shakespeare* (1817) the role of the revival of Elizabethan poetry is recognized. "Several of our bards," he says, "have in great degree reverted to the ancient school."[69] In Hazlitt's *Lectures on the English Poets* (1818) a new age dominated by Wordsworth is described quite clearly, with its sources in the French revolution, in German literature, and its opposition to the mechanical conventions of the followers of Pope and the old French school of poetry. An article in *Blackwood's* sees the connection between the "great change in the poetical temper of the country" and the Elizabethan revival. "A nation must revert to the ancient spirit of its own. The living and creative spirit of literature is its nationality."[70] Scott uses Schlegel extensively and describes the general change as a "fresh turning up of the soil" due to the Germans and necessitated by the "wearing out" of the French models.[71] Carlyle in his introduction to selections from Ludwig Tieck draws the English-German parallel quite explicitly:

67. Wordsworth, *Prose Works*, ed. Grosart, 2, 118, 124.

68. Review of Scott's edition of Swift, in *Edinburgh Review*, Sept. 1816; *Contributions to Edinburgh Review* (2nd ed. London, 1846), *1*, 158, 167.

69. London, 1817, p. 600.

70. *Blackwood's Magazine, 4*, (1818), 264–66.

71. In "Essay on Drama," contributed to *Encyclopedia Britannica*, Supplement, vol. 3, 1819; *Miscellaneous Prose Works* (Edinburgh, 1834), *6*, 380.

Neither can the change be said to have originated with Schiller and Goethe; for it is a change originating not in individuals, but in universal circumstances, and belongs not to Germany, but to Europe. Among ourselves, for instance, within the last thirty years, who has not lifted up his voice with double vigour in praise of Shakespeare and Nature, and vituperation of French taste and French philosophy? Who has not heard of the glories of old English literature; the wealth of Queen Elizabeth's age; the penury of Queen Anne's; and the inquiry whether Pope was a poet? A similar temper is breaking out in France itself, hermetically sealed as that country seemed to be against all foreign influences; and doubts are beginning to be entertained, and even expressed, about Corneille and the Three Unities. It seems to be substantially the same thing which has occurred in Germany . . . only that the revolution, which is here proceeding, and in France commencing, appears in Germany to be completed.[72]

All of this is broadly true and applicable even today and has been wrongly forgotten by modern sceptics.

Scott, in a retrospective "Essay on Imitations of the Ancient Ballads" (1830), also stressed the role of Percy and the Germans in the revival. "As far back as 1788 a new species of literature began to be introduced into the country. Germany . . . was then for the first time heard of as the cradle of a style of poetry and literature much more analogous to that of Britain than either the French, Spanish or Italian schools."

Scott tells of a lecture of Henry Mackenzie where the audience learned that the "taste which dictated the German compositions was of a kind as nearly allied to the English as their language." Scott learned German from Dr. Willich, who later expounded Kant in English. But, according to Scott,

72. *Works,* Centenary ed. (London, 1899), *German Romance, 1,* 261.

M. G. Lewis was the first who attempted to introduce something like German taste into English composition.[73]

Probably the most widely read of these pronouncements was T. B. Macaulay's account in his review of Moore's *Life of Byron*. There the period of 1750–80 is called the "most deplorable part of our literary history." The revival of Shakespeare, the ballads, Chatterton's forgeries, and Cowper are mentioned as the main agents of change. Byron and Scott are singled out as the great names. Most significantly, Macaulay realizes that "Byron, though always sneering at Mr. Wordsworth, was yet, though, perhaps unconsciously, the interpreter between Mr. Wordsworth and the multitude. . . . Lord Byron founded what may be called an exoteric Lake School—what Mr. Wordsworth had said like a recluse, Lord Byron said like a man of the world."[74] Macaulay thus long before he knew a term for it, recognized the unity of the English romantic movement.

James Montgomery, in his *Lectures on General Literature* (1833), described the age since Cowper as the third era of modern literature. Southey, Wordsworth, and Coleridge are called the "three pioneers, if not the absolute founders, of the existing style of English literature."[75]

The most boldly formulated definition of the new view is again in Southey, in the "Sketches of the Progress of English Poetry from Chaucer to Cowper" (1833). There the "age from Dryden to Pope" is called "the worst age of English poetry: the age of Pope was the pinchbeck age of poetry." "If Pope closed the door against poetry, Cowper opened

---

73. In new edition of *Minstrelsy of the Scottish Border* (1830), ed. T. Henderson (New York, 1931), pp. 535–62, especially pp. 549–50. On Willich, see my *Immanuel Kant in England* (Princeton, 1931), pp. 11–15.

74. *Edinburgh Review,* June 1831. Reprinted in *Critical and Historical Essays* (Everyman ed.) 2, 634–35.

75. Lectures given in 1830–31.

it."[76] The same view, though less sharply expressed, can be found with increasing frequency even in textbooks, such as Robert Chambers' *History of the English Language and Literature* (1836), in De Quincey's writings, and R. H. Horne's *New Spirit of the Age* (1844).

None of these publications use the term "romantic," but in all of them we hear that there is a new age of poetry which has a new style inimical to that of Pope. The emphasis and selections of examples vary, but in combination they say that the German influence, the revival of the ballads and the Elizabethans, and the French Revolution were the decisive influences which brought about the change. Thomson, Burns, Cowper, Gray, Collins, and Chatterton are honored as precursors, Percy and the Wartons as initiators. The trio, Wordsworth, Coleridge, and Southey, are recognized as the founders and, as time progressed, Byron, Shelley, and Keats were added in spite of the fact that this new group of poets denounced the older for political reasons. Clearly, such books as those of Phelps and Beers merely carry out, in a systematic fashion, the suggestions made by the contemporaries and even the actual protagonists of the new age of poetry.

This general scheme is, to my mind, still substantially valid. It seems an unwarranted nominalism to reject it completely and to speak, as Ronald S. Crane does, of "the fairy tales about neoclassicism and romanticism"[77] in the eighteenth century. Not much seems accomplished by George Sherburn when he avoids the term in an excellent summary of what is generally called the romantic tendencies of the late eighteenth century, since he is admittedly confronted with the same problems and facts.[78]

76. In Southey's ed. of *The Works of Cowper, 3,* 109, 142.
77. *Philological Quarterly, 22* (1943), 143, in a review of an article by Curtis D. Bradford and Stuart Gerry Brown, "On Teaching the Age of Johnson," in *College English, 3* (1942), 650–59.
78. In a *Literary History of England,* ed. A. C. Baugh (New York,

One must grant, of course, that many details of the books of Phelps and Beers are mistaken and out of date. The new understanding of neoclassical theory and the new appreciation of eighteenth-century poetry, especially of Pope, have led to a reversal of the value judgments implied in the older conceptions. Romantic polemics give frequently a totally distorted picture of neoclassical theory, and some modern literary historians seem to have misunderstood the eighteenth-century meaning of such key terms as "reason," "nature," and "imitation." Investigations have shown that the revival of Elizabethan, medieval, and popular literature began much earlier than has been assumed. Objections against slavish imitation of the classics and strict adherence to the rules were commonplaces of English criticism, even in the seventeenth century. Many supposedly romantic ideas on the role of genius and imagination were perfectly acceptable to the main neoclassical critics. Much evidence has been accumulated to show that many of the precursors of romanticism—Thomson, the Wartons, Percy, Young, Hurd—shared the preconceptions of their age and held many basic neoclassical critical convictions, and cannot be called "revolutionaries" or "rebels."

We grant many of these criticisms and corrections of the older view. We may even side with the modern neoclassicists who deplore the dissolution of their creed and the extravagances of the romantic movement. One should also grant that the hunt for "romantic" elements in the eighteenth century has become a rather tiresome game. A book such as Eric Partridge's *Eighteenth Century English Poetry* (1924) tried to identify "romantic" lines in Pope with great self-assurance. Partridge tells us that "nearly one-fifth of the total number of lines in *Eloisa to Abelard* are indisputably either markedly

---

1948), p. 971n. The "part" is called "The Disintegration of Classicism," the chapter "Accentuated Tendencies," terms which give away the argument against preromanticism.

romantic in themselves or clearly romantic in tendency." He
singles out lines in Dyer's *Fleece* as "romantic."[79] There are
several German theses which break up an eighteenth-century
critic or poet into his wicked pseudo-classical and his virtu-
ous romantic halves.[80]

Nobody has ever suggested that the precursors of romanticism were conscious of being precursors. But their anticipations of romantic views and devices are important, even if it
can be shown that these pronouncements, taken in their total
context, need to be interpreted differently and were innocuous from a neoclassical point of view. The fact that a later
age could fasten on certain passages in Young or Hurd or
Warton is relevant—not the intentions of Young, Hurd, or
Warton. It is the right of a new age to look for its own
ancestors and even to pull passages out of their context. One
can prove, as Hoyt Trowbridge has done,[81] that Hurd's total
theory was neoclassical; but, in the perspective of a new age,
only a few passages from the *Letters on Chivalry and Romance* mattered—Hurd's saying that the *Faerie Queene*
"should be read and criticised under the idea of a Gothic,
not a classical poem" and his plea for the "pre-eminence of
the Gothic manners and fictions as adapted to the end of
poetry, above the classic."[82] The argument against the very
existence of romanticism in the eighteenth century is based
on the prejudice that only the totality of a writer's works is
the criterion of judgment, while in the many instances which
are constantly being produced to show that individual ro-

79. London, 1924, pp. 72, 172. Lines 209–13, 385–89 of Dyer's
poem are called "romantic."

80. E.g. J. E. Anwander, *Pseudoklassizistisches und Romantisches
in Thomsons Seasons* (Leipzig, 1930); Sigyn Christiani, *Samuel
Johnson als Kritiker im Lichte von Pseudo-Klassizismus und Romantik* (Leipzig, 1931).

81. "Bishop Hurd: A Reinterpretation," *PMLA, 58* (1943), 450–
65.

82. Ed. Edith Morley (Oxford, 1911), pp. 115, 128.

mantic ideas can be traced to the seventeenth century or beyond, the opposite method is employed—an atomistic view which ignores the question of emphasis, place in a system, frequency of occurrence. Both methods have been manipulated interchangeably.

The best solution seems to say that the student of neoclassical literature is right in refusing to see every figure and idea merely in terms of the role it may have played in the preparation of romanticism. But this refusal should not amount to a denial of the problem of the preparation of a new age. One could also study the new age for its survivals of the neoclassical norms,[83] a point of view which could prove illuminating, though it could hardly be considered of equal standing. Time flows in one direction and mankind for some reason (craze for novelty, dynamism, creativity?) is interested more in origins than in residues. If there were no preparations, anticipations, and undercurrents in the eighteenth century which could be described as pre-romantic, we would have to make the assumption that Wordsworth and Coleridge fell from heaven and that the neoclassical age was unperturbedly solid, unified, and coherent in a way no age has ever been before or since.

An important compromise has been propounded by Northrop Frye.[84] He argues that the second half of the eighteenth century is a "new age" which has "nothing to do with the Age of Reason. It is the age of Collins, Percy, Gray, Cowper, Smart, Chatterton, Burns, Ossian, the Wartons and Blake." "Its chief philosopher is Berkeley and its chief prose writer Sterne." "The age of Blake," he concludes, "has been rather unfairly treated by critics, who have tended to see in

83. Suggested by Louis Landa in *Philological Quarterly*, 22 (1943), 147. Cf. Pierre Moreau, *Le Classicisme des romantiques* (Paris, 1932).

84. In *Fearful Symmetry: A Study of William Blake* (Princeton, 1947), especially p. 167.

it nothing but a transition with all its poets either reacting against Pope or anticipating Wordsworth." Mr. Frye unfortunately ignores the fact that Hume rather than Berkeley dominated the philosophy of the age and that Dr. Johnson was then very much alive. Blake remained totally unknown in his time. In Thomas Warton, certainly, we have a recognition of classical standards and a tempered appreciation of Gothic picturesqueness and sublimity, a theory of a double standard of poetry which apparently was held by him without a feeling of contradiction.[85] Still, the contradictions are inherent in the whole position and it is hard to see what can be objected to calling it "pre-romantic." One can observe a process by which these scattered and underground tendencies strengthen and collect; some writers become "doubles," houses divided, and thus, seen from the perspective of a later time, can be called "pre-romantic." We can, it seems, go on speaking of "pre-romanticism" and romanticism, since there are periods of the dominance of a system of ideas and poetic practices which have their anticipations in the preceding decades. The terms "romantic" and "romanticism," though late by the dates of their introduction, were everywhere understood in approximately the same sense and are still useful as terms for the kind of literature produced after neoclassicism.

2

The Unity of European Romanticism

If we examine the characteristics of the actual literature which called itself or was called "romantic" all over the continent, we find throughout Europe the same conceptions of poetry and of the workings and nature of poetic imagination, the same conception of nature and its relation to man,

85. Cf. fuller discussion in my *Rise of English Literary History* (Chapel Hill, 1941), especially pp. 185–86.

and basically the same poetic style, with a use of imagery, symbolism, and myth which is clearly distinct from that of eighteenth-century neoclassicism. This conclusion might be strengthened or modified by attention to other frequently discussed elements: subjectivism, mediævalism, folklore, etc. But the following three criteria should be particularly convincing, since each is central for one aspect of the practice of literature: imagination for the view of poetry, nature for the view of the world, and symbol and myth for poetic style.

German literature is the clearest case; in both so-called romantic schools we find a view of poetry as knowledge of the deepest reality, of nature as a living whole, and of poetry as primarily myth and symbolism. This would hardly need to be argued with anyone who had read only Novalis. But it is impossible to accept the common German view that romanticism is the creation of the Schlegels, Tieck, Novalis, and Wackenroder. If one looks at the history of German literature between the date of Klopstock's *Messiah* (1748) and the death of Goethe (1832), one can hardly deny the unity and coherence of the whole movement which, in European terms, would have to be called "romantic." Some German scholars, such as H. A. Korff,[86] recognize this and speak of "Goethezeit" or "deutsche Bewegung," terms which, however, obscure the international character of the changes.

One must, of course, grant distinctions between the different stages of the development. There was the "storm and stress" movement in the seventies which exactly parallels what today is elsewhere called "pre-romanticism." It was more radical and violent than anything corresponding in England or France, but it must be recognized as substantially the same movement, if we realize that the most important single influence was that of Rousseau and understand the

86. *Geist der Goethezeit: Versuch einer ideellen Entwicklung der klassisch-romantischen Literaturgeschichte* (5 vols. Leipzig, 1923–57).

extraordinary extent to which the ideas of Herder were prepared by the English and Scottish critics of the eighteenth
century. The usual German terminology, "die Klassiker," is
grossly misleading, since the authors grouped together as
the German "classics" form two quite distinct groups; Lessing and Wieland belong to neoclassicism, while Herder
was an extremely irrationalistic pre-romanticist, as were the
early Goethe and Schiller. Only these last two authors went
through a phase of "classicism," and that for the most part
only in their theories. It is hard to find anything classical
in Schiller's practice. The nostalgic hymn, "Die Götter
Griechenlands," is rather a typical romantic dream. Goethe,
while under the impression of his trip to Italy, for a time
expounded a classical creed, especially in his writings on
the plastic arts; and he wrote some works which must be
considered in any history of neoclassicism: *Iphigenie* (1787),
*Römische Elegien, Achilleis, Hermann und Dorothea, Die
natürliche Tochter* (1804), possibly *Helena.* Still, however
successfully their classical spirit could be defended, Goethe's
greatest works are the subjective lyrics, *Faust,* the very influential *Meister,* and of course, *Werther.* It seems a strange
preconception of many Germans to judge their greatest
writer only according to one stage in his development and
in accordance with his quite derivative and conventional
taste in the fine arts. All the artistic power of Goethe is in
the lyrics, in *Faust,* and in the novels, where there is scarcely
any trace of classicism. If we examine Goethe's views of
nature, it is obvious that he was an enemy of the Newtonian
cosmology, the eighteenth-century world machine, and that
he not only defended poetically a dynamic, organic view of
nature, but also attempted to buttress it by scientific experi-
ments and speculations (the *Theory of Colors,* the *Metamorphosis of Plants*) and by the use of concepts such as
teleology, polarity, and so forth. Goethe's views are not

identical with those of Schelling, but they are not easy to distinguish from them, and Schelling was the father of German *Naturphilosophie.* Goethe was also a symbolist and mythologist both in theory and practice. He interpreted language as a system of symbols and images. All philosophizing about nature was to him only anthropomorphism.[87] Goethe was apparently the first to draw clearly the distinction between symbol and allegory.[88] He attempted to create new myths, such as the Mothers in the second part of *Faust,* and tried to define poetically the relation of "Gott und Welt." One could use as a commentary to these poems the neo-Platonic cosmology Goethe claimed was his own at the age of twenty-one.[89] Goethe's one abstractly philosophical paper clearly formulates what even in 1812 he declared to have been "der Grund seiner ganzen Existenz," i.e. to see God in nature and nature in God.[90] Thus, Goethe perfectly fits into the European romantic movement which he, as much as any single writer, helped to create.

There was, one must admit, a pronounced stage of Hellenism in the German movement; its roots are in Winckelmann, an ardent student of Shaftesbury, and this Hellenic enthusiasm early became extremely fervid in Germany. Its main documents are Schiller's "Die Götter Griechenlands," Höl-

87. To Riemer, *Gespräche,* ed. F. Biedermann, *1* (Leipzig, 1909), 505. See *Farbenlehre,* Didaktischer Teil, sec. 751. Jubiläumsausgabe, *40,* 87.

88. Curt Richard Müller, *Die geschichtlichen Voraussetzungen des Symbolbegriffs in Goethes Kunstanschauung* (Leipzig, 1937); Maurice Marache, *Le Symbole dans la pensée et l'œuvre de Goethe* (Paris, 1960).

89. *Dichtung und Wahrheit,* Jubiläumsausgabe, *23,* 163 ff. Suggested by Arnold's *Kirchen- und Ketzergeschichte.*

90. The so-called "Philosophische Studie," written in 1784–85, published in 1891. See *Sämtliche Werke,* Jubiläumsausgabe, ed. Eduard von der Hellen, *39,* 6–9. See also Korff, *3,* 35–36.

derlin's *Hyperion* and *Archipelagus,* some of the writings of
Wilhelm von Humboldt, Goethe's *Winckelmann und sein
Jahrhundert,* and the early writings of Friedrich Schlegel.
Still, one need not speak of a "Tyranny of Greece over
Germany."[91] There was, after all, a comparable Hellenic
enthusiasm in France and England. It seems a mistake to
underrate these parallel developments because they did not
find such embodiment as in Germany's Goethe. French neo-
Hellenism has at least one great poet, André Chénier. One
cannot ignore the Hellenic enthusiasms and interests of even
Chateaubriand and Lamartine, or the "Dionysiac" conception of Greek mythology charmingly expressed by Maurice
de Guérin. We must not forget the Greek revival in painting
and sculpture: Canova, Thorwaldsen, Ingres, Flaxman, none
of whom were Germans.

In England, the role of romantic Hellenism has been
studied only recently;[92] it was widespread in the eighteenth
century and finds poetic expression of great power in Byron,
Shelley, and Keats. The whole of neo-Hellenism, German,
English, and French, is not necessarily contradictory of
romanticism. Homer was interpreted as a primitive poet.
Leopardi, arguing against romanticism, appealed to a pastoral, romanticized, primitive Greece.[93] Surprisingly early
the "Orphic," orgiastic side of Greek civilization was recognized: by Friedrich Schlegel, by Schelling, by Maurice de
Guérin.[94] The conception of antiquity emerging from Keats'

91. The title of E. M. Butler's book (Cambridge, 1935).

92. See Harry Levin, *The Broken Column, a Study in Romantic
Hellenism* (Cambridge, Mass., 1931), and Bernard H. Stern, *The
Rise of Romantic Hellenism in English Literature, 1732–86* (Men-
asha, Wis., 1940).

93. "Discorso di un Italiano intorno alla poesia romantica"
(1818). First published in Leopardi, *Scritti vari inediti* (1906).

94. See esp. Walther Rehm, *Griechentum und Goethezeit: Geschichte eines Glaubens* (Leipzig, 1936). On French developments,

Hyperion is far removed from any eighteenth-century neo-classicism.

If this view that a large part of Hellenism is romantic is justified, it will be possible to minimize the excessive stress the Germans have traditionally put on the supposed conflict between their "classicism" and "romanticism." This conflict was in part purely personal, as a detailed history of the relations between Goethe and Schiller and the Schlegels shows,[95] and in part it expressed a return of the so-called romantics to the ideals of the *Sturm und Drang* which Goethe and Schiller had attempted, somewhat too strenuously, to repudiate. Still, there is a fundamental unity in the whole of German literature from roughly the middle of the eighteenth century to the death of Goethe. It is an attempt to create a new art different from that of the French seventeenth century; it is an attempt at a new philosophy which is neither orthodox Christianity nor the Enlightenment of the eighteenth century. This new view emphasizes the totality of man's forces, not reason alone, nor sentiment alone, but rather intuition, "intellectual intuition," imagination. It is a revival of neo-Platonism, a pantheism (whatever its concessions to orthodoxy), a monism which arrived at an identification of God and the world, soul and body, subject and object. The propounders of these ideas were always conscious of the precariousness and difficulty of these views, which frequently appeared to them only as distant ideals; hence the "unending desire" of the German romantics, the stress on evolution, on art as a groping towards the ideal. Exoticism of many kinds is part of the reaction against the

see Henri Peyre, *L'Influence des littératures antiques sur la littérature française moderne: État des travaux* (New Haven, 1941), esp. p. 63 and references there given.

95. See Josef Körner, *Romantiker und Klassiker: Die Brüder Schlegel in ihren Beziehungen zu Schiller und Goethe* (Berlin, 1924).

eighteenth century and its self-complacency; the suppressed forces of the soul seek their analogies and models in prehistory, in the Orient, in the Middle Ages, and finally in India, as well as in the unconscious and in dreams.

The German romantic writers are the contemporaries of the flowering of German music: of Beethoven, Schubert, Schumann, Weber, and others, many of whom used German poetry of the age as texts for their songs or, like Beethoven, as inspiration for their symphonies. The fact of this collaboration is significant but hardly sufficient to make it the distinguishing characteristic of all romanticism.[96] Such an emphasis obscures the international character of the movement, since the collaboration with music was practically nonexistent in England and fairly late and slight in France. It points to the undeniable fact that romanticism in Germany was far more pervasive than in the other countries and that it affected all human endeavors—philosophy, politics, philology, history, science, and all the other arts—there much more thoroughly than elsewhere. But in this respect also the difference between Germany and the other countries is only relative. There was a romantic philosophy, philology, history, politics, and even science, not to speak of painting and music, in other countries, especially in France (Delacroix, Berlioz, Michelet, Cousin). The apparent isolation of Germany is exaggerated by German writers who see in romanticism a purely German style, and by antiromantics and recently by anti-Hitler propagandists who want to prove that all the ills of the last two centuries came from Germany. The only view which takes account of all factors holds that romanticism is a general movement in European thought and art and that it has native roots in every major country. Cultural revolutions of such profound significance are not accomplished by mere importations.

96. As in Richard Benz, *Deutsche Romantik* (Leipzig, 1937).

Romanticism was more completely victorious in Germany than elsewhere for very obvious historical reasons. The German Enlightenment was weak and of short duration. The Industrial Revolution was late in coming. There was no leading rationalistic bourgeoisie. Both the derivative, unoriginal Enlightenment and the peculiarly rigid religious orthodoxies seemed unsatisfactory. Thus social and intellectual causes opened the way for a literature which was created mostly by unattached intellectuals, tutors, army surgeons, salt-mine officials, court clerks, and the like, who revolted against both feudalism and middle-class ideals. German romanticism, more so than English and French, was the movement of an intelligentsia which had loosened its class ties and hence was particularly apt to create a literature remote from ordinary reality and social concerns. Still, the aestheticism and lack of social "engagement" of writers such as Goethe has been very much exaggerated. One hears too much about the "Olympian" Goethe. It is not realized that the quotation "ein garstig Lied, pfui, ein politisch Lied!" is the dramatic pronouncement of a student in "Auerbachs Keller."

While it would be absurd to deny the special features of the German romantic age (we may pause to reflect that every age has its special features), almost all its views and techniques can be paralleled elsewhere. It is no denial of originality to see that the great German writers drew freely on foreign sources (Rousseau, English preromanticism) or on sources in the remote past, both foreign and native, which had been available to the other European nations: neo-Platonism, Giordano Bruno, Böhme, a reinterpreted Spinoza, Leibniz. The Germans, in turn, influenced other countries; but their influence, for obvious chronological reasons, comes too late to make them the only source of the turn towards the ideas and poetic myths usually called romantic. In England, Böhme was important for Blake,

Schelling and August Wilhelm Schlegel for Coleridge, Bürger and Goethe for Scott (though hardly centrally so),
Goethe and Jean Paul for Carlyle. But the German influence on Wordsworth, Shelley, Keats, and even Byron is
negligible. In France, German influences came much later;
A. W. Schlegel, we have shown, was very important for the
introduction of the new critical terminology. German interests are strong in Nodier, in Gérard de Nerval, and in Quinet,
who studied Herder and Creuzer. Some argument can be
made for the importance of the German song (*Lied*) for
the French romantic lyric;[97] but certainly the central figures,
Chateaubriand, Lamartine, Vigny, Hugo, Balzac, Sainte-
Beuve have few German affinities, and similarities must be
explained by identical antecedents in England and an analogous literary and cultural situation.

As for France, our view is blurred by the official insistence
on beginning the romantic movement with the triumph of
Hernani (1830), a minor event in a later perspective, which
obscures the fact that, outside of the drama or rather the
Parisian official stage, a profound change had come over
French literature many years before. This has been widely
recognized in France, even though the centenary of romanticism was celebrated in 1927. The very first historian of
romanticism in France, F. R. de Toreinx, says that romanticism was born in 1801, that Chateaubriand was its father,
Madame de Staël its godmother (he is silent about the
mother). In 1824 *La Muse Française* noticed the decisive
role of Rousseau and Bernardin de St. Pierre; Alfred Mi-
chiels, in his *Histoire des idées littéraires en France* (1842),
was of the opinion that the whole of romanticism can be
found in Sébastien Mercier.[98] Some have tried to find the

97. See Gertrud Sattler, *Das deutsche Lied in der französischen
Romantik* (Bern, 1932).
98. See André Monglond, *Le Préromantisme français* (Grenoble,
1930), *1*, x.

ancestors of romanticism even further back in the past; Faguet interpreted French poetry around 1630 with reference to Lamartine, and Brunetière claimed to see the germs of melodrama in *Phèdre*.[99] But more sober views have prevailed. The romantic elements in French eighteenth-century literature have been investigated quite systematically and, on the whole, convincingly; there is today some very fine work by Pierre Trahard and André Monglond[1] on the history of sentimentalism, usually traced back at least as far as Prévost. Daniel Mornet has studied the reawakening of the feeling for nature and Gilbert Chinard has devoted much attention to French exoticism and primitivism.[2] Auguste Viatte has shown, most impressively, the large undercurrent of illuminism and theosophy in eighteenth-century France.[3] Saint-Martin assumes a large role not only for France (De Maistre, Ballanche), but also for Germany (Hamann, Baader, even Goethe, Novalis). Rousseau, of course, has never ceased to attract attention; he has even been made the wellspring of all romanticism, by friends like J.-J. Texte or by enemies who try to reduce romanticism to Rousseauism.[4] But Rousseau is unduly overrated if he is made the originator of attitudes which he helped popularize but did not invent. Still, all these scattered French studies

99. See Émile Faguet, *Histoire de la poésie française de la renaissance au romantisme* (Paris, n.d.), *2*, 145, 171 ff.; *3*, 185. See also *Petite Histoire de la littérature française* (Paris, n.d.), pp. 100–01; Ferdinand Brunetière, *Conférences de l'Odéon. Les Époques du théâtre français* (Paris, 1901), p. 179.

1. Pierre Trahard, *Les Maîtres de la sensibilité française au XVIIIe siècle*, (4 vols. Paris, 1931–33), and Monglond, *ibid.*

2. Daniel Mornet, *Le Sentiment de la nature en France de J.-J. Rousseau à Bernardin de St. Pierre* (Paris, 1907); Gilbert Chinard, *L'Amérique et le rêve exotique* (Paris, 1911).

3. *Les Sources occultes du romantisme*, 2 vols. (Paris, 1928).

4. *J.-J. Rousseau et les origines du cosmopolitisme littéraire* (Paris, 1895); and the books by Irving Babbitt, Pierre Lasserre, and the Baron Seillière.

show isolated anticipations of romantic attitudes, ideas, sentiments, rather than a real romantic literature in eighteenth-century France. That such a literature existed has best been demonstrated by Kurt Wais,[5] who has shown that there was a whole group of French writers who attacked the *philosophes* and the neoclassical tradition, stressed primitivism, thought that there is cultural decay rather than progress, attacked science, felt well inclined toward religion and even toward superstition and the marvelous. Many of the authors quoted are very minor and even minimal; Ramond de Carbonnières' *Les dernières aventures du jeune d'Olban* (1781) is only a mediocre imitation of *Werther*. But Wais has established that there was a widespread "irrationalism" in writers like Mercier, Chassaignon, Loaisel de Tréogate, and others, which can be compared with the German *Sturm und Drang*.

This French preromantic movement received a temporary setback through the Revolution, which fostered classicism and rationalism, and by the Empire, which also had its official classicism. But among the *émigrés* romanticism flourished. Madame de Staël was the propagandist of the German romantics. Chateaubriand cannot be made out a classicist, whatever his interests in classical antiquity and his reservations against Shakespeare or against many of his contemporaries. *Le Génie du Christianisme* (1802) is a romantic poetics. If we apply our tests, it is obvious that Chateaubriand expounds an organic, symbolic order of nature, that he is a mythologist and symbolist *par excellence*. But Madame de Staël and Chateaubriand were by no means alone in their time; even Chénier conceived the idea of a new mythic poetry, especially in the fragment *Hermès*.[6] In Sénancour's *Obermann* (1804) we find the romantic view of nature in

5. *Das antiphilosophische Weltbild des französischen Sturm und Drang (1760–89)*, (Berlin, 1934).

6. "Il faut magnifiquement représenter la terre sous l'emblème métaphorique d'un grand animal qui vit, se meut, est sujet à des

full bloom. "La nature sentie n'est que dans les rapports humains, et l'éloquence des choses n'est rien que l'éloquence de l'homme. La terre féconde, les cieux immenses, les eaux passagères ne sont qu'une expression des rapports que nos cœurs produisent et contiennent."[7] Obermann constantly finds in external things analogies which give us the feeling of a universal order. Even flowers, a sound, a smell, a gleam of light become the "materials which an external idea arranges like figures of an invisible thing." The states of mind described by Sénancour are extraordinarily similar to Wordsworth's, but unlike Wordsworth (not to speak of Novalis' "magic" idealism) Sénancour experiences them almost as a curse. He complains bitterly that fate has condemned him to have only a "dream of his existence."[8] His art is rather that of passive rêverie.

In Charles Nodier also we find the whole repertory of romantic themes and ideas. Nodier was a quite technical entomologist who mythologized the world of insects. He sees in nature an alphabet which needs deciphering. In the world of insects and infusoria he finds a grotesque parallel to the forms of human art, and in the universe a process of *"syn-génésie,"* a fantastic evolution toward a human Utopia. Nodier knew Swedenborg and Saint-Martin, and used the work of an Italian physiologist, Malpighi. He wrote romantic fairy tales (*La Fée aux Miettes*) and fantasies such as *Lydie ou la Résurrection* (1839), which has obvious affinities with Novalis' *Hymnen an die Nacht.*[9]

---

changements, des révolutions, des fièvres, des dérangements dans la circulation de son sang." In *Œuvres,* ed. Henri Clouard, *1* (Paris, 1927), 161–62.

7. Ed. G. Michaut (Paris, 1911), *1*, 132, Letter 36.

8. See Albert Béguin, *L'Âme romantique et le rêve* (Paris, 1946), pp. 332–33.

9. See Walter Mönch, *Charles Nodier und die deutsche und englische Literatur* (Berlin, 1931).

Lamartine's *Harmonies poétiques et religieuses* (1830) ties completely into our scheme; one could hardly find a more precise expression of the romantic view of nature as a language, as a concert of harmonies. The whole universe is conceived of as a system of symbols, correspondences, emblems, which at the same time is alive and pulsates rhythmically. The task of the poet is not only to read this alphabet, but to vibrate with it, to sense and reproduce its rhythm. *La Chute d'un Ange* (1838) has a mythological conception of the epic similar to Ballanche; there is the scale of being, there is the concept of the transformation of each atom and element into thought and sentiment.[10]

Vigny is different. He does not accept the romantic concept of nature, but embraces a dualism of man and nature, a pessimistic titanism which is a continuous protest against the order of nature. Nature is dead, silent, and even hostile to man. But this sharp ethical dualism of man versus nature is, in Vigny, combined with a totally romantic symbolism: "The men of greatest genius are those who made the justest comparisons. They are the branches to which we can cling in the void which surrounds us. . . . Each man is nothing but an image of an idea of the general mind."[11] Many of Vigny's poems are organized around such symbols as *Le Cor, La Neige, La Bouteille à la mer*. Vigny's preoccupation with myth is obvious; he planned a most ambitious series which was to include a Last Judgment and "Satan Sauvé." Only *Eloa,* a "mystery," and *Le Déluge* were carried out.

10. Pierre Maurice Masson, in *Œuvres et maîtres* (Paris, 1923), traces Lamartine's slow growth towards romantic symbolism. Albert J. George, *Lamartine and Romantic Unanimism* (New York, 1940), studies, under this anachronistic term, evidence for his monism, pantheism, etc.

11. *Journal d'un poète,* ed. F. Baldensperger (London, 1928), pp. 17, 136.

Victor Hugo, later in his life, became the most ambitious mythologist, symbolist, prophet of a new religion, of all the romantics. His fame has declined in the twentieth century, but recently several attempts have been made to rescue these late works—parts of the *Légende des Siècles, La Fin de Satan, Dieu*. These attempts emanate not only from academic scholars, but also from surrealist poets.[12] They stress the mythic, eerie, grand, and sometimes absurd late Hugo. He fits into our scheme beautifully, whatever we may think of the quality of the poetry. Historians of ideas "have marvelled at the unperturbed serenity of a synthesis which does not flinch before self-contradiction, which, at once pantheist and deist, shows God disseminated in the universe and yet transcendent and personal; which draws from all sources, from the modern Platonists and Pythagoreans . . . Swedenborg, Ballanche, from the contemporary Illuminati, from Cabbalists, but persists in wresting originality out of a many-sided indebtedness." Hugo expounds a panpsychism of nature; a conviction of omnisentience (e.g. *Le Sacre de la Femme*), of the "victory of unity over diversity, of All over the ephemeral, the victory of universal and palpitating life over all that limits, curtails, frustrates, and denies."[13] In *Le Satyre* the satyr is haled before the gods and asked to sing in order to amuse the contemptuous Olympians. "Le satyre chanta la terre monstrueuse." His stature increases in singing, he becomes an incarnation of nature and life. The faun declares himself in the concluding line: "Place à tout! Je suis Pan, Jupiter, à genoux!" In *La Fin de Satan*, Satan is pardoned and dies in a surprising conclusion, God saying: "Satan est mort! renais, o Lucifer céleste!" Evil is reabsorbed

12. *La Bouche d'ombre*, ed. Henri Parisot, preface by Léon-Paul Lafargue (Paris, 1947).

13. Quoted from Herbert J. Hunt, *The Epic in Nineteenth Century France* (London, 1941), pp. 282, 293.

because Satan actually loved God, was himself a part of the providential scheme. In *Dieu,* Hugo passes in review the different philosophies he rejects or ridicules: atheism, scepticism, dualism, Greek polytheism, the Hebrew Jehovah. A spiritual pantheism is expounded by an angel: "Tous les êtres sont Dieu; tous les flots sont la mer." The poem concludes in a hymn to God, who is conceived as a bewildering series of contradictions, a dazzling light which is, at the same time, darkness. "Rien n'existe que Lui; le flamboiement profond." In Hugo, then, all the romantic convictions and themes are summarized: organic, evolving nature, the view of poetry as prophecy, the view that symbol and myth are the instruments of poetry. In Hugo the reconciliation of opposites, the stress on the grotesque and evil ultimately absorbed in the harmony of the universe, is particularly clear and was clear even in his early aesthetic theories, as in the preface to *Cromwell.* His prophetic fervor, intensity, and grandiose gestures may have become pretentious and absurd to generations who have lost this view of poetry. But Hugo marshalled all the possible arguments for the romantic view of nature, for man's continuity with nature, the great scale of nature, and the final perfection of man.

Balzac is not usually considered a romantic and he may not be one in many aspects of his stupendous work. But E. R. Curtius[14] has rightly stressed an aspect which must have struck every reader of the *Human Comedy*—Balzac's interest in magic and the occult. A study of Balzac's religious views reveals that he declared himself a Swedenborgian many times. In *Louis Lambert,* which contains much that is autobiography, there is an exposition of a system which must be substantially Balzac's and exuberant praise of Swedenborg as the "Buddha of the North." *Seraphita* also is full of Swedenborgianism, a theosophical and pantheistic philosophy of immanence, which Balzac must have considered

14. *Balzac* (Bonn, 1923).

compatible with Catholicism and his specific endorsement of political Catholicism. Whatever Balzac's exact religious views, he certainly held this organic view of nature which he calls *magisme*. He was deeply impressed by contemporary biology, especially by Geoffroy Saint-Hilaire and his view that there is only *one* animal. He was absorbed and taken in by all forms of magnetism, mesmerism, and phrenology, all of which uphold the "unity of nature." Like the romantics, Balzac had a theory of intuition, to which he applies the queer term, *spécialité*, distinguishing it from instinct and abstraction.[15] He was also an ardent mythologist, giving a symbolic interpretation to all rites, cults, myths, mysteries of religion, and creations of art. "Today hieroglyphics are not any more impressed in Egyptian marble, but in mythologies which are unified worlds." Balzac said of *La Peau de Chagrin,* "tout y est mythe et figure."[16] He himself constantly gave symbolic interpretations; e.g. *La Vieille fille* contains a strange symbolic use of *Orlando Furioso.* Though wide stretches of Balzac's work may not show it, he was inspired by a peculiar type of romantic metaphysics, physics, or energetics, with its supposed laws of compensations, polarities, fluids, etc.

Among the authors less well known today many fit in with our criteria. Pierre-Simon Ballanche had a mystical, Pythagorean conception of nature and the harmony of the spheres (the seven numbers produce an endless concert); an apocalypse is presented in which matter will be spiritualized by a new magnetism and the animals disappear as their life, by assimilation, becomes the life of man. Ballanche was not only a mythologist and fantastic philosopher of nature but also a symbolist who, long before Mallarmé, conceived the unity of the senses.[17]

15. *Louis Lambert,* fragment 16.
16. Curtius, *Balzac,* pp. 69–70.
17. "Tous les sens se réveillent réciproquement l'un l'autre. Il y

Edgar Quinet is related to Ballanche and, of course, to the Germans. To him, religion was the business of the poet; the poet destroys the fixed symbols of dogma in order to renew them. Quinet believed also in some future universal epic which will "reconcile all legends by fusing them into one."[18]

Maurice de Guérin also fits into our scheme. He shows the major points of agreement: the views of the substantial unity of nature, the continuity in the chain of creation, the primacy of the intuitive faculty in man, which is especially active in poets, whose role is to decipher the "flottant appareil de symboles qu'on appelle l'univers." His sense of identity with nature is finely expressed in his journal. "Se laisser pénétrer à la nature . . . s'identifier au printemps . . . aspirer en soi toute la vie . . . se sentir à la fois fleur, verdure, oiseau, chant, fraîcheur, élasticité, volupté, sérénité." Guérin wants to "sentir presque physiquement que l'on vit de Dieu et en Dieu." He aspired to create neopagan myths, like *Le Centaure*, and to spiritualize nature, as in the *Méditation sur la mort de Marie;* he had the romantic thirst to ascend to the origins of mankind and of himself as a child, to find the "point de départ de la vie universelle."[19]

Gérard de Nerval is the most mystical, "supernatural," of the French romantics, the nearest to the most fantastic Germans whom he knew and loved. The symbolists have recognized him as their precursor. *Aurélia,* especially, is a series of visions and dreams which attempt to change the whole life

---

aurait là, en quelque sorte, des onomatopées de couleurs, tant tout est harmonie dans l'homme et dans l'univers." Hunt, *op. cit.,* p. 99. From *La Ville des Expiations.*

18. "Concilier toutes les légendes en les ramenant à une seule," from Avant-propos to *Merlin,* quoted in Hunt, p. 137.

19. Journal, Dec. 10, 1834; March 25, 1833; March 21, 1833, in *Œuvres,* ed. H. Clouard (Paris, 1930), *1,* 253, 167, 147.

of the author himself into a myth. Nerval, exactly like Keats, believed in the literal truth of anything imagination has invented. The whole of Nerval's work is a world of dream symbols and myths. He is full of Swedenborgianism and other occult beliefs; nature is emblematic through and through. He speaks of "a vast conspiracy of all animate beings to reestablish the world in its first harmony": "How can I have existed so long, I said to myself, outside Nature without identifying myself with her? Everything lives, everything acts, everything corresponds; the magnetic rays emanating from myself or others traverse unimpeded the infinite chain of created things; it is a transparent network which covers the world, and its fine threads communicate from one to another to the planets and the stars. I am now a captive on the earth, but I converse with choiring stars, who share my joys and sorrows!"[20]

I have already suggested some of the sources of French romanticism—Swedenborg, Saint-Martin, the Germans. But we must realize that in all phases of French thought there was a considerable parallel activity. In history Michelet propounded a "historical symbolism." The numerous neo-Catholic French thinkers shared many of the main romantic tenets and motifs. There is "striking similarity between the doctrines of Hegel and Bonald."[21] Joseph de Maistre, in his youth at least, was steeped in the mythical, Masonic, and Illuminati ideas of the time, and they left strong traces on his mature thought. A letter to Bonald states that "the physical world is nothing but an image or, if you prefer, the formula, a repetition of the spiritual world." Matter does not exist independently of mind. Catholicism does not totally reject polytheism; it rather explains and corrects the Graeco-

20. *Aurélia,* trans. Richard Aldington (London, 1932), pp. 51–52.
21. See George Boas, *French Philosophies of the Romantic Period* (Baltimore, 1925), p. 73.

Roman mythology. "The name of God, no doubt, is exclusive and incommunicable; still, there are many gods in heaven and earth. There are intelligences, better natures, deified men. The gods of Christianity are the saints."[22]

The whole eclectic movement, fed as it is in part from German sources, especially Schelling, fits into our scheme, and much in the French science of the time, particularly biology, helps to re-create the whole mental "climate" in which French romanticism flourished.

Turning to England, we can see a complete agreement with the French and the Germans on all essential points. The great poets of the English romantic movement constitute a fairly coherent group, with the same view of poetry and the same conception of imagination, the same view of nature and mind. They share also a poetic style, a use of imagery, symbolism, and myth, which is quite distinct from anything that had been practiced by the eighteenth century, and which was felt by their contemporaries to be obscure and almost unintelligible.

The affinity of the concepts of imagination among the English romantic poets scarcely needs demonstration. Blake considers all nature to be "imagination itself." Our highest aim is:

> To see a World in a Grain of Sand:
> And a Heaven in a Wild Flower,
> Hold Infinity in the palm of your hand
> And Eternity in an hour.[23]

Thus imagination is not merely the power of visualization, somewhere in between sense and reason, which it had been to Aristotle or Addison, nor even the inventive power of the

22. *Le Pape*, in *Œuvres*, *4*, 541, quoted by Viatte, *2*, 80.
23. "Auguries of Innocence," *Poetry and Prose of William Blake*, ed. Geoffrey Keynes (New York, 1927), p. 118.

poet, which by Hume and many other eighteenth-century theorists was conceived of as a "combination of innate sensibility, the power of association, and the faculty of conception,"[24] but a creative power by which the mind "gains insight into reality, reads nature as a symbol of something behind or within nature not ordinarily perceived."[25] Thus imagination is the basis of Blake's rejection of the mechanistic world picture, the basis of an idealistic epistemology—

> The Sun's Light when he unfolds it
> Depends on the Organ that beholds it;[26]

and, of course, the basis of an aesthetics, the justification of art and his own peculiar kind of art. This conception of imagination sufficiently justifies the necessity of myth and of metaphor and symbol as its vehicle.

The concept of the imagination in Wordsworth is fundamentally the same, though Wordsworth draws more heavily on eighteenth-century theories and compromises with naturalism. Still, Wordsworth cannot be explained entirely in Hartley's terms;[27] imagination is for him "creative," an insight into the nature of reality and hence the basic justification of art. The poet becomes a living soul who "sees into the life of things." Imagination is thus an organ of knowledge which transforms objects, sees through them, even if they are only the "meanest flower" or the humble ass, an idiot boy, or simply a child: "mighty prophet, seer blest."

The whole of the *Prelude* is a history of the poet's imagination which, in a central passage of the last book, is called

24. Walter J. Bate's description in *From Classic to Romantic* (Cambridge, Mass., 1946), p. 113.

25. I. A. Richards, *Coleridge on Imagination* (London, 1935), p. 145.

26. "For the Sexes: The Gates of Paradise," *Blake*, p. 752.

27. As Arthur Beatty attempted in *William Wordsworth: His Doctrine and Art in Their Historical Relations* (2nd ed. Madison, 1927).

> Another name for absolute power
> And clearest insight, amplitude of mind,
> And Reason in her most exalted mood.[28]

In a letter to Landor, Wordsworth tells him that "in poetry it is the imaginative only, i.e. that which is conversant or turns upon Infinity, that powerfully affects me." "All great poets are in this view powerful Religionists."[29]

It is hardly necessary to explain what a central role the imagination plays in Coleridge's theory and practice. There is a book by I. A. Richards, *Coleridge on Imagination,* and recently R. P. Warren has carefully related the theory to the *Rime of the Ancient Mariner.*[30] The key passage in *Biographia Literaria* on primary and secondary imagination is too well known to need quoting.[31] It is Schellingian in its formulation—on the whole, Coleridge's theory is closely dependent on the Germans. His term for "imagination," the "esemplastic power," is a translation of "Einbildungskraft," based on a fanciful etymology of the German.[32] But, when Coleridge ignores his technical jargon, as in the ode *Dejection* (1802), he still speaks of the "shaping spirit of the imagination," of imagination as a "dim analogue of creation, not all that we *believe,* but all that we can *conceive* of crea-

28. *Prelude,* XIV, 190 ff.

29. Jan. 21, 1824. In *Letters: Later Years,* ed. E. de Selincourt (Oxford), *1,* 134–35.

30. *The Rime of the Ancient Mariner: With an Essay by Robert Penn Warren* (New York, 1946).

31. *Biographia Literaria,* ed. J. Shawcross, *2* (Oxford, 1907), 12. T. S. Eliot quoted it in "Andrew Marvell" (1921), reprinted in *Selected Essays* (London, 1932), p. 284; also I. A. Richards in *Principles of Literary Criticism* (London, 1924), p. 242. It has since been repeated ad nauseam.

32. "Einbildungskraft" is interpreted by Coleridge as "In-eins-Bildung." But the prefix "ein" has nothing to do with "in-eins."

tion."[33] If Coleridge had not known the Germans, he would have been able to expound a neo-Platonic theory, just as Shelley did in his *Defense of Poetry*.

Shelley's *Defense of Poetry* is almost identical, in general conception, with Coleridge's theory. Imagination is the "principle of synthesis." Poetry may be defined as the "expression of the imagination." A poet "participates in the eternal, the infinite, and the one." Poetry lifts the veil from the "hidden beauty of the world, and makes familiar objects be as if they were not familiar." "Poetry redeems from decay the visitations of the divinity in man." To Shelley imagination is creative, and the poet's imagination is an instrument of knowledge of the real. Shelley, more sharply than any other English poet with the exception of Blake, states that the poetic moment is the moment of vision; that the words are but a "feeble shadow," that the mind in composition is a "fading coal."[34] In Shelley we find the most radical divorce between the poetic faculty and will and consciousness.

The affinities and fundamental identities of Keats' views are obvious, though Keats (under the influence of Hazlitt) has more of the sensationalist vocabulary than either Coleridge or Shelley. But he also says: "What the imagination seizes as Beauty must be Truth whether it existed before or not."[35] Clarence D. Thorpe, in analyzing all of Keats' relevant scattered pronouncements, concludes: "Such is the power of creative imagination, a seeing, reconciling, combining force that seizes the old, penetrates beneath its surface, disengages the truth slumbering there, and, building

33. Jan. 15, 1804. In *Letters*, ed. E. H. Coleridge, 2 (London, 1890), 450.

34. Shelley's *Literary and Philosophical Criticism*, ed. J. Shawcross (London, 1909), pp. 131, 155, 153.

35. Letter to B. Bailey, Nov. 22, 1817, in *Letters*, ed. M. B. Forman (4th ed. London, 1952), p. 67.

afresh, bodies forth anew a reconstructed universe in fair
forms of artistic power and beauty."[36] This could be a summary of the theories of imagination of all the romantic poets.

Clearly, such a theory implies a theory of reality and,
especially, of nature. There are individual differences among
the great romantic poets concerning the conception of nature.
But all of them share a common objection to the mechanistic
universe of the eighteenth century—even though Wordsworth admires Newton and accepts him, at least in the orthodox interpretation. All romantic poets conceived of nature
as an organic whole, on the analogue of man rather than a
concourse of atoms—a nature that is not divorced from
aesthetic values, which are just as real (or rather more real)
than the abstractions of science.

Blake stands somewhat apart. He violently objects to the
eighteenth-century cosmology, personified by Newton.

May God us keep
From Single Vision and Newton's sleep.[37]

Blake's writings are also full of condemnations of Locke and
Bacon, atomism, deism, natural religion, and so forth. But
he does not share the romantic deification of nature; he comments expressly on Wordsworth's preface to the *Excursion*:
"You shall not bring me down to believe such fitting and
fitted."[38] To Blake nature is everywhere fallen. It fell with
man; the fall of man and the creation of the physical world
were the same event. In the Golden Age to come, nature will
(with man) be restored to her pristine glory. Man and nature
are, in Blake, not only continuous, but emblematic of each
other:

36. *The Mind of John Keats* (Oxford, 1926), p. 126.
37. Letter to T. Butts, Nov. 22, 1802, *Blake,* p. 1068.
38. Ibid., p. 1026 (written in 1826).

> Each grain of Sand,
> Every Stone on the Land,
> Each rock and each hill,
> Each fountain and rill,
> Each herb and each tree,
> Mountain, hill, earth, and sea,
> Cloud, Meteor, and Star
> Are Men Seen Afar.[39]

In *Milton* especially, nature appears as man's body turned inside out. The ridges of mountains across the world are Albion's fractured spine. Nothing exists outside Albion; sun, moon, stars, the center of the earth, and the depth of the sea were all within his mind and body. Time even is a pulsation of the artery, and space a globule of blood. The crabbed symbolism, the strident tone have kept these later poems from being widely read; but the books by Damon, Percival, Schorer, and Frye[40] have shown the subtlety and coherence of Blake's speculations which set him in the great tradition of *Naturphilosophie* as it comes down from Plato's *Timaeus* to Paracelsus, Böhme, and Swedenborg.

In Wordsworth's conception of nature there is a shift from something like animistic pantheism to a conception reconcilable with traditional Christianity. Nature is animated, alive, filled with God or the Spirit of the World; it is mysteriously present, it gives a discipline of fear and ministry of pleasure.[41] Nature is also a language, a system of symbols. The rocks, the crags, the streams on Simplon Pass

39. Letter to T. Butts, Oct. 2, 1800, ibid., 1052.
40. S. Foster Damon, *William Blake* (Boston, 1924); William C. Percival, *William Blake's "Circle of Destiny"* (New York, 1938); Mark Schorer, *William Blake* (New York, 1946); Northrop Frye, *Fearful Symmetry: A Study of William Blake* (Princeton, 1947).
41. Excellent discussions in J. W. Beach, *The Concept of Nature in Nineteenth-Century English Poetry* (New York, 1936), and in R. D. Havens, *The Mind of a Poet* (Baltimore, 1941).

Were all like workings of one mind, the features
Of the same face, blossoms upon one tree;
Characters of the great Apocalypse
The types and symbols of Eternity.[42]

We would misunderstand idealistic epistemology if we questioned the "objectivity" which Wordsworth ascribes to these conceptions. It is a dialectical relation, not a mere subjectivist imposition, in spite of such passages as

. . . from thyself it comes, that thou must give,
Else never canst receive.[43]

The mind must collaborate and it is its very nature that it should be so.

. . . my voice proclaims
How exquisitely the individual Mind
(And the progressive powers perhaps no less
Of the whole species) to the external World
Is fitted:—and how exquisitely, too . . .
The external world is fitted to the Mind;
And the creation (by no lower name
Can it be called) which they with blended might
Accomplish.[44]

The ancestry of these ideas in Cudworth, Shaftesbury, Berkeley, and others is obvious; there are certain poetic anticipations in Akenside and Collins; but, in Wordsworth, a natural philosophy, a metaphysical concept of nature, enters poetry and finds a highly individual expression—the brooding presence of the hills, of the firm, eternal forms of nature, combined with a vivid sense of the almost dreamlike unreality of the world.

The general concept of nature he shares with his friend

42. *Prelude,* VI, 636 ff.
43. Ibid., XII, 276–77.
44. Preface to *Excursion. Poetical Works,* ed. E. de Selincourt and H. Darbishire (Oxford, 1949), 5, 5.

Coleridge. We could easily match all the fundamental concepts of Wordsworth in Coleridge; probably their phrasing is due to the influence of Coleridge, who early was a student of the Cambridge Platonists and of Berkeley.

> The one Life within us and abroad . . .
> And what if all of animated nature . . .
> Plastic and vast, one intellectual breeze.
> At once the Soul of each, and God of all . . .

the "eternal language, which thy God utters. . . ." "Symbolical, one mighty alphabet," and the conception of subject-object relation:

> We receive but what we give
> And in our life alone does Nature live![45]

—these are quotations from the early poetry. The later Coleridge developed an elaborate philosophy of nature which leans heavily on Schelling's and Steffens' *Naturphilosophie*.[46] Nature is consistently interpreted by analogy with the progress of man to self-consciousness, and Coleridge indulges in all the contemporary speculative chemistry and physics (electricity, magnetism) to buttress a position which is near to vitalism or panpsychism.

Echoes of this contemporary science also permeate Shelley's conceptions and even images. There are many allusions in his poetry to chemical, electrical, and magnetic theories—to theories expounded by Erasmus Darwin and Humphrey Davy.[47] But, in general terms, Shelley mainly echoes Words-

45. From "The Eolian Harp," "Frost at Midnight," "The Destiny of Nations," and "Dejection," *The Poems*, ed. E. H. Coleridge (Oxford, 1912), pp. 101–02, 132, 242, 365.

46. *The Theory of Life* is nothing but a patchwork of translated passages. See Henri Nidecker, "Praeliminarium zur Neuausgabe der Abhandlung über *Lebenstheorie* (*Theory of Life*) von Samuel Taylor Coleridge," *Bericht der philosophisch-historischen Fakultät der Universität Basel*, Heft 5 (Basel, 1927), pp. 7–12.

47. Much evidence in C. Grabo, *A Newton among Poets: Shelley's Use of Science in Prometheus Unbound* (Chapel Hill, 1930).

worth and Coleridge on the "spirit of nature." There is the
same concept of the vitality of nature, its continuity with
man, its emblematic language. There is also the concept of
the cooperation and interrelation of subject and object, as in
the beginning of *Mont Blanc*:

> The everlasting universe of things
> Flows through the mind, and rolls its rapid waves,
> Now dark—now glittering—now reflecting gloom—
> Now lending splendor, where from secret springs
> The source of human thought its tribute brings
> Of waters,—with a sound but half its own.

This seems to say: There is nothing outside the mind of man,
but the receptive function of the stream of consciousness is
very much larger than the tiny active principle in the mind.

> My own, my human mind, which passively
> Now renders and receives fast influencings,
> Holding an unremitting interchange
> With the clear universe of things around.

Here we have, in spite of the stress on the passivity of the
mind, a clear conception of a give and take, of an interchange
between its creative and purely receptive principles. Shelley
conceives of nature as one phenomenal flux; he sings of
clouds, wind, and water rather than, like Wordsworth, of
the mountains or the "soul of lonely places." But he does not,
of course, stop with nature, but seeks the higher unity behind
it:

> Life, like a dome of many-colored glass,
> Stains the white radiance of Eternity.[48]

In the highest ecstasy, all individuality and particularity are
abolished by the great harmony of the world. But in Shelley,
in contrast to Blake or Wordsworth who calmly look into the
life of things, the ideal itself dissolves; his voice falters; the

48. *Adonais,* lines 462–63.

highest exaltation becomes a total loss of personality, an instrument of death and annihilation.

In Keats, the romantic conception of nature occurs, but only in attenuated form, though it would be hard to deny the poet of *Endymion* or the "Ode to a Nightingale" an intimate relation to nature and to the nature mythology of the ancients. *Hyperion* (1820) obscurely hints at an optimistic evolutionism, as in the speech of Oceanos to his fellow Titans:

> We fall by course of Nature's law, not force . . .
> As thou wast not the first of powers
> So art thou not the last . . .
> So on our heels a fresh perfection treads.
> . . . for 'tis the eternal law
> That first in beauty should be first in might.[49]

But Keats, possibly because he was a student of medicine, was least affected by the romantic conception of nature.

This conception occurs, though only fitfully, in Byron, who does *not* share the romantic conception of imagination. It is present especially in the third canto of *Childe Harold* (1818), written in Geneva when Shelley was his constant companion:

> I live not in myself, but I become
> Portion of that around me; and to me
> High mountains are a feeling.

Byron mentions:

> . . . the feeling infinite, so felt
> In solitude where we are least alone;
> A truth which through our being then doth melt
> And purifies from self.[50]

But generally Byron is rather a deist who believes in the New-

49. Book II, lines 181–90, 189, 212, 228–29.
50. *Childe Harold*, canto III, stanzas 72, 90.

tonian world machine and constantly contrasts man's passion and unhappiness with the serene and indifferent beauty of nature. Byron knows the horror of man's isolation, the terrors of the empty spaces, and does not share the fundamental rejection of the eighteenth-century cosmology nor the feeling of continuity and basic at-homeness in the universe of the great romantic poets.

This conception of the nature of poetic imagination and of the universe has obvious consequences for poetic practice. All the great romantic poets are mythopoeic, are symbolists whose practice must be understood in terms of their attempt to give a total mythic interpretation of the world to which the poet holds the key. The contemporaries of Blake began this revival of mythic poetry—which can be seen even in their interest in Spenser, in *Midsummer Night's Dream* and *The Tempest,* in the devils and witches of Burns, in the interest of Collins in Highland superstitions and their value for the poet, in the pseudo-Norse mythology of Gray, and in the antiquarian researches of Jacob Bryant and Edward Davies. But the first English poet to create a new mythology on a grand scale was Blake.

Blake's mythology is neither classical nor Christian, though it incorporates many Biblical and Miltonic elements. It draws vaguely on some Celtic (Druidical) mythology or rather names, but essentially it is an original (possibly a too original) creation which tries to give both a cosmogony and an apocalypse: a philosophy of history, a psychology, and (as has been recently stressed) a vision of politics and morals. Even the simplest of the *Songs of Innocence* and *Songs of Experience* are permeated by Blake's symbols. His last poems, such as *Jerusalem,* require an effort of interpretation which may not be commensurate to the aesthetic rewards we get; but Northrop Frye has certainly shown convincingly that Blake was an extraordinarily original thinker who had ideas on cycles of culture, metaphysical theories of time, speculations about the universal diffusion throughout primitive society of archetypal myths and rituals which may be frequently confused and dilettantish, but which should not prove incomprehensible to an age which has acclaimed Toynbee, Dunne on time, and has developed modern anthropology.

Wordsworth, at first sight, is the romantic poet farthest removed from symbolism and mythology. Josephine Miles in her study, *Wordsworth and the Vocabulary of Emotion,*[51] has taken him as the prime example of the poet who states emotions, names them specifically. But Wordsworth does stress imagery in his theory and is by no means indifferent to mythology. He plays an important part in the new interest in Greek mythology interpreted in terms of animism. There is the sonnet, "The World Is too Much with Us," and there is a passage in the fourth book of the *Excursion* (1814) which celebrates the dim inklings of immortality that the Greek sacrificing a lock in a stream may have had. There is the later turning to classical mythology, "Laodamia" and the "Ode to Lycoris," poems which Wordsworth defended also for their material "which may ally itself with real sentiment."

But, most important, his poetry is not without pervading symbols. Cleanth Brooks has shown convincingly how the "Ode: Intimations of Immortality" is based on a double, contradictory metaphor of light and how even the sonnet "Upon Westminster Bridge" conceals an all-pervasive figure.[52] *The White Doe of Rylstone* may be really allegorical, in an almost medieval sense (the doe is like an animal in a bestiary), but even this late piece shows Wordsworth's endeavor to go beyond the anecdotal or the descriptive, beyond the naming and analyzing of emotions and states of mind.

In Coleridge a theory of symbolism is central; the artist discourses to us by symbols, and nature is a symbolic language. The distinction between symbol and allegory is, in Coleridge, related to that between imagination and fancy

51. Berkeley, 1942.
52. *The Well Wrought Urn* (New York, 1947).

(which, in some ways, can be described as a theory of imagery), genius and talent, reason and understanding. In a late discussion he says that an allegory is but a translation of abstract notions into a picture language, which is itself nothing but an abstraction from objects of sense. On the other hand, a symbol is characterized by a translucence of the special in the individual, or of the general in the special, or of the universal in the general; above all, a symbol is characterized by the translucence of the eternal through and in the temporal. The faculty of symbols is the imagination. Coleridge condemned classical as distinct from Christian mythology in many early pronouncements; but later he became interested in a symbolically reinterpreted Greek mythology and wrote a queer piece "On the *Prometheus* of Aeschylus" (1825), which is closely dependent on Schelling's treatise, *Über die Gottheiten von Samothrace* (1815).[53]

The early great poetry of Coleridge is certainly symbolic throughout. R. P. Warren has recently given an interpretation of the *Ancient Mariner,* which may go too far in detail, but is convincing in the general thesis—the whole poem implies a concept of "sacramentalism," of the holiness of nature and all natural beings, and is organized on symbols of moonlight and sunlight, wind and rain.[54]

That Shelley is a symbolist and mythologist needs no argument. Not only is Shelley's poetry metaphorical through and through, but he aspires to create a new myth of the redemption of the earth which uses classical materials very freely, e.g. in *Prometheus Unbound* (1820), in the "Witch of Atlas," and in *Adonais* (1821). This last poem can be easily misinterpreted if it is seen merely as a pastoral elegy in the

---

53. *The Statesman's Manual,* in *Complete Works,* ed. Shedd, *1* (New York, 1853), 437–38; W. K. Pfeiler, "Coleridge and Schelling's *Treatise on the Samothracian Deities," Modern Language Notes, 52* (1937), 162–65.

54. New York, 1946.

tradition of Bion and Moschus. Through Shelley's poetry runs a fairly consistent system of recurrent symbols: the eagle and the serpent (which has Gnostic antecedents), temples, towers, the boat, the stream, the cave, and, of course, the veil, the cupola of stained glass, and the white radiance of eternity.[55]

> Death is the veil which those who live call life:
> They sleep and it is lifted.[56]

In Shelley the ecstasy takes on a hectic, falsetto tone, the voice breaks at the highest points; he swoons, "I faint, I fail!" "I fall upon the thorns of life! I bleed."[57] Shelley would like us to transcend the boundaries of individuality, to be absorbed into some nirvana. This craving for unity explains also one pervading characteristic of his style; synaesthesia and the fusing of the spheres of the different senses in Shelley is paralleled in his rapid transitions and fusions of the emotions, from pleasure to pain, from sorrow to joy.

Keats is a mythologist, too. *Endymion* and *Hyperion* are eloquent witnesses. There is in Keats the recurrent symbolism of moon and sleep, temple and nightingale. The great odes are not merely a series of pictures, but symbolic constructions in which the poet tries to state the conflict of artist and society, time and eternity.

Byron also—as Wilson Knight has shown extravagantly in *The Burning Oracle*[58]—can be interpreted in these terms: *Manfred* (1817), *Cain, Heaven and Earth,* and even *Sardanapalus* (1821). The great poets are not alone in their time. Southey wrote his epics, *Thalaba, Madoc* (1805), *The Curse of Kehama* (1810), on mythological themes from

55. On Shelley's symbols, see A. T. Strong, *Three Studies in Shelley* (London, 1921), and W. B. Yeats' essay in *Ideas of Good and Evil* (1903).
56. *Prometheus Unbound,* III, scene 3, lines 113–14.
57. "The Indian Serenade," "Ode to the West Wind."
58. London, 1939.

ancient Wales and India. Thomas Moore gained fame with
the Oriental pseudo-splendor of *Lalla Rookh* (1817), Mrs.
Tighe's *Psyche* influenced Keats. Finally, in 1821, Carlyle
published *Sartor Resartus,* with its philosophy of clothes, and
in which a whole chapter is called "Symbolism." Whatever
the level of penetration, there is a widespread return to the
mythic conception of poetry which had been all but forgotten
in the eighteenth century. Pope at most could conceive of
burlesque machines such as the sylphs in the *Rape of the
Lock* or the grandiose, semiserious last yawn of Night at the
conclusion of the *Dunciad.*[59]

It could be argued that these romantic attitudes, beliefs,
and techniques were confined to a small group of great poets
and that, on the whole, the England of the early nineteenth
century shared many points of view with the Age of Reason.
One may grant that the English romantic movement was
never as self-conscious or, possibly, as radical as the German
or French movements, that eighteenth-century attitudes were
far more influential and widespread than on the continent,
e.g. in philosophy where utilitarianism and Scottish common-
sense philosophy held sway, and that the English romantic
theory of poetry is a curious amalgamation of sensualism and
associationism, inherited from the eighteenth century and the
new or old Platonic idealism. The only major writer who
propounded a coherent "idealistic" system was Coleridge,
and his "system" or plan for a system was largely an importation from Germany. But there is a good deal of evidence
among the minor writers also that the intellectual atmosphere
was changing in England. Some of the minor proponents of
Kant, such as the curious jeweler, Thomas Wirgman, may
be cited.[60] There was much romantic science, biology, and
chemistry in England, of which we know very little today.

59. W. K. Wimsatt's excellent "The Structure of Romantic Nature
Imagery," in *The Age of Johnson: Essays Presented to C. B. Tinker*
(New Haven, 1949), pp. 291–303, certainly supports my argument.
60. See my *Immanuel Kant in England* (Princeton, 1931).

If we examine the literary ideas and scholarship of the time, we can trace the changes which occurred somewhat earlier on the continent. The romantic conception of folklore can be found, e.g. in the remarkable preface to the second edition of Thomas Warton's *History of English Poetry,* by Richard Price (1824); Price knew the Schlegels, the brothers Grimm, and even Creuzer's *Symbolik.*[61] In 1827 William Mother-well, the first faithful editor of the Scottish ballads, spoke of popular poetry as "that body of poetry which has inwoven itself with the feelings and passions of the people, and which shadows forth as it were an actual embodiment of their Universal mind, and its intellectual and moral tendencies."[62] Much research in minor writers and periodicals would be needed to substantiate this fully, but enough evidence has been produced to show that England also underwent the change of intellectual atmosphere which was general in Europe.

Much space would be required to examine all the other European literatures adequately from this point of view. Italy has sometimes been considered an exception; it has even been denied that it had any "real" romanticism.[63] But, while one may grant the strong survivals of neoclassicism, the peculiarly vehement political orientation, and the absence of some themes of the Northern romantic literatures, Italy cannot be considered to deviate from the pattern. Leopardi certainly is in profound agreement with his great contemporaries across the Alps, even though his literary theories have many neoclassical traits. For his romantic concept of nature the early poem *L'infinito* (1819) is evidence.[64] His specula-

---

61. W. C. Hazlitt's ed. (London, 1871), pp. 11, 27n.

62. *Minstrelsy: Ancient and Modern* (Glasgow, 1827), p. v.

63. E.g. Gina Martegiani, *Il Romanticismo italiano non esiste* (Florence, 1908).

64. The poem ends thus:

> Così tra questa
> Immensità s'annega il pensier mio,
> E il naufragar m'è dolce in questo mare.

tions on the great poetic harmony, the "effetto poetico" of the totality of nature, and his nostalgia for early Greece link him with the Germans. Foscolo and Manzoni, both as critics and as artists, are part and parcel of the European romantic movement. Gioberti expounded an aesthetics similar to Schelling's.

Allison Peers has argued that Spanish romanticism was of very short duration and disintegrated very soon after its triumph in 1838.[65] This may be true of romanticism as a "school," but hardly of romantic Spanish literature of the nineteenth century. Espronceda, especially, seems to fit our pattern very closely.

In the Scandinavian countries, German romanticism, especially Schelling, was most influential. Among the Swedes a whole group of critics viewed the work of art as a symbol of the universe.[66] *Naturphilosophie* was widely accepted, and mythologizing was at the very center of the whole Nordic revival.

The Slavic romantic movements present special features and special problems. The Russians drew heavily on the Germans, especially on Schelling and Hegel.[67] Lermontov fits into our pattern as does, of course, Vladimir Odoevsky, whose stories of artists, such as "Johann Sebastian Bach," are full of the theory of correspondences, the view of art as a mediator between man and nature.[68] Pushkin, to a certain

---

On Leopardi's myth, see K. Vossler, *Leopardi* (Munich, 1923), p. 192.

65. *A History of the Romantic Movement in Spain* (2 vols. Cambridge, 1940).

66. See especially Albert Nilsson, *Svensk Romantik. Den Platonske Strömingen. Kellgren—Franzén—Elgström—Hammersköld —Atterborn—Stagnelius—Tegnér—Rydberg* (Lund, 1916).

67. See Thomas G. Masaryk, *The Spirit of Russia* (2 vols. London, 1919); Dimitri Chizhevsky, *Gegel' v Rossii* [Hegel in Russia] (Paris, 1939).

68. *Romanticheskie povesti* [Romantic stories] (Leningrad, 1929).

extent, is an exception; his clear form seems neoclassical and recent Russian literary scholarship excludes him from the romantic movement.[69] But this is hardly warranted if one considers not only the usually quoted affinities with Byron, but recognizes also Pushkin's nature symbolism, which has been studied, possibly oversubtly, by Gershenzon, or if one considers his myth of the destructive statue, in the *Stone Guest,* the *Bronze Horseman,* and the *Tale of the Golden Cockerel.*[70]

Polish romantic literature is the most romantic of all minor literatures: Mickiewicz and Slowacki share fully the romantic view of nature, the romantic concept of the imagination, the use of symbol and mythology, and express them even extravagantly. So do such Polish romantic thinkers as Hoene-Wroński. The Czech romantic movement has at least one great poet, Karel Hynek Mácha, who shares the concept of nature, of imagination, and of symbol with his German and Polish contemporaries.[71] One important argument for the coherence and unity of the European romantic movement emerges from an investigation of the minor literatures—the "predictability" of their general character. If we had never heard anything about the Czech romantic movement, it would still be possible, within limits, to assert the presence and absence of certain themes, views, and techniques.

My conclusion concerning the unity of the romantic movement may be distressingly orthodox and even conventional.

69. Viktor Zhirmunsky, *Valeri Bryusov i nasledie Pushkina* [V. B. and Pushkin's Heritage] (Petrograd, 1922); and Boris Eikhenbaum, "Problemy poetiki Pushkina" [Problems of Pushkin's Poetics], in *Skvoz' Literaturu* (Leningrad, 1924).

70. Mikhael O. Gershenzon, *Mudrost' Pushkina* [Pushkin's Wisdom] (Moscow, 1919); Roman Jakobson, "Socha v symbolice Puškinově" [The Statue in Pushkin's Symbolism], *Slovo a slovesnost, 3* (Prague, 1937), 2–24.

71. See my "Mácha and Byron," *Slavonic Review, 15* (1937), 400–12.

But it seems necessary to reassert it, especially in view of Lovejoy's famous attack. "On the Discrimination of Romanticisms" proves, it seems to me, only that Joseph Warton was an early naturalistic preromanticist, that Friedrich Schlegel was a highly sophisticated, self-conscious intellectual, and that Chateaubriand held many classicist views on literary criticism and on Shakespeare. The fact that Chateaubriand was conservative and Hugo ended in liberalism does not disrupt the continuity of French romanticism as a literary movement. On the whole, political criteria seem grossly overrated as a basis for judging a man's basic view of the world and artistic allegiance.

I do not, of course, deny differences between the various romantic movements, differences of emphasis and distribution of elements, differences in the pace of development, in the individualities of the great writers. I am perfectly aware that the three groups of ideas I have selected have their historical ancestry before the Enlightenment and in undercurrents during the eighteenth century. The view of an organic nature descends from neo-Platonism through Giordano Bruno, Böhme, the Cambridge Platonists, and some passages in Shaftesbury. The view of imagination as creative and of poetry as prophecy has a similar ancestry. A symbolist, and even mythic, conception of poetry is frequent in history, e.g. in the baroque age with its emblematic art, its view of nature as hieroglyphics which man and especially the poet is destined to read. In a sense, romanticism is the revival of something old, but it is a revival with a difference; these ideas were translated into terms acceptable to men who had undergone the experience of the Enlightenment. It may be difficult to distinguish clearly between a romantic and a baroque symbol, the romantic and the Böhmean view of nature and imagination. But for our problem we need only know that there is a difference between the symbol in Pope and in Shelley. This can be described; the change from the type of imagery and symbolism used by Pope to that used by Shelley is an empirical fact of history. It seems difficult to deny that we are confronted with substantially the same fact in noting the difference between Lessing and Novalis or Voltaire and Victor Hugo.

Lovejoy has argued that the "new ideas of the period were in large part heterogeneous, logically independent and sometimes essentially antithetic to one another in their implications."[72] If we look back on our argument it will be obvious that this view must be mistaken. There is, on the contrary, a profound coherence and mutual implication between the romantic views of nature, imagination, and symbol. Without such a view of nature we could not believe in the significance of symbol and myth. Without symbol and myth the poet would lack the tools for the insight into reality which he claimed, and without such an epistemology, which believes in the creativity of the human mind, there would not be a living nature and a true symbolism. We may not accept this view of the world for ourselves—few of us can accept it literally today—but we should grant that it is coherent and integrated and, as I hope to have shown, all-pervasive in Europe.

We can then go on speaking of romanticism as one European movement, whose slow rise through the eighteenth century we can describe and examine and even call, if we want to, preromanticism. Clearly there are periods of the dominance of a system of ideas and poetic practices; and clearly they have their anticipations and their survivals. To give up these problems because of the difficulties of terminology seems to me tantamount to giving up the central task of literary history. If literary history is not to be content to remain the usual odd mixture of biography, bibliography, anthology, and disconnected emotive criticism, it has to study the total

72. "The Meaning of Romanticism for the Historian of Ideas," *Journal of the History of Ideas*, 2 (1941), 261.

process of literature. This can be done only by tracing the sequence of periods, the rise, dominance, and disintegration of conventions and norms. The term "romanticism" posits all these questions, and that, to my mind, is its best defense.

Romanticism Re-examined

The preceding essay has elicited many comments and much has been said, independently, to substantiate and to modify the view of the nature and unity of romanticism there propounded. A re-examination of the whole question may be welcome.

Lovejoy has not defended his thesis, but he has reasserted it: in the preface to a little book, *The Reason, The Understanding and Time* (1961),[1] which analyzes some ideas of Schelling, Jacobi, Schopenhauer, and Bergson, Lovejoy reprints the crucial passages of his earlier essays in order to justify his avoidance of calling these philosophers "romantic." Ronald S. Crane, whom I had quoted dismissing "the fairytales about neoclassicism and romanticism in the eighteenth century."[2] commented at some length on my article: he did not object to historical generalizations which would describe the change in the terms I had selected, but he considered my "passion for unity" excessive. He demanded "literal proof": he wants me to show "sameness in the literal sense" of the terms of "imagination," "nature," and "symbol" in all the writers discussed.[3] Crane has set me an impossible task: I do not see how anybody can prove a literal identity exclusive of all individuality. This would imply a monolithic period such as could not be found at any time in history. In all my writings I have consistently argued for a period con-

1. Baltimore, 1961.

2. Quoted above, p. 156 from *Philological Quarterly*, 22 (1943), 143.

3. In *Philological Quarterly*, 29 (1950), 257–59

cept which allows for the survival of former ages and the anticipations of later ones. "Period" demands the dominance (but not the total tight dictatorial rule) of a set of norms which, in the case of romanticism, are provided sufficiently by similar or analogous concepts of the imagination, nature, symbol, and myth. I am content with Crane's admission of such generalizations, and I grant that Lovejoy, in *The Great Chain of Being* and in some later papers, actually operates with concepts such as "organicism, dynamism, and diversitarianism" which are descriptive of what usually is called "romantic." The mere avoidance of the term in Lovejoy's new book on Schelling and his followers solves nothing.

Morse Peckham, in a widely noted article, "Toward a Theory of Romanticism" (1951),[4] wanted, he says, "to reconcile Lovejoy and Wellek, and Lovejoy with himself" by singling out the criterion of "organic dynamism" as the definition of romanticism. Peckham thus accepts the concept of nature and imagination as described in my article but drops the concern for symbol and myth. Peckham introduces a new concept, "negative romanticism," that is, despairing, nihilistic romanticism. The argument runs that positive romanticism does not fit Byron, but that "negative romanticism" does. I am supposed to be unable "to come to terms" with this phenomenon. Still, it seems to me that little has been accomplished by calling familiar states of mind—*Weltschmerz, mal du siècle,* pessimism—"negative" romanticism. It seems a purely verbal solution: as if we should call naturalism "negative symbolism," or symbolism "negative naturalism." By showing the coherence of the point of view which other writers as well as I have called "romanticism"—its organicism, its use of the creative imagination, its symbolic and mythic procedures—we have excluded nihilism, "alienation" from our definition. A man who considers nature dead and inimical to man, who considers imagination merely a

4. In *PMLA, 61* (1951), 5–23.

combinatory associative power, and who does not use symbolic and mythic devices is not a romanticist in the sense
in which Wordsworth, Novalis, and Hugo are romantic.

Since the 1951 article Morse Peckham has changed his
mind. In a new essay, "Towards a Theory of Romanticism.
Reconsiderations" (1961),[5] Peckham abandons his early
scheme in favor of a grandiose cultural history of the modern
age, which he has also developed in a book, *Beyond the
Tragic Vision* (1962).[6] Peckham now calls romanticism enlightenment, as he has been apparently deeply impressed by
Ernest Tuveson's *The Imagination as a Means of Grace:
Locke and the Aesthetics of Romanticism* (1960).[7] But
Tuveson, though excellent on Lockean influences on eighteenth-century British aesthetics, cannot show that imagination was considered a "means of grace" at that time. In any
case, the break with the Lockean tradition is precisely a
crucial test of romantic aesthetics. I need only allude to
Coleridge's rejection of Locke or to Schelling's view of
Locke's "bestialities" reported by Henry Crabb Robinson.[8]
Be that as it may, Peckham now believes the essence of
romanticism to be the imposition of order on chaos: a heroic
anti-metaphysical subjectivism which reminds one rather of
Bertrand Russell's "A Freeman's Worship" than of the outlook of a Wordsworth, Friedrich Schlegel, or Lamartine.
Peckham takes a quite unjustified view of Kant as a kind of
pragmatist. "Romanticism learns from Kant," he says, "that
it can do entirely without constitutive metaphysics and can
use any metaphysic or world hypothesis as supreme fiction."
I am not aware of a single writer in the late eighteenth or

5. In *Studies in Romanticism, 1* (1961), 1–8.
6. New York, 1962.
7. Berkeley, 1960.
8. Coleridge's views of Locke are collected in Roberta F. Brinkley,
Coleridge on the Seventeenth Century (Durham, N.C., 1955), pp.
67–109. For Schelling on Locke, see *H. C. Robinson in Germany,*
ed. E. Morley (Oxford, 1929), p. 118, letter dated Nov. 14, 1802.

early nineteenth century to whom this description would apply. Who then rejected the possibility of metaphysics or treated it as supreme fiction? Not even Friedrich Schlegel, whose theory of irony exposed him to the charge of "probabilism," opportunism, and aestheticism. I am afraid Peckham's "reconsiderations" do not contribute to a better definition of "romanticism": it seems only right that he avoids the term in *Beyond the Tragic Vision*.

Reading Peckham one is tempted to give up the problem in despair. We might come to agree with Lovejoy or even with Valéry, who warns us that it "is impossible to think seriously with words such as Classicism, Romanticism, Humanism, or Realism. One cannot get drunk or quench one's thirst with labels on a bottle."[9] But of course these terms are not labels: they have a range of meaning very different from Pabst Blue Ribbon or Liebfrauenmilch. Modern logicians tell us that all definitions are verbal, that they are "stipulated" by the speaker. We certainly cannot prevent communists from calling dictatorship "popular democracy," a baby from calling any strange man "daddy," or even Peckham from calling romanticism "enlightenment." But "there is a sense" —I am quoting Wilbur Urban—"in which the distinction between verbal and real definition is a valid one. . . . There comes a point at which such variation ceases to be merely inconvenient and unpragmatic; it becomes unintelligible. It leads to a *contradictio in adjecto,* in which intrinsic incompatibility between the subject and predicate of the defining proposition destroys the meaning by an implicit denial."[10] We can dismiss theories which will insist on calling romanticism enlightenment. We need not even consider our task

9. *Mauvaises Pensées* (Paris, 1942), p. 35: "Il est impossible de penser sérieusement avec les mots comme Classicisme, Romantisme, Humanisme, Réalisme. On ne s'enivre ni ne se désaltère avec des étiquettes de bouteille."

10. *The Intelligible World* (New York, 1929), p. 124.

identical with that of the lexicographer, who has to document the full range of usage of a term. We shall rather try to show that there is a growing area of agreement and even convergence among the definitions or, more modestly, descriptions of romanticism as they have been attempted by responsible scholars in recent decades in several countries. Incidentally, I hope, the survey will bring out the differences in methods and approaches characteristic of literary scholarship in Germany, France, England, and the United States. But precisely the varieties of national traditions which are often only in tenuous contact with each other will make the basic consensus about the nature of romanticism stand out all the more convincingly.

In Germany in the early twenties a whole series of books was devoted specifically to definitions of the nature or essence of romanticism. Germans operate, or rather operated, with dichotomics, thesis and antithesis, vast contrasts such as idea and form, idea and experience, rationalism and irrationalism, perfection and infinitude, etc. Max Deutschbein in *Das Wesen des Romantischen* (1921),[11] aims at a phenomenological intuition of the essence of romanticism by showing the agreement between English and German romanticism in their concept and use of the synthetic imagination: the union of opposites, the finite and infinite, eternity and temporality, universality and individuality. The scheme serves the conclusion that English poetry translated German theory into practice, but, of course, the amazing identities which Deutschbein finds between German and English romanticism are often due to the fact that his crown witness on the English side, Coleridge, is simply paraphrasing Schelling. Still, this neglected little book stressed one central and valid concept: the reconciling, synthetic imagination as the common denominator of romanticism.

The scheme of contrasts elaborated by Fritz Strich in

11. Coethen, 1921.

*Deutsche Klassik und Romantik: oder Vollendung und
Unendlichkeit* (1922)[12] has a different starting point. Strich
wants to transfer Wölfflin's *Kunstgeschichtliche Grundbegriffe* (1915) to the history of literature. Wölfflin ingeniously
contrasted Renaissance and baroque art on purely structural
grounds such as "open" or "closed" form. Strich ties the contrast between classical and romantic art rather to man's quest
for permanence or eternity.[13] Eternity can be achieved either
in perfection or in infinitude. The history of man oscillates
between these two poles. "Perfection wants repose. Infinitude: movement and change. Perfection is closed, infinitude
open. Perfection is clear, the Infinite is dark. Perfection seeks
the image, infinitude the symbol."[14] The transfer of Wölfflin's categories from art history to literature is accomplished
ingeniously, but one wonders whether the description of romanticism as dynamic, open form, unclear, symbolic, and
the like does more than line up romanticism with the baroque
and with symbolism in the series of polar alternations between intellect and feeling which are supposed to constitute
the history of Europe. It is the old separation into sheep and
goats: a schematic device which obscures the historical par-
ticularities of the romantic age in distinction from other open

12. Munich, 1922.
13. Strich seems to have elaborated a suggestion from Heine's
Romantische Schule (1833). See *Sämtliche Werke,* ed. O. Walzel,
7 (Leipzig, 1910), 14: "Die klassische Kunst hatte nur das Endliche
darzustellen, und ihre Gestalten konnten identische sein mit der Idee
des Künstlers. Die romantische Kunst hatte das Unendliche und
lauter spiritualistische Beziehungen darzustellen oder vielmehr anzu-
deuten, und sie nahm ihre Zuflucht zu einem System traditioneller
Symbole oder vielmehr zum Parabolischen."
14. Strich, pp. 7–8: "Vollendung ist unwandelbare Ruhe. Unendlichkeit: Bewegung und Verwandlung. Vollendung ist geschlossen,
Unendlichkeit aber offen. Vollendet ist die Einheit. . . . Vollendet ist
die Klarheit, unendlich aber das Dunkel. . . . Vollendet also ist das
Bild, unendlich aber das Sinnbild."

form, dynamic, symbolic styles. Strich and his many follow-ers have been extraordinarily successful in bringing out these very broad changes in feelings and art forms which were hardly perceived before Wölfflin and others devised the vo-cabulary for their description.

The whole enterprise is apparently still a novelty in the United States: thus the philosopher W. T. Jones in his new book, *The Romantic Syndrome* (1961),[15] makes the most extravagant claims for his discovery of a scheme which is very similar to that of many Germans. According to Jones romanticism is dynamic rather than static, prefers disorder to order, continuity to discreteness, soft focus to sharp focus, has an inner rather than an outer bias, and prefers another world to this world.[16] Jones seems unaware of the many typologies of this kind in Germany. The names of Dilthey, Spranger, Jaspers, Jung, and Nohl do not occur anywhere in the book.[17] The only theory known to Jones seems to be Wölfflin's, to whom he refers in a footnote. Wölfflin's cate-gories, Jones admits, "seem related to my axes," but Jones thinks that it is his discovery that "these categories permit a cross-medium comparison between artistic productions and literay and philosophical works."[18] Jones' analysis of art works, of the contrast between Dürer and Rubens, Bel-lini and El Greco, is completely dependent on Wölfflin. The application to romantic poetry, which interests us here, never gets beyond the simplest observations. Romantic poetry prefers the misty, the hazy, the dim, the soft focus

15. The Hague, 1961

16. Ibid., p. 118.

17. See Wilhelm Dilthey, "Die Typen der Weltanschauung" (1911), in *Gesammelte Schriften*, 8 (Leipzig, 1931), 75–118; Eduard Spranger, *Lebensformen* (Halle, 1914); Karl Jaspers, *Psy-chologie der Weltanschauungen* (Berlin, 1919); C. G. Jung, *Psy-chologische Typen* (Zürich, 1921); Herman Nohl, *Stil und Weltan-schauung* (Jena, 1923).

18. Jones, p. 48.

(Wölfflin's unclearness). Inner bias is illustrated easily, so is preference for disorder, love of continuity, the other world, etc. Most of these are familiar themes and Jones' examples seem often ill chosen. He uses, for instance, quotations from Goethe's *Faust* without heeding the dramatic context.[19] Jones' main contribution to typology is the ominous suggestion that it needs verification by quantification: the idea that a team of researchers should, for instance, make a count of soft focus imagery in all the poems published in a given year. Jones imagines that by such statistical methods it would be possible to give an objective date for the rise of romanticism.[20] I shall not urge the difficulties and uncertainties of this enterprise: the impossibility of establishing criteria for what is soft focus in imagery and for defining an image, and of counting them in every poem in all languages. One must rather reject the whole ideal of knowledge implied: the fashionable faith in statistics, the denial of the crucial issue of value and individuality.

The many German definitions of romanticism were surveyed by Julius Petersen in *Die Wesensbestimmung der deutschen Romantik* (1926).[21] Petersen welcomed each and every approach, including the racial, which makes romanticism peculiarly German, and the regional, which makes it East German in particular. But at the time of his writing the tide was beginning to turn. More and more reservations against the whole method were being voiced both inside and outside of Germany. Martin Schütze, a professor of German at the University of Chicago, made in his *Aca-*

19. E.g. Faust's speech answering Margaret's question about his belief: "Wer darf ihn nennen?" must not be interpreted as a profession of Goethe's faith as Jones assumes (p. 131). Faust tries to avoid a clear answer.

20. Pp. 227 ff.

21. Leipzig, 1926.

demic Illusions (1933)—a neglected book now happily again available in a reprint[22]—trenchant criticisms of the whole German phantasmagoria of polarities. Emil Staiger, just before the outbreak of the second World War, announced in the preface to *Die Zeit als Einbildungskraft des Dichters* (1939) that the task of literary study is "interpretation," and he dismissed influences, biography, psychology, sociology, and typology from the inner sanctum.[23] In his late years at Harvard Karl Vietor voiced his conviction that "the age of the *geistesgeschichtlich* approach and its methods is at an end."[24]

As far as I can ascertain, only two new German books about the nature of romanticism have appeared since the end of the war. Adolf Grimme, in *Vom Wesen der Romantik* (1947),[25] defines romanticism as a breakthrough of what he calls "the vegetative strata of the soul": the preconscious rather than the subconscious. The preconscious includes the imagination, which is raised to consciousness by romanticism. Grimme is more interesting in his theoretical defense of the method of phenomenology. A single example, he argues, must suffice, as we cannot deduce or generalize about romanticism before we know what is meant by romanticism. The aim of a verbal definition is illusory: we can only point to what is romantic as we can point to the color red. In a collection of lectures, *Romantik* (1948), the well-known Jesuit philosopher Romano Guardini comes to a similar con-

22. Chicago, 1933, new ed., Hamden, Conn., 1962, with preface by René Wellek.
23. Zürich, 1939: "Einleitung: Von der Aufgabe und den Gegenständen der Literaturwissenschaft."
24. "Deutsche Literaturgeschichte als Geistesgeschichte," in *PMLA*, 60 (1945), 899–916; 914: "Die Epoche der geisteswissenschaftlichen Betrachtungsweise und ihrer Methoden ist offenbar abgeschlossen."
25. Braunschweig, 1947.

clusion: romanticism is "an upsurge of the unconscious and primitive."[26]

The comparisons with English romanticism made in Germany have become very cautious. Horst Oppel, in "Englische und deutsche Romantik" (1956),[27] makes much of the differences between the two countries: the prevalence of an empirical philosophy in England, the uniqueness of the German fairy tale, the rarity of romantic irony in England, and so forth. A British professor of German writing in German, Eudo C. Mason, has recently elaborated on this theme in *Deutsche und englische Romantik* (1959).[28] He rightly emphasizes the very different historical situation of the English romantic poets, who were not confronted with such overpowering figures as those of Goethe and Schiller in Germany. He points to features in German romanticism such as a nihilistic daring, satanism, decadentism, and extreme aestheticism, which go far beyond the bourgeois limitations of a Wordsworth or Coleridge. Mason makes much of the almost complete lack of understanding and contacts between the two countries. To my mind he overemphasizes the timidity, orthodoxy, and prudery of the English poets. He plays up the role of Henry Crabb Robinson as the only person of the time who understood both Wordsworth and the German romantics, though he must admit that Robinson was historically quite ineffective and that his published articles hardly reflect the presumed depth of his understanding. Robinson's attempt, in 1829, to convert Goethe to Words-

26. "Erscheinung und Wesen der Romantik," in *Romantik. Ein Zyklus Tübinger Vorlesungen,* ed. Theodor Steinbüchel (Tübingen, 1948), pp. 237–49.

27. In *Die Neueren Sprachen,* Heft 10 (1956), pp. 457–75, Reprinted in *The Sacred River: Studien und Interpretationen zur Dichtung der englischen Romantik* (Frankfurt, 1959), pp. 5–24.

28. Göttingen, 1959.

worth by recruiting Ottilie von Goethe was pitifully inept. There was, one must conclude, no real meeting of minds (though a few physical encounters) between Coleridge and Tieck, or Coleridge and August Wilhelm Schlegel. But surely the problem of the affinity between German and English romanticism cannot be disposed of by showing that contemporary contacts were tenuous and personal sympathies far from perfect.

There is, of course, plenty of research and interpretation in Germany of individual romantic writers, but on the whole a strange silence has settled around the question of the nature or essence of romanticism.

In France the situation is very different. Paul Van Tieghem attempted a synthesis of all European romantic literatures in *Le Romantisme dans la littérature européenne* (1948).[29] Van Tieghem aims at writing literary history on a truly international scale: he draws liberally also from the small European literatures, including the Slavic and Scandinavian. He deliberately ignores national frontiers and orders his facts not according to a linguistic atlas but by a psychological and aesthetic map of tendencies and tastes. Categories such as "the feeling for nature," "religion," "love," "exoticism," "historicism" assemble a mass of information, but unfortunately never rise to any higher level of generalization. Oddly enough, Van Tieghem can say that "the suppression of the mythological style is probably the most universal trait of formal romanticism."[30] Van Tieghem, though learned and acutely aware of the unity of Europe, lacks the *esprit de finesse* and remains disconcertingly ex-

29. Vol. 76 of *L'Evolution de l'humanité,* ed. Henri Beer (Paris, 1948).

30. Ibid., p. 14: "La suppression de ce style [mythologique] conventionel est peut-être le caractère le plus universel du romantisme formel."

ternal.[31] An examination of recent definitions of romanticism by Jean-Bertrand Barrère lists nothing new. [32] He prefers to engage in a discussion of the different stages of French romanticism: a historical task which is not our concern.

Much more exciting and original are the studies of the group of critics who call themselves critics of consciousness or the Geneva school. They seem to live in a world quite different from that of the older academic scholars. Albert Béguin's *L'Âme romantique et le rêve* (1939)[33] studies German romanticism and the French writers who, in his opinion, went the same way, Rousseau, Sénancour, Nodier, Maurice de Guérin, Hugo, Nerval; he glances at Baudelaire, Rimbaud, Mallarmé, and Proust. Béguin is not particularly concerned with influences: his motivation is ultimately religious. "The greatness of romanticism" resides for him in "its having recognized and affirmed the profound resemblance of poetic states and the revelations of a religious order."[34] But Béguin is also a scholar interested in defining the essence of romanticism. Romanticism is to him a myth: man invents myths in order to overcome his solitude and to reintegrate himself into the whole. He invents myths in a double sense: he finds them in the treasure house of history and discovers them in dreams and the unconscious. Béguin distinguishes three ro-

31. A similar book is Giovanni Laini's *Il Romanticismo europeo* (2 vols. Florence, 1959), wide-ranging but purely external. It begins with anticlassical polemics in the fifteenth century and ends with present-day romanticism.

32. "Sur quelques Définitions du romantisme," *Revue des sciences humaines,* Fsc. 62–63 (1951), pp. 93–110.

33. 2 vols. Marseille, 1937. I quote the new ed. (Paris, 1946) in one volume, which unfortunately drops the critical apparatus and the bibliography.

34. Ibid., p. 401: "La grandeur du romantisme restera d'avoir reconnu et affirmé la profonde ressemblance des états poétiques et des révélations d'ordre religieux."

mantic myths: those of the soul, of the unconscious, and of poetry. Poetry is the only answer to the elemental anguish of the creature enclosed in his temporal existence. The analogical concept of the universe is assumed: the structure of our mind and our total being and its spontaneous rhythms are identical with the structure and the great rhythms of the universe.[35] Béguin's horizon is confined to German and French literature. He focuses on the German theorists, speculative philosophers, and doctors of the unconscious, and studies sympathetically such writers as Jean Paul, Novalis, Brentano, Arnim, and E. T. A. Hoffmann. A student of English romanticism might conclude that he singles out the most irrationalistic writers and isolates the dream, the night, the unconscious unduly, but I believe that even for a parallel study of English developments we would find in Béguin the finest understanding of the nature of the romantic imagination and its rootedness in a sense of the continuity between man and nature and the presence of God.

Georges Poulet, in his books and articles mainly concerned with the feeling of time and space, supports Béguin's conclusions by a somewhat different method. The early books, *Etudes sur le temps humain* and *La Distance intérieure* (1950, 1952), are both devoted to individual French writers, though the appendix to the English translation of *Studies in Human Time* contains thumbnail sketches of American writers from Emerson to Henry James and T. S. Eliot.[36] But in an article, "Timelessness and Romanticism" (1954),[37] and in a section, "Le Romantisme," of the new book, *Les Métamorphoses du cercle* (1961),[38] Poulet generalizes about romanticism boldly. The article in the *Journal*

35. Ibid., pp. 395–96, 400–01.
36. Paris, 1950 and 1952; Eng. trans. Elliott Coleman, *Studies in Human Time* (Baltimore, 1956).
37. In *Journal of the History of Ideas*, *15* (1954), 3–22.
38. Paris, 1961.

of the History of Ideas tries to define the specific experience of time common to many Romantics: to Rousseau, Coleridge, De Quincey, Baudelaire. They all seem to have experienced paramnesia, the sensation of *dejà vu*, the total recollection which does not appear to be recollected; they all aimed at least at the total exclusion of the past from the present by a perfect absorption in the present, as if time stood still and became eternity. But Poulet rightly emphasizes that this romantic experience is not identical with its philosophical source: the neo-Platonic "simultaneous and perfect possession of an interminable life." The romantics did not want to describe in their poems an ideal world or the abstract existence of God. They wanted to express their own concrete experiences, their own personal apprehension of human timelessness. "In brief, paradoxically, they brought Eternity into Time."[39] In the new book Poulet defines romanticism in somewhat different terms: as a consciousness of the fundamentally subjective nature of the mind, as a withdrawal from reality to the center of the self, which serves as starting point of a return to nature. Poulet draws his examples of this back-and-forth movement of the mind mainly from French writers, but also from Coleridge and Shelley, quoting and using ingeniously but overinsistently the figures of the circle and circumference. Shelley's saying that "poetry is at once the centre and the circumference of knowledge" pleases him as much as Coleridge's admiring an old coach wheel. "See how the rays proceed from the centre to the circumference, and how many different images are distinctly comprehended at one glance, as forming one whole, and each part in some harmonious relation to each and all." The wheel is the symbol of beauty, of organic wholeness, of the unity of the universe.[40]

39. *Journal of the History of Ideas*, 15 (1954), 7.
40. Quoted in *Métamorphoses du cercle,* p. 148, from *The Defense of Poetry,* and on p. 155 from Coleridge, *Miscellanies Aesthetic and Literary* (London, 1911), p. 20.

Poulet's conception of criticism had originally excluded the possibility of such generalizations about a period: each author, according to Poulet, lived in his particular world construed by his own "consciousness." The task of the critic is to enter this individual consciousness.[41] But apparently Poulet now conceives of these consciousnesses as unified in an all-embracing spirit of the time: he boldly generalizes about the Renaissance, the baroque, and romanticism. Romanticism—not only French or German but all romanticism —is defined by this effort to overcome the opposition of subject and object, of center and circumference, in a personal experience.

The same view is advanced by Albert Gérard in *L'Idée romantique de la poésie en Angleterre* (1955),[42] summarized in an article "On the Logic of Romanticism" (1957).[43] Gérard also rejects as inadequate the older generalizations about romanticism: its emotionalism, cult of spontaneity, primitivism, and the like, and he examines minutely, by traditional methods, the views common to Wordsworth, Coleridge, Shelley, and Keats (Byron is expressly excluded) of the poetic experience as a form of knowledge, an intuition of cosmic unity conceived as a matter-spirit continuum. The philosophy of creativity, the union of subject and object, the role of the symbol and myth are expounded by Gérard with ample documentation. The results will strike us as not particularly new. Gérard brings, however, welcome corroboration to recent students of romantic theory. I need only allude to Meyer H. Abrams' *The Mirror and the Lamp* (1953)[44] and

41. For a trenchant criticism of Poulet's method see Leo Spitzer, "A propos de la Vie de Marianne," in *Romanische Literaturstudien* (Tübingen, 1959), pp. 248–276, and my review in *Yale Review, 46* (1956), 114–19.

42. Paris, 1955.

43. In *Essays in Criticism, 7* (1957), 262–73.

44. New York, 1953; cf. my review in *Comparative Literature, 6* (1954), 178–81.

to the second volume of my *History of Modern Criticism*.[45] Abrams emphasizes the shift from imitation theory to theory of expression, from the mirror to the lamp: or rather, from the mechanistic metaphorical analogies of neoclassical theory to the biological imagery of the romanticists. He pays some attention to the German background of English theories. In my own book I give a full exposition of the Germans and distinguish between a romantic movement in a wider sense, as a revolt against neoclassicism, and a romantic movement in a more special sense, as the establishment of a dialectical and symbolist view of poetry. It thus seems a firmly established fact that there was a coherent romantic theory of poetry which has been defined and analyzed.

Poetic theory implies a philosophical attitude and a poetic practice, certainly in the romantic age. An agreement on the basic outlook of the romantics on reality and nature and on the main devices used by the romantic poets has also been reached among recent English and American students. What matters in a study of poetry is the function of the romantic view of nature. "The Structure of Romantic Nature Imagery" (1949) was explored by W. K. Wimsatt: he shows how the metaphor organizes a romantic nature poem, how, e.g. the landscape in Coleridge's sonnet "To the River Otter" is "both the occasion of reminiscence and the source of the metaphors by which reminiscence is described," how the romantic poems blur the distinction between literal and figurative because the poet wants to read a meaning into the landscape, but also wants to find it there.[46] Meyer H. Abrams, in "The Correspondent Breeze: A Romantic Metaphor" (1957), shows how this recurrent image represents "the chief theme of continuity and interchange between outer motions and interior life and powers" in many important

45. Vol. 2, *The Romantic Age* (New Haven, 1955).
46. In *The Verbal Icon: Studies in the Meaning of Poetry* (Lexington, Ky., 1954), pp. 103–16, esp. p. 109.

romantic poems, such as Coleridge's "Dejection: An Ode" and Wordsworth's *Prelude*.[47] Abrams refuses to be drawn into inferences about archetypal patterns: he argues that this mode of reading eliminates the individuality of a poem and threatens to nullify even its status as a work of art. Several other sensitive studies, mostly concerned with Wordsworth, have recently led to the same conclusion: e.g. Geoffrey Hartman's paper "A Poet's Progress: Wordsworth and the *Via naturaliter negativa*" (1962) describes how Nature itself led the poet beyond nature. But the Nature is not Nature as such, but Nature indistinguishably blended with Imagination or, as Hartman formulates it paradoxically, "the Imagination experienced as a power distinct from Nature opens the poet's eyes by putting them out."[48] Another writer, Paul de Man, in a paper entitled "Symbolic Landscape in Wordsworth and Yeats" (1962), describes this double vision which allows Wordsworth to see landscapes as "objects as well as entrance gates to a world lying beyond visible nature." Wordsworth's transcendental vision is contrasted with Yeats' emblematic landscape.[49] David Ferry, in *The Limits of Mortality: An Essay on Wordsworth's Major Poems* (1959), seems to overstate Wordsworth's hatred for the mortal limitations of man: he misconceives his mood, I believe. But he sees that nature is, in Wordsworth, a "metaphor for eternity, for the absence of death," that "the theory of symbolism posits as its ground the double consciousness . . . whereby the objects of nature may have individual and particular identity in themselves as objects, yet will stand 'figuratively' for the whole of which they really are part."[50] In Earl Wasserman's turgid and

47. In *The Kenyon Review, 19* (1957), 113–30, quoted from reprint in *English Romantic Poets: Modern Essays in Criticism*, ed. M. H. Abrams (New York, 1960), pp. 37–54, esp. p. 39.

48. In *Modern Philology, 59* (1962), 214–24, esp. p. 224.

49. In *In Defense of Reading*, ed. Reuben A. Brower and Richard Poirier (New York, 1962), pp. 22–37, esp. p. 28.

50. Middletown, Conn., 1959, pp. 16, 37.

forced interpretations, both in the book on Keats, called *The Finer Tone* (1953), and in the more recent *The Subtler Language* (1959), we find this awareness that the poetic act is creative both of a cosmic system and of the poem made possible by that system. Wasserman hardly overstates romantic individualism when he says that "the creation of a poem is also the creation of the cosmic wholeness that gives meaning to the poem, and each poet must independently make his own world picture, his own language within language."[51] This ambition justifies the romantic concern for symbolism and mythology, and for a symbolism and mythology which is individual and private, relies on personal vision, and hence is open to the most diverse and often contradictory interpretations. The most influential study of romantic key images and myths was G. Wilson Knight's *Starlit Dome* (1941).[52] We all have learned from Wilson Knight: I suspect that even Georges Poulet has read him with profit. His spatial approach, the way of seeing "a poem or a play at once in a single view, like a patterned carpet,"[53] has become the model of many later readings. But most of us have become increasingly dissatisfied with the arbitrariness of his associations, the intrusion of a crude psychoanalysis and of a strangely misused Nietzsche. Few of us can share the odd exaltation of Byron to a symbolist and prophet, to the greatest man after Christ. But in the chapter "The Wordsworthian Profundity" Knight comes to the right conclusion that Wordsworth aims at a "fusion of mind with nature to create the living paradise," to which, however, in Knight's opinion, Shelley and Keats "bear stronger *immediate* witness" than Wordsworth.[54] Knight's themes have been pursued by others, often with a different emphasis: W. H.

51. Baltimore, 1953 and 1959; see *The Subtler Language,* p. 186.
52. Oxford, 1941, new ed. London, 1959.
53. Ibid., p. xii, from the introduction by W. F. Jackson Knight.
54. Ibid., p. 82.

Auden's *The Enchaféd Flood: the Romantic Iconography of the Sea* (1950) centers on the longing for the sea from Wordsworth to Mallarmé, with emphasis on *Moby Dick*. Auden sees a dialectic of consciousness and unconsciousness: "Romanticism means the identification of consciousness and sin: the Romanticist yearns for innocence because he is" traveling farther and farther from "unconsciousness."[55] In the introduction to the fourth volume of *Poets of the English Language* (1950), Auden states the same conclusion somewhat differently: as self-consciousness is the noblest human quality, the artist as the most conscious man becomes the romantic hero. But "the idol of consciousness is a pantheistic god immanent in nature."[56] In the same year, F. W. Bateson concluded that "the nature-symbol, the synthetic link between the conscious and the subconscious mind, is the basic unit of Romantic poetry."[57] Also R. A. Foakes' *The Romantic Assertion* (1958) describes the romantic system of symbols as serving the "vision of harmony." In a rather obvious way this romantic "vocabulary of assertion" is contrasted with the modern poetry of conflict and irony.[58] On the other hand, Frank Kermode, in his *Romantic Image* (1957), derives the modern symbol, mainly in Yeats, directly from romanticism. "The Symbol of the French is the Romantic Image writ large and given more elaborate metaphysical and magical support." But Kermode considers Symbolism a "great and in some ways noxious historical myth" and wants to destroy the idea of the supernatural image and what he considers its inevitable accompaniment: the alienated artist, the artist as a pretentious prophet and seer.[59]

55. New York, 1950, p. 150.

56. Ed. W. H. Auden and Norman Holmes Pearson (New York, 1950), pp. xv–xvi.

57. In *English Poetry: A Critical Introduction* (London, 1950), p. 126.

58. London, 1958, pp. 50, 182.

59. London, 1957, pp. 5, 166.

An opposite and emphatically positive evaluation of romantic mythology is made in Harold Bloom's *The Visionary Company* (1961), a book which interprets closely all the main romantic poems with less polemical fervor than his earlier work on *Shelley's Mythmaking* (1959).[60] Bloom exalts Blake and Shelley. Their vision is interpreted as gnostic rapture transcending that of the more nature-bound Wordsworth and Keats. I find many of Bloom's readings totally unconvincing. Thus, he invokes Blake's inept picture of the tiger—"a shabby pawn-shop sort of stuffed tiger, more an overgrown house-cat"—to misread the whole poem as a mockery revealing "a state of being beyond either Innocence or Experience, a state where the lamb can lie down with the tiger."[61] Nor are Wordsworth or Keats interpreted rightly: Bloom minimizes both the Christian and the Hellenic components of romanticism. He sees only the prophetic, the visionary of the company.[62] We shall not, I think, make much progress with the problem of romanticism if we seek its prototype in such an exceptional and lonely figure as Blake, who seems to me rather a survival from another century, however much he may also anticipate the issues of our own time.

What is called romanticism in England and on the Continent is not the literal vision of the mystics but the concern for the reconciliation of subject and object, man and nature, consciousness and unconsciousness to which we have returned several times. It is well brought out in three recent studies which deal with both English and Continental romanticism. E. D. Hirsch, in *Wordsworth and Schelling* (1960),[63] defines the convergence of these strikingly different figures in a whole spectrum of ideas: the way of reconciling time

60. New Haven, 1959.
61. Garden City, N. Y., 1961, p. 31.
62. Cf. the review by Paul de Man in *The Massachusetts Review*, *3* (1962), 618–23.
63. New Haven, 1960.

and eternity, the immanent theism, the dialectic which favors what Hirsch calls "both/and thinking," the fear of alienation, the concept of living nature, and the role of the imagination which makes explicit the implicit unity of all things. Hirsch construes a typology which he derives from Karl Jaspers' *Psychologie der Weltanschauungen* (1919), and thus he avoids the question of common sources and influences. Surely, however, we must assume that the neo-Platonic tradition and the nature mysticism of Jakob Boehme translated into eighteenth-century terms lie behind both Wordsworth and Coleridge, as well as Schelling.

Paul de Man, in an article "Structure intentionelle de l'Image romantique" (1960),[64] redefines the romantic nature image. He uses passages about the high Swiss mountains from Rousseau, Wordsworth, and Hölderlin to show the peculiar paradox of the romantic poet's nostalgia for the object. Language strives to become nature. The words must, in a phrase of Hölderlin's, "arise like flowers" (*wie Blumen entstehn*). "Sometimes romantic thought and poetry seem about to surrender so completely to the nostalgia for the object that it becomes difficult to distinguish between object and image, between imagination and perception, between expressive and constitutive language and mimetic and literal language." De Man thinks of passages in Wordsworth and Goethe, Baudelaire and Rimbaud, where the "vision becomes almost a presence, a real landscape." But he argues that even the most extreme believer in the magic of language, Mallarmé, never doubted the intrinsic ontological primacy of the natural and earthly object. But the attempt of language to approach the ontological status of the object fails. Contradicting his statement a few pages before, de Man concludes that we have misunderstood these poets if we call them "pantheists" while "they are probably the first writers

64. *Revue internationale de philosophie, 14* (1960), 68–84, esp. pp. 74–75, 83.

who, within the Western Hellenic and Christian tradition, have in their poetic language questioned the ontological primacy of the sensible object." Though de Man seems to waver on the issue of the romantics' precise view of nature, he strongly corroborates our central theme. The reconciliation of art and nature, language and reality *is* the romantic ambition.

In a recent essay, "Romanticism and 'Antiself-Consciousness' " (1962), Geoffrey Hartman has generalized about the common elements in English and German romanticism. The peculiarly romantic remedy for the human predicament is the attempt "to draw the anti-dote to self-consciousness from consciousness itself." The idea of a return to nature or naiveté via knowledge is common to German and English romanticism. He concludes that "to explore the transition from self-consciousness to imagination, and achieve that transition while exploring it is the most crucial Romantic concern." The modern writer, while pursuing the same aim, has lost faith in the role of nature.[65]

In all of these studies, however diverse in method and emphasis, a convincing agreement has been reached: they all see the implication of imagination, symbol, myth, and organic nature, and see it as part of the great endeavor to overcome the split between subject and object, the self and the world, the conscious and the unconscious. This is the central creed of the great romantic poets in England, Germany, and France. It is a closely coherent body of thought and feeling. We can, of course, still insist that there is also a unity of romanticism on the lowest literary level: in the renascence of wonder, in the Gothic romance, in the interest in folklore and in the Middle Ages. H. H. Remak, in "West-European Romanticism: Definition and Scope" (1961), has recently drawn up a large synoptic table where he lists many criteria proposed and answers "yes" or "no" whether they

65. In *The Centennial Review,* 6 (1962), 553–65.

apply to Germany, France, England, Italy, or Spain. He comes to the welcome conclusion that "the evidence pointing to the existence in Western Europe of a widespread, distinct, and fairly simultaneous pattern of thought, attitudes, and beliefs associated with the connotation 'Romanticism' is overwhelming,"[66] though Italy and Spain were the countries least affected by romanticism. But his tables have the drawback of being atomistic: the implication and coherence of the concepts of nature, imagination, and myth are not shown, and such old criteria as "liberalism" or "vagueness," and such ideas as "rhetoric" or "greater positive emphasis on religion" are given an undeserved status.

I prefer not to be called "the champion of the concept of a pan-European Romanticism."[67] I would not be understood minimizing or ignoring national differences or forgetting that great artists have created something unique and individual. Still, I hope to have shown that in recent decades a stabilization of opinion has been achieved. One could even say (if we did not suspect the word so much) that progress has been made not only in defining the common features of romanticism but in bringing out what is its peculiarity or even its essence and nature: that attempt, apparently doomed to failure and abandoned by our time, to identify subject and object, to reconcile man and nature, consciousness and unconsciousness by poetry which is "the first and last of all knowledge."[68]

66. In *Comparative Literature: Method and Perspective,* ed. Newton P. Stallknecht and Horst Frenz (Carbondale, Ill., 1961), pp. 223–59.

67. Ibid., p. 227.

68. Preface to the 2nd ed. of *Lyrical Ballads* (1800), in *Poetical Works,* ed. E. de Selincourt, 2 (Oxford, 1944), 396.

The Concept of Realism in
Literary Scholarship

The discussion of the concept of realism is today, over a hundred years after the French debate, again topical. In the Soviet Union, in all the satellite countries and, I presume, even in China "realism" or rather "socialist realism" is installed officially as the only permissible literary doctrine and method. Its exact meaning, history, and future is being debated endlessly, in a flood of writings, the extent of which we can hardly imagine here in the West, where we need not follow every sinuosity of the party line and, happily, do not have to write and to criticize with constant regard to authorities, censors, resolutions, prescriptions, and exhortations.

If the debate on realism were merely a matter of concern for Soviet critics and writers we might ignore it or deplore it as an oddity of the cultural situation of the Soviet bloc. We might explain contemporary Russian painting as a "cultural lag," as an enforced survival of nineteenth-century taste in genre and color lithography, or we might account for the novels about cement making, dam building, partisan fighting, and party meetings as an attempt to produce a propaganda art comprehensible to the vast masses only recently admitted to literacy.

But this, I believe, would be a serious error of judgment. The Russian debate raises fundamental aesthetic issues and questions the basic presuppositions of modern art and aesthetics, particularly in the formulation given to it by the Hungarian Marxist Georg Lukács. Lukács is exceptional among Marxists for his knowledge of the German tradition and owes some of his success to his skill in combining realism with classicism. Still, one should recognize that the re-emergence and reformulation of the problem of realism appeals to a potent tradition in history, not only in Russia where the so-called radical critics of the sixties anticipated its position, or even to the mainly French realist move-ment of the nineteenth century, but to all literary and art history. Realism in the wide sense of fidelity to nature is indubitably a main stream of the critical and creative tradi-tion of both the plastic arts and literature. I need allude only to what seems the faithful, almost literal realism of much Hellenistic or late Roman sculpture or to much of Dutch painting, or, in literature, to scenes in the *Satyricon* of Petronius, to medieval *fabliaux,* to the bulky corpus of the picaresque novel, to the circumstantial minuteness of Daniel Defoe, or the bourgeois drama of the eighteenth century— to limit my examples to writings preceding the nineteenth century. Even more relevantly to our discussion the dominance of the concept of "imitation" in all criti-cal theory since Aristotle testifies to the enduring concern of the critic with the problem of reality. In painting, an-cient theory was preoccupied with the achievement of literal naturalism, even deception and delusion; we all know the anecdotes about the birds who started to peck at the painted cherries or about the painter Parrhasius who tricked his rival Zeuxis into trying to pull a painted curtain from his picture.

In the history of literary criticism the concept of imita-tion was, whatever its exact meaning in Aristotle may have been, often interpreted as literal copying, as naturalism. In neoclassical theory naturalistic arguments were the main support for the three unities. D'Aubignac, in his *Pratique du théâtre* (1657) consistently argued that the time of action should be limited to three hours, the actual time of representation. The unity of place is defended with the naturalistic argument that the same image (the stage) cannot represent two different things. Diderot pushed naturalism as literal deception to astonishing extremes. In reporting a performance of his play *Le Père de famille* he is pleased to relate that "hardly had the first scene been played before one believed oneself in a family circle and forgot that one was in a theater." Similar naturalistic standards are common in such supposedly neoclassical critics as Dr. Johnson and even Lessing.[1]

The strength of this tradition must not be underrated. It has on its side some very simple truths. Art cannot help dealing with reality, however much we narrow down its meaning or emphasize the transforming or creative power of the artist. "Reality," like "truth," "nature," or "life," is, in art, in philosophy, and in everyday usage a value-charged word. All art in the past aimed at reality even if it spoke of a higher reality: a reality of essences or a reality of dreams and symbols.

But it is not my aim in this essay to discuss this eternal realism, the whole fundamental epistemological problem of the relation of art to reality. I shall be content with raising the question of realism in the nineteenth century, anchored in a particular moment of history, referable to a well-known body of texts. In other contexts I have made a defense of the use of such period terms, which must, it seems to me, be secured against two dangers: one, the extreme nominalism which considers them mere arbitrary linguistic labels, a tradition prevalent in English and American scholarship, and the other, very common in Germany, of considering such terms as almost metaphysical entities whose essences can be known only by intuition. I shall make some common sense distinctions and lead slowly to a con-

1. See my *History of Modern Criticism, 1* (New Haven, 1955), 14–15, 47–48.

crete description of the period concept of realism, which I shall regard as a regulative concept, a system of norms dominating a specific time, whose rise and eventual decline it would be possible to trace and which we can set clearly apart from the norms of the periods that precede and follow it.[2]

We must distinguish this system of norms from the history of the term "realism." This history, like the history of criticism in general, will help us in understanding the aims of a period, the self-consciousness of its authors, but does not necessarily bind us. Theory and practice diverge often in literary history, and theory might get along without a specific term. Still, there is some use in knowing the history of a term if only to avoid uses which run contrary to history. We can, no doubt, use a term in a sense quite different from its original meaning but it seems as unwise as if we should insist on calling a dog a cat.

The term "realism" existed in philosophy long ago with a meaning very different from ours. It meant the belief in the reality of ideas and was contrasted with nominalism, which considered ideas only names or abstractions. I am not acquainted with a study of the semantic changes which must have occurred in the eighteenth century. Thomas Reid's realism would be an instance of the reversal of meaning in philosophy. In the *Critique of Judgement* (1790) Kant speaks of the "idealism and realism of natural purposes," and Schelling, in his early paper "Vom Ich in der Philosophie" (1795), defines pure realism as "positing the existence of the non-ego,"[3] But Schiller and Friedrich

2. See my *Theory of Literature* (2nd ed. New York, 1956), pp. 252 ff.; "The Theory of Literary History," *Travaux du cercle linguistique de Prague*, 4 (1936), 173–91; "Periods and Movements in Literary History," in *English Institute Annual 1940* (New York, 1941), pp. 73–93, and some modifications in "The Concept of Evolution in Literary History," above.

3. Kant, *Kritik der Urteilskraft*, Par. 72. "Idealismus und Realismus der Naturzwecke," see also Par. 58, *Werke*, (Wiesbaden, 1957),

Schlegel seem the first to apply the term to literature. In 1798 Schiller refers to the French as "better realists than idealists." He takes from that "a victorious argument that realism cannot make a poet," and about the same time Friedrich Schlegel paradoxically asserts that "all philosophy is idealism and there is no true realism except that of poetry." In Schlegel's "Gespräch über die Poesie" (1800) one of the interlocutors is praised for choosing Spinoza in order to "show the primitive source of poetry in the mysteries of realism."[4] Schelling once, in his *Lectures on the Method of Academic Study* (1802), mentions even "poetic realism" but he refers there to Plato's "polemic against the poetic realism," which surely means no more than "realism" in poetry and not any special brand of realism.[5] The term is fairly frequent among the German romanticists but has not crystalized to mean either specific writers or a specific period or school.

In France the term was applied to concrete literature as

5, 453, 506–07; Schelling, *Sämmtliche Werke* (Stuttgart, 1856), 1. Abtheilung. *1*, 213: "Der reine Realismus setzt das Daseyn des Nicht-Ichs überhaupt"; cf. pp. 211, 212.

4. Schiller to Goethe, April 27, 1798: "Bessere Realisten als Idealisten" . . . "Ich nehme daraus ein siegendes Argument, dass der Realism [sic] keinen Poeten machen kann." Cf. letter of January 5 commenting on *Wallenstein*: "Es ist eine ganz andere Operation, das Realistische zu idealisieren, als das Ideale zu realisieren." Friedrich Schlegel, "Ideen," no. 96 from *Seine prosaischen Jugendschriften*, ed. J. Minor, *2* (Vienna, 1882), 299: "Alle Philosophie ist Idealismus und es giebt keinen wahren Realismus als den der Poesie," and ibid. *2*, 365: "um uns den Urquell der Poesie in den Mysterien des Realismus zu zeigen."

5. 14. Vorlesung, *Werke*, ed. M. Schröter, *3*, 368. Strangely enough both Brinkmann and Markwardt consider this passage an anticipation of Ludwig's "poetischer Realismus" and make much of the ignorance of other scholars who consider the term Ludwig's invention (Markwardt, 608–09, 632, Brinkmann, 3–4).

early as 1826. A writer in the *Mercure français* asserts that "this literary doctrine which gains ground every day and leads to faithful imitation not of the masterworks of art but of the originals offered by nature could very well be called realism. According to some indications it will be the literature of the nineteenth century, the literature of the true."[6] Gustave Planche, in his time an influential anti-romantic critic, used the term realism from about 1833 onwards almost as an equivalent of materialism, particularly for the minute description of costumes and customs in historical novels. Realism worries, he says, about "what escutcheon is placed over the door of a castle, what device is inscribed on a standard, and what colors are borne by a lovesick knight."[7] Clearly with Planche realism means almost the same as "local color," exactitude of description. Hippolyte Fortoul in 1834 complains for instance of a novel by A. Thouret that it is written "with an exaggeration of realism which he borrowed from the manner of M. Hugo."[8] Realism at that time is thus merely a feature observed in the method of writers whom we would today call romantic, in Scott, in Hugo, or in Mérimée. Soon the term

6. *13* (1826), quoted by Borgerhoff, "*Réalisme* and Kindred Words," *PMLA*, *53* (1938), 837–43: "Cette doctrine littéraire qui gagne tous les jours du terrain et qui conduirait à une fidèle imitation non pas des chefs-d'œuvre de l'art mais des originaux que nous offre la nature, pourrait fort bien s'appeler le réalisme: ce serait suivant quelques apparences, la littérature du XIXe siècle, la littérature du vrai."

7. "Moralité de la poésie," in *Revue des deux mondes*, 4th ser., *1* (1835), 259: "Quel écusson était placé à la porte du château, quelle devise était inscrite sur l'étendard, quelles couleurs portées par l'amoureux baron." Quoted from Borgerhoff.

8. "Revue littéraire du mois," in *Revue des deux mondes*, 4 (1 Nov. 1834), 339: "M. Thouret a écrit son livre avec une exagération de réalisme, qu'il a emprunté à la manière de M. Hugo"; from Weinberg, p. 117 (see below).

was transferred to the minute description of contemporary manners in Balzac and Murger but its meaning crystalized only in the great debates which arose in the fifties around the paintings of Courbet and through the assiduous activity of a mediocre novelist, Champfleury, who in 1857 published a volume of essays with the title *Le Réalisme,* while a friend of his, Duranty, edited a short-lived review *Réalisme* between July 1856 and May 1857.[9] In these writings a definite literary creed is formulated which centers on a very few simple ideas. Art should give a truthful representation of the real world: it should therefore study contemporary life and manners by observing meticulously and analyzing carefully. It should do so dispassionately, impersonally, objectively. What had been a widely used term for any faithful representation of nature now becomes associated with specific writers and is claimed as a slogan for a group or movement. There was wide agreement that Mérimée, Stendhal, Balzac, Monnier, and Charles de Bernard were the precursors while Champfleury and later Flaubert, Feydeau, the Goncourts, and the younger Dumas were the exponents of the school, though Flaubert, for instance, was annoyed at the designation and never admitted it for himself.[10] There is a remarkable, tiresomely monotonous agreement in the contemporary discussion of the main features of realism. Its numerous enemies judged the same traits negatively, complaining, for instance, about the excessive use of minute external detail, of the neglect of the ideal, and seeing the vaunted impersonality and objectivity as a

9. See Bernard Weinberg, *French Realism: The Critical Reaction, 1830–1870* (New York, 1937); H. U. Forest, " 'Réalisme,' Journal de Duranty," *Modern Philology, 24* (1926), 463–79.

10. The list from Weinberg. On Flaubert see Maxime du Camp, *Revue des deux mondes, 51* (June 1882), 791: "Le mot (Réalisme) le blessa et, dans son for intérieur, il ne l'a jamais admis."

cloak for cynicism and immorality. With the trial of Flaubert in 1857 for *Madame Bovary* the volume of discussion becomes so large and so repetitious that we need not trace the history of the term in France any further.

Obviously the French debate or battle soon found its echoes in other countries. We must, however, sharply distinguish between the use of the term "realism" in reporting French developments and the adoption of the term as a slogan for a local school of realistic writing. The situation in the main countries varies greatly in this respect. In England there was no realist movement of that name before George Moore and George Gissing, late in the eighties.

But the terms "realism" and "realist" occur in an article on Balzac as early as 1853 and Thackeray was called, rather casually, "chief of the Realist school" in 1851. George Henry Lewes seems to have been the first English critic who systematically applied standards of realism, for instance, in a severe review, "Realism in Art: Recent German Fiction" (1858). There Lewes trounces Freytag and Ludwig as unrealistic and mawkish, praises Paul Heyse and Gottfried Keller, and boldly proclaims "Realism the basis of all Art." In David Masson's *British Novelists and their Styles* (1859) Thackeray is contrasted as "a novelist of what is called the Real school" with Dickens, "a novelist of the Ideal or Romantic school," and the "growth among novel-writers of a wholesome spirit of Realism" is welcomed. Realistic criteria such as truth of observation and a depiction of commonplace events, characters, and settings are almost universal in Victorian novel criticism.[11]

11. "Balzac and his Writings," *Westminster Review, 60* (July and October 1853), 203, 212, 214; "William Makepeace Thackeray and Arthur Pendennis, Esquires," *Fraser's Magazine, 43* (January 1851), 86; Lewes, *Westminster Review, 70* (October 1858), 448–518, esp. 493; Masson (Cambridge, 1859), pp. 248, 257; see Robert

The situation in the United States was very similar: in 1864 Henry James recommended "the famous 'realistic system' "—obviously referring to the French—for study to a fellow novelist, Miss Harriet Prescott, who, he complained, had not "sufficiently cultivated a delicate perception of the actual."[12] But only W. Dean Howells, writing in 1882, speaks of Henry James as the "chief exemplar" of an American school of realism and from 1886 onwards propagated realism as a movement of which he counted himself and James as the chief proponents.[13]

In Germany there was, I believe, no self-conscious realist movement, though the term was used occasionally. In 1850 Hermann Hettner spoke of Goethe's realism. For F. T. Vischer, Shakespeare was the supreme realist.[14] Otto Ludwig devised the term "poetischer Realismus" in order to contrast Shakespeare with the contemporary French movement.[15] Julian Schmidt used the term in articles in *Die Grenzboten* from 1856, and in his history of German literature (1867) for what is usually called "Das Junge Deutschland."[16] Even in Marxist theory the term arrives very late. I cannot find it in early pronouncements of either Marx or

Gorham Davis, "The Sense of the Real in English Fiction," *Comparative Literature, 3* (1951), 200–17, and Richard Stang, *The Theory of the Novel in England 1850–1870* (London, 1959), p. 148.

12. Reprinted in *Notes and Reviews,* ed. Pierre de Chaignon La Rose (Cambridge, Mass., 1921), pp. 23, 32.

13. "Henry James Jr.," *Century Magazine, 25* (1882), 26–28.

14. Hettner, "Die romantische Schule," *Schriften zur Literatur* (Berlin, 1959), p. 66; Vischer, "Shakespeare in seinem Verhältnis zur deutschen Poesie" (1844), in *Kritische Gänge, 2* (Stuttgart, 1861), 1–62, does not use the term. In the preface of the 1861 reprint Vischer regrets that "der Ausdruck realistisch noch nicht im Gebrauche war" when he wrote the article.

15. *Gesammelte Schriften,* ed. A. Stern, *5* (Leipzig, 1891), 264 ff.

16. *Die Grenzboten, 14* (1856), 486 ff; "Die Realisten 1835–1841" in Julian Schmidt, *Geschichte der deutschen Literatur seit Lessings Tod* (3rd vol., *Die Gegenwart, 1814–1867*) (5th ed. Leipzig, 1867).

Engels. It was in 1888 that Engels, in an English letter to Miss Harkness commenting on her novel, *The City Girl,* complains that it is "not quite realistic enough. Reality, to my mind, implies, besides truth to detail, the truthful reproduction of typical circumstances."[17] A later letter uses the term milieu and shows, as does the emphasis on type and on Balzac, the influence of Taine.[18]

In Italy, De Sanctis defended Zola in 1878 and thought realism an "excellent antidote for a fantastic race fond of phrasemaking and display." But later he recoiled before the spread of naturalism and positivistic science, lectured on the need of the "ideal," and deplored the new "animalism."[19] The Italian realistic novelists invented a new term, "verismo," and the most prominent theorist of the group, Luigi Capuana, came to reject all "isms" indignantly, both for himself and his great friend Giovanni Verga.[20]

In Russia the situation was again different: there Vissarion Belinsky had adopted Friedrich Schlegel's term "real poetry" as early as 1836; he applied it to Shakespeare, who "reconciled poetry with real life," and Scott, "the second Shakespeare, who achieved the union of poetry with life."[21] After 1846 Belinsky spoke of Russian writers such

17. *Über Kunst und Literatur,* ed. Michail Lipschitz (Berlin, 1948), pp. 103–04.

18. To Hans Starkenburg, Jan. 25, 1894, in *Dokumente des Sozialismus,* ed. Eduard Bernstein, *2* (1903), 73–75.

19. "Studio sopra E. Zola" (1877) in *Saggi critici,* ed. L. Russo, *3* (Bari, 1956), 234–76; cf. ibid., 299, end of the essay on *L'Assommoir* (1879): "Per una razza fantastica, amica delle frasi e della pompa." The lecture, "L'ideale" (1877) in *La Poesia cavalleresca e scritti vari,* ed. M. Petrini (Bari, 1954), pp. 308–13, and "Il Darwinismo nell'arte" (1883), in *Saggi critici, 3,* 325.

20. *Gli 'ismi' contemporanei (Verismo, simbolismo, idealismo, cosmopolitismo) ed altri saggi* (Catania, 1898).

21. *Sobranie sochinenii,* ed. F. M. Golovenchenko, *1* (Moscow, 1948), 103, 107–08.

as Gogol as the "natural school."[22] Belinsky determined the views of the radical critics of the sixties but, among them, only Dimitri Pisarev used the term as a slogan. Realism for him is, however, simply analysis, criticism. "A realist is a thinking worker."[23] Dostoevsky attacked the radical critics sharply in 1863. He always disapproved of photographic naturalism and defended the interest in the fantastic and exceptional. In two well-known letters Dostoevsky asserted that he had "quite different conceptions of reality and realism than our realists and critics. My idealism is more real than their realism." His realism is pure, a realism in depth while theirs is of the surface. N. N. Strakhov, in his biography, reports Dostoevsky as saying: "they call me a psychologist: mistakenly. I am rather a realist in a higher sense, i. e. I depict all the depths of the human soul."[24] Similarly, Tolstoy disapproved of the radical critics and showed a violent distaste for Flaubert though, surprisingly enough, he praised Maupassant and wrote an introduction to a Russian translation. Though truth and truth of emotion is mandatory for Tolstoy in *What is Art?*, the word "realism" does not occur in his writings prominently at all.[25]

This short sketch of the use and spread of the term "realism" would be out of focus if we did not remark on

22. Ibid., *3*, 649; see note on p. 902 referring to Bulgarin's use of the term earlier in the same year.

23. *Sochineniya. Polnoe sobranie,* ed. F. Pavlenkov, *4* (4th ed. St. Petersburg, 1904–7), 68.

24. Letter to A. N. Maykov, 11/23 Dec. 1868, in *Pisma,* ed. A. S. Dolinin, *2* (Moscow, 1928–34), 150, and letter to N. N. Strakhov, 26 Feb./10 March 1869, ibid., 169; N. N. Strakhov and O. Miller, *Biografiya, pisma . . .* (St. Petersburg, 1883), p. 373.

25. E.g. Tolstoy's introduction to S. T. Semenov's *Peasant Stories* (1894) ridicules *La Légende de Julien l'hospitalier;* see *What is Art?* and *Essays on Art,* Eng. trans. A. Maude (Oxford, 1930), pp. 17–18; the introduction to Maupassant (1894), ibid., pp. 20–45.

the term "naturalism," which was in constant competition with "realism" and was often identified with it. It is an ancient philosophical term for materialism, epicureanism, or any secularism. In a literary sense it can be found again in Schiller, in the preface to the *Bride of Messina* (1803) as something which Schiller finds worth combating, as in poetry "everything is only a symbol of the real."[26] Heine, in a passage of the 1831 *Salon* which profoundly impressed Baudelaire, proclaimed himself a "supernaturalist in art" in contrast to his "naturalism" in religion.[27] But again the term, widely used for faithful adherence to nature, crystalized as a specific slogan only in France. It was captured by Zola, and since the preface to the second edition of his novel *Thérèse Raquin* (1868) it became more and more identified with his theory of the scientific, experimental novel. But the distinction between "realism" and "naturalism" was not stabilized for a long time. Ferdinand Brunetière in his *Le Roman naturaliste* (1883) discusses Flaubert, Daudet, Maupassant, George Eliot as well as Zola under this title. The separation of the terms is only a work of modern literary scholarship.

Thus the contemporary uses of the terms "realism" and "naturalism" should be distinguished from the process by which modern literary research has imposed the term "realism" or "realist period" on the past. The two processes are of course not independent of each other: the original suggestion comes from the contemporary debates. But still the two are not entirely the same. Again, the situation varies greatly in the different countries.

In France the term "realism" with a distinct later stage of "naturalism" seems firmly established. In particular the

26. *Sämtliche Werke,* ed. Güntter-Witkowski, *20* (Leipzig, 1909–11), 254: "Alles ist nur ein Symbol des Wirklichen."
27. *Salon* (1831), in *Werke,* ed. O. Walzel, *6* (Leipzig 1912–15), 25: "In der Kunst bin ich Supernaturalist."

books by Pierre Martino, *Le Roman réaliste* (1913) and
Le Naturalisme français (1923), have confirmed the distinction: "naturalism" is the doctrine of Zola; it implies a
scientific approach, it requires a philosophy of deterministic
materialism while the older realists were far less clear or
unified in their philosophical affiliations. In France there
is one good book, Gustave Reynier's *Les Origines du roman réaliste* (1912), which traces the method of realism
from the *Satyricon* of Petronius to Rabelais, the Spanish
Celestina, and the French literature about peasants and
beggars in the sixteenth century. Reynier both in his examples and in his exclusions anticipates Auerbach on some
points: realism must not be satirical or comical to qualify
as such.

In England the use of the term "realism" as a period
concept is still very rare. The standard histories of English
literature of the early twentieth century, the *Cambridge
History of English Literature* and Garnett and Gosse, use
the term only very occasionally. Gissing is called a "realist"
because of Zola's influence and we hear that "Ben Jonson
set out to be what we now call a 'realist' or 'naturalist.' "[28]
It needed an American scholar, Norman Foerster, to suggest that the term "Victorian" should be replaced by
"realist."[29]

In American literary scholarship the position is quite
the reverse of the English position. There "realism" is
firmly established, mainly, I believe, since Vernon Parrington gave the title *The Beginnings of Critical Realism*
(1930) to the third volume of his *Main Currents of*

28. On Gissing, *Cambridge History of English Literature, 14,* 458;
on Ben Jonson, R. Garnett and E. Gosse, *English Literature. An Illustrated Record, 2* (1903–4), 310.

29. *The Reinterpretation of Victorian Literature,* ed. Joseph E.
Baker (Princeton, 1950), pp. 58–59.

American Thought. There is a recent collective volume, *Transitions in American Literary History* (1954), which manipulates the period concept almost with the assurance of a German literary historian. Realism, unlike naturalism, is not primarily engaged in social criticism, it is argued, but concerns itself with the conflict between the inherited American ideals of faith in man and the individual and the pessimistic, deterministic, creed of modern science.[30] Charles Child Walcutt in *American Literary Naturalism* (1956) has well described what he called its "divided stream," "the mixture of fervid exhortation with concepts of majestic inevitableness."[31]

In Germany, Richard Brinkmann, in *Wirklichkeit und Illusion* (1957), has recently surveyed the German discussions of realism, rejecting them all in favor of his own theory, and Bruno Markwardt, in the fourth volume of his very learned *Geschichte der deutschen Poetik* (1959), has studied the most casual pronouncements of fifth-rate writers, classifying their theories into the strangest pigeonholes. There is a "Frührealismus," a "religiös-ethischer Realismus," an "Idealrealismus," there is "der konzentrierende Typ des Realismus," "der konsequente, besonnene Realismus," "der naturalistische Realismus,"[32] etc., etc., until one's head spins with the dance of bloodless categories and one ceases to notice that Markwardt, hails as discoveries the hoariest commonplaces about life, truth, verisimilitude, and objectivity.[33] Markwardt is resolutely provincial: nothing has ever happened outside Germany, and Aristotle (though mentioned several times) has never thought about imitation of nature, probability or pathos. The French do

---

30. Robert O. Falk, "The Rise of Realism," in *Transitions in American Literary History*, ed. H. H. Clark (Durham, N. C., 1954).

31. Minneapolis, Minn., 1956, p. 9.

32. Berlin, 1959, pp. 96, 102, 216, 378, 291, and passim.

33. See e.g. pp. 615, 660, 680, 691, e.g. no satire in Thackeray, p. 666.

not exist: Flaubert, Taine, the Goncourts do not occur in the very complete index.

At the other extreme stands Erich Auerbach's *Mimesis* (1946). Auerbach has an international horizon and is so suspicious of the categorizing of *Geistesgeschichte* that it is difficult to discover what he means by "realism." He tells us himself that he would like to have written his book without using any "general expressions." I have shown elsewhere[34] that Auerbach tries to combine two contradictory conceptions of realism; firstly something which might be called existentialism: the agonizing revelations of reality in moments of supreme decisions, in "limiting situations": Abraham about to sacrifice Isaac, Madame du Chastel deciding not to rescue her son from execution, the Duke of Saint-Simon asking the Jesuit negotiator how old he is. There is, however, a second realism in Auerbach, the French nineteenth-century realism, which he defines as depicting contemporary reality, immersed in the dynamic concreteness of the stream of history. Historicism contradicts existentialism. Existentialism sees man exposed in his nakedness and solitude, it is unhistorical, even anti-historical. These two sides of Auerbach's conception of realism differ also in their historical provenience. "Existence" descends from Kierkegaard, whose whole philosophy was a protest against Hegel, the ancestor of historicism and *Geistesgeschichte*. In Auerbach's sensitive and learned book "realism" has assumed a very special meaning: realism must not be didactic, moralistic, rhetorical, idyllic, or comic. Thus he has nothing to say of the bourgeois drama or the English realistic novel of the eighteenth and nineteenth century; the Russians are excluded and so are all the Germans of the nineteenth century as either didactic or idyllic. Only passages in the Bible and Dante, and among

34. "Auerbach's Special Realism," *Kenyon Review, 16* (1954), 299–307.

moderns, Stendhal, Balzac, Flaubert, and Zola live up to Auerbach's requirements.

Richard Brinkmann's *Wirklichkeit und Illusion* (1957) also arrives at an idiosyncratic conclusion. He ignores the historical debate and focuses on an ingenious analysis of three German stories: Grillparzer's *Armer Spielmann* (1848), Otto Ludwig's *Zwischen Himmel und Erde* (1855) and Edward von Keyserling's *Beate und Mareile* (1903). Brinkmann argues that the acme of realism is reached in Keyserling's story, as there the narrator limits himself to the representation of the feelings of a single fictional figure, the hero, a Prussian *Junker* wavering between two women. Realism or rather reality is found ultimately in the stream of consciousness technique, in the attempt to "dramatize the mind," a technique which actually achieved the most radical dissolution of ordinary reality. Brinkmann is well aware of the paradox of this "reversal," by which the attention to the factual and the individual finally led to something as "unrealistic" in the traditional sense as in Joyce, Virginia Woolf, and Faulkner. Brinkmann does not analyze a single text which could be called strictly "realistic," partly because in the body of the book—in spite of the international perspective of the conclusion—his attention is so completely limited by the German horizon that he is concerned only with German latecomers and derivatives. The conclusion that "the subjective experience . . . is the only objective experience"[35] identifies impressionism, the exact notation of mental states of mind, with realism and proclaims it the only true realism. The accepted nineteenth-century meaning of realism is turned upside down. It is replaced by an individualizing, atomistic, subjective realism that refuses to recognize an objective order of things: it is even solipsism

35. Tübingen, 1957, p. 298: "Das Subjektive, das subjektive Erleben, die subjektive Erkenntniss, der subjektive Trieb sind—zugespitzt formuliert—das einzig Objektive."

in the sense of Pater or Proust. The individual is called the "only reality" as in existential philosophy. *Lieutenant Gustl* by Arthur Schnitzler rather than *Die Buddenbrooks,* both dated 1901, is the culmination point of German realism. Bergson rather than Taine or Comte would be its philosopher.[36]

In Germany everybody is on his own and looks for realism wherever he wants to find it. In Italy, with the exception of Marxist critics, there is no problem of realism. Croce has taken care of that: there is no nature or reality outside the mind and the artist need not worry about the relationship. "Realism" is (like romanticism) only a pseudo-concept, a category of obsolete rhetoric.[37]

In Russia realism is everything. There they hunt for realism even in the past. Pushkin and Gogol are realists, and as in Germany they quarrel and quibble about "critical realism," "radical democratic realism," "proletarian realism," and "socialist realism," its last stage, which according to Timofeyev's authoritative *Theory of Literature* is the "fulfilment of all art and literature."[38]

Among the Marxists Georg Lukács has developed the most coherent theory of realism: it starts with the Marxist dogma that literature is a "reflection of reality" and that it will be the truest mirror if it fully reflects the contradictions of social development, that is, in practice, if the author shows an insight into the structure of society and the future direction of its evolution. Naturalism is rejected as concerned with the surface of everyday life and with the aver-

36. Ibid., pp. 319, 327.
37. Croce, *Estetica* (Bari, 1950), p. 118; "Breviario di estetica," in *Nuovi saggi di estetica* (Bari, 1948), pp. 39–40; "Aestetica in nuce," in *Ultimi saggi* (Bari, 1948), p. 21.
38. L. I. Timofeyev, *Teoriya literatury* (Moscow, 1938), quoted in Rufus W. Mathewson, Jr., *The Positive Hero in Russian Literature* (New York, 1958), p. 7.

age, while realism creates types which are both representative and prophetic. Lukács assembles a number of criteria which allow him to judge literature in terms of its "progressiveness" (which might be unconscious, even contra to the political opinions of the author) and in terms of the inclusiveness, representativeness, self-consciousness, and anticipatory power of the figures created by the great realists. Though there is much purely political polemic in Lukács and the criteria are predominantly ideological, "popular front," and later "cold war," Lukács at his best reformulates the "concrete universal" and renews the "ideal type" problem so closely in relation with the main tradition of German aesthetics that Peter Demetz could speak of him as achieving "a renaissance of originally idealistic aesthetics in the mask of Marxism."[39]

This little survey of contemporary uses of the term and modern interpretations of the concepts, besides its intrinsic interest, aims at establishing two points: the self-consciousness of a time has no power to bind modern scholars like ourselves, concerned with the task of periodization. We cannot limit ourselves to writers who called themselves realists nor can we be content with the theories developed at the time. On the other hand the enormous variety of often quite contradictory opinions in modern scholarship as to the content and reference of the concept should serve as a warning that we should best not lose touch with the basic theories of the time and the acknowledged masterpieces. But while we cannot be bound by a study of the application of the term in its time, we have, I think, also to recognize the importance of self-consciousness when it is felt and even formulated without the terms which we use today. The time

39. "Zwischen Klassik und Bolschewismus. Georg Lukács als Theoretiker der Dichtung," *Merkur, 12* (1958), 501–15: "Eine Renaissance der ursprünglich idealistischen Aesthetik in der Maske des Marxismus."

around the July revolution of 1830 was generally considered as the end of an epoch, as the dawn of a new age in literature also. Heine's formula, "das Ende der Kunstperiode," is just as valid for France as for Italy or England. We do not need the term "realism": it might in Germany be Wienbarg's "poetry of life" or Gervinus' intense feeling for the change demanded of Germany from art to politics. It might in France be the slogan "être de son temps" or the utilitarian ideals of the Saint-Simonians or Leroux; in England it might lie in Carlyle's turning to the only Poem Reality, and in Russia it might be Belinsky's last phase, his exaltation of Pushkin's turn to real life, his praise of the young Dostoevsky (so quickly retracted) for his *Poor People* or of Turgenev for the first *Sportsman's Sketches*. In short, there was a universal feeling for the end of romanticism, for the rise of a new age concerned with reality, science, and this world. Similarly we could document the realization in the late eighteen nineties that realism and naturalism had run their course and would be replaced by a new art, symbolic, neoromantic or whatever else it might call itself.

We can now approach our final, most important task, the description (I don't say definition) of a meaningful period concept of realism which could stand the test of the requirements we have established: it must not be merely the description of a style of literature which occurred in all times and ages, as we are not trying to establish a typology of literature, but a period concept. If it is to be a significant period concept it must be clearly distinguished from the period concepts with which it will be compared and contrasted, from classicism and romanticism. And if it is to be a period concept it cannot be conceived so narrowly that it would exclude writers who dominated the time and seem most representative and typical of it.

Let us start with something very simple and say that realism is "the objective representation of contemporary social reality." This, I admit, says little and raises such questions as what is meant by "objective" and what is meant by "reality." But we must not rush to consider ultimate questions but see this description in a historical context as a polemical weapon against romanticism, as a theory of exclusion as well as inclusion. It rejects the fantastic, the fairytale-like, the allegorical and the symbolic, the highly stylized, the purely abstract and decorative. It means that we want no myth, no *Maerchen*, no world of dreams. It implies also a rejection of the improbable, of pure chance, and of extraordinary events, since reality is obviously conceived at that time, in spite of all local and personal differences, as the orderly world of nineteenth-century science, a world of cause and effect, a world without miracle, without transcendence even if the individual may have preserved a personal religious faith. The term "reality" is also a term of inclusion: the ugly, the revolting, the low are legitimate subjects of art. Taboo subjects such as sex and dying (love and death were always allowed) are now admitted into art.

On this point the French situation is somewhat peculiar: through the authority of French classicism the ancient theory of the three levels of style had held its sway much longer. The low was kept in its place: it could be used only in satire, in the burlesque, and in the comic. The breakdown of the three levels of style is one of the main themes of Auerbach's great book. But in focusing so exclusively on France, where neoclassicism survived longest for political reasons, throughout the Revolution and the Napoleonic empire and even after the Restoration, Auerbach makes the breakdown of the levels of style, the mixing of genres and thus the appearance of a serious realism far too sudden a phenomenon, due only to Stendhal and Balzac. In England the situation was very different; there Shakespeare had mixed the styles and genres thoroughly and only by declar-

ing that everything didactic and moralistic is excluded
from realism can Auerbach dismiss Defoe, Richardson and
Fielding, and the whole domestic tragedy of the English as
irrelevant. Moreover, I doubt whether the French realists
were so completely nondidactic as Flaubert's theory claims
to be, and it seems to me inadvisable to exclude such writers
as George Eliot or Tolstoy, despite their didactic intention,
from a concept of realism.

We must recognize that in our original definition, "the
objective representation of contemporary social reality,"
didacticism is implied or concealed. In theory, completely
truthful representation of reality would exclude any kind of
social purpose or propaganda. Obviously the theoretical difficulty of realism, its contradictoriness, lies in this very
point. This may be blatantly obvious to us but it is a simple
fact of literary history that the mere change to a depiction
of contemporary social reality implied a lesson of human
pity, of social reformism and criticism, and often of rejection and revulsion against society. There is a tension between description and prescription, truth and instruction,
which cannot be resolved logically but which characterizes
the literature of which we are speaking. In the new Russian
term "socialist realism" the contradiction is confessed quite
openly: the writer ought to describe society as it *is* but he
must also describe it as it should or will be.

This conflict explains the crucial importance of the concept of "type" for the theory and practice of realism, because
"type" constitutes the bridge between the present and the
future, the real and the social ideal. "Type" as a term has a
complex history which I can trace here only very briefly.
In Germany, Schelling used it in the sense of a great universal figure of mythical proportion: Hamlet, Falstaff, Don
Quixote, Faust are types.[40] In this sense the term was im-

40. See my *History of Modern Criticism, 2,* 77.

ported into France by Charles Nodier in an essay, "Des Types en littérature" (1832)[41] and it is used pervasively in Hugo's strange rhapsody on Shakespeare (1864). Don Juan, Shylock, Achilles, Iago, Prometheus, and Hamlet[42] are his examples of "types," Adams—archetypal patterns we might say today. But parallel with this development the term "type" emerges as meaning "social type." It replaced the older word "caractère," which had assumed the meaning of individual character and lost the association with Theophrastus and La Bruyère. Balzac in the preface to the *Comédie humaine* (1842) considers himself a student of social types, and George Sand in the preface to her novel, *Le Compagnon du tour de France* (1851), clearly conceives of "type" as a social model worthy of imitation in life.[43] In early realist theory the descriptive usage predominates. In Taine this theory of social types is combined with the Hegelian ideal. At times Taine uses types as sources to discover social stratification and he goes through the characters in La Fontaine's fables, in Shakespeare, in Balzac and Dickens with this question in mind. In the lectures *De l'idéal en art* (1867) Taine, however, distinguishes types within a scale of social beneficence and exalts heroes as "types" and models for society. In flat contradiction to his usual admiration for the great passionate criminal or monomaniac, Taine has to rank types in a scale which leads from ideal women such as Miranda, Imogen, and Goethe's Iphigenie to martyrs and finally to heroes of the ancient epics: Siegfried, Roland, and the Cid. "Farther up, and in a higher sphere, are the saviors and gods of Greece, of Ju-

---

41. In *Rêveries littéraires, morales, et fantastiques* (Brussels, 1832), pp. 41–58.

42. On Hugo see my *History*, 2, 257–58.

43. For Balzac, George Sand, see my "Hippolyte Taine's Literary Theory and Criticism," in *Criticism*, 1 (1959), 16–17.

dea and Christianity." Oddly enough, in Taine, God becomes a type, a hero, a model, an ideal.[44]

This emphasis on type had also appeared in Russian
literary thought: Belinsky had used the term in its German
romantic sense. An article on Gogol (1836) defines the
primary task of the artist as the creation of types, figures
who, although individuals, still have universal significance.
Hamlet, Othello, Shylock, and Faust are Belinsky's examples, to which he adds, rather surprisingly, Gogol's Lieutenant Pirgorod, the hero of the story "Nevsky Prospekt,"
as a "type of types," a "mystical myth."[45] Dobrolyubov
(1836–61) seems, however, to have been the first critic in
Russia or elsewhere to point out social types as revealing an author's characteristic vision independently of or
even contrary to his conscious intentions. Dobrolyubov
distinguishes between the overt and the latent meaning
of a work of fiction and sees social types as crystalizing
points of social change. Unfortunately, in his critical practice, he was unable to hold steadily to this central insight
and often thought of types merely as "facilitating the formation of correct ideas about things and the dissemination
of these ideas among men,"[46] The artist should be a moralist and at the same time a scientist. Science and fiction
should merge, but to Dobrolyubov "science" is simply
"correct," that is, revolutionary, radical, social, and moral
thought. What seems a Platonic fusion of the true, the
good, and the beautiful becomes simply didacticism and
often a crude allegorizing for quite immediate polemical
purposes. Thus the lazy nobleman Oblomov from Gon-

44. Ibid., p. 18; from *De l'Idéal* (Paris, 1867), pp. 107-08: "Plus
haut encore et dans un ciel supérieur sont . . . les sauveurs et les dieux
de la Grèce . . . de la Judée et du christianisme."

45. Belinsky, *Sobranie sochinenii, 1* (Moscow, 1948), 136–37.

46. Dobrolyubov, *Izbrannye sochineniya,* ed. A. Lavretsky (Moscow, 1947), p. 104.

charov's novel is a "type" in this sense of a warning example, an allegory of Russian backwardness, in complete oblivion of the actual text. Dobrolyubov's main rival, Dimitri Pisarev (1840–68), interpreted Bazarov, the hero of Turgenev's *Fathers and Sons,* as the type of the new man, the herald of the new generation. In Bazarov, Pisarev discovered himself and his generation, in a genuine act of self-recognition and self-criticism, an almost unique case which seems to me a justification of the method which treats a fictional figure quite apart from the overt intentions of the author.[47] Critics in Russia, I believe, more than elsewhere, have concentrated on this problem of the hero, both the negative and the positive hero; the "superfluous man" whom they found in Pushkin's Onegin, in Lermontov's Pechorin, and in Goncharov's Oblomov, the positive hero whom they hailed in Bazarov, the Nihilist, or in Rakhmetov, the improbably tough revolutionary in Chernyshevsky's novel *What Is to Be Done?* This incredibly bad novel altered, however, the whole direction of the lives of important people. Lenin saw in Rakhmetov his ideal and so did Dimitrov, the Bulgarian communist of the Leipzig trial.[48] "Type," "typicalness," was discussed recently by another expert in aesthetics of short duration, Georgi Malenkov, as the central, political problem of realism.[49] It certainly formulates the problem of universality and particularity, the concrete universal of Hegel, and it states the problem of the hero, of his representativeness and hence of the social challenge implied in a work of fiction.

The emphasis on type is almost universal in realist theory;

47. Pisarev, "Bazarov" (1862), "The Realists" (1864), in *Sochineniya,* ed. Pavlenkov, vol. 2.
48. From Mathewson, *The Positive Hero,* pp. 104–06.
49. Georgi Malenkov, Report to the 19th Party Congress (5 Oct. 1952), in Martin Ebon, *Malenkov: Stalin's Successor* (New York, 1953), p. 227.

that even the prescriptive type is not unknown in Western literatures is obvious if we only reflect on Aeneas or the chivalric hero or any saint in legend, or think of Robinson Crusoe or Werther, all of whom have become models in real life. In the nineteenth century the theory of types was, as far as I know, opposed only by De Sanctis, the great Italian critic who taught Croce to emphasize the concrete and the individual in art. De Sanctis argues that "to say that Achilles is the type of force and courage, and that Thersites is the type of cowardice, is inexact, as these qualities may have infinite expression in individuals. Achilles is Achilles and Thersites is Thersites." At most De Sanctis would consider type the result of a process of dissolution achieved by time, in which individuals such as Don Quixote, Sancho Panza, Tartuffe, and Hamlet are reduced in the popular imagination to mere types and thus deprived of their individuality.[50] The main theorist of Italian realism, Luigi Capuana, shares this view. Apparently drawing on De Sanctis he declared flatly that "type is an abstract thing; it is a usurer, but not Shylock; it is a suspicious man, but not Othello; it is a hesitant, chimera-chasing man, but not Hamlet."[51]

Type, in spite of its didactic and prescriptive implications, preserves, however, the all-important association with objective social observation. "Objectivity" is certainly the other main watchword of realism. Objectivity means again

50. *La Giovinezza di Francesco De Sanctis,* ed. P. Villari (18th ed. Naples, 1926), p. 314: "Dire che Achille è il tipo della forza e del corragio, e che Tersite è il tipo della debolezza e della vigliaccheria, è inesatto, potendo queste qualità avere infinite espressioni negl'individui: Achille è Achille, e Tersite è Tersite." See also *Lezioni sulla Divina Commedia,* ed. M. Manfredi (Bari, 1955), p. 350.

51. *Gli 'ismi' contemporanei,* p. 46: "Il tipo è cosa astratta: è l'usuraio, ma non è Shylock: è il sospottoso, ma non è Othello: è l'esitante, il chimerizzante, ma non è Amleto."

something negative, a distrust of subjectivism, of the romantic exaltation of the ego: in practice often a rejection of lyricism, of the personal mood. In poetry the Parnassians wanted and achieved *impassibilité,* and in fiction the main technical demand of realist theory came to be impersonality, the complete absence of the author from his work, the suppression of any interference by the author. The theory had its main spokesman in Flaubert but it was also the preoccupation of Henry James—and Friedrich Spielhagen in Germany devoted a whole book to its defense.[52] Spielhagen appeals to epic theory, particularly to Wilhelm von Humboldt's essay on *Hermann und Dorothea* (1799), though the emphasis on the complete objectivity of the epic was elaborated of course before, for instance by Goethe and the Schlegels,[53] who could have found their model in Aristotle's praise of Homer. About the same time, in German theory and in English opinion, the complete objectivity of Shakespeare, his aloofness and superiority to his creation was constantly being celebrated. The contrast between objective and subjective poetry, implied also in Schiller's essay on *Naive and Sentimental Poetry,* was made particularly explicit by Friedrich Schlegel. The ancients, in his view, were objective, disinterested, impersonal, the moderns subjective, interesting, personal. We should realize, however, that in Friedrich Schlegel the demand for objectivity is confined to the epic and the drama; he contrasts the novel, which the realists consider the most objective genre, with the epic: it should rather express a subjective mood, like his own *Lucinde* or the novels of Sterne and Diderot.[54] In the other important Ger-

---

52. Friedrich Spielhagen, *Beiträge zur Theorie und Technik des Romans* (1883). Note the earlier article. "Über Objektivität im Roman" (1863), in *Vermischte Schriften, 1* (Berlin, 1864), 174–97.

53. See my *History, 2,* 50–51.

54. Ibid., 19–20.

man aestheticians of the time the same stress on objectivity is common. Solger's "irony" is the irony of Sophocles and Shakespeare, the highest objectivity of the artist.[55] Schopenhauer constantly distinguishes between poets of the first rank, objective poets such as Shakespeare and Goethe, and mere "ventriloquists," poets of the second rank, such as Byron, who speak only of themselves through the mouths of their characters.[56] In Hegel the same theories of the objectivity of the epic and of great classical art are expounded very prominently.[57]

In England, Coleridge took up the terms objective-subjective, reproduced the epic theory, and praised Shakespeare as a "Spinozistic deity—an omnipresent creativeness."[58] Coleridge's early friend William Hazlitt plays constant variations on the contrast between the objective poets, Shakespeare and Scott, and the subjective, Byron and Wordsworth. Scott, he tells us, is never "this opaque, obtrusive body getting in the way and eclipsing the sun of truth and nature."[59] There is a similar praise of the objective poets, Goethe and Shakespeare, in Carlyle, and his exact contemporary Keats defined the poetical character in these terms: "he has no self . . . it is everything and nothing . . . it has as much delight in conceiving an Iago as an Imogen."[60]

One cannot be sure of the exact ways in which these theories filtered into France and into the theory of the novel. The old image of the mirror is still at the center of Stendhal's theory of the novel. In a famous epigraph to a

55. Ibid., 300.
56. Ibid., 310.
57. Ibid., 324 ff.
58. *Specimens of the Table Talk* (London, 1851), p. 71; see my *History, 2,* 162.
59. *Complete Works,* ed. Howe, *16* (London, 1930), 401; see my *History, 2,* 202.
60. Ibid., *2,* 214; *Letters,* ed. M. B. Forman (Oxford 1952), p. 227 (October 27, 1818).

chapter of *Le Rouge et le noir* Stendhal called the novel a "mirror walking down the road" reflecting, one assumes, even the puddles on it, and he had used the same figure in the preface to the earlier novel *Armance*. "Is it the fault of the mirror that ugly people have passed in front of it? On whose side is the mirror?"[61] But this recommendation of literal and total imitation becomes in Flaubert and Henry James a very self-conscious prescription for the suppression of the author. The author must not comment, must not erect sign-posts telling us how we are to feel about his characters and events. For Henry James this principle is the sharp dividing line between old and new fiction. Trollope is criticised for "taking a suicidal satisfaction in reminding the reader that the story he was telling was only, after all, a make-believe." Trollope, James complains, "admits that the events he narrates have not really happened, and that he can give his narrative any turn the reader may like best. Such a betrayal of a sacred office seems to me, I confess, a terrible crime." James on the other hand commends Turgenev for being "superior to the strange and second-rate policy of explaining or presenting [his characters] by reprobation or apology." James is highly dogmatic about this method, which is to his mind absolutely necessary to the achievement of illusion in fiction, despite the fact that, unlike Flaubert, he recognizes the impossibility and even falsity of aiming at complete impersonality. "Vision and opportunity reside in a personal sense and a personal history," he tells us, "and no short cut to them in the interest of plausible fiction has ever been discovered."[62]

61. Ch. 13: "Un roman: c'est un miroir qu'on promène le long d'un chemin"; preface to *Armance*: "Est-ce leur faute si des gens laids ont passé devant ce miroir? De quel part est un miroir?" See my *History*, 2, 412.

62. *Partial Portraits* (London, 1919), pp. 116, 379; *The Future of the Novel*, ed. L. Edel (New York, 1956), p. 232; *Notes on Novelists* (New York, 1916), p. 36.

The short cuts discovered (or at least believed to be) were Flaubert's *impassibilité*, the Goncourts' exact notation, and Zola's scientific procedure. In any case Joseph Warren Beach is right in saying: "In a bird's eye view of the English novel from Fielding to Ford" (and he could have added the French, the German, the Russian, the American, etc.) "the one thing that will impress you more than any other is the disappearance of the author."[63] Fielding, Scott, Dickens, Trollope, Thackeray tell us constantly what they think of their figures and what we are to think about them. Thackeray deliberately, lovingly fingers his puppets. George Eliot tells us exactly why she does not like her frivolous, shallow, and pretty Hetty Sorrel. Laurence Sterne, a century before, had outrageously parodied all the conventions of the realist novel and had disrupted all illusion quite deliberately, juggling with the number captions of his chapters, inserting black, blank, and even marble pages and drawing a funny twisted line of the future progress of his story. The contrast with a novel such as Maupassant's *Bel-Ami* is certainly striking. Here we get the straight-faced story of a cad whose success with women leads him to wealth and honors. In the last scene, without a word of condemnation from the author, the hero is getting married to the young and wealthy daughter of his mistress in the fashionable church of La Madeleine.

Still, despite the view so fervently held by writers such as Flaubert and James (and in Italy, Verga), I hesitate to include "objectivity," in the sense of absence of the author, as an indispensable criterion of realism. It would force us to exclude Thackerary and Trollope, George Eliot and Tolstoy from realism. Käte Hamburger in her *Logik der Dichtung* (1957) has well brought out the fact that so called romantic irony, the appearance of the poet, the break of the illusion, might rather emphasize and underline the illusion of fictionality which is the aim of the novelist. The cap-

63. *The Twentieth Century Novel* (New York, 1932), p. 14.

riccios, the arabesques of the narrator do not necessarily disturb the impression of reality.[64] Certainly Sancho Panza, Uncle Toby, Becky Sharp seem more alive, more "real" than many a figure in a completely objective novel by Henry James or Joseph Conrad. Besides, the objectivity of narration, the whole attempt to approximate the novel to drama which reached such extremes as the almost completely dialogized novel, *The Awkward Age* (1899) of James, or the novel in dialogue by Pérez Galdós, *Realidad* (1890), does not necessarily mean an increase of realism in the sense of "faithful representation of social reality." The furthest consequences of the method, the stream of consciousness, the dramatizing of the mind, actually dissolve outer reality. The stream of consciousness represents rather an inward turn toward a subjective, symbolic art which is at the other pole of realism.[65]

One last criterion promises well: it is the demand that realism be "historistic." In Stendhal's *Le Rouge et le noir* (1830) man is represented, in the words of Erich Auerbach, as "embedded in a total reality, political, social, economic, which is concrete and constantly evolving."[66] Julien Sorel is placed in vital relationship to the France of the Restoration, just as Balzac sets his action within a changing society after the fall of Napoleon, or Flaubert places Frédéric Moreau in the time of the 1848 revolution. Balzac in particular has learned from the historical novel; he began as an imitator of Scott, in *Les Chouans*, and there is some truth in saying that his descriptive and analytical method is

---

64. Stuttgart, 1957, pp. 86–87.

65. Cf. L. E. Bowling, "What is the Stream of Consciousness Technique?" *PMLA*, 65 (1950), 337–45, and Melvin Friedman, *Stream of Consciousness: A Study in Literary Method* (New Haven, 1955).

66. *Mimesis* (Bern, 1946), p. 409; Eng. trans. W. R. Trask (Princeton, 1953), p. 463: "Eingebettet in eine konkrete, ständig sich entwickelnde politisch-gesellschaftlich-ökonomische Gesamtwirklichkeit."

the method of Scott applied to contemporary society. Balzac has also learned from the historians, particularly Michelet: he can speak of an "opposition of historical colors" in describing two characters,[67] and he uses historical contrasts continuously. We may remember in *Cousine Bette* the amusing discussion of the two ways of making love, before the Revolution and after the Restoration. Love-making used to be fun under the *ancien régime* and M. Hulot, the old rake, cannot understand Madame Marneffe with her conventions of the poor feeble woman, the "sister of charity."[68] But granted that this sense of history is vividly present in Balzac, and possibly in Zola and Flaubert, we may very well doubt whether the bulk of realist authors would meet the requirement of "historicism": I do not think merely of a writer such as Jane Austen, from whose novels we could not guess the existence of a French Revolution or the Napoleonic wars, or of Stifter or Raabe, who are idyllic and could be described as *Biedermeyer,* or judged by Lukács as examples of the German *Misère*. Even Tolstoy cannot be described as "historistic" in this sense. His view of man is radically antihistorical: he would like to deprive him of all institutions, historical memories, and prejudices, even of society, and reduce him to his elements. In short, Tolstoy is a thoroughgoing Rousseauist, and yet cannot and should not be excluded from "realism."[69]

We have to come to a disconcertingly trivial conclusion. Realism as a period concept, that is as a regulative idea, an ideal type which may not be completely fulfilled by any single work and will certainly in every individual work be combined with different traits, survivals from the past,

67. Ibid., p. 424: "L'opposition des teintes historiques," in *La vieille Fille*.

68. *Cousine Bette,* ch. 9.

69. On Tolstoy, see Isaiah Berlin, *The Hedgehog and the Fox* (Oxford, 1953).

anticipations of the future, and quite individual peculiarities, realism in this sense means "the objective representation of contemporary social reality." It claims to be all-inclusive in subject matter and aims to be objective in method, even though this objectivity is hardly ever achieved in practice. Realism is didactic, moralistic, reformist. Without always realizing the conflict between description and prescription it tries to reconcile the two in the concept of "type." In some writers, but not all, realism becomes historistic: it grasps social reality as dynamic evolution.

If we survey this assemblage of related traits we must ask the last question: does it meet the criterion that it should distinguish this particular period from the other periods in literary history? There seems no difficulty in a comparison with romanticism: realism definitely breaks with the romantic exaltation of the ego, with the emphasis on imagination, the symbolic method, the concern for myth, the romantic concept of animated nature. The difference between realism and classicism both in the French and German sense is less clear-cut. Classicism, like realism, wants to be objective, wants to arrive at the typical, and it is certainly didactic. But obviously realism rejects the "ideality" of classicism: it interprets "type" as a social type and not as universally human. Realism rejects the assumption of classicism that there is a scale of dignity in subject matter; it breaks with the levels of style and the social exclusions inherent in classicism. If we include in classicism the English eighteenth century it will, however, be more difficult to differentiate nineteenth-century realism very clearly from it. There is, no doubt, a direct continuity, both in ideology and artistic method, between the English novel of the eighteenth century, Fielding and Richardson in particular, and the nineteenth-century novel, which is usually called "realistic." What is new in the nineteenth century is due largely to the historical position of its productions, to its consciousness of the upheavals at the turn of the eighteenth and nineteenth centuries: the industrial revolution, the victory of the bourgeoisie (anticipated in England during the eighteenth century), the new historical sense which came with it, the far greater consciousness that man is a being living in society rather than a moral being facing God, and the change in the interpretation of nature which shifts from the deistic, purposeful, even though mechanistic world of the eighteenth century to the far more unhuman, inhuman order of deterministic nineteenth-century science. Yet in spite of these historical differences, I cannot see why Richardson and Fielding should not, stylistically, artistically deserve the designation "realist."

I said "deserve" almost inadvertently, but I want, in conclusion, to make it clear that I do not consider realism the only and ultimate method of art. It is, I should emphasize, only one method, one great stream which has its marked limitations, shortcomings, and conventions. In spite of its claim to penetrate directly to life and reality, realism, in practice, has its set conventions, devices, and exclusions. For example, on the stage realism often meant no more than the avoidance of certain improbabilities, of old stage conventions, the chance meeting, the listening at doors, the too obviously contrived contrasts of older drama. Ibsen's stage devices can be described as clearly as Racine's. Naturalistic novels in retrospect are disconcertingly similar in structure, style, and content. Still, the pitfall of realism lies not so much in the rigidity of its conventions and exclusions as in the likelihood that it might, supported as it is by its theory, lose all distinction between art and the conveyance of information or practical exhortation. When the novelist attempted to be a sociologist or propagandist he produced simply bad art, dull art; he displayed his materials inert and confused fiction with "reportage" and "documentation."

In its lower reaches realism constantly declined into journalism, treatise writing, scientific description, in short, into non-art; at its highest, with its greatest writers, with Balzac and Dickens, Dostoevsky and Tolstoy, Henry James and Ibsen, and even Zola it constantly went beyond its theory: it created worlds of imagination. The theory of realism is ultimately bad aesthetics because all art is "making" and is a world in itself of illusion and symbolic forms.

The Revolt Against Positivism in Recent European Literary Scholarship

In Europe, especially since the first World War, there has been a revolt against the methods of literary study as practiced in the second half of the nineteenth century: against the mere accumulation of unrelated facts, and against the whole underlying assumption that literature should be explained by the methods of the natural sciences, by causality, by such external determining forces as are formulated in Taine's famous slogan of *race, milieu, moment*. In Europe, this nineteenth-century scholarship is generally called "positivism": a convenient label which is, however, somewhat misleading, as by no means all older scholars were positivists in the sense of actually believing in the teachings of Comte and Spencer. If we analyze the state of scholarship at the beginning of the twentieth century, we recognize that the reaction since the twenties has been directed against three or four fairly distinct traits of traditional literary studies. There is, first, petty antiquarianism: "research" into the minutest details of the lives and quarrels of authors, parallel hunting, and source digging—in short, the accumulation of isolated facts, usually defended on the vague belief that all these bricks will sometime be used in a great pyramid of learning. It is this characteristic of traditional scholarship that has elicited most derisive criticism, but it is in itself, a harmless and even useful human activity which dates back at least as far as the Alexandrian scholars and the medieval monks. There will always be pedants and antiquaries; and their services, properly sifted, will always be needed. However, a false and pernicious "historicism" is frequently connected with this "factualism": the view that no theory or no criteria are needed in the study of the past and the view that the present age is unworthy of study or is inaccessible to study by scholarly methods. Such an exclusive "historicism" has justified a refusal even to analyze and criticize literature. It has led to a complete resignation in face of all aesthetic problems, to extreme skepticism, and hence to an anarchy of values. The alternative to this historical antiquarianism was late nineteenth-century aestheticism: it stresses the individual experience of the work of art, which is, without doubt, the presupposition of all fruitful literary study, but which in itself can lead only to complete subjectivism. It cannot bring about such a formulation of a systematic body of knowledge as will, necessarily, always remain the aim of literary scholarship. This aim was sought after by nineteenth-century scientism, by the many attempts to transfer the methods of natural science to the study of literature. This was the intellectually most coherent and respectable movement in nineteenth-century scholarship. But also here we have to distinguish several motives: one was the attempt to emulate the general scientific ideals of objectivity, impersonality, and certainty—an attempt, on the whole, supporting pre-scientific factualism. Then there was the effort to imitate the methods of natural science by a study of causal antecedents and origins which, in practice, justified the tracing of any kind of relationship as long as it was possible on chronological grounds. Applied more rigidly, scientific causality was used to explain literary phenomena by determining causes in economic, social, and political conditions. Other scholars tried even to introduce the quantitative methods of science: statistics, charts, and graphs. And finally there was a most ambitious group which made a large-scale attempt to use biological concepts in the tracing of the evolution of literature. Ferdinand Brunetière and John Addington Symonds conceived of the evolution of genres on the analogue of biological species. Thus students of literature became scientists, or rather would-be scientists. As they were late in the field and handled an intractable material, they were usually bad or second-rate scientists who felt apologetic about their subject and only vaguely hopeful about their methods of approach. This is certainly a somewhat oversimplified characterization of the situation of literary scholarship around 1900; but I dare say we all recognize its survivals today, in America and elsewhere.

In Europe, the revolt against this positivism was variously instigated. Something must have been due to the general change in the philosophical atmosphere: the old naturalism was thrust into the background in most countries when Bergson in France, Croce in Italy, and a host of men in Germany (and to a lesser extent in England) overthrew the dominance of the old positivistic philosophies in favor of a wide variety of idealistic or at least boldly speculative systems like those, to name only English examples, of Samuel Alexander and A. N. Whitehead. Especially in Germany, psychology overcame the old sensationalism and associationism by such new concepts as the *Gestalt* or *Struktur*. The natural sciences also underwent a profound transformation which it would be difficult to summarize briefly but which meant a loss of the old certainty about preconceptions on matter, the laws of nature, causality, and determinism. The fine arts themselves and the art of literature reacted against realism and naturalism in the direction of symbolism and other "modernisms" whose victory must, however slowly or indirectly, have influenced the tone and attitude of scholarship.

But, most importantly, a group of philosophers offered a positive defense of the methods of the historical sciences, which they contrasted sharply with the methods of the physical sciences. I can do little more than indicate some of their solutions, since a detailed discussion would involve such intricate questions as the classification of the sciences and the nature of scientific method. In Germany, as early as 1883, Wilhelm Dilthey[1] worked out the distinction between the methods of natural science and those of history in terms of a contrast between causal explanation and comprehension. The scientist, Dilthey argued, explains an event by its causal antecedents, while the historian tries to understand its meaning in terms of signs or symbols. The process of understanding is thus necessarily individual and even subjective. A year later, Wilhelm Windelband,[2] the well-known historian of philosophy, attacked the view that the historical sciences should imitate the methods of the natural sciences. The natural scientists, he argued, aim to establish general laws, while the historians try rather to grasp the unique and nonrecurring fact. Windelband's view was elaborated and somewhat modified by Heinrich Rickert,[3] who drew the line not so much between generalizing and individualizing methods, as between the sciences of nature and the sciences of culture. The moral sciences, he argued, are interested in the concrete and individual. Individuals, however, can be discovered and comprehended only in reference to some scheme of values, which is merely another name for culture. In France, A. D. Xénopol[4] distinguished between the natural sciences as preoccupied

1. *Einleitung in die Geisteswissenschaften* (Berlin, 1883).

2. *Geschichte und Naturwissenschaft* (Strassburg, 1894), reprinted in *Präludien, 1* (Tübingen, 1907).

3. *Die Grenzen der naturwissenschaftlichen Begriffsbildung,* (Tübingen, 1921).

4. *Les Principes fondamentaux de l'histoire* (Paris, 1894), 2nd ed., with title *La Théorie de l'histoire* (Paris, 1908).

with the "facts of repetition" and history preoccupied
with the "facts of succession." Finally in Italy, Benedetto
Croce[5] made even more sweeping claims for the method
of history. All history is to him contemporaneous, an act
of the spirit, knowable because created by man and hence
known far more certainly than the facts of nature. There
are many other theories of this type which have one feature in common: they all make a declaration of independence for history and the moral sciences against their sub-
jection to the methods of the natural sciences. They all
show that these disciplines have their own methods or
could have their own methods just as systematic and rigor-
ous as those of the natural sciences. But their aim is
different, and their method is distinct; and thus there is no
need to ape and envy the natural sciences. All these theories also agree in refusing to accept an easy solution which
many scientists and even scholars in the humanities seem
to favor. They refuse to admit that history or the study of
literature is simply an art, namely, a nonintellectual, non-
conceptual enterprise of free creation. Historical as well
as literary scholarship, though not natural science, is a
system of organized knowledge with its own methods and
aims, not a collection of creative acts or records of merely
individual impressions.

Let us now glance at the different countries of Europe
to see how far their reactions have gone in each case and
what alternatives have been proposed to the methods of
nineteenth-century literary scholarship. I shall be forced
to ignore or pass over lightly some countries; but, in spite
of these limitations, something like a spiritual map of Europe should emerge if literary scholarship is at all an
indication of the general intellectual situation of a country.

I shall begin with France since France seems to me the

5. *Teoria e storia della storiografia* (Bari, 1917), Eng. trans. Douglas Ainslie, *History: Its Theory and Practice* (New York, 1923).

country least affected by this revolt. The reasons for this possibly surprising French conservativism are not far to seek. France was never overwhelmed by the invasion of organized German literary factualism; and her literary historians, however naturalistic in their aims, preserved an admirable aesthetic and critical sense. Ferdinand Brunetière, though deeply influenced by biological evolutionism, managed to remain a classicist and a Catholic; and Gustave Lanson combined a scientific ideal with conceptions of a national soul and its spiritual aspirations. Factualism most nearly triumphed in France just after the first World War: the heavily documented *thèse;* the wide ramifications of a well-organized school of comparative literature, inspired by Fernand Baldensperger; the successes of scholars who furnished extremely elaborate editions of French classics;[6] the theories of Daniel Mornet, who demanded an "integral" literary history of the minor and even minimal authors— all these are symptoms that France tried to catch up with the purely historical scholarship of the nineteenth century But also in France there are signs of a change which tends, as everywhere, in two directions: towards a new synthesis and a new analysis. French literary historians excelled especially in boldly sketched intellectual histories. For instance, Paul Hazard's *La Crise de la conscience européenne*[7] is a skillful exposition of the change which came over Europe at the end of the seventeenth-century, and Hazard works with the conception of a European mind incomprehensible to the old positivistic methods. Naturalism was also thrown to the winds in the studies by professed Catholics such as Etienne Gilson[8] of the effects of scholasticism

6. For instance, Abel Le Franc's *Rabelais,* Pierre Villey's edition of the *Essais* of Montaigne, Daniel Mornet's edition of Rousseau's *Nouvelle Héloise.*

7. 3 vols. Paris, 1934, Eng. trans. *The European Mind: The Critical Years, 1680–1715* (New Haven, 1953).

8. *Les Idées et les lettres* (Paris, 1932).

on literature or by Abbé Bremond[9] in his voluminous *Literary History of the Religious Sentiment in France*. In more narrowly literary studies, Louis Cazamian[10] has even tried to construct a speculative scheme of a psychological evolution of the history of English literature conceived as a series of increasingly speedy oscillations of the English national mind between the poles of sentiment and intellect. Whatever we may think of the success of the scheme in its particular application (and I for one feel that it does violence to the complex reality of literary changes), here was at least an attempt at an almost metaphysical philosophy of history applied to literature. Paul Van Tieghem[11] has promoted the conception of "general literature," opposed to the isolated and isolating study of influences as practiced by the comparatists: a concept which assumes the unity of the Western European literary tradition. His own practice is, however, disappointingly conventional, since he merely traces literary fashions such as Ossianism through all European countries. Also in more purely analytical studies of literature I know of little evidence of a complete reorientation. The method of *explication de textes* (which must be welcomed as an early progenitor of the wholesome back-to-the-text movement in recent literary studies) is too narrowly philological and exegetical to be more than a useful device of literary pedagogy.

Things look very different in Italy. There the influence

9. *L'Histoire du sentiment religieux en France* (11 vols. Paris, 1923-33), partial Eng. trans. as *A Literary History of Religious Thought in France* (3 vols. New York, 1928–36).

10. *L'Évolution psychologique de la littérature en Angleterre* (Paris, 1920), and the second half of E. Legouis and L. Cazamian, *Histoire de la littérature anglaise* (Paris, 1924), Eng. trans. H. D. Irvine (2 vols. London, 1926–27).

11. "La Synthèse en histoire littéraire: Littérature comparée et littérature générale," *Revue de synthèse historique, 31* (1921). *Le Préromantisme* (3 vols. Paris, 1924–47).

of an idealist philosopher who was himself a distinguished historian and literary critic has transformed literary studies. Benedetto Croce[12] wrote frequently on questions of literary scholarship from his first booklet on literary criticism in 1894 until his death in 1952, consistently arguing against the mechanical and uncritical practices of the routine scholarship of his time. He revived interest in Francesco de Sanctis, the Hegelian historian of Italian literature. He focused attention sharply on the aesthetic and theoretical problems of literature without losing a very intense sense of the past. He himself contributed notably to literary criticism with studies of Dante, Ariosto, Shakespeare, Corneille, Goethe, and a very severe review of nineteenth-century poetry. In detail, however, many of his theories seem to me steps in a wrong direction. His theory of art as expression led to a dismissal of such real questions as literary genres or literary evolution. His sharp distinction[13] between poetry and literature seems quite untenable. Croce demands a history of poetry which would be little more than applied poetics, and a history of literature which would be a part of the history of civilization. It seems impossible to uphold such a distinction, breaking up literature into a series of peaks of poetry and into valleys divided by some impenetrable bank of clouds. Croce's excessive individualism and expressionism explain why recent Italian scholarship has turned largely to an aesthetic and spiritual biography. Bertoni, Donadoni, Luigi Russo, and the more independent Borgese have all produced rather monographs and critical essays than literary history. One

12. "La critica letteraria" (1894), reprinted in *Primi Saggi* (Bari 1919); *La Poesia di Dante* (Bari, 1920); *Ariosto, Shakespeare e Corneille* (Bari, 1920); *Goethe* (Bari, 1919); *Poesia e non poesia* (Bari, 1923).

13. *La Poesia. Introduzione alla Critica e Storia della Poesia e della Letteratura* (Bari, 1936).

of the most gifted critics, Mario Praz,[14] even represents a return to a spiritualized psychography. His studies of Marlowe, Donne, and Crashaw as well as the book called in English *The Romantic Agony,* but more correctly described by its Italian title as treating of *Flesh, Death, and the Devil in Romantic Literature,* are fine achievements of a subtly psychoanalytical method. On the whole, the new idealism seems to have prevailed in Italy almost completely: it has even permeated literary journalism and that refractory science, linguistics. Its general speculative method has affected even those who have remained unconvinced by the systems of Croce or Gentile.

The situation in England is less easily classifiable. In England there prevail two traditions in literary scholarship: pure antiquarianism, which, with the method of the new "bibliography" (textual and "higher" criticism, mostly of Shakespeare) as practiced by W. W. Greg and Dover Wilson, became very influential in recent decades, and the personal critical essay which frequently degenerated into the display of sheer irresponsible whimsicality. In England the distrust of the intellect and of any organized knowledge has gone apparently further than in any other country, at least in academic scholarship. Resignation in the face of any more difficult and abstract problem, unlimited skepticism as to the possibilities of a rational approach to poetry, and hence a complete absence of any thinking on fundamental problems of methodology seem to have been characteristic, at least of the older group of scholars. To take one example: H. W. Garrod[15] asserts that poetry is

14. "Christopher Marlowe," *English Studies, 13* (1931); *Secentismo e Marinismo in Inghilterra* (Florence, 1925); *La Carne, la Morte e il Diavolo nella Letteratura Romantica* (Milan, 1930); cf. Eng. trans. Angus Davidson, *The Romantic Agony* (London, 1933).

15. *The Profession of Poetry* (Oxford, 1929), p. 47; *Poetry and the Criticism of Life* (Oxford, 1931), pp. 156–57.

"a subtle something or nothing" and that criticism is best which is written with the "least worry of head, the least disposition to break the heart over ultimate questions." Those who occasionally reflected on the implications of their work end either, like Sir Arthur Quiller-Couch, in a vague religious mysticism, or, like F. L. Lucas,[16] in pure aesthetic impressionism and subjectivism.

But also in England a reaction has taken place which has gone in two different directions: one is the method of I. A. Richards, propounded in his *Principles of Literary Criticism* (1924) and best applied in his *Practical Criticism* (1929). Richards is, of course, primarily a psychologist and semanticist who is interested in the therapeutic effects of poetry, in the reader's response and the patterning of his impulses. The implications of his theory are entirely naturalistic and positivistic; at times he refers us, with an almost desperate naïveté, to the "hidden jungles of neurology." It is difficult to see of what use this supposedly poised state of mind of the reader is for the study of literature, as Richards himself has to admit that it can be induced by almost any object or movement, irrespective of its aesthetic intent. But every theory which puts the onus on the effects in the individual mind of the reader is bound to lead to a complete anarchy of values and ultimately to barren skepticism. Richards has himself drawn this conclusion, saying that "it is less important to like 'good' poetry and to dislike 'bad' than to be able to use them both as a means of ordering our minds."[17] This would mean that poetry is good or bad according to my momentary psychic needs; and anarchy is the logical consequence of refusing to see the objec-

16. *The Poet as Citizen and other Papers* (Cambridge, 1934), p. 134; and F. L. Lucas, "Criticism," in *Life and Letters*, 3 (1929), 433–65; *The Criticism of Poetry* (London, 1933).

17. *Principles of Literary Criticism* (London, 1924), p. 120; *Practical Criticism* (London, 1929), p. 349.

tive structure of a work of art. Luckily, in his critical practice Mr. Richards ignores his theory most of the time. He has understood the wholeness and multiple meaning of a work of art and has inspired others to put his techniques of analysis of meaning to new uses.

His best pupil, William Empson, has done in his *Seven Types of Ambiguity*[18] more than anybody else to inaugurate the subtle and sometimes even overingenious analyses of poetic diction and its implications which are flourishing today both in England and in the United States. F. R. Leavis, former editor of the Cambridge *Scrutiny* and influential teacher, has applied the methods of Richards with much sensitiveness and has combined them with a revaluation of the history of English poetry begun, with dogmatic assurance, in the essays of T. S. Eliot.[19] Without giving up Richards' methods of interpreting poetry, Leavis has abandoned his pseudo-scientific apparatus. Without giving up Eliot's critical attitude towards modern civilization, Leavis has refused to follow him into the camp of Anglo-Catholicism. His stress on the unity of a work of art, his conception of tradition, his sharp rejection of an artificial distinction between literary history and criticism are all leading traits of the antipositivistic movement. Geoffrey Tillotson[20] has also applied the methods of close inspection of the text derived from Richards to the poetry of Pope with great sensitivity and much power of discrimination. But in the

18. (London, 1930); see also *Some Versions of Pastoral* (London, 1935).

19. *How to Teach Reading* (London, 1932); *New Bearings in English Poetry* (London, 1932); *Revaluation: Tradition and Development in English Poetry* (London, 1936). See my paper "Literary Criticism and Philosophy," *Scrutiny*, 5 (1937), 375–83.

20. *On the Poetry of Pope* (Oxford, 1939); *Essays in Criticism and Research* (Cambridge, 1942); cf. my review in *Modern Philology, 41* (1944), 261–63.

preface to a volume of *Essays in Criticism and Research* he has defended a confused theory of historical reconstruction, and his own practice remains mostly on a level of atomistic uncorrelated observations.

A different approach to literary study in England is affiliated with the revival of neo-Hegelianism and its conception of dialectical evolution. The great medievalist, W. P. Ker,[21] in his last books, began to expound the conception of an evolution of genre as an almost Platonic pattern. Learnedly and skillfully, C. S. Lewis, in his *Allegory of Love,*[22] has combined an evolutionary scheme of genre history with the history of man's attitude towards love and marriage. Lewis, furthermore, has argued wittily against the "personal heresy in criticism," the common overrating of the biographical and psychological context of literature. It seems a pity that Lewis, in his recent work, has come to the defense of genteel convention and has attacked most that is vital in modern literature. The one Englishman who has shown a clear awareness of the problem of a history of literature which would not be a mere mirror of social change is F. W. Bateson, to whom all English scholars owe a debt of gratitude for editing the *Cambridge Bibliography of English Literature.* In *The English Language and English Poetry,*[23] he has criticized the "absence of all discrimination and the total lack of a sense of proportion in modern scholarship" and the mistake of nineteenth-century historians of regarding literature as simply the product of social forces. His own remedy, a history of English poetry

21. *Form and Style in Poetry,* ed. R. W. Chambers (London, 1928).

22. Oxford, 1936; C. S. Lewis and E. M. Tillyard, *The Personal Heresy: A Controversy* (Oxford, 1934); *Rehabilitations* (London, 1939).

23. Oxford, 1934.

in close connection with linguistic change, is less convincing as Mr. Bateson thus reintroduced a one-sided dependence of literary evolution on a single outside force. But he has at least radically broken with positivistic preconceptions and suggested the central problem of a genuine literary history.

Also in the history of ideas closely connected with literary history, new viewpoints and methods begin to prevail in England. Basil Willey's *Seventeenth Century Background*[24] is written almost as if to illustrate the thesis of T. S. Eliot about the unified sensibility of the seventeenth century and its disintegration in its latter half. Willey's book certainly implies a strongly antinaturalistic conception of human history and poetry. On the whole, however, the revolt against positivism in England is unsystematic, erratic, and frequently quite unclear as to its philosophical implications and affiliations. Theory seems still too much obsessed by a vaguely neurological psychology. But at least dissatisfaction with the old type of scholarship is widespread.

The situation is very different in Germany. There, more so than in any other country, a veritable battle of methods was fought from the beginning of the twentieth century. Germany, which had been the motherland of philology and has been the bastion of philological literary history in the nineteenth century, reacted most sharply and most violently against its methods. This reaction went in all possible directions, going, as it is apparently usual in Germany, to almost unimaginable extremes. One group moved furthest in its contempt for traditional scholarship: the circle which gathered around the poet Stefan George and cultivated an abject adoration for his mission, an extravagant heroworship for a few great figures of the past, and a studied

24. London, 1934. *The Eighteenth Century Background* (London, 1940) is less distinguished.

neglect of the ordinary processes of patient research and slow induction. Friedrich Gundolf[25] is their greatest scholar; his complete disdain of footnotes and references should not disguise his extraordinary learning. His earliest book on *Shakespeare and the German Spirit* is, to my mind, his best. It is a history of the influence of Shakespeare on German literature conceived of as a play and tension of spiritual forces illustrated by brilliant stylistic analyses of German translations and imitations. In his later books on Goethe, George, and Kleist, Gundolf developed a method of spiritual biography which he called statuesque and monumental. Mind and work are conceived as a unity and interpreted in a scheme of dialectical opposites which construct a myth or legend rather than a living man. Ernst Bertram,[26] a follower of Gundolf, has openly called his book on Nietzsche an attempt at a mythology.

Far less purely intuitive and arbitrary in their constructions are the German scholars whose interest centered on the problem of style, which is, of course, conceived by them not in purely descriptive terms but as the expression of a mind or a recurrent artistic or a unique historical type. German scholars in the Romance languages, partly under the influence of Croce, have developed a type of linguistics which they call "idealistic," where linguistic and artistic creation are identified. Karl Vossler[27] has given examples of such studies, which interpret, for instance, the whole development of French civilization in terms of a close unity between linguistic and artistic evolution; and Leo

25. *Shakespeare und der deutsche Geist* (Berlin, 1911); *Goethe* (Berlin, 1916); *George* (Berlin, 1920); *Heinrich von Kleist* (Berlin, 1922).

26. *Nietzsche, Versuch einer Mythologie* (Berlin, 1920).

27. *Frankreichs Kultur im Spiegel seiner Sprachentwicklung* (Heidelberg, 1913); *Positivismus und Idealismus in der Sprachwissenschaft* (Heidelberg, 1904).

Spitzer[28] has studied the style of many French authors in order to arrive at psychological and typological conclusions. Among students of German literature, attempts were rather made to define broadly historical stylistic types. Oskar Walzel[29] was, I believe, the first to apply the stylistic criteria evolved by the art historian, Heinrich Wölfflin,[30] to the history of literature. Through him and several others the term "baroque" spread to the history of literature, and periods and styles of literary history were described in terms of the corresponding periods of art history. Fritz Strich[31] has applied the method with the greatest success in a book on *German Classicism and Romanticism*. According to Strich, the baroque characteristics hold good of romanticism, the Renaissance, of classicism. Strich interprets Wölfflin's contraries of closed and open form as analogues to the opposition between the complete classical form and the open, unfinished, fragmentary, and blurred form of romantic poetry expressive of man's longing for the infinite. In detail, Strich is full of subtle remarks and observations, but his general construction will not withstand closer criticism. Of more permanent value are several excellent stylistic histories of genres produced in Germany: Karl Vietor's *History of the German Ode*[32] and Günther Müller's *History of German Song*,[33] and the many studies of single literary

28. *Stilstudien* (2 vols. Munich, 1928); *Romanische Stil- und Literaturstudien* (2 vols. Marburg, 1931).

29. *Wechselseitige Erhellung der Künste* (Berlin, 1917); *Gehalt und Gestalt im Kunstwerk des Dichters* (Berlin-Potsdam, 1923); *Das Wortkunstwerk* (Leipzig, 1926).

30. *Kunstgeschichtliche Grundbegriffe* (Munich, 1915); Eng. trans. M. D. Hottinger, *Principles of Art History* (London, 1932).

31. *Deutche Klassik und Romantik, oder Vollendung und Unendlichkeit* (Munich, 1922).

32. *Geschichte der deutschen Ode* (Munich, 1923).

33. *Geschichte des deutschen Liedes* (Munich, 1925).

devices such as Hermann Pongs' *The Image in Poetry*.[34] With Vossler and Strich analysis of style clearly passes into general intellectual history.

This general intellectual history is another extremely diversified and productive movement in German scholarship. Partly it is simply the history of philosophy as mirrored in literature which is now being studied by men of real philosophical training and insight. In this field Wilhelm Dilthey was a leader; Ernst Cassirer, Rudolf Unger, and, in classical philology, Werner Jaeger—to name only a few —can point to achievements probably unequaled in the history of literary scholarship.[35] Partly there developed, mostly owing to the efforts of Rudolf Unger,[36] a less purely intellectualist approach to the history of attitudes toward such eternal problems as death, love, and fate. Unger, who has strong religious interests, has given an example of the method in a little book tracing the changes and continuities of the attitude toward death in Herder, Novalis, and Kleist; and his followers, Paul Kluckhohn[37] and Walther Rehm,[38] have developed the method on a large scale in studies of the concept of death and love, which are conceived as having their own logic and dialectical evolution. These scholars are writing a history of sensibility and sentiment as mirrored in literature rather than a history of literature itself.

34. *Das Bild in der Dichtung* (2 vols. Marburg, 1927–34).

35. *Gesammelte Schriften* (12 vols. Berlin, 1923–36); Ernst Cassirer, *Idee und Gestalt* (Berlin, 1921), *Freiheit und Form* (Berlin, 1922); Rudolf Unger, *Hamann und die deutsche Aufklärung* (2 vols. Halle, 1911); Werner Jaeger, *Paideia: Die Formung des griechischen Menschen*, (3 vols. Berlin, 1934–47), Eng. trans. G. Highet, *Paideia: The Ideals of Greek Culture* (3 vols. New York, 1939–44).

36. *Herder, Novalis, Kleist* (Frankfurt, 1922); *Literaturgeschichte als Problemgeschichte* (Berlin, 1924).

37. *Die Auffassung der Liebe in der Literatur des achtzehnten Jahrhunderts und in der Romantik* (Halle, 1922).

38. *Der Todesgedanke in der deutschen Dichtung* (Halle, 1928).

But most German literary historians have come to cultivate the "history of the spirit," *Geistesgeschichte,* which
aims to reconstruct, to quote one exponent, the "spirit of a
time from the different objectifications of an age—from religion through literature and the arts down to costumes and
customs. We look for the totality behind the objects, and
explain all facts by the time-spirit."[39] Thus a universal
analogizing between all human activities is at the very center of the method which has stimulated a flood of writings
on the "Gothic" man, the spirit of the baroque, and the
nature of romanticism. In a wider field, Oswald Spengler's
Decline of the West is the best known example. In German
literary history, a book by H. A. Korff,[40] *The Spirit of the
Age of Goethe,* might be singled out as a boldly speculative attempt which manages to keep in touch with the
texts and facts of literary history. The Hegelian Idea is the
hero of the book, and its dialectical evolution through its
symbolical expression in individual works of art is traced
with great skill and surprising lucidity. Unquestionably the
method can be and has been abused. To give only one
example: Paul Meissner's book[41] on the English literary
baroque has used the simple formula of antithesis and tension quite uncritically. He pursues it through all human
activities from traveling to religion, from diary writing to
music. All the wealth of materials is neatly ordered into

39. M. W. Eppelsheimer, "Das Renaissanceproblem," *Deutsche
Vierteljahrschrift für Literaturwissenschaft und Geistesgeschichte
11* (1933), 497.

40. *Geist der Goethezeit, Versuch einer ideellen Entwicklung der
klassisch-romantischen Literaturgeschichte* (5 vols. Leipzig, 1923,
1930, 1940, 1953, 1957).

41. *Die geisteswissenschaftlichen Grundlagen des englischen Literaturbarocks* (Berlin, 1934). A fuller discussion of *Geistesgeschichte*
may be found in my "Parallelism between Literature and the Fine
Arts," in *English Institute Annual, 1941* (New York, 1942), and in
my and Austin Warren's *Theory of Literature* (New York, 1949).

categories such as expansion and concentration, macrocosmos and microcosmos, sin and salvation, faith and reason. Meissner never raises the obvious question whether the same scheme of contraries could not be extracted from any period or whether the same material could not be arranged into a very different scheme of contraries. There are many books of this type in Germany, for example, Max Deutschbein's[42] or Georg Stefansky's[43] volumes intuiting the essence of romanticism. They sometimes abound in learning and insight but construct fantastic houses of cards. The many writings by Herbert Cysarz[44] which include books on experience and idea in German literature, on German baroque poetry, and on Schiller are probably the most pretentious examples of wide learning, considerable speculative power, and even critical sensibility gone wild in an orgy of oracular declamation and abstract hair splitting.

Seemingly on the opposite pole of these metaphysical intuitionists we find a whole group of German scholars who have tried to rewrite the history of German literature in terms of its biological and racial affiliations. One might list them among the belated positivists and pseudo-scientists, if their concept of the German race or tribe were not essentially ideological and even mystical. A writer whose original affiliations were conservative and Catholic, Josef Nadler,[45] has written a new history of German literature "from below," according to the tribes, districts, and cities, always constructing tribal souls of the different German "regions."

42. *Das Wesen des Romantischen* (Cöthen, 1921).

43. *Das Wesen der deutschen Romantik* (Stuttgart, 1923).

44. *Erfahrung und Idee* (Vienna, 1921); *Deutsche Barockdichtung* (Leipzig, 1924); *Literaturgeschichte als Geisteswissenschaft* (Halle, 1926); *Schiller* (Halle, 1934).

45. *Literaturgeschichte der deutschen Stämme und Landschaften* (4 vols. Regensburg, 1912–28); A later nazified edition is called *Literaturgeschichte des deutschen Volkes* (4 vols. 1938–42); cf. also *Die Berliner Romantik* (Berlin, 1921).

Actually, his main thesis is a somewhat fantastic philosophy of German history: Western Germany, which has been settled since Julius Caesar, tried to recapture classical antiquity in German classicism; Eastern Germany, Slavic in its racial basis and Germanized securely only since the eighteenth century, tried rather, through the romantic period, to recapture the culture of medieval Germany. Romanticists, according to Nadler, come all from the East of Germany; and if they don't (as, unfortunately for his theory, a good many don't) they are simply not genuine romanticists. But it would be unfair to Nadler not to stress his genuine merits: he has revived interest in the submerged and neglected Catholic South, he has a fine power of racy characterization and a sense for locality which is not at all useless in the study of the older frequently very local German literature. His conceptions seem to have prepared the way for Nazi literary history. Their point of view has come to the fore only since 1933, when fanatics and opportunists began to discover the possibilities of Nazi ideology for the purposes of literary history. The more obvious features of their revaluation of literary history need no description: their elimination or denigration of Jews, their stress on the anticipation of Nazi doctrines in the past, their contortions in fitting inconvenient but unavoidable figures like Goethe into this pattern.[46] It would be, however, an error to consider Nazi literary history simply as racialist, a pseudo-scientific explanation of literary processes. Most German literary historians of the 1930s and 1940s managed to combine racialism with old romantic conceptions of the national soul, and even with categories derived from *Geistesgeschichte* and the history of artistic styles. Though I do not wish to deny that individuals continued to produce good

46. H. G. Atkins, *German Literature through Nazi Eyes* (London, 1941).

work in the established methods and that some non-Nazis paid merely lip-service to the official creed, the general level of German literary scholarship declined seriously in the period from 1933 to 1945. A mixture of resentful propaganda, racial mysticism, and romantic boasting characterized its standard productions. Happily, since the end of the war, a reaction against the type of criticism fostered by the Third Reich has been in full force. On the whole, Germany represented the most baffling variety of schools and methods, a lively debating ground and experimenters' shop, in which everybody seems to have been sharply aware of the philosophical issues involved and was filled with a proud consciousness of the importance of literary scholarship.

Probably the least known developments are those of the Slavic countries. This is in part due simply to the linguistic barriers and, of course, also to the very real gulf which has divided Western Europe from Russia, especially since the Bolshevik revolution. Russia, during the nineteenth century, produced a fine school of comparative literary historians, headed by Alexander Veselovsky,[47] who tried to write a natural history of literary forms drawing very largely from their studies of the abundant Slavic folklore. Besides, there flourished a metaphysical, or rather ideological, criticism which many English readers will know from one example: Nikolay Berdayev's book on Dostoevsky.[48] In reaction against this either naturalistic-biological or religious-metaphysical study of literature, there arose, around 1916, a movement which called itself "formalism." It is mainly opposed to the prevailing didacticism of Russian literary criticism; and, under the Bolsheviks, it was

47. *Istoricheskaya Poetika* (Historical Poetics), ed. V. Zhirmunsky (Leningrad, 1940).
48. Eng. trans. (from the French) Donald Attwater (New York, 1934).

no doubt also a silent protest against or at least an escape from Marxist historical materialism prescribed by the party. The school of Formalists was suppressed around 1930; and there are, I believe, no open practitioners left in present-day Russia. Formalism was affiliated with Russian Futurism and, in its more technical aspects, with the new structural linguistics. The literary work of art is conceived by them as the "sum of all the devices employed in it"; metrical structure, style, composition, all elements usually called form, but also the choice of topic, characterization, setting, plot, usually considered matter, are all treated equally as artistic means to the achievement of a certain effect. All these devices have a double character: organizing and de-forming. If, for example, a linguistic element (sound, sentence construction, etc.) is used just as it is in common language it will not attract attention; but as soon as the poet distorts it, by subjecting it to a certain organization, it will attract attention and thus become the object of aesthetic perception. The work of art and its specific "literariness" is resolutely put into the center of literary studies, and all its biographical and social relationships are minimized or considered as purely external. All the formalists have developed methods of astonishing ingenuity for analyzing sound-patterns, metrical systems of the different languages, principles of composition, types of poetic diction, etc., mostly in close collaboration with the new functional linguistics which developed "phonemics," now flourishing also in America. To give a few examples: Roman Jakobson[49] has put metrics on an entirely new basis by rejecting the purely acoustic or musical methods and by studying it in close connection with meaning and the phonetic system of the different languages. Viktor Shklovsky[50] has analyzed types of fiction and their technical devices in such terms

49. See esp. *O cheshskom stiche* (On Czech Verse) (Berlin, 1923).
50. *O Teoriyi prozy* (The Theory of Prose) (Moscow, 1925).

as the "deformation" of ordinary time sequence, the accumulation of obstacles for delaying action, etc. Osip Brik[51] has specialized in ingenious studies of sound-patterns which he sees as determining and being determined by diction and meter. Viktor Zhirmunsky and Boris Tomashevsky[52] have studied the theory and history of Russian versification and rhyme. Eikhenbaum and Tynyanov[53] have applied these techniques to an investigation of Russian works of literature which has put its history into a completely new light. The Russian formalists have also faced most resolutely and clearly the problem of literary history conceived as distinct from a mere history of manners and civilization in the mirror of literature. Profiting from Hegelian and Marxist dialectic but rejecting its universalizing dogmatism, they have written histories of genres and devices in purely literary terms. Literary history is for them the history of literary tradition and of literary devices. Each work of art is studied against the background of or as a reaction against preceding works of art, as the formalists conceive of the evolution of literature as a self-evolving process which maintains only external relations to the history of society or the individual experiences of the authors. New forms appear to them apotheoses of inferior genres. For example, Dostoevsky's novels are simply exalted crime stories, and Pushkin's

51. Papers in Opoyaz: *Sbornik pro teoriyi poeticheskogo yazyka* (A symposium on the theory of the language of poetry) (Leningrad, 1916, 1917, and 1919); The last volume is called *Poetika*.

52. Viktor Zhirmunsky, *Rifma, yeye istoriya i teoriya* (Rhyme: Its History and Theory) (Leningrad, 1923); *Byron i Pushkin* (Leningrad, 1924); Boris Tomashevsky, *Russkoye stikhoslozhenye* (Russian Metrics) (Leningrad, 1923); *Teoriya literatury* (Leningrad, 1925).

53. Boris Eikhenbaum, *Molodoy Tolstoy* (The Young Tolstoy) (Leningrad, 1922); *Literatura: teoriya, kritika, polemika* (Leningrad, 1926); *Lev Tolstoy* (2 vols. Leningrad, 1931); Yuriy Tynyanov, *Problema stikhotvornogo jazyka* (The Problem of Poetic Language). (Leningrad, 1924).

lyrics are glorified album verses. The more conservative wing among the group has done excellent work even on such traditional questions as the influence of Byron on Pushkin, which Zhirmunsky conceived of not as a series of parallel passages but as the relation of two totalities. The more brilliant and more radical members have not avoided the dangers of shrill overstatement and rigid dogmatism. They certainly minimized the philosophical and ethical aspects of literature. But Russian formalism was, at least, an important antidote against the official Marxist interpretation of literature. The average Marxist critic seems to me only a revived positivist. He usually indulges in more or less ingenious exercises in the game of fixing this or that literary work of art in this or that particular stage of economic development. The causal relationship between society and literature is put in crudely deterministic terms. But the subtler practitioners, such as P. Sakulin, remained literary while being genuinely preoccupied with sociology. Sakulin's *History of Russian Literature*[54] traces the history of art in close connection with the audience and class to which it appealed and to the social strata from which the artists were derived. The process is seen as a dialectical tension of art and society and as the successive rise of the lower classes to literary productivity.

Russian formalism influenced profoundly the two other Slavic countries I know. In Poland, Roman Ingarden[55] has written an extremely subtle analysis of the poetic work of art, using the terminology of German phenomenology as developed by Edmund Husserl. Ingarden conceives of the work of art as a system of strata which rise from the sound

54. *Geschichte der russischen Literatur* (Berlin, 1927), in Oskar Walzel's *Handbuch der Literaturwissenschaft.*
55. *Das dichterische Kunstwerk* (Halle, 1931); *O poznawaniu dziela literackiego* (About Knowing a Literary Work of Art) (Lwów, 1937).

pattern towards the metaphysical qualities which emerge finally from its totality. Ingarden is a speculative philosopher remote from the practice of literary history. More technical literary history had been primarily ideological and nationalistic. But Manfred Kridl[56] has produced and inspired many formalistic studies employing the Russian methods and has written a powerful attack on the study of literature by nonliterary methods. His own "integrally literary" method minimizes the social bearings of literature consistently and revolts against the confusion of methods prevalent in most literary history.

Czechoslovakia, the last country on our list, was fortunate to receive one of the most original and productive members of the Russian formalist school, Roman Jakobson. Jakobson was able to affiliate with a group of Czechs who, even before his arrival, had reacted against the dominant historical, ideological, or psychological methods of the study of literature. The Prague Linguistic Circle was organized in 1926 under the chairmanship of Vilém Mathesius. The members of the circle applied the methods of literary study developed by the Russians to new materials but also tried to reformulate them more philosophically. They replaced the term "formalism" by "structuralism" (which in English has its own difficulties), and they combined the purely formalistic approach with sociological and ideological methods. The most productive member of the school was Jan Mukařovský,[57] who has not only produced brilliant studies of individual works of poetry, the history of Czech metrics,

56. *Wstęp do badań nad dzielem literackiem* (Introduction to the Investigation of the Literary Work of Art) (Wilno, 1936).

57. *Máchův Máj, Estetická studie* (Mácha's May, An Aesthetic Study) (Prague, 1928); *Estetická funkce, norma a hodnota jako sociální fakty* (Aesthetic Function, Norm and Value as Social Facts) (Prague, 1936); "L'Art comme fait sémiologique," in *Actes du huitième congrès international de philosophie* (Prague, 1936), 1065–72.

and poetic diction, but also has speculated interestingly on fitting the formalistic theory into a whole philosophy of symbolic forms, and on combining it with a social approach which would see the relationship between social and literary evolution as a dialectical tension. I trust that my view is not falsified by years of membership in the Prague circle, if I express my conviction that here in the close cooperation with modern linguistics and with modern philosophy were the germs of a fruitful development of literary studies.

Our survey of the new methods of literary study practiced in Europe had to be very hasty and even sketchy. A whole volume could be written on each individual country.[58] But perhaps this sketch has suggested at least some feeling of the bewildering variety of methods which are, or rather were, being cultivated in Europe. It may have pointed out at least some of the major, very striking differences among seven European countries. Possibly it has also suggested some fundamental similarities among these movements. Their directions are not only negative ones of reaction. There is a new will for synthesis, for speculative daring, for philosophical penetration; and there is also a new desire for closer and closer analysis of the actual work of art in its

58. I know of no similar survey of recent scholarship. Individual countries or groups of scholars are treated in Phillipe van Tieghem's *Nouvelles Tendances en histoire littéraire* (Paris, 1930); J. Petersen's *Die Wesensbestimmung der deutschen Romantik* (Leipzig, 1926); Werner Mahrholz's *Literaturgeschichte und Literaturwissenschaft* (2nd ed. Leipzig, 1932); Martin Schütze's *Academic Illusions* (Chicago, 1933); H. Rossner's *Georgekreis und Literaturwissenschaft* (Frankfurt, 1938); Horst Oppel's *Die Literaturwissenschaft in der Gegenwart* (Stuttgart, 1939); V. Zhirmunsky, "Formprobleme in der russischen Literaturwissenschaft," *Zeitschrift für slavische Philologie, 1* (1925); Nina Gourfinkel, "Nouvelles Méthodes d'histoire littéraire en Russie," *Le Monde Slave, 6* (1929); Manfred Kridl, "Russian Formalism," *American Bookman, 1* (1944); Max Wehrli, *Allgemeine Literaturwissenschaft* (Bern, 1951); Victor Erlich, *Russian Formalism* (The Hague, 1955).

totality and unity. Both these expansions and concentrations are healthy signs, though I am the last to deny that, in its extreme forms, the reaction has its own dangers. Bold speculations, sweeping vistas, subtle analyses, and sensitive judgments may make us forget the necessity of a solid understructure in a wide knowledge of relevant facts which the old philology, at its best, tended to produce. We want not less scholarship and less knowledge, but more scholarship, more intelligent scholarship, centered on the main problems which arise in the study of literature, both as an art and as an expression of our civilization.

The Crisis of Comparative Literature

The world (or rather our world) has been in a state of permanent crisis since, at least, the year 1914. Literary scholarship, in its less violent, muted ways, has been torn by conflicts of methods since about the same time. The old certainties of nineteenth-century scholarship, its ingenuous belief in the accumulations of facts, any facts, in the hope that these bricks will be used in the building of the great pyramid of learning, its trust in causal explanation on the model of the natural sciences, had been challenged sharply even before: by Croce in Italy, by Dilthey and others in Germany. Thus no claim can be made that recent years have been exceptional or even that the crisis of literary scholarship has reached anywhere a point of solution or even temporary accommodation. Still, a re-examination of our aims, and methods is needed. There is something symbolic to the passing, in the last decade, of several of the masters: Van Tieghem, Farinelli, Vossler, Curtius, Auerbach, Carré, Baldensperger, and Spitzer.

The most serious sign of the precarious state of our study is the fact that it has not been able to establish a distinct subject matter and a specific methodology. I believe that the programmatic pronouncements of Baldensperger, Van Tieghem, Carré, and Guyard have failed in this essential task. They have saddled comparative literature with an obsolete methodology and have laid on it the dead hand of nineteenth-century factualism, scientism, and historical relativism.

Comparative literature has the immense merit of com-

bating the false isolation of national literary histories: it is
obviously right (and has brought a mass of evidence to
support this) in its conception of a coherent Western tradition of literature woven together in a network of innumerable
interrelations. But I doubt that the attempt to distinguish
between "comparative" and "general" literature, made by
Van Tieghem, can succeed. According to Van Tieghem
"comparative" literature is confined to the study of interrelations between *two* literatures while "general" literature is
concerned with the movements and fashions which sweep
through *several* literatures. Surely this distinction is quite
untenable and impracticable. Why should, say, the influence
of Walter Scott in France be considered "comparative" literature while a study of the historical novel during the Romantic age be "general" literature? Why should we distinguish
between a study of the influence of Byron on Heine and the
study of Byronism in Germany? The attempt to narrow
"comparative literature" to a study of the "foreign trade"
of literatures is surely unfortunate. Comparative literature
would be, in subject matter, an incoherent group of unrelated fragments: a network of relations which are constantly
interrupted and broken off from meaningful wholes. The
comparatiste qua *comparatiste* in this narrow sense could
study only sources and influences, causes and effects, and
would be even prevented from investigating a single work of
art in its totality as no work can be reduced entirely to foreign influences or considered as a radiating point of influence only toward foreign countries. Imagine that similar
restrictions would be imposed on the study of the history
of music, the fine arts, or philosophy! Could there be a congress or even a periodical exclusively devoted to such a
mosaic of questions as, say, the influence of Beethoven in
France, of Raphael in Germany, or even Kant in England?
These related disciplines have been much wiser: there are
musicologists, art historians, historians of philosophy, and

they do not pretend that there are special disciplines such as comparative painting, music, or philosophy. The attempt to set up artificial fences between comparative and general literature must fail because literary history and literary scholarship have one subject: literature. The desire to confine "comparative literature" to the study of the foreign trade of two literatures limits it to a concern with externals, with second-rate writers, with translations, travelbooks, "intermediaries"; in short, it makes "comparative literature" a mere subdiscipline investigating data about the foreign sources and reputations of writers.

The attempt to set apart not only the subject matter but also the methods of comparative literature has failed even more signally. Van Tieghem sets up two criteria which supposedly distinguish comparative literature from the study of national literatures. Comparative literature is concerned, he tells us, with the myths and legends which surround the poets and it is preoccupied with minor and minimal authors. But it is impossible to see why a student of a single national literature should not do the same: the image of Byron or Rimbaud in England or France has been successfully described without much regard to other countries and, say, Daniel Mornet in France or Josef Nadler in Germany have shown us that one can write national literary history with full attention to ephemeral and forgotten writers.

Nor can one be convinced by recent attempts by Carré and Guyard to widen suddenly the scope of comparative literature in order to include a study of national illusions, of fixed ideas which nations have of each other. It may be all very well to hear what conceptions Frenchmen had about Germany or about England—but is such a study still literary scholarship? Is it not rather a study of public opinion useful, for instance, to a program director in the Voice of America and its analogues in other countries? It is national psychology, sociology, and, as literary study, nothing else but a revival of the old *Stoffgeschichte*. "England and the English in the French novel" is hardly better than "the Irishman on the English stage" or "the Italian in Elizabethan drama." This extension of comparative literature implies a recognition of the sterility of the usual subject matter—at the price, however, of dissolving literary scholarship into social psychology and cultural history.

All these flounderings are only possible because Van Tieghem, his precursors and followers conceive of literary study in terms of nineteenth-century positivistic factualism, as a study of sources and influences. They believe in causal explanation, in the illumination which is brought about by tracing motifs, themes, characters, situations, plots, etc., to some other chronologically preceding work. They have accumulated an enormous mass of parallels, similarities, and sometimes identities, but they have rarely asked what these relationships are supposed to show except possibly the fact of one writer's knowledge and reading of another writer. Works of art, however, are not simply sums of sources and influences: they are wholes in which raw materials derived from elsewhere cease to be inert matter and are assimilated into a new structure. Causal explanation leads only to a *regressus ad infinitum* and besides, in literature, seems hardly ever unequivocally successful in establishing what one would consider the first requirement of any causal relationship: "when X occurs, Y must occur." I am not aware that any literary historian has given us proof of such a necessary relationship or that he even could do so, as the isolation of such a cause has been impossible with works of art which are wholes, conceived in the free imagination, whose integrity and meaning are violated if we break them up into sources and influences.

The concept of source and influence has of course worried the more sophisticated practitioners of comparative literature. For instance, Louis Cazamian, commenting on Carré's book *Goethe en Angleterre,* sees that there is "no assurance that this particular action made this particular difference." He argues that M. Carré is wrong in speaking of Goethe's "having, indirectly, provoked the English romantic movement" merely because Scott translated *Goetz von Berlichingen.*[1] But Cazamian can only make a gesture toward the idea, familiar since Bergson, of flux and becoming. He recommends the study of individual or collective psychology which, with Cazamian, means an elaborate, totally unverifiable theory of the oscillations of the rhythm of the English national soul.

Similarly also, Baldensperger, in his programmatic introduction to the first number of *Revue de littérature comparée* (1921) saw the dead end of literary scholarship preoccupied with tracing the history of literary themes. They can never establish, he admits, clear and complete sequences. He rejects also the rigid evolutionism propounded by Brunetière. But he can substitute for it only the suggestion that literary study should be widened to include minor writers and should pay attention to contemporaneous evaluations. Brunetière is too much concerned with masterpieces. "How can we know that Gessner played a role in general literature, that Destouches charmed the Germans more than Molière, that Delille was considered as a perfect and supreme poet in his time as Victor Hugo was later and that Heliodorus counted perhaps as much as Aeschylus in the heritage of antiquity?" (p. 24). Baldensperger's remedy is thus again attention to minor authors and to the bygone fashions of literary taste. A historical relativism is implied: we should study the standards of the past in order to write "objective" literary history. Comparative literature should plant itself "behind the scenes and not in front of the stage" as if in literature the play were not the thing. Like Cazamian, Baldensperger makes a ges-

1. "Goethe en Angleterre, quelques réflexions sur les problèmes d'influence," *Revue Germanique, 12* (1921), 374–75.

ture toward Bergson's becoming, the incessant movement, the "realm of universal variation" for which he quotes a biologist as a parallel. In the conclusion of his manifesto Baldensperger abruptly proclaims comparative literature a preparation for a New Humanism. He asks us to ascertain the spread of Voltaire's skepticism, of Nietzsche's faith in the superman, of the mysticism of Tolstoy: to know why a book considered a classic in one nation is rejected as academic in another, why a work despised in one country is admired elsewhere. He hopes that such researches will furnish our dislocated humanity with a "less uncertain core of common values" (p. 29). But why should such erudite researches into the geographical spread of certain ideas lead to anything like a definition of the patrimony of humanity? And even if such a definition of the common core were successful and would be generally accepted, would it mean an effective New Humanism?

There is a paradox in the psychological and social motivation of "comparative literature" as practised in the last fifty years. Comparative literature arose as a reaction against the narrow nationalism of much nineteenth-century scholarship, as a protest against the isolationism of many historians of French, German, Italian, English, etc., literature. It was cultivated often by men who stood themselves at the crossroads of nations or, at least, on the borders of one nation. Louis Betz was born in New York of German parents and went to Zurich to learn and teach. Baldensperger was of Lothringian origin and spent a decisive year in Zürich. Ernst Robert Curtius was an Alsatian convinced of the need of better German-French understanding. Arturo Farinelli was an Italian from Trento, then still "irredenta," who taught at Innsbruck. But this genuine desire to serve as a mediator and conciliator between nations was often overlaid and distorted by the fervent nationalism of the time and situation. Reading Baldensperger's autobiography, *Une Vie parmi d'autres*

(1940, actually written in 1935), we feel the basic patriotic impulse behind his every activity: his pride in foiling German propaganda at Harvard in 1914, in refusing to meet Brandes in 1915 in Copenhagen, in going to liberated Strasbourg in 1920. Carré's book on *Goethe in England* contains an introduction arguing that Goethe belongs to all the world and to France in particular as a son of the Rhineland. After the second World War Carré wrote *Les Écrivains français et le mirage allemand* (1947) where he tried to show how the French nourished illusions about the two Germanies and were always taken in at the end. Ernst Robert Curtius thought of his first book, *Die literarischen Wegbereiter des neuen Frankreichs* (1918), as a political action, as instruction for Germany. In a postscript to a new edition written in 1952, Curtius declared his early concept of France an illusion. Romain Rolland was not the voice of the new France as he had thought. Like Carré, Curtius discovered a "mirage" but this time it was a French *mirage*. Even in that early book Curtius had defined his conception of a good European: "Ich weiss nur eine Art ein guter Europäer zu sein: mit Macht die Seele seiner Nation haben, und sie mit Macht nähren von allem, was es Einzigartiges gibt in der Seele der anderen Nationen, der befreundeten oder der feindlichen."[2] A cultural power politics is recommended: everything serves only the strength of one's nation.

I am not suggesting that the patriotism of these scholars was not good or right or even high-minded. I recognize civic duties, the necessity of making decisions, of taking sides in the struggles of our time. I am acquainted with Mannheim's sociology of knowledge, his *Ideology and Utopia,* and understand that proof of motivation does not invalidate the work of a man. I clearly want to distinguish these men from the base corruptors of scholarship in Nazi Germany or from the

2. *Französischer Geist im zwanzigsten Jahrhundert* (Bern, 1952), p. 237.

political doctrinaires in Russia who, for a time, declared "comparative literature" taboo and called anybody who would say in print that Pushkin drew the story of "The Golden Cockerel" from Washington Irving a "rootless cosmopolitan kowtowing to the West."

Still, this basically patriotic motivation of many comparative literature studies in France, Germany, Italy, and so on, has led to a strange system of cultural bookkeeping, a desire to accumulate credits for one's nation by proving as many influences as possible on other nations or, more subtly, by proving that one's own nation has assimilated and "understood" a foreign master more fully than any other. This is almost naively displayed in the table of M. Guyard's little handbook for students: it has neat empty boxes for the unwritten *thèses* on Ronsard in Spain, Corneille in Italy, Pascal in Holland, etc.[3] This type of cultural expansionism can be found even in the United States which, on the whole, has been immune to it partly because it had less to boast of and partly because it was less concerned with cultural politics. Still, for instance, the excellent cooperative *Literary History of the United States* (ed. R. Spiller, W. Thorp, et al., 1948) blithely claims Dostoevsky as a follower of Poe and even of Hawthorne. Arturo Farinelli, a comparatist of the purest water, described this situation in an article contributed to the *Mélanges Baldensperger* (1930) entitled "Gl'influssi letterari e l'insuperbire delle nazioni." Farinelli very appropriately comments on the absurdity of such computations of cultural riches, of the whole creditor and debtor calculus in matters of poetry. We forget that "the destinies of poetry and art are fulfilled only in the intimate life and the secret accords of the soul."[4] In an interesting article Professor Chinard has most opportunely pronounced the principle of "no debts" in

3. M.-F. Guyard, *La Littérature comparée* (Paris, 1951), pp. 124–25.
4. *1*, 273.

the comparison of literatures and quoted a fine passage from Rabelais on an ideal world without debtors and creditors.[5]

An artificial demarcation of subject matter and methodology, a mechanistic concept of sources and influences, a motivation by cultural nationalism, however generous—these seem to me the symptoms of the long-drawn-out crisis of comparative literature.

A thorough reorientation is needed in all these three directions. The artificial demarcation between "comparative" and "general" literature should be abandoned. "Comparative" literature has become an established term for any study of literature transcending the limits of one national literature. There is little use in deploring the grammar of the term and to insist that it should be called "the comparative study of literature," since everybody understands the elliptic usage. "General" literature has not caught on, at least in English, possibly because it has still its old connotation of referring to poetics and theory. Personally I wish we could simply speak of the study of literature or of literary scholarship and that there were, as Albert Thibaudet proposed, professors of literature just as there are professors of philosophy and of history and not professors of the history of English philosophy even though the individual may very well specialize in this or that particular period or country or even in a particular author. Fortunately, we still have no professors of English eighteenth-century literature or of Goethe philology. But the naming of our subject is an institutional matter of academic interest in the most literal sense. What matters is the concept of literary scholarship as a unified discipline unhampered by linguistic restrictions. I cannot thus agree with Friederich's view that comparatists "cannot and dare not

5. "La Littérature comparée et l'histoire des idées dans l'étude des relations franco-américaines," in *Proceedings of the Second Congress of the International Comparative Literature Association,* ed. Werner P. Friederich, *2* (Chapel Hill, 1959), 349–69.

encroach upon other territories," i.e. those of the students of English, French, German, and other national literatures. Nor can I see how it is even possible to follow his advice not to "poach in each other's territory."[6] There are no proprietary rights and no recognized "vested interests" in literary scholarship. Everybody has the right to study any question even if it is confined to a single work in a single language and everybody has the right to study even history or philosophy or any other topic. He runs of course the risk of criticism by the specialists, but it is a risk he has to take. We comparatists surely would not want to prevent English professors from studying the French sources of Chaucer, or French professors from studying the Spanish sources of Corneille, etc., since we comparatists would not want to be forbidden to publish on topics confined to specific national literatures. Far too much has been made of the "authority" of the specialist who often may have only the bibliographical knowledge or the external information without necessarily having the taste, the sensibility, and the range of the non-specialist whose wider perspective and keener insight may well make up for years of intense application. There is nothing presumptuous or arrogant in advocating a greater mobility and ideal universality in our studies. The whole conception of fenced-off reservations with signs of "no trespassing" must be distasteful to a free mind. It can arise only within the limits of the obsolete methodology preached and practiced by the standard theorists of comparative literature who assume that "facts" are to be discovered like nuggets of gold for which we can stake out prospectors' claims.

But true literary scholarship is not concerned with inert facts, but with values and qualities. That is why there is no distinction between literary history and criticism. Even the simplest problem of literary history requires an act of judg-

6. *Yearbook of Comparative and General Literature*, 4 (1955), 57.

ment. Even such a statement that Racine influenced Voltaire
or Herder influenced Goethe requires, to be meaningful, a
knowledge of the characteristics of Racine and Voltaire,
Herder and Goethe, and hence a knowledge of the context
of their traditions, an unremitting activity of weighing, com-
paring, analysing, and discriminating which is essentially
critical. No literary history has ever been written without
some principle of selection and some attempt at characterization and evaluation. Literary historians who deny the importance of criticism are themselves unconscious critics, usually
derivative critics who have merely taken over traditional
standards and accepted conventional reputations. A work of
art cannot be analyzed, characterized, and evaluated without
recourse to critical principles, however unconsciously held
and obscurely formulated. Norman Foerster in a still perti-
nent booklet, *The American Scholar,* said very cogently that
the literary historian "must be a critic *in order* to be a historian."[7] In literary scholarship theory, criticism, and history
collaborate to achieve its central task: the description, interpretation, and evaluation of a work of art or any group of
works of art. Comparative literature which, at least with its
official theorists has shunned this collaboration and has clung
to "factual relations," sources and influences, intermediaries
and reputations as its only topics, will have to find its way
back into the great stream of contemporary literary scholarship and criticism. In its methods and methodological reflections comparative literature has become, to put it bluntly, a
stagnant backwater. We can think of many scholarly and
critical movements and groupings during this century quite
diverse in their aims and methods—Croce and his followers
in Italy, Russian formalism and its offshoots and developments in Poland and Czechoslovakia, German *Geistesgeschichte* and stylistics which have found such an echo in the
Spanish-speaking countries, French and German existen-

7. Chapell Hill, 1929, p. 36.

tialist criticism, the American "New Criticism," the myth criticism inspired by Jung's archetypal patterns, and even Freudian psychoanalysis or Marxism: all these are, whatever their limitations and demerits, united in a common reaction against the external factualism and atomism which is still fettering the study of comparative literature.

Literary scholarship today needs primarily a realization of the need to define its subject matter and focus. It must be distinguished from the study of the history of ideas, or religious and political concepts and sentiments which are often suggested as alternatives to literary studies. Many eminent men in literary scholarship and particularly in comparative literature are not really interested in literature at all but in the history of public opinion, the reports of travelers, the ideas about national character—in short, in general cultural history. The concept of literary study is broadened by them so radically that it becomes identical with the whole history of humanity. But literary scholarship will not make any progress, methodologically, unless it determines to study literature as a subject distinct from other activities and products of man. Hence we must face the problem of "literariness," the central issue of aesthetics, the nature of art and literature.

In such a conception of literary scholarship the literary work of art itself will be the necessary focus and we will recognize that we study different problems when we examine the relations of a work of art to the psychology of the author or to the sociology of his society. The work of art, I have argued, can be conceived as a stratified structure of signs and meanings which is totally distinct from the mental processes of the author at the time of composition and hence of the influences which may have formed his mind. There is what has been rightly called an "ontological gap" between the psychology of the author and a work of art, between life and society on the one hand and the aesthetic object. I have

called the study of the work of art "intrinsic" and that of its
relations to the mind of the author, to society, etc., "ex-
trinsic." Still, this distinction cannot mean that genetic relations should be ignored or even despised or that intrinsic
study is mere formalism or irrelevant aestheticism. Precisely
the carefully worked out concept of a stratified structure of
signs and meanings attempts to overcome the old dichotomy
of content and form. What is usually called "content" or
"idea" in a work of art is incorporated into the structure of
the work of art as part of its "world" of projected meanings.
Nothing would be further from my mind than to deny the
human relevance of art or to erect a barrier between history
and formal study. While I have learned from the Russian
formalists and German *Stilforscher*, I would not want to confine the study of literature either to the study of sound, verse,
and compositional devices or to elements of diction and syntax; nor would I want to equate literature with language. In
my conception these linguistic elements form, so to say, the
two bottom strata: the sound stratum and that of the units of
meaning. But from them there emerges a "world" of situations, characters, and events which cannot be identified
with any single linguistic element or, least of all, with any
element of external ornamental form. The only right conception seems to me a resolutely "holistic" one which sees the
work of art as a diversified totality, as a structure of signs
which, however, imply and require meanings and values.
Both a relativistic antiquarianism and an external formalism
are mistaken attempts to dehumanize literary study. Criticism cannot and must not be expelled from literary scholarship.

If such a change and liberation, such a reorientation
toward theory and criticism, toward critical history should
take place, the problem of motivation will take care of itself.
We still can remain good patriots and even nationalists, but
the debit and credit system will have ceased to matter. Illu-

sions about cultural expansion may disappear as may also illusions about world reconciliation by literary scholarship. Here, in America, looking from the other shore at Europe as a whole we may easily achieve a certain detachment, though we may have to pay the price of uprootedness and spiritual exile. But once we conceive of literature not as an argument in the warfare of cultural *prestige,* or as a commodity of foreign trade or even as an indicator of national psychology we shall obtain the only true objectivity obtainable to man. It will not be a neutral scientism, an indifferent relativism and historicism but a confrontation with the objects in their essence: a dispassionate but intense contemplation which will lead to analysis and finally to judgments of value. Once we grasp the nature of art and poetry, its victory over human mortality and destiny, its creation of a new world of the imagination, national vanities will disappear. Man, universal man, man everywhere and at any time, in all his variety, emerges and literary scholarship ceases to be an antiquarian pastime, a calculus of national credits and debts and even a mapping of networks of relationships. Literary scholarship becomes an act of the imagination, like art itself, and thus a preserver and creator of the highest values of mankind.

American Literary Scholarship

In 1900 a type of philological scholarship imported from Germany had triumphed in American graduate schools and in the production of American literary scholars. The decisive years were the eighties and nineties of the last century. In 1850 there were only eight graduate students in the whole of the United States, three at Harvard and three at Yale. In 1852, Daniel C. Gilman, later to become the first president of Johns Hopkins, could get no graduate instruction either at Yale or Harvard: he had difficulty in persuading one professor to read a little German with him.[1] With the exception of the great scholars, George Ticknor of Harvard, whose major work, *The History of Spanish Literature* (1849–63), was widely used, and Francis Child, also of Harvard, who edited the *Scottish and English Popular Ballads* (1857–58), there were no "producing" scholars in the modern languages in America, no periodicals, and no university presses.

The situation changed rapidly in the last decades of the nineteenth century. In 1876 the Johns Hopkins University was founded expressly for the providing of graduate instruction on the German model. Soon the other universities followed, expanding their graduate instruction so rapidly that by 1900 there were 5,831 graduate students (of all subjects) in the United States. In 1883 the Modern Language Association was founded. At first, it was only a small group of teachers who were interested in the discussion of questions of classroom instruction and grammar, but it grew rapidly

1. Daniel C. Gilman, *The Launching of a University* (New York, 1906), p. 8.

and completely changed its character. In 1927 the Association voted to replace the original definition of its purpose as "the *study* of modern languages and literatures" by the "advancement of *research* in the modern languages and literatures"; but long before, certainly by 1900, this stress on research had become predominant. Several periodicals exclusively devoted to the publication of the results of academic scholarship in the modern languages were founded: *Publications of the Modern Language Association* in 1886, *Modern Language Notes* in 1886, the *Journal of English and Germanic Philology* in 1897, and *Modern Philology* in 1903. University presses were established, mainly after the 1890s, and several series of publications were devoted to printing doctoral dissertations. The *Yale Studies in English,* now running to over one hundred and fifty volumes, was begun in 1898. The fabulous growth of the American university libraries and, later, the founding of research libraries such as the Folger and the Huntington libraries, both mainly devoted to English Renaissance literature, stimulated the expansion of research. Today American libraries are so well equipped and so well administered that for most purposes they are preferable to European libraries. If we look at these achievements we can understand the enthusiasm with which, at the height of the movement, its leaders contemplated its success. Here are a few passages from the presidential address of Thomas R. Price of Columbia University, delivered at the annual meeting of the Modern Language Association in 1901:

> As teachers of the modern languages, in our survey of our own Association and of the American university system, we must all feel a certain warmth of exhilaration. The progress that our favorite studies have been making is so splendid. With that period of forty years . . . there has been a steady current of progress, so vast

an improvement in our methods of instruction, so vast
an increase in the magnitude of our work, in the number of pupils, in the size and qualification of our pro-
fessorial force. There has been, indeed, in this wide
enthusiasm for the spreading and elevation of modern
language instruction, an intellectual movement that
may fairly be compared with the enthusiasm in the
days of the renaissance . . . In country villages I found
the same ardor for our special studies as in great universities. No man that has shared in this movement can
fail to feel a noble joy in such a display of energy and
in such an achievement of results.[2]

Something happened to this "renaissance" in these last
sixty years. The ardor, and that not only of the villagers,
went out of it. By the mid-century, philological scholarship,
though still entrenched in most graduate schools, was definitely on the defensive; its exclusive rule of the American
universities was broken; and everywhere, especially among
the younger men of the staff and the students, dissatisfaction
with the system became so widespread that it seemed merely
a matter of time when it could be seen as a historical phenomenon of American cultural history.

We can explain its triumph about 1900. It was not only
owing to the importation of German scholarship and to the
prestige of Germany at that time. It also met a contemporary
intellectual and social situation. It satisfied the nostalgia for
the past, especially the European past and the Middle Ages,
and at the same time it met the desire for facts, for accuracy,
for the imitation of the "scientific method" which had ac-
quired such overwhelming prestige through the success of
modern technology so particularly conspicuous in the United
States. The critical relativism implied in the method of studying literature through its historical antecedents, its open

2. *PMLA, 16* (1901), 77–91.

abdication before the task of evaluation, also fitted into the pattern of a civilization disoriented or skeptical in its judgments of values. The enormous possibilities of production, of production in quantities, and of a standardization of the products were aids to victory, for bulk in production was an industrial ideal, and the convenient grading of teachers was a practical necessity. The useless antiquarianism, the dreary factualism, the pseudo-science combined with anarchical skepticism and a lack of critical taste characteristic of this scholarship must be apparent to almost everybody today. The system has become almost too easy a target for ridicule. Yet one must recognize that, out of inertia, it perpetuates itself even today, and that it has still some attractions for those who are enamored of its mechanical perfection and its tone of detachment, and for those who are merely docile and industrious.

Whatever the abuses of the system, one should recognize that they represent the decadence of a worthy ideal, that of philology conceived as a total science of a civilization, an ideal originally formulated for the study of classical antiquity and then transferred by the German romanticists to the modern languages. In the programmatic statements by leading American scholars, we actually find such ambitious formulations: for example, in Albert S. Cook's *The Higher Study of English* (1908) or in Edwin Greenlaw's *Province of Literary History* (1931). But while one may recognize that the standards and aims professed in these books are broad and humane, in actuality there was a divorce between theory and practice. Albert S. Cook himself published mainly editions, studies, and notes on Anglo-Saxon literature, many of them on trivial and minute points. His editions of classics of criticism (Sidney, for instance) are school texts containing little editorial matter. His occasional critical pronouncements echo Arnold and his dubious theory of "touchstones." Edwin Greenlaw did, for the most part, highly competent studies of the political allegory in Spenser. The gestures towards criticism, synthesis, the history of the human mind, remained mostly gestures or the private virtues of an individual who was unable to make his ideas effective institutionally.

The original conceptions and aims of a humane literary scholarship were constantly forgotten. The romantic stress on origins coming from Herder led in practice to the strange overrating of the study of Anglo-Saxon and early forms of medieval languages, specialties which were (and in some places continue to be) imposed on most American students of literature. The requirements in Anglo-Saxon grammar and the history of English phonology not only diverted energies from literary pursuits but deterred many students from completing their professional studies. The romantic concept of the evolution and the continuity of literature decayed so quickly that nothing was left of it save the superstition that works of literature could be reduced to compounds of parallels and sources. The evolutionary conception still survived after 1900 in the writings of Francis Gummere on the *Origins of Poetry* and on the *Popular Ballad*; but as the evolutionary concept had become far too strongly subservient to biological analogues, it was soon discarded and today seems completely incomprehensible, to the degree that the writing of narrative literary history has become an almost lost art. The romantic conception of original genius degenerated into the excesses of biographical gossip-mongering, the feverish interest in trivial anecdotes, or the constant assumption that a work of literature is an autobiographical document. The ideal of a general history of culture embodied in the literature led—especially among English and American scholars —to the indiscriminate expansion into miscellaneous social history. Papers on the "Origin of the Long-bow," theses on "The Military Profession in the Sixteenth Century," great works such as *Witchcraft in Old and New England* brought about a complete obliteration of boundaries and confusion of methods. The romantic ideal of the study of a national spirit led, in practice, to the isolation of the study of one national literature, to the obscuring of the unity of European literature, to the neglect of comparative literature, to the Anglomania, Germanophilia, and Francophilia of many teachers, and finally to the new provincialism of many specialists in American literature. What had been a worthy ideal in the minds of the founders, the Grimms, Boeckh, Diez, became sheer Alexandrianism, an antiquarianism without sense of direction and purpose.

The reasons for this decay are obvious: some are not American but European also; they are due to the general decay of the romantic ideal and its replacement by pseudo-scientific mass production. But the American cultural situation accelerated the decay. Teutonic racialism, the inspiration of the founders of Germanistics, was, for obvious reasons, a very artificial growth in America; and so was romantic medievalism, which has no roots in a largely Protestant and commercial society. The social and institutional reasons for the decay were also greater than in Europe. The American colleges and universities were far more isolated from their cultural surroundings than the metropolitan universities of the European continent (Paris or Prague, for instance). Thus they were an invitation to cultivate the academic ivory tower, to defend the professor's self-esteem and social status by indulgence in "mysteries" incomprehensible and useless outside of the university, useless even to the majority of the students who went out to teach composition, language, and literature in the small colleges and state universities. The separation between the practice of literature and academic scholarship also became wider with the rise of literary naturalism and American regionalism with their descent into the slums and stockyards, farms and mines, and with their distrust of Europe, the intellect, tradition, and learning in general.

Still, whatever the waste of the academic system and the shoddiness of its run-of-the-mill products may be, it would be entirely unjust to ignore the achievement, within its limits, of American philological scholarship during the last sixty years. Especially in the field of English literature, American technical scholarship became indispensable and surely outstripped comparable British scholarship, and not merely quantitatively. Work in German, French, Italian, and Spanish by Americans is still frequently on a lower level of competence; and remoter fields (such as Slavic) are only beginning to be cultivated. The inferior state of studies in the non-English literatures is the result, in part, of the natural handicap with which every foreigner starts in studying a literature not his own, and in part of the preoccupation of American foreign literature teachers with the teaching of elementary language courses, but also, more deeply, of the "provincialism" of the student of foreign literatures. Most students of French and German quite uncritically adopted the methods and standards of the country whose literature they were studying. They thus developed a position of inferiority toward German and French scholarship, and were driven into a peculiar isolation in their own surroundings. Leo Spitzer, himself a prominent German émigré, commented wisely on a situation in which departments of foreign literatures "are usually enclaves in American universities, very much to the detriment of an indigenous American development."[3] As Henry C. Hatfield[4] pointed out, studies in things German are badly handicapped by their dependence on German values and standards. This is, of course,

3. *Deutsche Monatshefte, 48* (1946), 477.
4. "Studies of German Literature in the United States," *Modern Language Review, 43* (1948), 353–92.

the result of the early specialization which prevents the American student of things German or French from having a firm grasp on English and American literature and from thus achieving a coherent outlook of his own from which he can interpret the foreign literature. Especially in German studies, the highly metaphysical, frequently Hegelian, presuppositions of German *Geistesgeschichte* proved indigestible and unassimilable to American students, who at the same time were unable to replace them by anything of their own tradition.

The reaction against this philological scholarship in America is not merely of recent date. It is possible to distinguish between different motives of opposition and different movements in the revolt. In a roughly chronological order we would have to begin with the objections which came from the survivors of the older, more humane, but also more dilettantish, scholarship, of those who had preserved a continuity with the tradition of the British universities. The memoirs of men who have described their years of study around the turn of the century—Bliss Perry in *And Gladly Teach,* William Lyon Phelps in his *Autobiography,* and H. S. Canby in *Alma Mater*—voice deep discontent with the ruling methods and illustrate the evils of the system by anecdotes and sketches of classroom masters and tyrants. But they and their sympathizers were unable to offer any remedy or alternative except "appreciation," a romantic enthusiasm for the good and the beautiful, sweetness unaccompanied by light. Phelps was the first teacher to offer a course in the contemporary novel (1895-96—promptly dropped at the insistence of his superiors who threatened him with dismissal)[5] and the first American academic scholar to write on the Russian novelists (1911); but the love of literature which Phelps and comparable teachers instilled in their students was without critical

5. William L. Phelps, *Autobiography with Letters* (New York, 1939), p. 301.

standards. Such teachers, whatever their use to undergraduates, could not contribute to literary scholarship conceived
of as a body of knowledge. Some of the exponents of the
philological method were able to combine their "austere"
scholarship with such "appreciation." They taught graduate
students bibliography and sources, "Shakespeare on the graduate level" (that is, the distinctions of quartos and folios,
sources, stage conditions), and meanwhile they read poetry
to undergraduates in a trembling or unctuous voice. Sentimentalism and antiquarianism are not incompatible, even
philosophically.

Far more promising was the movement of the New Humanists, led by Irving Babbitt and Paul Elmer More, and
later by Norman Foerster. Irving Babbitt's *Literature and
the American College* (1908) and Norman Foerster's *American Scholar* (1929) are indictments of the philological
scholarship still cogent today. The New Humanists had an
ideal to offer which was not mere "appreciation": they had
an ideal of criticism, a strict regard for tradition, an interest
in philosophical ideas as they appear in literature, a new
neoclassical taste reacting against romanticism. Babbitt's
Masters of Modern French Criticism (1912) and his *Rousseau and Romanticism* (1919) are books of real critical
power and acumen. Marred though they are by frequent
obtuseness in the reading of texts and by lack of sensibility,
they have a power of abstraction and generalization and a
fervid "engagement" in ideas unknown to earlier American
scholarship. The neohumanist movement, after a short period of great public attention around 1929, became quies-
cent. But Babbitt at Harvard, More at Princeton, Stuart
Sherman at Illinois, and Foerster at North Carolina and Iowa
awakened many students to the futility of much conventional
scholarship and to the urgency of great ideas in literature.
The reasons for the failure of the movement to capture the
universities are, however, obvious: the social conservatism

of the New Humanists ran counter to the temper of a nation plunged into the depression, their rigid moralism violated the nature of literature as an art, and their hostility to the contemporary arts cut them off from literature as a living institution. Babbitt's philosophical and religious principles, which appealed for corroboration to Confucian and Buddhist thought, were too exotic and too austere to become a reforming power; his literary views were too closely related to the French antiromanticism of men like Charles Maurras, Lasserre, and Seillière to be immediately relevant to the American literary scene. After the period of his *Shelburne Essays,* Paul Elmer More became a historian of Greek philosophy and of Christian theology, and his attempts to come to terms with modern writers such as Joyce or Eliot were unsatisfactory. Stuart Sherman went to New York and, becoming a journalist, lost distinction in emphatic gusto.

Other attempts at changing the orientation of literary study in the American university also failed—or failed, at least, to be generally effective. In the thirties the Marxist approach to literature excited widespread interest; and, outside of the Academy or on its fringes, some Marxist criticism was produced. But possibly for political reasons, it produced hardly any effect upon American academic scholarship. Granville Hicks' books, their most ambitious application in America, were neither learned nor bold enough to recommend themselves for imitation. Economic determinism and a basically political outlook were introduced into American studies rather through the success of Vernon Parrington's *Main Currents of American Thought* (1927–30). Here a vaguely sociological approach assumes the special form of propaganda for Jeffersonian democracy; the focus of the book is so extraliterary that American literature studies, as far as they followed him, were diverted from literary values into social history and the history of political ideas. On the whole, the sociological approach proved singularly unattractive to American literary scholarship and has produced relatively little work of real distinction.

The study of ideas in literature, of literature in relation to philosophy, is old, of course; and, in a technical sense, it was cultivated very strenuously in Germany during the last decades, in violent reaction against philological scholarship. But the German *Geistesgeschichte* had few echoes in this country, except among teachers of German: some of these were hostile, as witness Martin Schütze's brilliant attack, in *Academic Illusions* (1933), a book which offered one of the best analyses of the situation of literary scholarship, not only in Germany. As a movement, the "history of ideas," initiated by Arthur O. Lovejoy, made the strongest impression on students of literature in the United States. Lovejoy is a professional philosopher, and his method is that of a philosophical analysis of ideas with close attention to terminology and the contradictions of individual writers. He draws the rather artificial contrast between his method and the ordinary history of philosophy in that he studies "unit-ideas" rather than whole philosophical systems and gives attention to the dissemination of ideas through popular philosophers and poets. His method can be criticized for its excessive intellectualism: Lovejoy conceives of ideological change as a self-subsisting process and pays little attention to historical or psychological contexts. To him poetry is merely a document for intellectual history, and ideas in literature are "philosophical ideas in dilution."[6] Literature thus becomes the water added to philosophy, and the history of ideas imposes purely philosophical standards on works of imagination. Intellectual history is, of course, a high discipline, with exegetical value for the study of the history of literature. But it is no substitute for literary study. Among American literary scholars there are actually few historians of ideas in Lovejoy's sense: Louis

6. Arthur O. Lovejoy, *The Great Chain of Being* (Cambridge, Mass., 1936), p. 17.

Bredvold, Marjorie Nicolson, Perry Miller come to mind.

Clearly, the greatest hope for a reconstitution of literary study in America lies in the critical movement developed in the last twenty-five years outside of the universities. It seems current to speak of the movement as the "New Criticism," a term which J. C. Ransom used on the title page of a book, published in 1941, discussing three critics—I. A. Richards, T. S. Eliot, and Yvor Winters; and these are there discussed with considerable reservations; but the term is often used now for any critic in the general tradition established by Richards and Eliot. This is unfortunate, for the phrase obscures the very great diversities and differences among the critics, giving the erroneous impression that these critics form a "school" or even a coterie. Only the four Southern critics, J. C. Ransom, Allen Tate, R. P. Warren, and Cleanth Brooks, have had close personal associations and show close coherence of outlook; and even they are far from subscribing to an unchanging position. J. C. Ransom especially goes his own way in his later speculations. The other critics grouped with the New Critics are often quite isolated, like Yvor Winters, who has developed a coherent and impressive but extremely doctrinaire view of the history of American and English poetry, and Kenneth Burke, who has evolved a system of critical theory so widely expanded that it has become, in intention, a whole philosophy of culture, utilizing semantics, Marxism, psychoanalysis, and anthropology. Edmund Wilson has used any and all methods in turn: his first book, *Axel's Castle* (1931), was an exposition of the Symbolist movement, which, though highly sympathetic and perceptive, concluded with a dirge on its supposed demise. He has since used Marxism and psychoanalysis quite eclectically and has declined into journalism and "Europe Without Baedeker." R. P. Blackmur, who began as an extremely close reader and analyst of texts, has been moving into statements of a general critical theory and has broadened his "practical criticism" to include moral and ideological discussions of the novels of Dostoevsky.

Still, in a general history of American criticism we can see that the new critics all react against a common preceding situation. They were all dissatisfied with the impressionistic, vaguely romantic, and sentimental "appreciation" prevalent inside and outside of the universities; and they disapproved of the purely journalistic criticism associated with Mencken and his praise of the American naturalistic novel; they felt uncomfortable with the New Humanist movement because of its hostility to contemporary writing and its rigidly moralistic view of literature. Tate, Blackmur, Kenneth Burke, and Winters even contributed to a symposium attacking the neo-humanist movement.[7]

In reaction against this situation they turned largely, at first at least, to a study of poetry, especially modern poetry, concentrating on the actual texts of the works under inspection and stressing the peculiarity of a work of art which they conceived of as comparatively independent of its background in history, biography, and literary tradition. In this turn to the text, this stress on the unity of a work of art, this refusal to reduce literature to its causes can be found what may be described as the common denominator of the new critics. But, among them there are, at least, two groups: those who have more and more brought to bear on literature all kinds of knowledge—psychoanalysis in particular, Marxism, and recently anthropology; and those who have tried to study literature primarily as an aesthetic fact. The first group has again used the literary work as a point of individual departure for general speculations on man and the universe, the ego, and society; while the other group has stayed more clearly within the precincts of literature, practicing techniques of close analysis. But it seems a mistake to charge even these

7. Clinton H. Grattan, ed., *The Critique of Humanism* (New York, 1930).

latter critics with "aestheticism" and even "formalism." None of them is an "aesthete": for their critical standards everywhere imply a philosophical, political, and religious point of view. The Southern group is preoccupied with the problem of modern urban and commercial civilization and its impact on tradition. Even when in appearance they are inspecting mainly what seem to be poetic devices such as ambiguities and paradoxes, they aim at a discussion of the general value, coherence, and maturity of a work of art—values which are human and social. They refuse to confuse the realm of art (which is not exempt from humanity) with the realms of thought or ethics, and understand that the meaning of a work of literature arises from its formal whole.

The antecedents and philosophical premises of the critical movement are quite various. T. S. Eliot is, of course, the great initiator; and Eliot's critical ideas have their antecedents in Babbitt at Harvard, in Hulme in England, and in Rémy de Gourmont in France. But Eliot's influence is combined with that of I. A. Richards, who yielded a method and procedure in many ways incompatible with Eliot's. While Eliot's early philosophical sympathies were with idealism (he expressed great interest in the Oxford Hegelian F. H. Bradley), Richards was a professed Benthamite, a physiological psychologist: only recently has he moved in the direction of idealism. The importance of Croce's *Estetica*, though not clearly traceable, must be assumed as background. However, there are no traces of the Crocean idealistic monism in the American critics nor are they interested in the problem of the development of literature, its dialectics, as the Russian formalists were; they all seem to accept Eliot's static view of literature as a timeless simultaneous order. They all react against the ruling philological scholarship to such an extent that they have lost all contact with modern linguistics. On these two points the American movement differs sharply from the analogous movements on the European Continent.

Still, it must strike every student of the cultural situation of the West as an almost mystical fact that in countries which had little or no direct contacts there arose the same kind of reaction against nineteenth-century positivistic scholarship. Of these movements the Russian formalists had the clearest, sharpest, and theoretically best-developed set of doctrines. In Germany the same tendency took rather the form of an interest in stylistics and in the parallelism between the arts and literature; and the Germans were extremely influential in the Spanish-speaking countries. The Russian, German, and Spanish movements differ from the American movement by their close association with linguistics, which has yielded excellent results, especially in the study of style and metrics; and in Europe these movements have been supported by new trends in linguistics running counter to the doctrinaire behaviorism of the predominant Yale school of linguists. The Italian and German movements are closely associated with idealistic philosophies and very conscious of their reaction against nineteenth-century positivism and naturalism, while the Russian movement has been professedly empirical and scientific. Still, whatever the differences, the assumptions and the direction of reaction against nineteenth-century scholarship are the same.

In America the movement has been less academic and more clearly concentrated on problems of criticism, while the Russians and Germans seem to cling, in practice, to historical relativism. Still, the American movement which arose outside of the Academy has increasingly found its way into the American universities and colleges. Ransom's plea for "Criticism, Inc." and Blackmur's for "A Featherbed for Critics" are being fulfilled, at least in part. Cleanth Brooks' remark, written as late as 1943, that the new critics "have next to no influence in the universities"[8] is obviously outdated. In most American universities, large and small, there

8. *Sewanee Review, 51* (1943), 59.

is a minority, especially in the English departments, which is deeply dissatisfied with the prevailing antiquarianism, and, among the younger members of the staff, critical interests are so widespread that it seems merely a matter of time when (and not whether) the graduate teaching of literature will pass into the hands of those who have broken with the ruling methods.

But if criticism is to transform American literary scholarship in the universities successfully, it must face a number of problems which its original propounders outside of the university had no need to face. If they abandon the old philology with its definite methods and body of knowledge they will have to replace it with a new body of doctrines, a new systematic theory, a technique and methodology teachable and transmissible and applicable to any and all works of literature. In this respect, much modern American criticism is still deficient or, it could be argued, has the virtue of this deficiency. Its vocabulary often differs far too sharply from author to author and even from essay to essay: its assumptions are rarely thought through in their philosophical implications and historical antecedents. Many American critics (Kenneth Burke is an extreme example) use a homemade terminology demanding a considerable effort of interpretation. They seem to feel the need of reformulating basic questions over and over again, to start *ab ovo* to think on aesthetic and critical problems which have a centuries-old history. They are thus open to misunderstanding by the wider public, which again and again is puzzled and misled by the novel uses of such terms as "form," "technique," "structure," "texture," "rhythm," or "myth." Thus a measure of agreement on basic issues of theory will have to be reached sooner or later. One can defend individual terminology up to a point; but indulgence in idiosyncrasies damages the cumulative effect of criticism.

Besides, modern criticism will have to reopen questions

which it has hitherto neglected or slighted for one reason or the other. Literary history is the most important of these. Literary history must not, as I showed in the first essay, be confused with antiquarianism. It needs rewriting with the new methods and a new emphasis and must not be left to the philologist or dilettante. Surely many of the greatest critics were also great literary historians: the Schlegels, Sainte-Beuve, De Sanctis, Taine, Brunetière, Croce. They were critical historians of literature. There are suggestions for the rewriting of the history of English poetry in some of the essays of F. R. Leavis, F. W. Bateson, and Cleanth Brooks, but they are only suggestions. It is possible to break away from the traditional literary history, an odd mixture of anthology, biography, social history, intellectual history, and criticism and to envisage a history of the art of literature written with critical insight, according to critical standards. While some modern critics have brought to bear all kinds of other types of knowledge on the understanding of literature, they seem to have neglected the illumination which can be brought to literature from the two fields which seem the nearest to the art of words: linguistics and aesthetics, including the aesthetics of the fine arts. Linguistics is especially indispensable for a study of style, diction, and meter; and the relations of literature to music and painting have hardly begun to be studied by modern methods. Finally, it seems both inevitable and most important that the methods of modern criticism should be applied to works remote in time and space, to older and to foreign literatures. The selection of European writers which have attracted the attention of modern critics in the United States is oddly narrow and subject to the distortion of a very local and temporary perspective.

If this consolidation and expansion are to succeed, they must draw on men in the universities, and especially on the young men. Within the universities some older men had begun to concern themselves with critical problems or, at least, with problems of close formal analysis even before the new critical movement. The studies of prose style by Morris W. Croll, or of the technique of prose fiction by J. W. Beach come to mind, also the many essays and books by E. E. Stoll stressing the role of theatrical convention, and criticizing ninteenth-century Shakespearian scholarship. But frequently the excursions of older men into literary criticism met with little success. Robert K. Root's sympathetic but slight book on Alexander Pope, or Hazelton Spencer's and Hardin Craig's books on Shakespeare are not impressive as examples of sensibility and penetration. But other scholars who started with historical studies of a more or less conventional kind have absorbed and applied the ideas of modern criticism and developed them, independently, in contact with texts from the past. F. O. Matthiessen, for instance, began with careful analytical work on Elizabethan translation and then wrote of T. S. Eliot, Henry James, and the whole American Renaissance critically and sensitively. Austin Warren began with a monograph in the history of criticism, analyzed the philosophical ideas of the elder Henry James, and reached criticism in a distinguished study of the poetry of Richard Crashaw. Increasingly, the younger men in the universities are becoming critics and interested in criticism without having lost the advantages of historical learning and training. The future belongs to them.

Finally, one source of possible academic reform should not be neglected: the presence, in the United States during the last two decades of some distinguished German, Spanish, and Russian émigrés who themselves shared directly in the development of the new methods in Europe. Even though some of the most distinguished of the scholars, e.g. Leo Spitzer, Erich Auerbach, Amado Alonso, are now dead, their work stands as a guide to be emulated with profit. Other émigrés are still active: Helmut Hatzfeld is an exponent of the German stylistics practiced by Spitzer and Auerbach;

Roman Jakobson was an original member of the Russian formalist group; and these men are not the only ones by far. The total work of such émigrés could be, if properly utilized, a contribution as great as that of other recent immigrants to this country to the study of the history of art or to the reorganization of musicology.

Thus, it is clear in what direction the reform of graduate study in English must move. The old Ph.D. degree must be changed radically. Its holder should be not an antiquarian specialist in a period but a "professional man of letters, a man who, in addition to English and American literature, knows literary theory, the modes of scholarship and criticism, who, without recourse to impressionism and 'appreciation,' can analyze and discuss books with his classes." The linguistic requirements should be changed by asking for a really advanced, literary knowledge of one or two of the great living languages of Europe. The thesis should be conceived of as flexibly as we can conceive of professional literary distinction. Its possible range should certainly include contemporary literature and allow the use of all the methods of literary criticism. There should be an increasing stress on training in other literatures, in aesthetics, in philosophy rather than in medieval philology. In short, a Ph.D. in literature rather than in English, French, or German philology is the ideal.[9]

But if this reform should be successful, we should also have to face the dangers with which it might be confronted and the excesses to which it might succumb. There may be something in the very nature of institutional academic life which will lead again to mechanization, ossification, to Alexandrianism in the bad sense. The danger of mere imitation and of routine repetition may become acute, though at a time fortunately still rather remote. More urgent is the danger that

9. The quotations are from my and Austin Warren's *Theory of Literature* (New York, 1949), pp. 292–93, 294.

in getting free of the past we may also get rid of its genuine virtues. The originators and leaders of the revulsion against philological scholarship (and I mean not only the "new" critics but also the neohumanists) have all been men of education and frequently of learning, men who had a sense of the past and who, with it, possessed an amount of information easy to underrate because they were apt to underrate it themselves. In present-day America students will have to face the problem that in learning certain techniques and discussing theoretical problems they may neglect to acquire basic facts and a knowledge of a map of literature which, even though but a map, has its uses. The appallingly bad secondary education of most American students puts a burden on the colleges which they are sometimes unable or unwilling to bear. Our graduate schools, if reformed, must face the problem that we need not less scholarship, but better, more intelligent, more relevant, and more critical scholarship.

Philosophy and Postwar
American Criticism

Criticism is discrimination, judgment, and hence applies and implies criteria, principles, concepts, and thus a theory and aesthetic and ultimately a philosophy, a view of the world. Even the criticism written "with the least worry of head, the least disposition to break the heart over ultimate questions"[1] takes a philosophical position. Even skepticism, relativism, impressionism appeal, at least silently, to some version of naturalism, irrationalism or agnosticism.[2]

American criticism since the end of the second World War is no exception. One could even say that compared to the critics who wrote up to about 1914, or even up to about 1932, American critics have become more clearly conscious of their philosophical affiliations and assumptions. Increasingly, one comes across such statements as that of Elder Olson: "criticism," he tells us, "is a department of philosophy. A given comprehensive philosophy invariably develops a certain view of art"[3]; or, in a new reversal of traditional views, criticism is simply considered a philosophy and even

1. H. W. Garrod, *Poetry and the Criticism of Life* (Oxford, 1931), pp. 156–57.
2. Cf. Benedetto Croce, "La critica letteraria come filosofia," in *Nuovi Saggi di estetica* (Bari, 1919).
3. R. S. Crane, ed., *Critics and Criticism* (Chicago, 1952), p. 547. Cf. e.g. Philip Blair Rice, *On the Knowledge of Good and Evil* (New York, 1955), p. 217: "To the extent that the critic has a consistent point of view, he is tacitly presupposing an aesthetic theory, whether he acknowledges the fact or not."

a form of theology, an all-inclusive system, a world hypothesis. Thirty years ago criticism was a lowly day-by-day activity of the reviewer or a little corner of academic concern; today it often makes the most grandiose claims, which far exceed even Arnold's hope for its salutary influence on the preservation of culture. It is serious praise that "criticism, ceasing to be one of several intellectual arts, is becoming the entire intellectual act itself" and that the critic is a "prophet, announcing to the ungodly the communication of men with ultimate reality."[4]

In my own experience of the American academic scene, the contrast between the Princeton of 1927-28, where even eminent scholars seemed hardly aware of the issues of criticism, and the Yale of 1962, where criticism and its problems are our daily bread and tribulation, is striking, and such an impression can easily be substantiated by a similar contrast between *The American Mercury* of 1927, a satirical organ devoted to muck-raking and the advancement of the naturalistic novel, and the 1962 quarterlies: *The Kenyon, The Hudson, The Sewanee, Criticism,* etc.

We could describe and analyze this change in a chronological order, expound, for instance, the doctrine of the New Criticism at the end of the war and then trace the diverse reactions against it and the alternatives offered for it: myth criticism, existentialism, and so forth. I have tried to do this, in an international context, in the following essay, "The Main Trends of Twentieth-Century Criticism," and again in a long contribution to a German encyclopedia of world literature.[5] There, necessarily, little room was left for recent developments in America: an expansion of the older treatments might be in order. But I shall try a some-

4. R. W. B. Lewis, "Casella as Critic: A Note on R. P. Blackmur," *Kenyon Review 13* (1951), 470, 473–74.

5. *Lexikon der Weltliteratur im 20. Jahrhundert, 2* (Freiburg, 1961), 178–261.

what different approach, which, I hope, will illuminate from a new angle the lay of the land and make the features of the landscape stand out in a stronger relief.

I propose to take the history of Western philosophy in its main representatives and currents—Plato, Aristotle, Thomism, British empiricism, Kant, Schelling, Hegel, etc. —in their chronological order and ask how far recent American critics profess allegiance to any of them or implicitly accept any of their general positions. In the space at my disposal I shall not be able to discuss all the important critics and books of the seventeen years since the war. I am aware that I can do little more than indicate the main types and trends and assign individual critics rather brusquely to one or the other position, without being able to make the necessary qualifications. Philosophical commitments in criticism, I realize, are often half-hearted: critical books are often hybrid and beset even by confusions and obscurities. Still, I hope to show the continuities of the main philosophical traditions, demonstrate some survivals from the past, point out some kinships and enmities of the mind. I want to achieve a "perspective by incongruity," the "sudden view of things from their reverse, usually unnoticed side" which Edward Bullough required for "psychical distance," and thus for all art.[6] I want what Pound calls "making strange" and Brecht *Verfremdung*.

Coleridge proclaimed that "every man is born either an Aristotelian or a Platonist," and Alfred North Whitehead has called the history of philosophy "a series of footnotes to Plato."[7] We could try separating the American critics into Platonists and Aristotelians, idealists and realists. But we would not get very far with such a simple dichotomy,

6. "Psychical Distance as a Factor in Art and an Aesthetic Principle," in *Aesthetics,* ed. E. M. Wilkinson (London, 1957), p. 95.

7. Coleridge, *Table Talk* (London, 1851), p. 100; A. N. Whitehead, *Process and Reality* (New York, 1929), p. 63.

and there are no Platonists left in a strict sense and very
few Aristotelians. But for my purpose I like to think of the
American neohumanist movement as Platonic, as certainly
Paul Elmer More was a close student of Plato. The neo-
humanist movement is defunct today, but its outlook survives in one American critic of stature, Yvor Winters. I am
aware that Winters in his youth contributed to an anti-
humanist symposium,[8] but since then he has expressed his
admiration for Irving Babbitt,[9] and he has, in general terms,
restated the moralism and antiromanticism of that group.
Most of Winters' work precedes 1945, but he has summarized his views in a long essay, *The Function of Criticism*
(1957), and has applied anew his principles to Hopkins,
Yeats, and Robert Frost, "the spiritual drifter."[10] Winters
asserts a firm belief in absolute values. "I am aware," he
says, "that my absolutism implies a theistic position, unfortunate as this admission may be. If experience appears to
indicate that absolute truths exist, that we are able to work
toward an approximate apprehension of them, but that they
are antecedent to our apprehension and that our apprehension is seldom or perhaps never perfect, then there is only
one place in which these truths may be located, and I see
no way to escape this conclusion."[11] A poem, he asserts
over and over again, is "a rational statement about a human
experience. It is a method for perfecting the understanding
and the moral discrimination."[12] It is judged by the rationality of its argument and the morality of its meaning, though
morality is seen as a balance of form and content, classical

8. "Poetry, Morality and Criticism," in *Critique of Humanism*,
ed. C. H. Grattan (New York, 1930), pp. 301–33.

9. *In Defense of Reason* (Denver, 1947), pp. 385–87, 568–69;
The Function of Criticism (Denver, 1957), pp. 11–13, 75.

10. *The Function*, pp. 157 ff.

11. Quoted in *Essays in Criticism, 12* (1962), 79.

12. *The Function*, p. 139.

order, control, equilibrium, and not as a bald didactic message. There is some harsh truth and hard common sense in Winters' attacks on Emerson, Poe, Whitman, Hawthorne and many other American writers as "obscurantists." Winters asserts a surprisingly modern taste in his appreciation of Valéry, Emily Dickinson, Bridges, and many of the less obvious Elizabethan poets, or in his reflections on prosody. But no American critic has indulged so unrestrainedly in the game of ranking: Elizabeth Daryush is "the finest British poet since T. Sturge Moore," Sturge Moore is a better poet than W. B. Yeats, and Adelaide Crapsey "certainly is an immortal poet," etc.[13] The epic and drama are dead, we are told. The novel is dying rapidly. History writing takes their place. Macaulay, oddly enough, appears as the great master.[14] Only the short reflective poem, like Valéry's *Ebauche d'un serpent*, has any future. There is no recourse against such dogmatism.

It is easy to find professed Aristotelians. A whole group of scholars at the University of Chicago during the 1940s called themselves neo-Aristotelians, and Aristotle's influence is felt even outside of the group. Gerald F. Else has written a voluminous commentary on the *Poetics* (1957). Francis Fergusson, whose central conception of tragedy is rather mythic, constantly appeals to Aristotle's analysis of dramatic structure. In an introduction to the *Poetics* he has drawn up an elaborate scheme to reconcile Aristotle's analysis of *Oedipus Rex* with the ritual forms of Greek drama as reconstructed by Gilbert Murray and his school.[15] Philip Wheelwright and Kenneth Burke have Aristotle constantly in mind. The Chicago Aristotelians, we should realize, do not commit themselves, in theory, to anything so crude as a doctrinaire acceptance of Aristotle's system. R. S. Crane,

13. *In Defense of Reason,* pp. 105, 490, 568.
14. *The Function,* pp. 74, 63 ff., 49 ff.
15. *Aristotle's Poetics* (New York, 1961), p. 40.

in his introduction to the programmatic volume, *Critics and Criticism* (1952), rather proclaims "a pluralistic and instrumentalist view of criticism," considers their Aristotelianism "a strictly pragmatic and not exclusive commitment," and admits even that this or any other interpreter's Aristotle "may not be Aristotle at all."[16] But in practice Crane's "method of multiple hypotheses"[17] is constantly abandoned by the Chicago Critics in favor of a dogmatic scheme which serves as a polemical instrument against the New Criticism and the propounders of symbolist and mythic interpretations of literature. Plot, character, genre are the central concepts, while language is relegated to the lowly position of a mere material cause or occasion of poetry. The Chicago Critics often embrace concepts common in Renaissance Aristotelianism. Language is to them inert matter like stone for the sculptor, and genre becomes a rigid scheme of definitions and exclusions. Elder Olson, in *Tragedy and the Theory of Drama* (1961), tells us that "the greater, and the chief part, of playwriting has nothing to do with words."[18] The *Divine Comedy* is classified as not "mimetic" but "didactic," not "symbolical" but only "allegorical."[19] I am not denying that the Chicago Critics have scored many points against the over-readings of the New Critics, especially against Robert Heilman's interpretations of *King Lear* and *Othello*.[20] One must, besides, be impressed by the extensive learning in the history of criticism shown particularly by R. S. Crane, Richard McKeon, and Bernard Weinberg. We owe to Weinberg a fully documented *History of Literary*

16. Pp. 9, 12–13, 17.

17. *The Languages of Criticism and the Structure of Poetry* (Toronto, 1953), p. 237.

18. Detroit, 1961, p. 9.

19. *Critics and Criticism*, pp. 590 ff.

20. *This Great Stage* (Baton Rouge, 1948); *The Magic in the Web* (Lexington, Ky., 1956).

Criticism in the Italian Renaissance (1961). But judged as an instrument of living criticism, the Chicago Aristotelianism seems to me, ultimately, only an ultra-academic exercise. The best practical application of the principles is Wayne Booth's *The Rhetoric of Fiction* (1961), which argues persuasively against the Jamesian dogma of the disappearance of the author from the novel, but ends with a distressingly Philistine plea for a sound and sane morality, to be clearly and publicly announced by the novelist. The only other book of practical criticism of the Chicago school is oddly enough, devoted to *The Poetry of Dylan Thomas* (1954). Elder Olson, who had attacked Empson for his ambiguities and ingenuities, indulges there enthusiastically in the same game, without any embarrassment at the contradiction. One can understand why other critics lose patience with the scientific pretensions of the Chicago school and occasionally even with their innocent godfather. Reuben Brower, a sensitive reader of poetry and close student of Alexander Pope, has even voiced the suspicion that "this excellent geometrician did not know what poetry was."[21] It simply won't do to make Aristotle again the master "di color che sanno." Too many things have happened since.

Surprisingly enough, there is no neo-Thomist criticism in the United States, though its founder, Jacques Maritain, lives among us and published, in English, *Creative Intuition in Art and Poetry* (1953). His new book could be interpreted as deserting Thomism for an almost Bergsonian intuitionism which in practice exalts French symbolism and even surrealism. There is, however, a strong intellectual ferment among Roman Catholics in the United States, and professed Catholics take part in literary criticism. Father William J. Lynch, for instance, in *Christ and Apollo* (1960), devised "dimensions" of the imagination which

21. "The Heresy of Plot," *English Institute Essays 1951* (New York, 1952), p. 59.

include the analogical, the theological, and the Christian in a scheme modeled on the fourfold method of medieval exegesis. Allen Tate, who is the most speculative mind among the Southern critics, had, even before his conversion to Roman Catholicism (1956), applied Maritain's doctrine of "angelism" to a confrontation between Dante's "symbolic" and Poe's "angelic imagination."[22] In Tate the hatred of science, the nostalgia for an organic society and religious view of the world, is combined with a somewhat paradoxical preoccupation with writers who reflect the dissolution of the tradition, with Poe, Emily Dickinson, T. S. Eliot, W. B. Yeats, and Hart Crane, a personal friend whose tragic fate documents for Tate the disintegration of any artist unsupported by a coherent tradition. But neither of these critics is a Thomist: Roman Catholicism rather provides a framework for a radical rejection of naturalism and positivism and a view of poetry as providing not only "complete knowledge" but revelation, absolute truth, even beatific vision.

These three philosophers, Plato, Aristotle and Thomas Aquinas, represent the old world of ideas about art and poetry. The new world arose in the eighteenth century, when neoclassical orthodoxy broke down and empiricism, sensualism, associationism, and their variants replaced it, at least in England. I don't want to suggest that anybody today embraces British eighteenth-century empiricism in its original form, but certainly a broad stream of aesthetic and critical thinking descends from there. Utilitarianism and positivism were its immediate heirs early in the nineteenth century, pragmatism followed closely, and behaviorism and logical positivism would hardly deny their ancestry. In its epistemological assumptions much literary scholarship and discussion is still positivistic, relying on a naive precritical conception of "fact" and assuming a simple mechanistic

22. Essays in *The Forlorn Demon* (Chicago, 1953).

concept of cause in biographical circumstances, literary influences, and social and historical backgrounds. The bulk
of conventional academic scholarship is confined within
this horizon even today. It hardly needs discussion in a survey of criticism. But later forms of positivistic thought have
assumed a great importance for the development of recent
American criticism. J. C. Ransom, in *The New Criticism*
(1941), starts his chapter on I. A. Richards by saying,
"The new criticism very nearly began with him"[23]; and certainly a good argument can be put up for the view that the
New Criticism *is* a peculiar combination of Richards and
T. S. Eliot. But Richards is an Englishman—though he has
been at the other Cambridge for thirty years—and most of
his writings precede 1945. Neither his only new critical
book, *Speculative Instruments* (1955), nor a few scattered
articles constitute a substantial change in his point of view.[24]
Richards has merely recognized that his earlier trust in the
advances of neurology was irrelevant: he still expounds the
view of art as a sort of emotional therapy, of the work as
a pattern of impulses, of poetry as emotive language,
pseudo-statement, or myth. Richards, like Dewey, denies
any difference between aesthetic and ordinary experience
and upholds a radical psychologism and hedonistic naturalism. Richards' interest in the meaning of meaning, in semantics, has proved his most fruitful contribution to criticism
proper. Such a critic as Cleanth Brooks, who does not share
Richards' philosophical assumptions, still uses his key terms:
attitudes, tensions, ambiguities, and irony.

The main attempt to erect a pragmatic and semantic
philosophy of criticism since Richards has been made by
Kenneth Burke. He resembles Richards in general orienta-

23. Norfolk, Conn., 1941, p. 3.
24. See "Emotive Language Still," *Yale Review,* (1949); "Poetic
Process and Literary Analysis," in *Style in Language,* ed. Thomas A.
Sebeok (New York, 1960); and "The Future of Poetry," in *The
Screens and Other Poems* (New York, 1960).

tion, but he tries to combine semantics with Marxism, Freudianism, and the philosophy of the "act" as expounded by George Herbert Mead, a follower of Dewey. Most of Burke's literary criticism belongs to his earlier years. Recently he has been engaged in devising a philosophical system which includes *A Grammar of Motives* (1945), *A Rhetoric of Motives* (1955), and *A Rhetoric of Religion* (1961). I cannot pretend to be able to follow Burke's acrobatics between the different activities of man; but I understand enough to see that a literary work is considered a "symbolic act," a personal ritual of purification which sublimates the poet's subconscious drives and affects society by its model "strategy" of "encompassing situations."[25] Literary criticism as judgment is completely lost sight of: no distinction between trash and Shakespeare is possible. The difference between literature and life, work and action is abolished. Burke's charts, hierarchies, pentads, bureaucracies have nothing to do with literature. When in recent years Burke has engaged a specific poetic text, he has produced only fanciful or heavy-footed Marxist or psychoanalytical interpretations. For instance, the "socioanagogic" interpretation of *Venus and Adonis* amounts to reducing this witty and sensual poem to a "concealed social allegory." The goddess represents a noblewoman in love with a commoner: the poem is "social lewdness" expressed in sexual terms.[26] In "Beauty is truth, truth beauty" Burke professes to find a punning scatological sense.[27] The albatross in the *Ancient Mariner* is "a synecdochic representative of [Coleridge's] Sarah," and the whole poem "a ritual for the redemption of his drug."[28] Burke has ceased to be a critic and has set up as an oracle of an abstruse philosophy.

The same thing has happened to Richard P. Blackmur,

25. *The Philosophy of Literary Form* (Baton Rouge, 1941), p. 1.
26. *A Rhetoric of Motives,* pp. 212-21.
27. Ibid., p. 204.
28. *The Philosophy of Literary Form,* pp. 72, 96.

except that we cannot be sure that there is any philosophy behind the oracular manner. Blackmur also began as an ingenious analyst of texts, but in his recent essays he has become vaguer and vaguer, talking teasingly in the cobwebby style of the very latest stage of Henry James. Even a fervent admirer spoke eleven years ago of his "hidden ball play,"[29] and the ball has become even more hidden as the years go by. Blackmur has voiced dissatisfaction with the limitations of the New Criticism, but has been unable to formulate a comprehensive theory of his own. He comes nearest to a general statement when he speaks of "language as gesture." Gesture is a term combining symbol and expression. Symbol is a "cumulus of meaning" which is achieved by all the devices of poetry: punning, rhyme, meter, tropes.[30] But most of the new essays collected in *Language as Gesture* (1952) and *The Lion and the Honeycomb* (1955) show a disconcerting loss of contact with any text and a random experimentation with many different terms and their contraries: symbol, myth, imagination, behavior, gesture, and even silence and "the grasp of unreason."[31] Blackmur, just because of his subtlety and versatility, illustrates the predicament of much recent American criticism: its involvement in a private world of concepts and terms, a groping toward a general philosophy of life or even theology by the avenue of literature, and a distrust of traditional methods which leads to a reliance on purely personal combinations and associations. In some of Blackmur's essays the privacy of terms and feelings has reached a fuzziness and blur so extreme that it seems impossible to keep up any interest in the solution of the metaphorical riddles propounded or to

29. R. B. W. Lewis, *Kenyon Review, 13* (1951), 463.

30. *Language as Gesture* (New York, 1952), p. 16.

31. See "The Language of Silence," *Sewanee Review, 63* (1955), 382–404; and "The Great Grasp of Unreason," *Hudson Review, 9* (1956–57), 488–503.

care for the opaque mysteries which are only pointed or
hinted at. It seems odd that a basically naturalistic philosophy should lead to such obeisances to the ultimate darkness.
But naturalism and agnosticism, pragmatism and irrationalism go together: William James was not averse to the
occult.

Another main strand of American criticism descends
rather from German idealism: from Kant, Schelling, and
Hegel. But we must make distinctions on this point. Kantian aesthetics survives only as a most general attitude: as a
recognition of the distinction between the true, the good
and the beautiful, of the autonomy of art, a basic insight
which is lost or rather purposely obliterated by Dewey,
Richards, and their followers. Actual Kantianism is alive
only in the modernized version of the German philosopher
Ernst Cassirer, who died in New York in 1945. But a kind
of neo-Kantian expressionism flourishes today. One influential aesthetician, Susanne K. Langer, has developed, in
Feeling and Form (1953), a theory of art as representa-
tional symbolism which draws on Cassirer's *A Philosophy
of Symbolic Forms*. Mrs. Langer, though largely concerned
with music and the fine arts, formulates a view of poetry
as the creation of symbols of feelings, a world of illusory
experience, of "semblance," of metaphor and myth. And
Eliseo Vivas, in his essays *Creation and Discovery* (1955),
is not very far removed from this point of view. "Poetry
uniquely reveals a world which is self-sufficient," a world
constituted by means of a symbolic process.[32] Imitation and
expression theories and all naturalistic explanations are
rejected. Literature does not give us knowledge in the narrow sense of the word. It is rather prior "in the order of
logic to all knowledge: constitutive of culture."[33] Vivas
elaborates a theory of the "intransitivity" of aesthetic exper-

32. New York, 1955, pp. 73–74.
33. Ibid., p. 127.

ience[34] which seems a restatement of Kant's "disinterested satisfaction," but he is by no means only engaged in a discussion of aesthetic generalities: he has written well of Dreiser, Henry James, Kafka, and Dostoevsky and has recently devoted a book to *D. H. Lawrence* (1960) which tries to distinguish between the shoddy ideology and the good art. The neo-Kantianism of Mrs. Langer and Eliseo Vivas is not, of course, unmixed. Vivas describes himself as an "axiological realist," and if I understand him correctly he has approached a position close to that of Allen Tate.[35]

Oddly enough, the most influential philosopher among the German idealists is Schelling, though his actual works are not read and little is available in translation. It is all due to Coleridge, who transmitted, digested, and combined his ideas with many other *motifs* of thought. Coleridge's paper "On Poesy and Art," which is being quoted constantly, is hardly more than a translation of a speech of Schelling's given at the Munich Academy, and central passages in *Biographia Literaria,* on the two imaginations, on the reconciliation of opposites, paraphrase Schelling very closely.[36] We do not have to make up our minds about the degree of Coleridge's dependence on Schelling to recognize that through Coleridge the central conceptions of German romantic criticism entered the American tradition: creative imagination, the reconciliation of opposites, art as an analogue of nature, the poem as an organic whole, symbol in contrast to allegory, and so forth. These ideas filtered down to American critics through many intermediaries; but T. S. Eliot especially quoted the crucial passages from Coleridge, and Richards, in *Coleridge on Imagination* (1934), tried

34. See Appendix to *D. H. Lawrence* (Evanston, Ill., 1960).

35. See the fervid tribute to Allen Tate, "Mi ritrovai per una selva oscura," *Sewanee Review, 67* (1959), 560–66.

36. See my *History of Modern Criticism, 2* (New Haven, 1955), 152 ff.

to translate Coleridge into terms acceptable to a naturalist. The Coleridge point of view is today most clearly represented by Cleanth Brooks. It is a precarious position: how can one reconcile a contextualist view of the work of art —its self-containedness, its organicity—with a meaningful relation to reality? Brooks analyzes poems as structures of opposites, tensions, paradoxes, and ironies with unparalleled skill. Paradox and irony are terms used by him very broadly. Irony is not the opposite of an overt statement, but "a general term for the kind of qualification which the various elements in a context receive from the context."[37] It indicates the recognition of incongruities, the union of opposites which Brooks finds in all good, that is, complex, "inclusive" poetry. Poetry must be ironic in the sense of being able to withstand ironic contemplation. The method works best when applied to Donne and Shakespeare, Eliot and Yeats, but in *The Well Wrought Urn* (1947), Brooks has shown that even Wordsworth and Tennyson, Gray and Pope yield to this kind of technique. Brooks attacks the "heresy of paraphrase," all attempts to reduce the poem to its prose content, and he has defended a well-defined absolutism: the need of judgment against the flaccid surrender to relativism and historicism. But in a number of essays, largely devoted to poems from the seventeenth century, Brooks has taken special pains to demonstrate that his absolutism of values is not incompatible with a proper regard for history.[38] Brooks joined forces with W. K. Wimsatt in writing *Literary Criticism: A Short History* (1957). Wimsatt, in the epilogue, formulates a syncretic creed which

37. *The Well Wrought Urn* (New York, 1947), p. 191.
38. E.g. "Literary Criticism," *English Institute Essays 1946* (New York, 1947) pp. 127–58; "The Quick and the Dead," in *The Humanities*, ed. Julian Harris (Madison, Wis., 1950), pp. 1–21; "Poet, Poem and Reader," in *Varieties of Literary Experience*, ed. S. Burnshaw (New York, 1962), pp. 95–114.

belies the "argumentative" concern voiced in the preface. Poetry, he concludes, is a "tensional unity of making with seeing and saying." All three major theories of poetry, the mimetic or Aristotelian, the emotive or Richardsian, and the expressionistic or Crocean must be respected: only metaphor is the pervasive principle of all poetry.[39] In his earlier work, collected as *The Verbal Icon* (1954), Wimsatt was primarily concerned with the objective structure of the work of art. He sharply dismissed the reliance on the intention of the author as the "Intentional Fallacy" and disparaged criticism according to the emotional effect of the work of art as the "Affective Fallacy." He uses the term "icon" suggested by Charles Morris as an alternative for the poetic symbol. In one brief passage of the epilogue of *Literary Criticism* Wimsatt suggests a parallel between his literary theory and the dogma of the Incarnation,[40] but it is an error committed by some reviewers who know of Wimsatt's Roman Catholicism to describe his critical position as religious or specifically Thomist. Both Wimsatt and Brooks, in difference from many of their fellow critics who have Arnoldian hopes for poetry replacing religion, keep a sharp distinction between aesthetics and theology and refuse to accept poetry as a substitute for religion. Quite rightly, they are not included in Richard Foster's *The New Romantics* (1962), which treats Richards, Vivas, Blackmur, and Tate as so many disguised Arnoldians. Brooks and Wimsatt have the peculiar merit of holding firmly to the aesthetic fact, of aiming at a theory of literature which will be literary.

On the whole, the relation of modern American criticism to the idealist tradition is puzzling. They draw, like Eliot, Brooks, or Wimsatt, concepts and terms from the romantic idealists, but these have somehow lost their metaphysical moorings in the new context. Benedetto Croce's aesthetic

39. New York, 1957, pp. 749, 750, 755.
40. P. 746.

must have had some influence in transmitting idealist conceptions, since it was expounded early by Joel Spingarn under the title of *The New Criticism* (1910). But Spingarn's version of Croce is diluted: it is simply a negation of rhetorical categories, of style, of genres, of the distinction between the arts and, in practice, a defense of impressionism. Richards dismissed Croce haughtily as appealing "exclusively to those unfamiliar with the subject, to the man of letters and the dilettante."[41] Only recently an Italian émigré scholar, G. N. Orsini, has written a full exposition of *Benedetto Croce* (1961) which does justice to his intricate system and to the wide range of his criticism. Hegel came to America directly from Germany in the nineteenth century, and a Hegelian movement was still represented early in this century by the commanding figure of Josiah Royce. From England, Hegelian *motifs* came with A. C. Bradley's *Shakespearean Tragedy* and Bernard Bosanquet's writings on aesthetics. A book such as Richard Sewall's *Vision of Tragedy* (1959) expounds the Bradleian view substantially unchanged. Wimsatt adopts the Hegelian term "concrete universal,"[42] but Hegel's dialectical method, not to speak of the details of the aesthetics, is entirely unknown in the United States.

The same is true of Marxism, at least in criticism. There was a Marxist movement in the thirties, and Marxist *motifs* and terms occur in the writings of Edmund Wilson and Kenneth Burke. But today no genuine Marxist criticism seems to be written in the United States. This is not, I think, due to McCarthyism or to anti-Soviet bias. It seems rather ignorance or lack of interest in the kind of criticism practiced by Georg Lukács or T. W. Adorno with such great acclaim on the Continent.

41. *The Principles of Literary Criticism* (London, 1924), p. 255n.
42. See "The Concrete Universal," in *The Verbal Icon* (Lexington, Ky., 1954), pp. 69–83.

Social criticism in the United States is rather anchored in a concern for the American liberal tradition and for an Arnoldian concept of culture. Genuine socialist affiliations are rare: F. O. Matthiessen professed a Christian socialism, though he was, in practice, a defender of Soviet policies even at the take-over of Czechoslovakia.[43] His only book within our purview, the posthumous study of *Dreiser* (1951), elaborately explains Dreiser's "symbolic" joining of the communist party and sympathetically studies a writer who must appear as the antipode of his early favorite, T. S. Eliot.

But the other social critics are liberal defenders of a free, critical, tolerant society which they want to preserve both against the evils of our vulgar mass culture and against reaction. Lionel Trilling, in his collections of essays, *The Liberal Imagination* (1950) and *The Opposing Self* (1955), is worried about the gulf between the rationality of his political convictions and the insights of modern literature represented by Proust, Joyce, Eliot, Kafka, Rilke, Gide and others. A man of modern sensibility, with a taste for Henry James and E. M. Forster and a dislike for naturalism, Trilling can only state his problem but not solve it, as he believes that ideas are emotions and that politics permeates literature. He has come to recognize the "fortuitous and the gratuitous nature of art, how it exists beyond the reach of the will alone,"[44] an insight buttressed by his understanding of Freud. The essay on Keats[45] shows his growing feeling for selves in opposition to general culture, for the alienation of the artist as a necessary device of his self-realization. A new essay, "The Modern Element in Modern Literature" (1961), raises again, in very personal terms, the question of the bitter hostility of the artist to

43. Cf. *From the Heart of Europe* (New York, 1948), esp. pp. 142 ff.

44. *The Liberal Imagination* (New York, 1950), p. 280.

45. In *The Opposing Self* (New York, 1955).

civilization, puzzling over the American phenomenon that students will take it all as a matter of course and will engage in the "acculturation of the anti-cultural, or the legitimization of the subversive."[46]

This seems an admirable phrase for what has happened to all the irrationalistic philosophies of Europe which came to the United States: romantic historicism, Schopenhauer, Nietzsche, Bergson, Freud, Jung, and existentialism. With few exceptions they became, at least in criticism, assimilated to the prevailing rationalist or pragmatist temper of the nation and certainly were rarely pushed to their irrationalist and often obscurantist extremes.

Much American criticism, especially criticism of American literature, assumes an attitude of romantic historicism. It is ultimately derived from the body of ideas developed by Herder and his successors, who looked for the organicity and continuity of literature as an expression of the national spirit, the folk. In America these ideas were early assimilated to the tradition of the Enlightenment which promoted the Revolution and were adapted to the particular conditions of the new continent: the classless society, the frontier, etc. Many recent critics are concerned with defining the nature of the American, the Americanism of American literature, often only dimly aware of how much is common to man, modern man, and common to Europe and America. Old ideas about national character are combined today with concepts derived from the prevalent theories about myth or even from existentialist phraseology. Old questions such as that concerning types in the novel, or the image of ideal man in literature are thus refurbished to the new taste. There is a whole spate of such books on American literature. Matthiessen's *American Renaissance* (1941), which precedes our era, is the initiating book: it combines an Eliotic concern for language and diction, symbolism and myth,

46. *Partisan Review, 28* (1961), 31.

with a fervent belief in the possibilities of democracy in America. The central theme has been approached by different authors from different angles. Charles Feidelson, in *Symbolism and American Literature* (1953), uses Cassirer, Susanne Langer and Whitehead. Literature is a verbal construct with hardly any relation to immediate social reality. Symbolism is conceived so broadly that no distinction between the early romantic Emersonian and Eliotic view can be made. The symbolistic method of Emerson, Melville, Hawthorne, Poe, and Whitman is their title to literary independence, the glory of American literature. Marius Bewley, in a book on Hawthorne and Henry James entitled *The Complex Fate* (1952), is preoccupied rather with the question of the American writer in Europe, his fate of "being an American, fighting against a superstitious valuation of Europe."[47] A second book, *The Eccentric Design* (1959), is concerned with the unhappy plight of the American writer, his isolation and rootlessness in his own country. Harry Levin's study of Hawthorne, Poe, and Melville, *The Power of Blackness* (1958), revolves around the somber title theme, which is studied sensitively and soberly. Richard W. B. Lewis, in *The American Adam* (1955), pursues the brighter theme of paradise, innocence, and the recovery of youth. In a flamboyant book, *Love and Death in the American Novel* (1960), Leslie A. Fiedler labors a psychoanalytical and social thesis: "the failure of the American writer to deal with adult heterosexual love and his consequent obsession with death, incest, and innocent homosexuality."[48] All these writers focus on what has been called the American Gothic fiction, "nonrealist, sadist and melodramatic— a literature of darkness and the grotesque in a land of light and affirmation."[49] A book devoted to *The Continuity of*

47. Quoting James, letter of Feb. 4, 1872, in *Letters, 1,* 13.
48. New York, 1960, p. xi.
49. Ibid., p. xxiv.

American Poetry (1961) by Roy Harvey Pearce uses cultural anthropology and existential terms for what, in the upshot, seems a high-minded romantic nationalism. The proposed aim of a fusion between the "Adamic" and the "mythic" means little more than the old aspiration to reconcile the individual and society, innocence and experience. Pearce's book simply ignores the fact that American poetry is English poetry, or rather, comfortably relegates this basic problem of a history of American poetry to the extraneous field of "comparative literature." Pearce's programmatic essay, "Historicism Once More,"[50] illustrates the current confusion between historicism, existentialism, and anthropology. Historicism means little more than a feeling for the actual existence of the past: its presence among us.

In Kantian, Coleridgean, and the historistic criticism we find "myth" used in the most diverse ways, but "myth" is also the central term for a type of criticism which has its antecedents in Nietzsche, Frazer, the Cambridge Greek scholars, and in Carl Jung. "Myth" thus has today so wide a range of meanings that it has become difficult to argue about it with any clarity of reference. The term appeals to many because it allows the discussion of themes and types, topics usually considered part of the "content" and thus not quite respectable to formalist critics. Huck Finn floating down the Mississippi with Jim is a "myth," and so is any truth which is generally accepted by its society. "Myth" can be simply a synonym for ideology. Richard Chase's *Quest for Myth* (1949) identifies all good, sublime literature with myth. The term may assume, however, more specific value for literary study when it refers to a system of archetypes recoverable in rituals and tales or to a scheme of metaphors, symbols, and gods created by a poet such as Blake or Yeats. From Jung comes the dangerously occult idea of a collective unconscious, of a racial memory

50. *Kenyon Review, 20* (1958), 554–91.

of which all literature is supposed to be a disguised expression. Myth criticism achieves its purpose when it shows the hidden pattern underlying every work of literature: e.g. the descent into hell, the purgatorial stair, the sacrificial death of the god. But one wonders whether anything important for literary criticism has been achieved by such a discovery. All literature is reduced to a few myths. "After decoding each work of art in these terms one is left with a feeling of monotony and futility. Poetry is revelation, but what does it reveal?"[51]

We must, however, make distinctions among the myth-critics. There are the allegorizers, who find the story of redemption all over Shakespeare or discover Swedenborgianism in the novels of Henry James. There are others who have preserved an aesthetic sense and judgment. Francis Fergusson's *Idea of a Theater* (1949) uses the results of the Cambridge school to consider the theater of all ages, from Sophocles to T. S. Eliot, as ritual. Even *Hamlet* appears as such a ritual performance in conflict with improvisation, while the drama of Racine and much modern theatre is criticised as arbitrary invention, as rationalistic contrivance with no proper relation to society. Fergusson has used this approach also for a very personal and somewhat tenuous interpretation of the *Purgatorio* as *Dante's Drama of the Mind* (1953).

Fergusson remains in many ways a man of the theater, of a poetic symbolist theater. Philip Wheelwright, in *The Burning Fountain* (1954), combines, rather, myth interest with semantics. Wheelwright is a student of Heraclitus, Aristotle, and Buddhism. Aesthetic contemplation, he tells us, is and should be "but a halfway house to mysticism."[52] Wheelwright is, fortunately, interested in the beginning of

51. Austin Warren, in R. Wellek and A. Warren, *Theory of Literature* (New York, 1949), p. 217.
52. Bloomington, Ind., 1954, p. 61.

the journey: what he calls the "plurisignation" of the poetic work, the ascent from literal meaning through metaphor and symbol to myth. In his new book, *Metaphor and Reality* (1962), the sequence is elaborated, and in the chapters of *The Burning Fountain* devoted to the *Oresteia* and *The Waste Land* thematic and mythic patterns are studied sensitively.

An all-embracing scheme is proposed in Northrop Frye's *Anatomy of Criticism* (1957). Frye began with an excellent interpretation of Blake's private mythology, *Fearful Symmetry* (1947). In *Anatomy of Criticism* literature is conceived as "existing in its own universe, no longer a commentary on life and reality, but containing life and reality in a system of verbal relationships." Literature "imitates the total dream of man," the "order of nature is imitated by a corresponding order of words." Criticism which clarifies this order should succeed in "reforging the links between creation and knowledge, art and science, myth and concept."[53] In practice Frye devises an enormously intricate scheme of modes, symbols, myths, and genres for which, however, the Jungian archetype is the basic assumption. Frye is not interested in causal explanation and rejects the collective unconscious as an unnecessary hypothesis. What concerns him is mostly a new theory of genres, of which there are four: comedy, romance, tragedy, and satire; and these correspond to the four seasons: spring, summer, autumn, and winter, the rhythm of nature. The method leads to the most surprising confrontations: thus, in comedy the myth of spring is recapitulated, and such completely different works as *Winter's Tale, Bleak House, Pamela,* and *The Rape of the Lock* are interpreted as variants of the Proserpine myth. All literature is finally part of the *Urmythos*. In Frye all distinctions of artistic value disappear: the simplest folk tale will fit just as well as *Hamlet*.

53. Princeton, N. J., 1957, pp. 118, 119, 122, 354.

In a "Polemical Introduction" Frye has excluded value judgment from his concept of criticism, as criticism "should show a steady advance toward undiscriminating catholicity."[54] But Frye, in practice, is a sensitive reader and ingenious theorist who imposes the fearful symmetry of his system by his power of discrimination and combination. One cannot help thinking that criticism, in Frye, has overreached itself and that a more modest concept of its aim would be wiser. Frye quotes, with apparent approval, Mallarmé's saying, "Tout, au monde, existe pour aboutir à un livre,"[55] but Frye's book is, we know all the time, his own *Anatomy*. The trouble with his speculations is that they are completely uncontrollable. On the analogy of the Freudian dream interpretation, they allow all manner of substitutions, condensations, and identifications. As Frye admits: "The literary universe is a universe in which everything is potentially identical with everything else."[56]

This method is also the bane of Freudian criticism which has "scientific" pretensions and a rationalistic philosophical basis. Freudian criticism, much more than Jungian criticism, is frighteningly obtuse to the text and dreary in its search for sexual symbolism. In the books of Arthur Wormhoudt, writing is spilling of mother's milk. Domes, mountains, pyramids, cups, and even trees and birds are all breast symbols.[57] In Charles Neider's book on Kafka, *The Frozen Sea* (1948), every protuberance and opening is read as male or female. But such total Freudians exist only on the fringes of literary criticism. No strictly Freudian critic has won any reputation. Freudian motifs and insights

54. Ibid., p. 25.
55. Ibid., p. 122.
56. Ibid., p. 124.
57. *The Demon Lover* (New York, 1949), pp. 6, 13; *The Muse at Length* (New York, 1953); *Hamlet's Mouse Trap* (New York, 1956).

have provided tools for other critics, who see the limitations of the method but use it as a technique of reading below the surface, as an unmasking. Freudian concepts or pre-conceptions organize many literary biographies and psychological interpretations. Even in this connection, however, Lionel Trilling, who praises Freud for having done "more for our understanding of art than any other writer since Aristotle,"[58] has stated convincingly the differences between art and neurosis, artistic creation and daydreaming.

Bergsonism is another European philosophy which has had important bearings on American criticism. I would class John Crowe Ransom, the supposed father of the New Criticism, as, at least originally, a Bergsonian. Ransom studied Greats at Oxford and knows much about Kant, Hegel, and Croce. Allen Tate, in an illuminating aside, has protested against the view that Ransom taught his disciples (Tate, R. P. Warren, Cleanth Brooks) the knowledge of good and evil. Rather, he taught them "Kantian aesthetics and a philosophy of dualism, tinged with Christian theology, but ultimately derived from the Nicomachean ethics."[59] But surely Bergson made the greatest impression on the early Ransom: Ransom's criticism of abstraction, his distinction between structure and the "irrelevant" texture of a poem, his attack on Platonic poetry in favor of a poetry of things, is Bergsonian (though some of it may come through T. E. Hulme and Imagism). After World War II, however, Ransom tried different approaches; at one time, for instance, he adopted a Freudian analogy for his distinction between structure and texture: the poem as structure, as thought-work, as prose-value belongs to the *ego*; the latent or suspected content, the texture, belongs to the *id*.[60] But Ransom

58. *The Liberal Imagination*, p. 161.
59. "A Southern Mode of the Imagination," in *The Carleton Miscellany, 1* (1960), 12.
60. "Poetry: The Final Cause," *Kenyon Review, 9* (1947), 654.

seems later to have dropped these ideas and in his recent writings has returned to his more rational defense of the concrete, of texture, of things and nature. He clings to a dualism of form and content and keeps his theory of poetry resolutely secular. The early attempt to set up a God with Thunder seems abandoned. In his rejection of organistic aesthetics Ransom preserves a very individual and isolated position in American criticism.

A new motif of American criticism in recent years is existentialism. I am not sure whether we can speak of a genuinely existential criticism. A concrete, knowing relation to either Heidegger or Sartre does not seem to exist. Existential criticism is a vocabulary, a mood, an attitude, or it should be described rather as "phenomenology," as the attempt to reconstruct the author's "consciousness," his relation to time and space, nature and society in the manner which has been demonstrated so successfully by recent French critics such as Georges Poulet and Jean-Pierre Richard. Geoffrey Hartman, in his *Unmediated Vision* (1954), studies poems by Wordsworth, Hopkins, Valéry, and Rilke in order to trace the dialectic of perception and consciousness, the process of "how an image before the eye becomes an idea in the mind."[61] In J. Hillis Miller's *Charles Dickens: The World of his Novels* (1959) a "preexistent psychological condition" of the writer is assumed by which he "apprehends and in some measure creates himself."[62] The interior landscape, the search for identity are the leading themes of an analysis of Dickens' fictional world.

In R. W. B. Lewis' *Picaresque Saint* (1959) the existential theme, the sense of nothingness, is shown to be transcended, in several modern novelists, by an "agonized dedication to life."[63] The type of the saintly rogue seems often forced on

61. New Haven, 1954, p. 123.
62. Cambridge, Mass., 1959, p. viii.
63. Philadelphia, 1959, p. 27.

the authors selected: Moravia, Camus, Silone, Faulkner, and Graham Greene. Lewis' motivation is really religious and political: optimistic in its conclusions. On the other hand, Ihab Hassan's *Radical Innocence: Studies in the Contemporary American Novel* (1962) looks only for anti-heroes, victims, pariahs. "They all share a vision of absurdity despite their radical apprehension of the Self." Hassan solemnly discusses such an inconsequential romp as Truman Capote's *Breakfast at Tiffany's* and returns again to the question of Americanism. The book concludes with a dusty answer: "Every one must rediscover America for himself—alone."[64] The theme of loneliness and despair informs also Murray Krieger's *The Tragic Vision* (1960). There the protagonist of tragedy is taken deliberately out of the context of tragedy as structure. The tragic hero (or rather "visionary") is the man of the "sickness unto death," of modern nihilism. Even Dostoevsky's Idiot is assimilated to this concept, and there is less trouble with the heroes of Kafka, Camus, Thomas Mann, and Melville. Krieger, who had before written an acute analysis of the New Criticism, *The New Apologists for Poetry* (1956), now advocates "thematics" as a supplement to formal criticism. A new dualism of form and content is adapted to a metaphysical dualism, a "vision of a final cosmic disharmony." Literature becomes the "only form of existential philosophy"[65]: philosophizing in existential terms is actually impossible, he asserts. You can convey the existential vision only in fictional terms. But one may ask how it can be conveyed, then, in terms of criticism? The irrationalistic argument fits existential criticism as well as philosophy: only a mood, an attitude remains.

If we look back at this panorama, or rather listen to the confusion of tongues in the new Tower of Babel, we cannot

64. Princeton, 1962, pp. 332, 336.
65. New York, 1960, pp. 245, 247.

be surprised at a growing feeling of bewilderment and in-
comprehension. A facile resignation, a crude anti-intellectualism and anti-criticism is in the air. It can be frankly and
grossly Philistine; it can be a blithe defense of amateurism,
impressionism, enthusiasm; it can be the skepticism and historical relativism of the scholar who sees critical theories
as so many rationalizations for a transient sensibility; or it
can be simply the disgust of poets and writers with the
critics' ubiquity and pretentiousness. Randall Jarrell, in
Poetry and the Age (1953), complained that "criticism
which began by humbly and anomalously existing for the
work of art, and was in part a mere by-product of philosophy
and rhetoric, has by now become, for a good many people, almost what the work of art exists for."[66] Karl Shapiro, in a
crude attack on what he considers the obnoxious clique of
Eliot and Pound, called *In Defense of Ignorance* (1960),
wants the critic to have "no system" and to leave philosophy
alone. He observes that "literary criticism hardly exists in
our time; what we have is culture criticism or theology, ill
concealed. The critic today uses literature only as a vehicle
for ideas; he has bigger fish to fry than poets."[67] There is
some justice in this observation. At every point recent criticism slides over into psychology, sociology, philosophy,
and theology. Only those who adhere to either the German
idealist tradition, in the Kantian or Coleridgean version,
or those who rediscover Aristotle, still keep a grasp on the
nature of art and recognize the necessity of an aesthetic and
the ideal of a study of literature as literature. But they are
today a small minority divided in itself. "Vision" is momen-
tarily the fashionable key-term, as "myth" was a little while
ago, and "ambiguity" and "irony" even earlier. I have no
sympathy with amateurism and anti-intellectualism, as I am

66. "The Age of Criticism," in *Poetry and the Age* (Vintage Book
ed. New York, 1955), p. 84.
67. New York, 1960, p. 8.

concerned with the theory of literature, with the development of a method or even methodology adequate to deal with literature and its values. I can understand that criticism needs constantly to draw on neighboring disciplines and needs the insights of psychology, sociology, philosophy, and theology. But I can also sympathize with a protest against the unlimited expansion of criticism and the abandonment of its central concern: the art of literature. It does seem to me an oddity of our time that "art" and "aesthetic" are sometimes considered to be outside of reality, life, and humanity: as if art were not part of life and did not give life coherence and meaning. But recent criticism—and not only criticism in America—looks constantly elsewhere, wants to become sociology, politics, philosophy, theology, and even mystical illumination. If we interpret philosophy in the wide sense, our title has announced a tautology or equation. Literary criticism has *become* philosophy. I wish, however, that criticism may preserve its original concern: the interpretation of literature as distinct from other activities of man. In short I hope our phrase will remain: "philosophy *and* literary criticism."

The Main Trends of
Twentieth-Century Criticism

Both the eighteenth and the nineteenth centuries have been called "the age of criticism": surely the twentieth century deserves this title with a vengeance. Not only has a veritable spate of criticism descended upon us, but criticism has achieved a new self-consciousness, a much greater public status, and has developed, in recent decades, new methods and new evaluations. Criticism, which even in the later nineteenth century was of no more than local significance outside of France and England, has made itself heard in countries that before seemed on the periphery of critical thought: in Italy since Croce, in Russia, in Spain, and, last but not least, in the United States. Any survey of twentieth-century criticism must take account of this geographical expansion and of the simultaneous revolution of methods. We need some principles of selection among the mountains of printed matter that confront us.

Obviously even today much criticism is being written that is not new: we are surrounded by survivals, leftovers, throwbacks to older stages in the history of criticism. Ordinary book reviewing still mediates between the author and the general public by the old methods of impressionistic description and arbitrary pronouncements of taste. Historical scholarship continues to be of great importance for criticism. There will always be a place for a simple comparison between literature and life: for the judging of current novels by standards of probability and accuracy of the social situations reflected in them. In all countries there are writers, and often good writers, who practice these methods marked out by nineteenth-century criticism: impressionistic appreciation, historical explanation, and realistic comparison. Let us recall the charming evocative essays of Virginia Woolf or the nostalgic vignettes of the American past by Van Wyck Brooks or the mass of social criticism of the recent American novel and allude to the contribution which historical scholarship has been making to a better understanding of almost all periods and authors of literary history. But at the risk of some injustice I shall try to sketch out what seem to me the new trends in twentieth-century criticism.

First of all, one is struck by the fact that there are certain international movements in criticism which have transcended the boundaries of any one nation, even though they may have originated in a single nation; one is struck by the fact that from a very wide perspective a large part of twentieth-century criticism shows a remarkable resemblance of aim and method, even where there are no direct historical relationships. At the same time, one cannot help observing how ingrained and almost unsurmountable national characteristics seem to be: how within this very wide range of Western thought with cross-currents from Russia to the Americas, from Spain to Scandinavia, the individual nations still tenaciously preserve their own traditions in criticism.

The new trends of criticism, of course, have also roots in the past, are not without antecedents, and are not absolutely original. Still, one can distinguish at least six general trends which are new in this last half-century: (1) Marxist criticism, (2) psychoanalytic criticism, (3) linguistic and stylistic criticism, (4) a new organistic formalism,

(5) myth criticism appealing to the results of cultural anthropology and the speculations of Carl Jung, and (6) what amounts to a new philosophical criticism inspired by existentialism and kindred world views. I shall take up these trends in the order I have mentioned them, which is roughly chronological.

In taste and in theory Marxist criticism grows out of the realistic criticism of the nineteenth century. It appeals to a few pronouncements made by Marx and Engels, but as a systematic doctrine it cannot be found before the last decade of the nineteenth century. In Germany Franz Mehring (1846-1916) and in Russia Georgi Plekhanov (1856-1918) were the first practitioners of Marxist criticism, but they were very unorthodox from the point of view of later Soviet dogma. Both Mehring and Plekhanov recognize a certain autonomy of art and think of Marxist criticism rather as an objective science of the social determinants of a literary work than as a doctrine which decides aesthetic questions and prescribes subject matter and style to authors.

Prescriptive Marxism is the result of much later developments in Soviet Russia. In the twenties there was still possible in Russia a considerable debate between different doctrines. Only about 1932 was devised and imposed the uniform doctrine which goes under the name of "socialist realism." The term covers a theory which asks the writer, on the one hand, to reproduce reality accurately, to be a realist in the sense of depicting contemporary society with an insight into its structure, and, on the other hand, asks the writer to be a socialist realist, which in practice means that he is *not* to reproduce reality objectively but must use his art to spread socialism: that is, communism, the party spirit, and the party line. Soviet literature, the authoritative theoretician declared, must be "instrumental in the ideological molding of the working masses in the spirit of socialism"—a command which fits Stalin's saying that writers are "engineers of the human soul." Literature is thus frankly didactic and even idealizing in the sense that it shows us life not as it is but as it ought to be according to Marxist doctrine. Good Marxist critics understand that art operates with characters and images, actions and feelings. The focus on the concept of "type" is the bridge between realism and idealism. Type does not mean simply the average or the representative, but rather the ideal type, the model or simply the hero which the reader is to imitate in actual life. Georgi Malenkov—briefly the great expert on aesthetics—proclaimed the typical to be "the basic sphere of the manifestation of party spirit in art. The problem of the type is always a political problem." Criticism in Russia is almost entirely criticism of characters and types: authors are taken to task for not depicting reality correctly, that is, for not assigning sufficient weight to the role of the party, or for not depicting certain characters favorably enough. Soviet criticism, especially since the second World War, is in addition highly nationalistic and provincial: no suggestion of foreign influences is tolerated and comparative literature is a subject on the blacklist. Criticism has become an organ of party discipline, not only in Russia and its many satellites but apparently also in China. Even the genuine insights of Marxism into social processes and economic motivations are hardly used today.

Marxism spread abroad, especially in the twenties, and found adherents and followers in most nations. In the United States there was a short-lived Marxist movement in the early thirties. Its best-known proponent, Granville Hicks, gave a remarkably innocuous reinterpretation of American literature; Bernard Smith's *Forces in American Criticism* (1939) is a bolder attempt to write a history of American criticism from a social point of view. But the influence of Marxist criticism extends far beyond the strict adherents of the doctrine. It is visible in certain stages of

the development of Edmund Wilson and Kenneth Burke.
In England Christopher Caudwell (1907–37) was the outstanding Marxist critic. His main book, *Illusion and Reality*
(1937), is actually a weird mixture of Marxism, anthropology, and psychoanalysis, a diatribe against individual-
istic civilization and false "bourgeois" freedom. But by far
the most outstanding Marxist critic today is Georg Lukács
(born 1885), a Hungarian who writes mostly in German.
He combines a thorough grasp of dialectical materialism
and its sources in Hegel with a real knowledge of German
literature. His many books, among them brilliant studies of
Goethe and His Age (1947) and of the *Historical Novel*
(1955), reinterpret the course of nineteenth-century literature in terms of realism, with emphasis on the social and
political implications but not without sensitivity to literary
values.

Marxism is at its best when it serves as a device to expose
the latent social and ideological implications of a work of
literature. The second of the six critical trends listed above,
psychoanalysis, although with very different assumptions,
serves the same general purpose: a reading of literature behind its ostensive surface, i.e. an unmasking. Freud himself
suggested the leading *motifs* of psychoanalytical criticism.
The artist is a neurotic who by his creative process keeps
himself from a crack-up but also from any real cure. The
poet is a daydreamer who publishes his phantasies and is
thus strangely socially validated. These phantasies, we all
know today, are based on childhood experiences and com-
plexes and can be found symbolized also in dreams, in
myths and fairly tales, and even in smoking-car jokes.
Literature thus contains a rich storehouse of evidence for
man's subconscious life. Freud drew the name of the Oedipus complex from a play by Sophocles and interpreted
Hamlet and *The Brothers Karamazov* as allegories of inces-
tuous love and hatred. But Freud had only slight literary

interests and always recognized that psychoanalysis did not solve the question of art. His followers have applied his methods systematically to an interpretation of literature: *Imago* (1912–38) was a German magazine devoted to these problems, and many of Freud's close followers have studied the subconscious meanings of works of art, the subconscious drives of fictional figures, and the subconscious intentions of authors.

Freudian psychoanalysis spread slowly around the world. Dr. Ernest Jones, an English physician who spent many years at Toronto, wrote as early as 1910 an article on "The Oedipus Complex as an Explanation of Hamlet's Mystery"; and in this country in 1912 Frederic Clark Prescott expounded the relation of "Poetry and Dreams" in psychoanalytical terms. Orthodox Freudian literary criticism usually indulges in a tiresome search for sexual symbols and very frequently violates the meaning and integrity of a work of art; but again, as with Marxism, the methods of psychoanalysis have contributed to the tools of many modern critics who cannot be simply called Freudians. Thus Edmund Wilson, in *The Wound and the Bow*, has skillfully used the Freudian method for a psychological interpretation of Dickens and Kipling, and in England Herbert Read has defended Shelley and interpreted Wordsworth with the insights of the same school.

A third trend of twentieth-century criticism could be called linguistic. It takes seriously the famous saying of Mallarmé that "poetry is not written with ideas but with words." But one must distinguish between several approaches in different countries. In Russia, during the first World War, a "Society for the Study of Poetic Language" (OPOJAZ) was organized which became the nucleus of the Russian formalist movement. In its early stages this group was primarily interested in the problem of poetic language, which the members conceived as a special language characterized by a purposeful "deformation" of ordinary speech by "organized violence" committed against it. They studied mainly the sound stratum of language—vowel harmonies, consonant clusters, rhyme, prose rhythm, and meter—and leaned heavily on the concept of the phoneme, developed at first by De Saussure and the Geneva school, and then by Russian linguists such as Trubetskoy. They devised many technical (even statistical) methods for the study of a work of literature, which they conceived, often mechanically, as a sum of its devices. They were positivists with a scientific ideal of literary scholarship.

In Germany, after the first World War, very different linguistic concepts were applied to the study of literature, mainly by a group of Romance scholars. In many finely analytical books, ranging widely from Dante to Racine and the Spanish poetry of solitude, Karl Vossler (1872–1949) drew on Croce's identification of language and art in order to study syntax and style as individual creation. Leo Spitzer (1887–1960) developed his method of interpreting style at first under the stimulus of Freud. The observation of a stylistic trait allowed him to infer the "biography of a soul"; but later Spitzer himself repudiated his earlier method and turned to a structural interpretation of literary works in which style is seen as the surface which, properly observed, leads the student to the discovery of a central motive, a basic attitude or way of viewing the world which is not necessarily subconscious or personal. Spitzer analyzed hundreds of passages of works of literature using grammatical, stylistic, and historical categories, with unparalleled ingenuity. Most of Spitzer's work concerns French, Spanish, and Italian literature, but during his later years, spent in the United States, he also interpreted poems by Donne, Marvell, Keats, and Whitman, and other English texts. Spitzer worked usually on a small scale, concentrating almost micrologically on specific passages. Erich Auerbach

(1892–1957) used essentially the same method. His *Mimesis* (1946) is a history of realism from Homer to Proust which always starts with individual passages analyzed stylistically in order to reflect on literary, social, and intellectual history. Auerbach's concept of realism is very special and possibly contradictory: it means to him both a concrete insight into social and political reality, and a sense of existence, understood tragically, as man in solitude facing moral decisions.

The German type of stylistics has had astonishing success in the Spanish-speaking world. Dámaso Alonso (born 1898) is the most distinguished practitioner who identifies literary criticism with stylistics and who has revalued Spanish poetry with a new taste for the Baroque, for Góngora and St. John of the Cross. Unfortunately Alonso often abandons linguistic and stylistic methods for gestures toward some ultimate ineffable mystical insight.

In the Anglo-Saxon world, surprisingly enough, no such linguistic and stylistic criticism took hold. Here the gulf between linguistics and literary criticism has widened deplorably. The critics are more and more ignorant of philology; and the linguists, especially the Yale school headed by the late Leonard Bloomfield, have expressly proclaimed their lack of interest in questions of style and poetic language. Interest in "language" is, however, prominent among English and American critics: but it is rather in "semantics," in the analysis of the role of "emotive" language contrasted with intellectual, scientific language. It is at the basis of the theories propounded by I. A. Richards.

I. A. Richards (born 1893) developed a theory of meaning which distinguishes among sense, tone, feeling, and intention, and emphasizes, in poetry, the ambiguities of language. In his *Practical Criticism* (1928) Richards analyzed, with great pedagogical skill, the various sources of our misunderstanding of poetry by using the papers of his students written on anonymous poems. But, unfortunately to my mind, the finely analytical work of Richards is overlaid by a theory of the psychic effect of poetry which seems to me not only erroneous but detrimental to literary study. Richards does not recognize a world of aesthetic values. Rather the only value of art is in the psychic organization it imposes on us: what Richards calls the "patterning of impulses," the equilibrium of attitudes that art induces. The artist is conceived almost as a mental healer and art as a therapy or a tonic for our nerves. Richards has not been able to describe this effect of art concretely, though he claims that art (in his sense) will replace religion as a social force. He has finally to admit that the desired balanced pose can be given by "a carpet, or a pot, by a gesture as well as by the Parthenon." It does not matter whether we like good or bad poetry as long as we order our minds. Thus Richards' theory—which is scientific in its pretensions and often appeals to future advances of neurology—ends in critical paralysis. It leads to a complete divorce between the poem as an objective structure and the reader's mind. Poetry is deliberately cut off from all knowledge and even reference to reality. Poetry, at most, elaborates the myths by which men live, even though these myths may be untrue, may be mere "pseudo-statements" in the light of science.

Richards' dissolution of poetry into an occasion for the ordering of our impulses, as a means toward mental hygiene seems to me a blind alley of literary theory. But Richards had the real merit of turning attention to the language of poetry. When his central psychological teaching was ignored, his method of analysis could be made to yield concrete results. This is precisely what William Empson (born 1906) did. Ignoring and later rejecting altogether Richards' emotive theory, he developed Richards' concept of the flexibility and ambiguity of poetic language by a technique of multiple definitions. *Seven Types of Ambiguity* (1930) pursues to the farthest ends the implications, poetic and social, of difficult, witty, metaphorical poetry by a method of verbal analysis which often loses all contact with the text and indulges in private associations. In his later books Empson combined this semantic analysis with ideas drawn from psychoanalysis and Marxism, and recently he has practically left the realm of literary criticism for a special kind of linguistic analysis which is often only a pretext for the fireworks of his wit and recondite ingenuity.

The Richardsian semantic analysis has had an important influence on several American critics who are usually called New Critics. Kenneth Burke (born 1897) combines the methods of Marxism, psychoanalysis, and anthropology with semantics in order to devise a system of human behavior and motivation which uses literature only as a document or illustration. The early Burke was a good literary critic, but his work in recent decades must rather be described as aiming at a philosophy of meaning, human behavior, and action whose center is not in literature at all. All distinctions between life and literature, language and action disappear in Burke's theory.

In Burke the expansion of criticism has reached its extreme limits. On the opposite pole is Cleanth Brooks (born 1906). He also starts with Richards but arrives at very different conclusions. He takes Richards' terminology, deprives it of its psychologistic assumptions, and transforms it into an instrument of analysis. This allows Brooks, while still talking of attitudes, to analyze poems concretely as structures of tensions: in practice, as structures of paradoxes and ironies. Brooks uses these terms very broadly. Irony indicates the recognition of incongruities, the ambiguity, the reconciliation of opposites which Brooks finds in all good, that is, complex poetry. Poetry must be ironic in the sense of being able to withstand ironic contemplation. The method, no doubt, works best when applied to Donne or Shakespeare, Eliot or Yeats, but in *The Well Wrought Urn* (1947) Brooks has shown that even Wordsworth and Tennyson, Gray and Pope yield to this kind of analysis. The theory emphasizes the contextual meaning of the poem, its wholeness, its organicity, and thus draws significantly on the central insight of what I called the fourth type of twentieth-century criticism: the new organistic and symbolistic formalism.

This organistic formalism has many antecedents: it started in Germany late in the eighteenth century and came to England with Coleridge. Through devious channels many of its ideas entered the theories of French symbolism late in the nineteenth century and, more directly, from Hegel and De Sanctis this organistic formalism found an impressive formulation in the aesthetics of Benedetto Croce. Coleridge, Croce, and French symbolism are the immediate antecedents of modern English and American so-called New Criticism, though strangely and surprisingly this tradition—idealistic in its philosophical assumptions—combined here with the positivistic psychology and utilitarian semantics of I. A. Richards.

Benedetto Croce (1866–1952) has completely dominated Italian criticism and scholarship for the last fifty years, but outside of Italy his theories have had only a negative influence. Even his propagandist in this country, the fine historian of Renaissance criticism, Joel E. Spingarn, hardly understood Croce's peculiar doctrines. *Estetica* (1902) propounds a theory of art as intuition which is at the same time expression. Art for Croce is not a physical fact, but purely a matter of the mind; it is not pleasure, it is not morality, it is not science and not philosophy. There is no distinction between form and content. The common view that Croce is a "formalist" or a defender of "art for art's sake" is mistaken. Art does play a role in society and can even be controlled by it. In his criticism Croce pays little attention to form in the ordinary sense but rather to what he calls the "leading sentiment." In Croce's radical monism there is no place for rhetorical categories, for style, for symbol, for genres, even for distinctions among the arts, because every work of art is a unique intuition-expression. For Croce, the creator, the work, and the reader are identified. Criticism can do little more than remove the obstacles to this identification, and pronounce whether a work is poetry or nonpoetry. Croce's position hangs together remarkably well and is not open to objections which neglect its basis in an idealistic metaphysics. If we demur that Croce neglects the medium or technique of art, he answers that "what is external is no longer a work of art." Literary history, psychology and biography, sociology, philosophical interpretation, stylistics, genre criticism—all are ruled out from Croce's scheme. We arrive at an intuitionism which, in Croce's critical practice, is hard to distinguish from impressionism. It isolates appealing passages or anthologizes arbitrarily from unargued pronouncements of judgment. Mainly due to the influence of Croce, Italian criticism today presents a situation very different from that in other countries. There is erudition, there is taste, there is judgment, but on the other hand there is no systematic analysis of texts, no intellectual history, no stylistics, except among a small group which is definitely anti-Crocean in outlook (Giuseppe de Robertis, Gianfranco Contini) and leans instead towards stylistics.

In Germany an organistic, symbolist concept of poetry revived as a consequence of French influence within the circle around the poet Stefan George. George's disciples elaborated the hints and sayings of the master into a body of criticism which, for the first time after a long period of philological factualism, asserted a critical creed with definite standards. Unfortunately the genuine insights of the school into the nature of poetry were marred by the doctrinaire tone of delivery, the aristocratic pretensions, and the often comically high-pitched, almost oracular solemnity of their pronouncements. By far the best of George's disciples was Friedrich Gundolf (1880–1931), who studied the influence of Shakespeare on German literature and wrote a large book on Goethe (1916). He tried to construe Goethe's "figure" as a unity of life and work, in terms of a scheme which allows a grading of his writings in three main categories: lyrical, symbolic, and allegorical. The book, though finely written and well composed, fails to convince. It transforms the eminently humane and even bourgeois figure of Goethe into a superhuman creator for creation's sake. But in the writings of Gundolf, in those of the sensitive and elegant Hugo von Hofmannsthal, and the violent, passionate Rudolf Borchardt (1871–1945), Germany has found its way back to the great tradition and a restatement of the age-old view of poetry as symbolism.

In France formalist criticism found its most impressive restatement in the writings of Paul Valéry (1871–1945). Valéry, in contrast to Croce, asserts the discontinuity of author, work, and reader. He stresses the importance of form divorced from emotion and takes poetry completely out of history into the realm of the absolute. For Valéry there is a deep gulf between creative process and work. At times it seems as if Valéry were hardly interested in the work but only in the process of creation. He seems to have been content to analyze creativity in general. Poetry is not inspiration, not dream, but making. It must be impersonal to be perfect. Emotional art seems to him always inferior. A poem should aim to be "pure," absolute poetry, free from factual, personal, and emotional admixtures. It cannot be paraphrased, it cannot be translated. It is a tight universe of sound and meaning, so closely interlocked that we cannot distinguish content and form. Poetry exploits the resources of language to the utmost, removing itself from ordinary speech by sound and meters and all the devices of imagery. Poetic language is a language within the language, language completely formalized. To Valéry poetry is both a calculus, an exercise, even a game, and a song, a chant, an enchantment, a charm. It is figurative and incantatory: a compromise between sound and meaning which, with its own conventions, even arbitrary conventions, achieves the ideal work of art, unified, beyond time, absolute. The novel, with its plot complications and irrelevances, and tragedy with its appeal to violent emotions, seem to Valéry inferior genres—not quite properly art. Valéry defends a position which seems extreme in its austerity and vulnerable for its discontinuities. But it has been fruitful in asserting a central concern of modern poetics: the discovery of pure representation, of the "unmediated vision" for which two other great poets of the century, Eliot and Rilke, were also searching.

The affinity with Eliot is obvious. In Eliot we find the English version of the formalist, symbolist theories. Eliot defined the enormous change of poetic taste in our time and asserted a return to a tradition which he calls "classical." Eliot's theory of poetry starts with a psychology of poetic creation. Poetry is not "the spontaneous overflow of powerful feelings," not the expression of personality, but is an impersonal organization of feelings which demands a "unified sensibility," a collaboration of intellect and feeling in order to find the precise "objective correlative," the symbolic structure of the work. In Eliot there is a certain conflict between an ideological classicism and his own spontaneous taste, which could be described as baroque and symbolist; and Eliot's increasing preoccupation with orthodoxy has led him to the mistaken introduction of a double standard in criticism: aesthetic and religious. He dissolves again the unity of the work of art that had been the basic insight of formalist aesthetics.

The impulses from Eliot and Richards were most effectively combined in England, at least, in the work of Frank Raymond Leavis (born 1895) and his disciples grouped around the magazine *Scrutiny* (1932–53). Leavis is a man of strong convictions and harsh polemical manners. He has in recent years sharply underlined his disagreements with the later development of Eliot and Richards. But his starting point is there: in Eliot's taste and Richards' technique of analysis. He differs from them mainly by a strong Arnoldian concern for a moralistic humanism. Leavis practices close reading, a training of sensibility, which has little use for literary theory or history. But "sensibility" with Leavis means also a sense of tradition, a concern for local culture, the organic community of the old English countryside. He has criticized the commercialization of English literary life and has defended the need of a social code and order, "maturity," "sanity," and "discipline." But these terms are purely secular and include the ideals of D. H. Lawrence. Leavis' concern with the text is often deceptive: he quickly leaves the verbal surface in order to define the peculiar emotions which an author conveys. He becomes a social and moral critic who, however, insists on the continuity of language and ethics, on the morality of form.

The so-called Southern critics share Leavis' general position between Eliot and Richards and share his concern with the evils of urbanization and commercialization, the need of a healthy society which alone can produce a vital literature. The Southern critics—John Crowe Ransom, Allen Tate, Cleanth Brooks, and R. P. Warren—differ from Eliot, however, by rejecting his emotionalism. They recognize that poetry is not merely emotive language but a particular kind of presentational knowledge. John Crowe Ransom (born 1888), in *The World's Body* (1938), argued that poetry conveys a sense of the particularity of the world. "As science more and more completely reduces the world to its types and forms, art, replying, must invest it again with a body." True poetry is metaphysical poetry, a new awareness of the "thinginess" of the world conveyed mainly by extended metaphor and pervasive symbolism. Ransom emphasizes the "texture" of poetry, its seemingly irrelevant detail, so strongly that he runs into the danger of a new split, within the work of art, between "structure" and "texture." Allen Tate (born 1899) is like Ransom preoccupied with the defense of poetry against science. Science gives us abstraction, poetry concreteness; science partial knowledge, poetry complete knowledge. Abstraction violates art. Good art proceeds from a union of intellect and feeling, or rather from a "tension" between abstraction and sensation.

There are other critics who cannot be discussed here at length who share, in general, this organistic symbolistic outlook: R. P. Blackmur (born 1904) who, however subtle a reader of poetry, seems in recent years more and more entangled in a private web of terms and elusive feelings; W. K. Wimsatt (born 1907) whose *Verbal Icon* (1954) is an attempt at a consolidation of the teachings of the New Criticism; and Yvor Winters (born 1900) who is much more rationalistic and moralistic than the other American critics but still shares their general taste and methods of analysis.

The New Criticism—whose basic insights seem to me valid for poetic theory—has, no doubt, reached a point of exhaustion. In some points the movement has not been able to go beyond its initial restricted sphere: its selection of European writers is oddly narrow. The historical perspective remains very short. Literary history is neglected. The relations to modern linguistics are left unexplored with the result that the study of style, diction, and meter remains often dilettantish. The basic aesthetics seems often without a sure philosophical foundation. Still the movement has immeasurably raised the level of awareness and sophistication in American criticism. It has developed ingenious methods for the analysis of imagery and symbol. It has defined a new taste averse to the romantic tradition. It has supplied an important apology for poetry in a world dominated by science. But it has not been able to avoid the dangers of ossification and mechanical imitation. There seems time for a change.

A polemical movement still within the limits of formalism, Chicago Aristotelianism has recently challenged the concern of the New Criticism with poetic language and symbolism. The Chicago school emphasizes plot, composition, and genre. The group has scored a good many points against the hunters of paradoxes, symbols, ambiguities, and myths. But neither R. S. Crane nor Elder Olson is able to offer any positive solutions beyond arid classifications of hero types, plot structures, and genres. The armature of scholarship hides an insensitivity to aesthetic values. It seems an ultra-academic exercise destined to wither on the vine.

Much more vital is the fifth trend on our list, myth criticism. It developed from cultural anthropology and the Jungian version of the subconscious as collective reservoir for the "archetypal patterns," and primordial images of mankind. Jung himself was cautious in applying his philosophy to literature, but in England and in the United States his caution was thrown to the winds and whole groups of critics have tried to discover the original myths of mankind behind all literature: the divine father, the descent into hell, the sacrificial death of the god, etc. In England Maud Bodkin, in *Archetypal Patterns in Poetry* (1934), studied, for instance, the "Ancient Mariner" and the *Waste Land* as poems of the rebirth pattern. In the United States myth criticism can be described as the most successful attempt to replace the New Criticism. It allows, to put it bluntly, the discussion of subject matter, of folklore, of themes and content that were slighted by the New Critics. The dangers of the method are obvious: the boundary lines between art and myth and even art and religion are obliterated. An irrationalistic mysticism reduces all poetry to a conveyor of a few myths: rebirth and purification. After decoding each work of art in these terms, one is left with a feeling of futility and monotony. Many of the writings of Wilson Knight, which extract an esoteric wisdom from Shakespeare, Milton, Pope, Wordsworth, and even Byron, are open to such objections. The best practitioners manage to combine the insights of myth criticism with a grasp on the nature of art. Thus Francis Fergusson, in his *Idea of a Theater* (1949), keeps his own version of Aristotelianism, and Philip Wheelwright, in *The Burning Fountain* (1954), his own insight into the semantics of poetry. Northrop Frye began with an excellent interpretation of the private mythology of Blake in his *Fearful Symmetry* (1947) and in his *Anatomy of Criticism* (1957) combines myth criticism with motifs from the New Criticism. The *Anatomy* aims at an all-embracing theory of literature of the most grandiose pretensions. A more modest view of the function of criticism seems to me wiser.

The other recent vital trend is existentialism, our sixth and last trend in twentieth-century criticism. Existentialism dominated the French and German intellectual scene after the second World War and is only now slowly receding. If we interpret it as a philosophy of despair, of "fear and trembling," of man's exposure to a hostile universe, the reasons for its spread are not far to seek. But the main work of Martin Heidegger (born 1889), *Sein und Zeit*, dates from 1927, and existentialist ideas have been familiar in Germany since the early twenties when Kierkegaard was in fashion. Heidegger's version of existentialism is a kind of new humanism, profoundly different from the far more gloomy French school with its dominant concept of "the absurd." Heidegger's influence on literary criticism is due rather to his vocabulary and his preoccupation with the concept of time than to his own eccentric interpretations of poems by Hölderlin and Rilke. In Germany existentialism in literary criticism has meant a turning to the text, to the object of literature: a rejection of the psychology and biography, the sociology and intellectual history with which German literary scholarship had been almost exclusively concerned. Max Kommerell (1902-1944), for instance, in his many close readings of poems studied poetry as self-knowledge, and Emil Staiger (born 1908) has interpreted time as a form of poetic imagination and has devised a scheme of poetics in which the main kinds, or rather modes —the lyric, the epic and tragic—are aligned with the three dimensions of the time concept. The lyric is associated with the present, the epic with the past, and the drama, strangely enough, with the future.

In France, Jean-Paul Sartre is the main expounder of existentialism, though most of us will remember him as a defender of art committed to its social responsibility. But Sartre's *Qu'est-ce que la littérature?* (1948) is an impassioned plea for a metaphysical conception of art. The right of pure poetry is recognized. The final goal of art is not very different from Schiller's aesthetic education: "to recover the world by making us see it not as it is, but as if it had its source in human freedom." Still, the imagination is suspect in Sartre: it creates a shadow-world of distortion, unreality, and illusion, shattered at the first contact with the absurdity and horror of actual existence.

Genuine existentialist criticism has been developed rather apart from Sartre, though often in combination with motifs derived from symbolism, surrealism, and Thomism. Marcel Raymond's *De Baudelaire au surréalisme* (1935) is the fountainhead of a conception of criticism which aims less at an analysis of a work of art than at the discovery of the particular "consciousness" and the existential feelings of the poets. Raymond traced here the myth of modern poetry to its source in Baudelaire. Albert Béguin (1901–57), in *L'Ame romantique et le rêve* (1939), went back to the dream world of the German romantics and in his later writings to the visionary Balzac, to Nerval and Lautréamont, more and more accepting a Catholic mysticism. Georges Poulet, in his *Études sur le temps humain* (1950), has analyzed the time concepts and feelings of French writers from Montaigne to Proust with dazzling ingenuity. Somewhat apart stands Maurice Blanchot who, acutely aware of the shortcomings of language, can ask such questions as "whether literature is possible," and meditate on essential solitude and the "space of death," using Mallarmé, Kafka, Rilke, and Hölderlin for his texts. Ideas from existentialist criticism have begun to filter into American critical writings. Geoffrey Hartman's subtle readings of Wordsworth, Hopkins, Valéry, and Rilke in *The Unmediated Vision* (1954) culminate in a concept of poetry as an understanding of existence in its immediacy; and J. Hillis Miller has applied Poulet's method to the study of time and space in the novels of Dickens (1959).

But while I sympathize with many insights of myth criticism and existentialism into the human soul and condition and admire some of the recent critics of these persuasions, I do not think that either myth criticism or existentialism offers a solution of the problems of literary theory. With mythology and existentialism we are back again at an identification of art with philosophy, or art with truth. The work of art as an aesthetic entity is broken up or ignored in favor of a study of attitudes, feelings, concepts, and philosophies of the poets. The act of creation and the poet rather than the work become the centers of interest. It still seems to me that formalistic, organistic, symbolistic aesthetics, rooted as it is in the great tradition of German aesthetics from Kant to Hegel, restated and justified in French symbolism, in De Sanctis and Croce, has a firmer grasp on the nature of poetry and art. Today it would need a closer collaboration with linguistics and stylistics, a clear analysis of the stratification of the work of poetry to become a coherent literary theory capable of further development and refinement, but it would hardly need a radical revision.

This survey of the main trends of twentieth-century criticism is necessarily something like a Cook's tour, or possibly like an airplane trip: only the main features of the landscape stand out and the selection of names is often arbitrary. I can plead only that its shortcomings are due to its very brevity and to the novelty of my task. I am not acquainted with any attempt, however brief, to survey the present scene on an international scale. But today more than ever this international perspective is needed in criticism.

A Bibliography of the Writings of
René Wellek

(as of December 31, 1963)*

A Books

1. *Immanuel Kant in England 1793–1838,* Princeton, Princeton University Press, 1931.
2. *The Rise of English Literary History,* Chapel Hill, The University of North Carolina Press, 1941.
3. *Theory of Literature* (with Austin Warren), New York, Harcourt, Brace, and Co., 1949.
   - 3a. *Teoria literaria.* Spanish translation by José Gimeno Capella, preface by Dámaso Alonso, Madrid, Editorial Gredos, 1953.
   - 3b. *Bun-gaku no ri-ron* (Theory of Literature), Japanese translation by Saburo Ota, Tokyo, Chi-kuma, 1954.
   - 3c. *Teoria della letteratura,* Italian translation by Pier Luigi Contessi, Società Editrice, Bologna, Il Mulino, 1956.
   - 3d. *Theory of Literature,* 2nd rev. ed., A Harvest Book, New York, Harcourt, Brace, and Co., 1956.
   - 3e. *Theorie der Literatur,* German translation by Edgar and Marlene Lohner, Bad Homburg, Hermann Gentner Verlag, 1959.
   - 3f. Korean translation by Chule Paik and Kim Byung-Chul, Shinku Moonhwa da Seoul, 1959.
   - 3g. Rev. Ed. of 3a, 1959.
4. *A History of Modern Criticism 1750–1950,* Vol. 1, The Later Eighteenth Century, New Haven, Yale University Press, 1955.

* The Bibliography does not list some 60 items in Czech (all published before 1939), but otherwise aims at completeness.

4a. *Geschichte der Literaturkritik 1750–1830,* German translation by Edgar and Marlene Lohner, Darmstadt, Hermann Luchterhand Verlag, 1959 (Vol. *2* is included).

4b. *Storia della critica moderna 1750–1950,* Vol. *2, Dall' Illuminismo al Romanticismo,* Italian translation by Agostino Lombardo, Bologna, Il Mulino, 1958.

4c. *Historia de la critica moderna 1750–1950,* Vol. *1,* Spanish translation by J. C. Cayol de Bethencourt, Madrid, Editorial Gredos, 1959.

5. *A History of Modern Criticism 1750–1950,* Vol. *2, The Romantic Age,* New Haven, Yale University Press, 1955.

5a. *Geschichte der Literaturkritik 1750–1830,* German translation by Edgar and Marlene Lohner, Darmstadt, Hermann Luchterhand Verlag, 1959 (Vol. *1* is included).

5b. *Storia della critica moderna,* Vol. *2, L'Età romantica,* Italian translation by Agostino Lombardo, Bologna, Il Mulino, 1961.

5c. *Historia de la critica Moderna,* Vol. *2,* Spanish translation by J. C. Cayol de Bethencourt, Madrid, Editorial Gredos, 1962.

B   Contributions to Books

1. "Carlyle and German Romanticism," *Xenia Pragensia Ernesto Kraus et Josepho Janko . . . Oblata* (Prague, Sumptibus Societatis Neophilologorum, 1929), pp. 375–403.

2. "Wordsworth's and Coleridge's Theories of Poetic Diction," *Charisteria Guilelmo Mathesio . . . Oblata* (Prague, 1932), pp. 130–34.

3. "The Pearl: An Interpretation of the Middle English Poem," *Studies in English by Members of the English Seminar of Charles University, 4* (Prague, 1933), 1–33.

4. "The Theory of Literary History," *Travaux du Cercle Linguistique de Prague, 6* (Prague, 1936), 173–91.

5. "Periods and Movements in Literary History," *English Institute Annual 1940* (New York, Columbia University Press, 1941), pp. 73–93.

6. "Literary History," *Literary Scholarship: Its Aims and Methods,* ed. Norman Foerster (Chapel Hill, University of North Carolina Press, 1941), pp. 91–103, 226–29, 239–55.

7. "The Parallelism Between Literature and the Arts," *English Institute Annual 1941* (New York, Columbia University Press, 1943), pp. 29–63.

8. "The Two Traditions of Czech Literature," *Slavic Studies,* ed. A. Kaun and E. J. Simmons (Ithaca, Cornell University Press, 1943), pp. 213–28.

9. "Development in Literature," *Dictionary of World Literature,* ed. Joseph T. Shipley (New York, Philosophical Library, 1943), pp. 156–58.

10. "Period in Literature," ibid, pp. 428–29. Reprinted in rev. ed., 1953, pp. 302–03.

11. "The Revolt Against Positivism in Recent European Literary Scholarship," *Twentieth Century English,* ed. W. S. Knickerbocker (New York, Philosophical Library, 1946), pp. 67–89.

12–53. "Czech Literature" and "Slovak Literature" and forty articles on the major figures of Czechoslovak literature since 1870, *Columbia Dictionary of Modern European Literatures,* ed. Horatio Smith (New York, Columbia University Press, 1947), pp. 185–91, 757–59, etc.

54. "Six Types of Literary History," *English Institute Essays 1946* (New York, Columbia University Press, 1947), pp. 107–26.

55. "Introduction" to Nikolay Gogol, *Dead Souls* (New York, Rinehart and Co., 1948), pp. v–xi.

56. "Czech Literature," *Collier's Encyclopedia, 6* (New York, R. F. Collier and Son, 1950), 211–12.

57. "Coleridge: Philosophy and Criticism," *The English Romantic Poets: A Review of Research,* ed. T. M. Raysor (New York, Modern Language Association, 1950), pp. 95–117.

57a. Rev. ed. of 57 (1956), pp. 110–37.

58. "Literary Scholarship," *American Scholarship in the Twentieth Century,* Library of Congress Series in American Civilization, ed. Ralph Gabriel (Cambridge, Massachusetts, Harvard University Press, 1954), pp. 111–45, 221–29.

59. "The Concept of Comparative Literature," *Yearbook of Comparative Literature*, ed. W. P. Friederich, 2 (Chapel Hill, University of North Carolina Press, 1953), 1–5.

60. "Modern Czech Criticism and Literary Scholarship," *Harvard Slavic Studies*, ed. Horace Lunt, 2 (Cambridge, Mass., Harvard University Press, 1954), 343–58.

61. "Social and Aesthetic Values in Russian Nineteenth-Century Literary Criticism: Belinskii, Chernyshevskii, Dobrolyubov, Pisarev," *Continuity and Change in Russian Thought*, ed. E. J. Simmons (Cambridge, Massachusetts, Harvard University Press, 1955), pp. 381–97.

62. "Masterpieces of Realism and Naturalism: Introductions to Balzac, Flaubert, Dickens, Dostoevsky, Tolstoy, Chekhov, Ibsen," *World Masterpieces*, ed. Maynard Mack, 2 (New York, W. W. Norton and Co., 1956), 1693–1727.

63. "The Concept of Evolution in Literary History," *For Roman Jakobson* (The Hague, Mouton and Co., 1956), pp. 653–61.

　　63a.　German translation by Paul Kruntorad, *Hefte für Literatur und Kritik, 1* (1961), 35–46.

64. "Kant's Aesthetics and Criticism," *The Philosophy of Kant and Our Modern World*, ed. Charles W. Hendel (New York, The Liberal Arts Press, 1957), pp. 65–89.

65. "Wilhelm Dilthey's Poetics and Literary Theory," *Wächter und Hüter, Festschrift für Hermann J. Weigand*, ed. Curt von Faber du Faur, Konstantin Reichardt, and Heinz Bluhm (New Haven, Department of Germanic Languages, 1957), pp. 121–32.

　　65a.　German translation by Edgar Lohner, *Merkur, 13* (1959), 426–36.

66. "The Crisis of Comparative Literature," *Proceedings of the Second International Congress of Comparative Literature*, ed. W. P. Friederich, 1 (Chapel Hill, University of North Carolina Press, 1959), 149–59.

　　66a.　German translation by Siegurd Burckhardt, *Wirkendes Wort, 9* (1959), 148–56.

67. "Style in Literature, Closing Statement," *Style in Language*, ed. Thomas A. Sebeok (Cambridge, Massachusetts, Technology Press & John Wiley and Sons, 1960), pp. 408–19.

68–70. "Letteratura ceca, Teatro, Letteratura slovacca," *Il Milione: Enciclopedia di Geografia,* 4 (Novara, Istituto Geografico de Agostini, 1960), 76–90.

71. "Literary Theory, Criticism, and History," *English Studies Today,* 2nd. ser., ed. G. A. Bonnard (Bern, Francke Verlag, 1961), pp. 53–65 [Identical with C 35].

72. "Emerson's Aesthetics and Literary Criticism," *Worte und Werte: Bruno Marckwardt zum 60. Geburtstag,* ed. Gustav Erdmann and Alfons Eichstaedt (Berlin, Walter de Gruyter, 1961), pp. 444–56.

73. "Literaturkritik," *Lexikon der Weltliteratur im 20. Jahrhundert,* 2 (Freiburg im Breisgau, Herder, 1961), 178–261.

74. "The Term and Concept of Literary Criticism," *Proceedings of the Third Congress of the International Association of Comparative Literature* (The Hague, Mouton and Co., 1962), pp. 35–47.

75. "Introduction: A Brief History of Dostoevsky Criticism," *Dostoevsky, A Collection of Critical Essays,* ed. René Wellek (Englewood Cliffs, N. J., Prentice Hall, 1962), pp. 1–15.

C Articles in Periodicals

1. "Ein unbekannter Artikel Savignys über die deutschen Universitäten," *Zeitschrift der Savigny—Stiftung für Rechtsgeschichte, 51* (1931), 521–37.

2. "The Cultural Situation in Czechoslovakia," *Slavonic Review, 14* (1936), 622–38.

3. "Karel Čapek," *Slavonic Review, 15* (1936), 191–206.

4 "Mácha and Byron," *Slavonic Review, 15* (1937), 400–12.

5. "Literary Criticism and Philosophy," *Scrutiny, 5* (1937), 375–83.

   5a. Reprinted in *The Importance of Scrutiny,* ed. Eric Bentley (New York, G. Stewart, 1948), pp. 23–30.

6. "Germans and Czechs in Bohemia," *German Life and Letters, 2* (1937), 14–24.

7. "Bohemia in English Civilization," *Central European Observer, 15* (1937), 21–22, 53–54, 107–08.

8. "Otokar Fischer," *Slavonic Review, 17* (1938), 215–18.

9. "Twenty Years of Czech Literature, 1918–38," *Slavonic Review, 17* (1939), 329–402.

10. "The Mode of Existence of a Literary Work of Art," *Southern Review, 7* (1942), 735–54.

   10a. Reprinted in *Critiques and Essays in Criticism, 1920–48,* ed. Robert W. Stallman (New York, Ronald Press, 1949), 210–23.

   10b. Reprinted in *The Problems of Aesthetics,* ed. E. Vivas and M. Krieger (New York, Rinehart and Co., 1953), 239–55.

11. "Van Wyck Brooks and a National Literature," *American Prefaces, 7* (1942), 292–306.

12. "The Nature and Scope of Literary History," *Huntington Library Quarterly, 6* (1942–43), 35–39.

13. "The Minor Transcendentalists and German Philosophy," *New England Quarterly, 15* (1942), 652–80.

14. "Emerson and German Philosophy," *New England Quarterly, 16* (1943), 41–62.

15. "Bohemia in Early English Literature," *Slavonic Review, 21* (1943), 114–46.

16. "Carlyle and the Philosophy of History," *Philological Quarterly, 23* (1944), 55–76.

17. "De Quincey's Status in the History of Ideas," *Philological Quarterly, 23* (1944), 248–72.

18. "The Philosophical Basis of Masaryk's Political Ideals," *Ethics, 55* (1945), 298–304.

19. "The Concept of Baroque in Literary Scholarship," *Journal of Aesthetics and Art Criticism, 5* (1946), 77–109.

20. "Studies in Eighteenth-Century English Literature, 1938–45," *Erasmus, 1* (1947), 11–24.

   20a. "English and American Studies of English Eighteenth-Century Literature During 1938–1945," *Philologica, 2* (supplement to Vol. *30* of *Časopis pro moderní Filologii,* Prague, 1947), 11–24 [Identical with 20].

21. "The Study of Literature in the Graduate School: Diagnosis and Prescription" (with Austin Warren), *Sewanee Review, 55* (1947), 610–26.

22. "Comparative Literature in General Education," *Journal of General Education, 2* (1948), 215–18.

23. "The Concept of 'Romanticism' in Literary History," *Comparative Literature, 1* (1949), 1–23, 147–72.

　23a. Partial reprint in *Romanticism: Points of View,* ed. Robert F. Gleckner and Gerald E. Enscoe (Englewood Cliffs, N. J., 1962), pp. 192–211.

24. "Literary History," part of "The Aims, Methods, and Materials of Research in the Modern Languages and Literatures," *PMLA, 67* (1952), 19–29.

25. "Benedetto Croce, Literary Critic and Historian," *Comparative Literature, 5* (1953), 75–82.

26. "Italian Criticism in the Romantic Age," *Orbis Litterarum, 9* (1954), 86–99, 158–66.

27. "Critica e teoria letteraria di Hegel," *Inventario, 6* (1954), 118–32 [Italian translation of ch. 12, Vol. *2, History of Modern Criticism*].

28. "The Criticism of T. S. Eliot," *Sewanee Review, 64* (1956), 398–443.

　28a. Japanese translation, *Americana, 3* (1957), 103–22.

29. "Francesco De Sanctis," *Italian Quarterly, 1* (1957), 5–43.

　29a. Italian translation by Piero Longanesi, *Convivium,* N. S., *3* (1957), 308–30.

30. "Walter Pater's Literary Theory and Criticism," *Victorian Studies, 1* (1957), 29–46.

31. "Concepts of Form and Structure in Twentieth-Century Criticism," *Neophilologus, 42* (1958), 1–11.

32. "Henry James's Literary Theory and Criticism," *American Literature, 30* (1958), 293–321.

33. "Hippolyte Taine's Literary Theory and Criticism," *Criticism, 1* (1959), 1–18, 123–38.

34. "Die Hauptströmungen der Literaturkritik des 20. Jahrhunderts," *Studium Generale, 12* (1959), 717–26 [Early version of C39].

35. "Literary Theory, Criticism, and History," *Sewanee Review, 68* (1960), 1–19 [Identical with B 71].

　35a. Italian translation by Antonio Russi, *Annali della Scuola Normale Superiore di Pisa,* 2nd ser., *24* (1960), 1–13.

35b. Japanese translation, *Americana, 7* (1961), 21–34.

36. "Italian Criticism after De Sanctis," *Italian Quarterly, 4* (1960), 30–54.

37. "The Concept of Realism in Literary Scholarship," *Neophilologus, 44* (1960), 1–20.

38. "Leo Spitzer (1887–1960)," *Comparative Literature, 12* (1960), 310–34.

39. "The Main Trends of Twentieth-Century Criticism," *Yale Review, 51* (1961), 102–18.

39a. Hebrew trans. in *Amoth, 1* (1962), 66–77.

40. "George Saintsbury," *English Miscellany, 12* (1961), 79–96.

D Reviews

1. Otokar Fischer, *Heine,* in *Euphorion, 25* (1924), 687–92.

2. Zdeněk Nejedlý, *T. G. Masaryk,* in *Slavonic Review, 14* (1936), 456–62.

3. Josef Šusta, *Soumrak Přemyslovců a jejich dědictví* (The Fall of the Premyslides and their Heritage), in *Slavonic Review, 15* (1937), 720–22.

4. *Československá vlastivěda* (A Survey of Czechoslovakia), in *Slavonic Review, 16* (1937), 230–41.

5. Konrad Bittner, *Deutsche und Tschechen,* in *Slavonic Review, 16* (1938), 481–84.

6. Max Brod, *Franz Kafka, Eine Biographie,* in *Scrutiny, 7* (1938), 86–89.

7. Ernst Kohn-Bramstedt, *Aristocracy and the Middle Classes in Germany,* in *Scrutiny, 7* (1938), 115–16.

8. Arthur R. Nethercot, *The Road to Tryermaine,* in *Modern Philology, 38* (1940), 218–21.

9. William J. Norton, *Bishop Butler, Moralist and Divine,* in *Journal of the Rutgers University Library, 4* (1940), 28–30.

10. R. L. Sharp, *From Donne to Dryden,* in *Philological Quarterly, 20* (1941), 90–92.

11. A. P. Comparetti, *Wordsworth's White Doe of Rylstone,* and M. R. Lowery, *Windows of the Morning,* in *Philological Quarterly, 20* (1941), 92–93.

12. Bertrand H. Bronson, *Joseph Ritson, Scholar-at-Arms*, in *Philological Quarterly, 20* (1941), 184–87.

13. Royal A. Gettmann, *Turgenev in England and America*, in *Russian Review, 1* (1941), 118–19.

14. F. W. Bateson, ed., *The Cambridge Bibliography of English Literature*, in *Philological Quarterly, 21* (1942), 251–56.

15. Elisabeth Haller, *Die barocken Stilmerkmale in . . . Thomas Burnet's "Theory of the Earth,"* in *Philological Quarterly, 21* (1942), 199–200.

16. Rudolph Stamm, *Der umstrittene Ruhm Alexander Popes*, in *Philological Quarterly, 21* (1942), 216–17.

17. Paul Hazard, *Le Problème du mal dans la conscience européenne du dix-huitième siècle*, in *Philological Quarterly, 21* (1942), 224–25.

18. Albert Schinz, *L'Etat présent des travaux sur J.-J. Rousseau*, in *Philological Quarterly, 21* (1942), 226–27.

19. Donald Stauffer, *The Art of Biography in Eighteenth-Century England*, in *Modern Philology, 39* (1942), 432–36.

20. James M. Osborn, *Dryden: Facts and Problems*, in *Modern Philology, 40* (1942), 104–07.

21. Henri Peyre, *Le Classicisme français*, in *Philological Quarterly, 22* (1943), 185–87.

22. Josephine Miles, *Wordsworth and the Vocabulary of Emotion*, in *Modern Language Notes, 58* (1943), 641–45.

23. Richard W. Armour, and R. F. Howes, *Coleridge the Talker*, in *Philological Quarterly, 22* (1943), 383–84.

24. Ernest C. Mossner, *The Forgotten Hume*, in *Philological Quarterly, 23* (1944), 167–69.

25. Joseph T. Shipley, ed., *Dictionary of World Literature*, in *Philological Quarterly, 23* (1944), 186–89.

26. Geoffrey Tillotson, *Essays in Criticism and Research*, in *Modern Philology, 41* (1944), 261–63.

27. Stephen A. Larrabee, *English Bards and Grecian Marbles*, in *Philological Quarterly, 22* (1944), 382–83.

28. Henri Peyre, *Writers and their Critics*, in *Modern Language Notes, 49* (1945), 166–68.

29. Giambattista Vico, *The Autobiography,* in *Philological Quarterly, 24* (1945), 166–68.

30. Ernst Cassirer, *Essay on Man,* in *Rocky Mountain Review, 9* (1945), 194–96.

31. F. C. Weisskopf, *Hundred Towers, A Czechoslovak Anthology,* in *Books Abroad, 19* (1945), 258–59.

32. Sigmund Skard, *Color in Literature,* in *American Literature, 19* (1947), 342–43.

33. Nathan C. Starrs, *The Dynamics of Literature,* in *Modern Language Notes, 61* (1947), 228.

34. Sir Herbert Grierson and J. C. Smith, *A Critical History of English Poetry,* in *Western Review, 12* (1947), 52–54.

35. Walter F. Schirmer, *Kurze Geschichte der englischen Literatur,* in *Journal of English and Germanic Philology, 48* (1948), 91–92.

36. Sidney Finkelstein, *Art and Society,* in *United States Quarterly Book List, 4* (1948), 13–14.

37. Ira O. Wade, *Studies on Voltaire,* in *Philological Quarterly, 27* (1948), 157–58.

38. Henri Grégoire and R. Jakobson, eds., *La Geste du Prince Igor,* in *Modern Language Notes, 51* (1948), 502–03.

39. Northrop Frye, *Fearful Symmetry: A Study of William Blake,* in *Modern Language Notes, 52* (1949), 62.

40. Howard M. Jones, *Theory of American Literature,* and Robert E. Spiller, et al., *Literary History of the United States,* in *Kenyon Review, 11* (1949), 500–06.

41. Albert C. Baugh, ed., *A Literary History of England,* in *Modern Philology, 47* (1949), 39–45.

42. A. O. Lovejoy, *Essays in the History of Ideas,* in *Germanic Review, 24* (1949), 306–10.

43. N. K. Gudzy, *History of Early Russian Literature,* L. Strakhovsky, ed., *A Handbook of Slavic Studies,* and Joseph S. Rouček, ed., *Slavonic Encyclopedia,* in *Comparative Literature, 2* (1950), 182–84.

44. F. Baldensperger, and Werner P. Friederich, *Bibliography of Comparative Literature,* in *Comparative Literature, 3* (1951), 90–92.

45. W. Eppelsheimer, *Handbuch der Weltliteratur,* in *Comparative Literature, 3* (1951), 185–86.

46. *Dizionario Letterario Bompiani,* in *Comparative Literature, 3* (1951), 364–66.

47. Kurt Wais, ed., *Forschungsprobleme der vergleichenden Literaturgeschichte,* in *Comparative Literature, 4* (1952), 277–79.

48. Rudolph Lutz, *S. T. Coleridge,* in *Journal of English and Germanic Philology, 52* (1953), 115–16.

49. Max Wehrli, *Allgemeine Literaturwissenschaft,* in *Erasmus, 6* (1953), 363–67.

50. Hill Shine, ed., *Carlyle's Unfinished History of German Literature,* in *Modern Language Notes, 56* (1953), 574.

51. Erich Auerbach, *Mimesis, the Representation of Reality in Western Literature,* in *Kenyon Review, 16* (1954), 299–307.
    51a. Italian translation by Piero Longanesi, *Il Verri* [Milan], *2* (1957), 13–24.

52. E. Jordan, *Essays in Criticism,* in *American Literature, 26* (1954), 122–23.

53. Isaiah Berlin, *The Hedgehog and the Fox,* in *Yale Review, 43* (1954), 607–09.

54. Meyer H. Abrams, *The Mirror and the Lamp,* in *Comparative Literature, 6* (1954), 178–81.

55. William E. Harkins, ed., *Anthology of Czech Literature,* in *American Slavic Review, 13* (1954), 618–19.

56. Waclaw Lednicki, *Russia, Poland and the West,* in *Comparative Literature, 6* (1954), 282–84.

57. D. Chizhevsky, *Outline of Comparative Slavic Literature,* in *Comparative Literature, 7* (1955), 166–67.
    57a. Russian translation, *Novyi Zhurnal, 40* (1955), 277–79.

58. Dorothy Brewster, *East-West Passage,* in *Russian Review, 14* (1955), 267–68.

59. Paul L. Garvin, *A Prague School Reader,* in *Language, 31* (1955), 584–87.

60. Charles E. Passage, *Dostoevski the Adapter*, in *Journal of English and Germanic Philology, 55* (1956), 173–77.

61. David Daiches, *Critical Approaches to Literature*, Murray Krieger, *The New Apologists for Poetry*, Milton C. Nahm, *The Artist as Creator*, Georges Poulet, *Studies in Human Time*, in *Yale Review, 46* (1956), 114–19.

62. Roy Pascal, *The German Sturm und Drang*, in *Erasmus, 9* (1956), 272–74.

63. J. C. LaDrière, *Directions in Contemporary Criticism and Literary Scholarship*, in *Journal of Aesthetics and Art Criticism, 15* (1957), 368.

64. Leslie Stephen, *Men, Books and Mountains*, S. Ullmann, ed., in *Victorian Newsletter, 11* (1957), 19–22.

65. Vladimir Seduro, *Dostoyevski in Russian Literary Criticism*, J. van der Eng, *Dostoevski Romancier*, in *The American Slavic Review, 17* (1958), 376–78.

66. Stanley Hubbard, *Nietzsche und Emerson*, in *Erasmus, 13* (1960), 134–36.

67. David Daiches, *A Critical History of English Literature*, in *Yale Review, 50* (1961), 416–20.

68. Peter H. Lee, *Studien zum Saenaennorae: Altkoreanische Dichtung; Studies in the Saenaennorae: Old Korean Poetry; Kranich am Meer*, in *Comparative Literature, 12* (1960), 376–77.

69. Robert E. Lane, *The Liberties of Wit*, in *Comparative Literature, 13* (1961), 370–71.

70. Newton P. Stallknecht and Horst Frenz, eds., *Comparative Literature*, in *Comparative Literature, 14* (1962), pp. 192–95.

71. Konrad Onasch, *Dostojewski-Biographie* in *Jahrbücher für Geschichte Osteuropas 10* (1962), 277–78.

E Miscellaneous

1. "A propos de Kant en Angleterre," *Revue de littérature comparée, 14* (1934), 372–76.

2. "The Yale Literary Magazine," *Yale Daily News, 58* (May 28, 1947), 6.

3. "The New Scholasticism? A Reply to Kenneth Neil Cameron," *College English, 13* (1951), 38–39.

4. "Comparative Literature in our Universities: Yale University," *Yearbook of Comparative and General Literature, 1,* Werner P. Friederich, ed. (Chapel Hill, 1952), 56–57.

5. "Preface" to Victor Erlich, *Russian Formalism, History-Doctrine* (The Hague, 1955), vii–viii.

6. "Croce, Wellek e Antoni," *Il Mondo,* 311–Anno VII, No. 5 (Rome, February 1, 1955), 7.

7. "Comment on Sven Eric Molin's 'Criticism in Vacuo,' " *The University of Kansas City Review, 24* (1958), 283–84.

8. "Obituary: Erich Auerbach (1892–1957)," *Comparative Literature, 10* (1958), 93–94.

9. The Pound Number, *Yale Daily News, 69* (December 15, 1958), 2.

10. "Addenda to Spitzer Bibliography," *Comparative Literature, 13* (1961), 378–79.

11. "A Reply to E. B. Greenwood's Reflections" [on "The Concept of Realism." Greenwood's article is published in *Neophilologus, 46* (1962), 89–97], in *Neophilologus, 46* (1962), 194–96.

12. "Preface" to Martin Schütze, *Academic Illusions in the Field of Letters and the Arts* (Hamden, Conn., 1962), pp. vii–viii.

Addenda

A3h. *Teoria da literatura,* Portuguese translation by José Palla e Carmo, Lisboa, Publicações europa-américa, 1962.

A3i. *Theory of Literature,* 3rd rev. ed., Harmondsworth, Middlesex, England, Penguin Books, 1963.

A6. *Essays on Czech Literature,* Introduction by Peter Demetz, The Hague, Mouton and Co., 1963.

C39b. ("Main Trends of Twentieth-Century Criticism"). Danish translation by Lars Peter Romhild, *Vindrosen, 9* (1962), 567–82.

C41. "Italian Criticism in the Thirties and Forties: from Scalvini to Tenca," *Italian Quarterly, 6* (1962), 3–25.

C42. "Some Principles of Criticism," *Times Literary Supplement,* July 26, 1963, p. 49.

C43. "Renato Poggioli (1907–1963)," *Comparative Literature Studies.* Special Advance Issue, 1963, pp. ix–xii.

D72. R. F. Christian, *Tolstoy's "War and Peace,"* in *Slavic Review, 22* (1963), 599–601.

D73. Robert Weimann, *"New Criticism" und die Entwicklung bürgerlicher Literaturwissenschaft,* in *American Literature, 35* (1963), 397–99.

E1a. "Literary Criticism and Philosophy," *Scrutiny, 6* (1937), 195–96.

E9a. "Correspondence" (Comment on letter by Bernard C. Heyl), *Sewanee Review, 68* (1960), 349–50.

Index of Names

Index of Topics and Terms